Self-Knowledge
and Resentment

Self-Knowledge
and Resentment

◆ ◆ ◆

Akeel Bilgrami

HARVARD UNIVERSITY PRESS

Cambridge, Massachusetts

London, England

2006

Library of Congress Cataloging-in-Publication Data

Bilgrami, Akeel, 1950–
Self-knowledge and resentment / Akeel Bilgrami.
p.   cm.
Includes bibliographical references (p.   ) and index.
ISBN-13: 978-0-674-02289-8 (alk. paper)
ISBN-10: 0-674-02289-0 (alk. paper)
1. Self-knowledge, Theory of.   2. Intentionality
(Philosophy)   I. Title.
BD438.5.B55   2006
128—dc22   2006041228

To Carol
with love and gratitude

Contents

Preface

ENCOURAGED BY SOME ideas in Kant on the subject of freedom and its relation to thought, this book argues that the notion of agency and the notion of intentionality are thoroughly normative notions, and that it is these notions so understood, that ground our intuition that self-knowledge has a special authority and transparency that no other knowledge possesses. Without these notions in place, it is very doubtful that self-knowledge can be said to be uniquely and radically set apart from other forms of knowledge, such as perceptual and inferential knowledge of the world and others. But once these notions, understood along these normative lines, are allowed, a right is given to the idea that our knowledge of our own minds, despite the fact of being 'knowledge', is not in any but the merest sense an epistemological notion. It is more that self-knowledge falls—freely and without any cognitive effort—out of the exercise of the most quotidian of our capacities: to act accountably in the world.

This large claim is the conclusion of an argument that *integrates* four themes that, at first sight, might appear to be miscellaneous. These are the themes of agency and the first person point of view, the irreducible nature of value, the irreducible nature of intentionality, and the special character of self-knowledge. All of these themes might and often have been presented as *problems* in philosophy; sometimes, if one is given to a certain prevalent form of naturalism, they have even been presented as mysteries to be solved or removed.[1] The thematic integrations are so vital to the book's work and framework that in a weak and heady moment I was actually tempted to give it the subtitle: "How to Reduce Four Mysteries to One." That corny and bombastic impulse passed almost as soon as it occurred, but what it tried to (atrociously) express is a sense of how I do in fact see the book's mission. It is a book whose argument should at the very least show that even if the reader does not go away with a sense of agreement with its account of self-knowledge, that is not an isolated disagreement but a broadly ideological one. She would have to register intrinsically related disagreements with a certain view of the nature of value, of intentionality, of agency and the first person.

The argument via these integrations takes roughly the following path through the book.

Chapter 1 lays out what it is that our intuitions about the special nature of self-knowledge amount to. It is argued that they amount to a conviction that two properties, transparency and authority, hold only of our knowledge of our own mental states, and the focus of the book is only on intentional states such as beliefs and desires. The chapter conveys the force of these intuitions not only by contrasting them in detail with more standard epistemological accounts (perceptual and inferential accounts) of self-knowledge that deny the intuitions but also by distancing the intuitions from their original doctrinal Cartesian setting, which had no explicit place for failures of self-knowledge such as, for instance, in self-deception. The chapter concludes by presenting two conditionals that respectively capture these two properties in a tentative form. The pledge is to give the conceptual grounds for these two conditionals over the next four chapters and in doing so present them in a less tentative, more conclusive formulation, thereby spelling out the special character of self-knowledge.

Chapters 2 and 3 provide the conceptual basis for transparency in an argument that owes to a normative conception of freedom or agency. Chapter 2 spells out that conception in some initial detail and argues for it along lines that owe greatly to Strawson's views on the subject, though with an important modification. The modification gives a clear sense to the idea that norm (or value) and agency are deeply integrated notions. The full nature of their integrated status is developed further in Chapter 5, but what is presented at this earlier stage is sufficient to provide the basis for an argument presented in the next chapter, Chapter 3, viz., that the conditional that captures transparency is true and can be asserted without any tentativeness if it is properly situated in considerations of such an integration of agency with value. Having shown this, there is an extensive demonstration at the end of the chapter of how transparency, so grounded, stands in stark contrast to other causal and perceptual accounts of self-knowledge that would deny its special character.

Chapters 4 and 5 provide the conceptual basis of authority. They involve a more complicated dialectic because authority, in general, is harder to ground in philosophical argument than transparency. Chapter 4 argues for the conclusion that agency, *normatively* understood along lines established in Chapter 2, is a necessary condition for thought or intentionality, at least of thought or intentionality at a level of sophistication in which it can be self-known. It does so by trying to imagine with as much sympathy and supporting argument as I can summon—but without eventual success—the thoughts of a figure of abject and comprehensive passivity, a subject who altogether lacks the first person point of view of agency. Chapter 5 argues that if it is indeed true that a subject without agency (normatively understood) cannot have thoughts and intentionality in the requisite sense, then a subject with such thoughts and intentionality must have states that are *themselves normative states.* Intentional states such as beliefs and desires are thereby integrated (literally identified) with value, i.e., with such normative states, by an argument that appeals to both G. E. Moore and Frege, and the argument also shows how other philosophers such as Davidson, who failed to see this, do not get fully right the normative nature of intentionality. The normative notion of agency as presented in Chapter 2 is then more fully developed in Chapter 5 by showing that to have such agency is to possess normative states of this kind that make a difference to the world by *'causing'* our *doings,* in a sense of 'cause' that is thoroughly non-naturalistic because it is a sense of 'doings' that is understood primarily in terms of the evaluative assessment of whether or not, as doings, they live up to the demands of these normative states of the doer that 'cause' them. Such a non-naturalism is shown to require and to derive from a perspectival duality that stresses a radical Spinozist contrast between the first person point of view of agency and engagement in which norms and values are in play and a third person point of view of detachment where they are not; and philosophers such as Davidson and McDowell are criticized for failing to ground non-naturalism in this perspectival duality and, as a result, for failing to give a satisfying account of how exactly it is that our intentional states, normatively understood, make a difference to the world via our agency by causing our actions. Finally, from all these points that integrate agency, intentionality, and value, it is concluded by further argument that subjects who possess intentional states in this specific normative sense are authoritative about them. The conditional for authority can now be asserted without tentativeness but only after one has seen through to its conceptual basis in such a view of the relations between agency, value, and thought or intentionality.

Chapter 6 recapitulates in summary the integrating strategy underlying these arguments that establish the two properties of transparency and authority, which make for the special character of self-knowledge, and it spells out some of their broadest implications for philosophy.

Finally, Appendix I addresses those cases of self-knowledge that are not special in the sense that has been presented in the main body of the book, that is to say, those cases of self-knowledge that are not a consequence of considerations of agency. These cases are like other forms of knowledge—such as perceptual and inferential knowledge—that are cognitively achieved. Psychoanalysis in particular is studied as an example of ways of gaining self-knowledge along lines that are more inferential, and it is shown, in general, how such forms of self-knowledge relate to the paradigmatic cases of self-knowledge that the book has established as being special.

The fact is—as I point out at the beginning of Chapter 1—that the interesting cases of self-knowledge for the lay reader (as for those with broad psychological and literary interests) are not the paradigmatic cases, where self-knowledge is presupposed by our agency, but the exceptional ones, where we are blocked for one psychological reason or another from knowing our mentality and have to make cognitive inferential efforts of various kinds to acquire knowledge of them. Quite apart from psychoanalysis, all sorts of puzzling questions (on the borderline of philosophy and other disciplines) emerge regarding the relation between these exceptional cases of self-knowledge and the paradigmatic ones, once one has shown the latter to be transparent and authoritative.

Here is one such question. Through the ages, it has been a standard technique in self-portraiture that the painter looks at himself in the mirror and paints what he sees. But the fact is that, given transparency, he knows himself 'from within', as it were, and so presumably there is some tension between the technique and such self-knowledge. This is a tension not much studied by art historians and theorists of art, but it would enrich their writing on the nature of self-portrait to reflect on it. Another question would be to look at a similar problem in the writing of autobiography, where it seems to the reader that such writing is best when it comes off as self-discovery rather than self-presentation. But if self-knowledge is paradigmatically as this book describes it (authoritative and transparent), then the writing should predominantly be a matter of self-presentation. Fascinating though they are, such questions will have to be left for other occasions. Appendix I merely sees through some rudimentary implications for the case of psychoanalysis. The point remains, though, that these questions could not even be posed if one did not have a firm understanding (that this book tries to provide) of what makes self-knowledge authoritative and transparent.

The book closes with Appendix II, in which an implication of the notion of commitments is briefly explained, in particular its relevance for the relation between an agency and our reasons for action. It offers the basis for a surprising re-orientation of the debate about internal and external reasons.

So, to repeat: it is the large claim of the book that our intuition that self-knowledge is in some sense unique—that it alone is authoritative and transparent—despite the manifest and ubiquitous fact of self-deception and other failures of self-knowledge, can best be retained if we situate self-knowledge in a normative setting, in particular, in normative notions of agency and mind. Self-knowledge, as I said, is a fallout of the fact that we are creatures with responsibility and with states of minds properly described in radically normative terms and not merely as motives and dispositions. Without this normative setting for the subject of self-knowledge, when it is viewed as a purely and primarily epistemological theme, the intuition is hard to sustain. Outside of the normative setting, the failures of self-knowledge take on a far more threatening significance, and the intuitions about authority and transparency begin to lose their grip. Because they pursue the subject outside this setting, there is something both right and honest, therefore, in the instincts of the philosophers whom I am opposing, who take the more standard perceptual and inferential view of self-knowledge. Threatened by the manifest evidence of our many failures of self-knowledge, they abandon the intuitions as Cartesian residues and give a purely epistemological account of self-knowledge in which these failures can be accounted for as they are in any knowledge based on perception and inference. The reader would be right to notice something damningly faint in this salute. Theirs is an honesty forced by an imperfect understanding of where self-knowledge is properly set.

There will be protest to be heard: How can self-knowledge, a kind of *knowledge* after all, not be an epistemological notion? A response can be constructed first by saying that if you thought it was primarily an epistemological notion, then the honest thing to do is to give up on the intuition that it is interestingly unique in some way. To want to have it both ways (preserving our intuition of uniqueness while claiming at the same time to do pure epistemology, devoid of practical categories of responsibility and irreducible normativity) is not possible and makes for much strain and inconsistency in one's philosophy.

This, then, encourages an approach that I will pursue in the book: preserve your intuitions of uniqueness by seeing self-knowledge in its normative setting, thereby transforming and transporting the very idea of such knowledge to a place outside epistemology in the standard sense. The approach is admittedly more radical than is usually found in the philosophical literature. As the view emerges, it not only establishes the properties of transparency and authority by arguing against perceptualist and inferentialist accounts of self-knowledge that deny these properties, but it does so in a way that goes further than other accounts that share a commitment to these properties of self-knowledge. By stressing the radically normative underpinnings of agency and thought, in a way that these other accounts do not, it provides an account of self-knowledge that even puts into doubt the aptness and usefulness to self-knowledge of epistemological notions of 'justification' or 'entitlement'. The aspiration is to preserve our intuitions about the special character of self-knowledge by peeling off from it all the epistemological trappings that accompany the idea of knowledge in general: that it is cognitively acquired; that it issues from perception, from inference; that it is reliabilistically justified; that it is even properly or usefully described as something that we are 'entitled' to on the basis of the presence of our intentional states. All that is replaced by an account of self-knowledge that turns on the relations self-knowledge bears to normatively understood notions of agency and mind. With all this peeled off, the only epistemological element left in the notion of self-knowledge is that it too traffics in truth-value-bearing states; i.e., like any knowledge, it consists of true (self-) belief. Now the protest "Surely self-knowledge, like any knowledge, is an epistemological notion" begins to sound as idle as the protest "Surely the last peel of an onion is an onion."

The main ideas of the book were first formulated over seventeen years ago and were published in very summary form in the appendix to my last book.[2] Since that time, I have presented these ideas to many philosophers in very many different places in the world, and have done much to fortify and elaborate them as a result of the discussions that followed. But there was much less anonymous advice as well.

I have had constant conversations for some twenty-eight years with Carol Rovane and less frequently (but over a longer period of time, since the days we were together at Oxford University in the early 1970s) with Stephen White. They have been so present in my intellectual life, generally, that there is no ordinary form of thanks that I could convey to them—not just for the instruction but for the pleasure of their company.

An essay by Crispin Wright in a volume of tributes to Noam Chomsky first formulated a set of conditionals to capture what is special about self-knowledge, and that immediately struck me as the right way to represent it. Though it will be apparent to readers of this book that my understanding and explanatory grounding of these conditionals is quite different from his, that still leaves it clear that my starting point on the subject owes to his illuminating way of casting the problem. I feel that I have taken the explanation of the conditionals measurably further than he has, but in case that sounds like a self-congratulatory comment, I should add that he thinks that it takes it further than we should take it. These are spirited disagreements, which we have conducted in a small and thoroughly enjoyable weekly reading group during his frequent visiting stints in universities in New York over the last many years. He also read the entire manuscript of this book with great care and commented extensively on all of its claims and arguments. Debts that one owes to one's philosophical colleagues for help of this kind cannot easily be repaid, and it seems to me the only thing one can do is to do such a thing for someone else sometime, if asked. John McDowell gave very shrewd and elaborate critical responses to many of the central ideas in the book in a "Reply" to my contribution to a volume of critical essays on him. In Section 4 of Chapter 5, many of his responses are addressed in detail. Although I am highly critical of him there, these are criticisms of someone with whose general philosophical views and intellectual temperament I have a great deal of sympathy. My valued colleagues Philip Kitcher and John Collins have commented on one or another aspect of the book's argument and helped to improve it. On one specific issue, having to do with supervenience, discussed in Chapter 5, I have had a long, drawn-out discussion with another colleague, David Albert, for many years—indeed, in some way or other, we have been talking and disagreeing about it fitfully and fruitfully (for me) since he first came and spoke at Columbia University twenty years ago. Garrett Deckel, who wrote a very interesting dissertation on the philosophical aspects of psychoanalysis, has helped me think through the issues on that subject in Appendix I. Allen Wood, Annalisa Coliva, Frank Jackson, and Patricia Kitcher also made helpful comments on some passages in the book. This is an opportunity to repeat my thanks to all of them.

The writings of P. F. Strawson, Tyler Burge, Sydney Shoemaker, Christopher Peacocke, Saul Kripke, and Robert Brandom, all of which get briefly discussed in the book, have given me much instruction. I have acknowledged (and sometimes recorded difference with) each of them in specific parts of the book; but since in order to avoid a certain clutter I have deliberately tried to avoid too much commentary on others who have written on the subject, I should like to acknowledge every one of them here as antecedents and influences on one or another element in the book.

For many years, Isaac Levi had the office next to mine at Columbia, and even the constant smell of his cigar was not an obstacle to some of the most intense and interesting (and often quarrelsome) philosophical discussions I have had over the last many years, in his office or mine. Despite the disagreement between us on some issues, Isaac's influence has been genuine and it has been deep.

Donald Davidson, who wrote a critical reply to one central strand in the book's argument and who is in turn criticized in the book, was an early but abiding influence. The more one looks around at contemporary philosophy, the more one realizes how much of what philosophers do today, even when they are openly critical or hostile to his ideas, is defined by or against his work. Davidson should have, but he never did worry that in this regard he had attained an almost Wittgensteinian status, the philosopher philosophers love to love or love to hate.

One of the main turns in my thinking that led to the formulation of the ideas in the second and fifth chapters of the book came to me after an instructive public exchange with Noam Chomsky at a symposium in New York almost two decades ago. Although these ideas are quite different from his, I should like to register a debt to the sharp stimulus of that occasion. I find it appalling how out of fashion his views are among philosophers. No doubt, his own impatience for much of contemporary philosophy is partly responsible for this. But no one writing today has such good philosophical instincts as he does. Chomsky is also a man of great and unusual courage. He has been a hero of mine from my mid-teens when I first went to college in Bombay. I can scarcely bear to think of the world without his voice, the more so now that the world is without the voice of my friend Edward Said.

Self-Knowledge
and Resentment

ONE

◆ ◆ ◆

What Makes Self-Knowledge Special?

1. A PHILOSOPHER—NOT one at large but one earning a salary at a university—often hopes fondly, but in all likelihood vainly, that some non-philosophers might also read his book. Should that happen with this book, I must warn against disappointing two natural expectations they might have.

First is the expectation that a book about self-knowledge will be about knowledge of something we call a 'self'. It is not that I have any prejudice or even skepticism about the concept of the self. Rather, since one cannot take up all issues in a single book, the specific focus here will be on our knowledge of our own states of mind. Even within that focus, the particular scrutiny will be on our knowledge of our intentional and propositionally specified states of mind, such as our beliefs and desires, and not on qualitative or phenomenal states of mind, such as pains and other kinds of sensation. Although I will use the usual term 'intentional states' to describe such states of mind, I should warn here too of a restriction. I will speak only to the more canonical such states—beliefs and desires, mainly—and not the entire range of intentional states. Extending the account given here to the other intentional states and eventually to qualitative states of mind is an important task but must await another occasion and effort.

Second, there is bound to be the expectation that a book on the subject of self-knowledge of our intentional states of mind will focus on the particularly interesting states of mind—the ones that reflect depth of character or strength of will; the ones that motivate heroic

1

striving or evil deeds; the ones that get repressed, create neuroses, and need psychoanalytical uncovering and treatment. Although, in Appendix I, I will say something about unconscious states of mind and about how to think philosophically about the kind of self-knowledge that is acquired when we employ various methods of discovering them and responding to them, much of the book will be about our knowledge of far less interesting states of mind. Why is that?

In general, there are often very interesting reasons for why we must sometimes spend a lot of time on the uninteresting aspects of a subject. A good deal of philosophy is defined by this mildly paradoxical method. In this sense the subject of self-knowledge is a peculiarly philosophical topic. It shares this with the subject of our knowledge of the external world. Non-philosophers are no more likely to be interested in our knowledge of our states of mind, in this sense, than they are likely to be interested in the historically much earlier theme in epistemology, our knowledge of the external world. Though, say, physicists are indeed interested in a variety of objects in the world external to us, as indeed are other sorts of non-philosopher, they are not particularly interested in the general question: what is it to have knowledge of the external world at all; what—as Kant put it—makes it possible; and therefore—as Kant also asked—what makes such sorts of knowledge as is found in physics itself possible? (I am deliberately avoiding putting this highly general question about the external world in the form philosophers have often put it, which is: Do we have a right to say that we have knowledge of the external world? Might it be that we have no such knowledge? One does not have to take up the issue of skepticism of our knowledge of the world or of our knowledge of our own thoughts in order to highlight the great generality of the question that philosophy raises in these areas that distinguishes its interests from the more specific questions that are of interest to the non-philosopher.) So the psychologist, the literary person, the historian, and the reflective person on the street may also be interested in self-knowledge of some highly interesting states of our minds—for example, the darker and murkier desires and beliefs studied by Freud or, more generally, those states of mind studied by the moralist who is interested in how and why we may be motivated in matters of public and personal import. But it is the philosopher alone who thinks that all these interests are just special cases of a much more general subject of self-knowledge. It is the philosopher who is interested not merely in such interesting things as his knowledge of his own attitudes toward his father who has influenced him, or toward a colleague who is jealous of him, but also in his knowledge of his present belief that it is now raining outside and his desire that he not get wet. The philosopher interested in self-knowledge is thus interested in self-knowledge at the highest level of generality, just as the philosopher interested in the external world is interested not specifically in quarks or in the flowers that he is about to buy for a person dear to him but in all or any objects in the world external to him.

I say all this at the very outset not merely to preempt the disappointment of a reader who may have opened a book bearing this title with a view to reading about something interestingly psychoanalytical or moral-psychological in its theme. Those themes do not surface for the first many pages of the book, and it is one of the possibly surprising claims of this book that the banal cases of self-knowledge that I do begin with, and that do not interest the non-philosopher, have certain very important and unnoticed properties that they share with the more interesting cases of self-knowledge. The uninteresting and interesting cases of self-knowledge are all alike in that they are closely tied to our practical and normative lives as free and responsible agents, and therefore *even the uninteresting cases* of conscious efforts at gaining self-knowledge are caught up with what might be thought of as therapy and self-improvement, in the most broadly conceived sense of those notions. But I am getting far ahead of myself.

2. As with so much else in modern philosophy, both for better *and* for worse, the story has its wellspring in Descartes. Here is a brisk trek back to these origins.

The subject of self-knowledge, as it has come to be discussed in our own times, grew out of a struggle to address a certain familiar problem about other minds. Other minds had first posed themselves to be a 'problem' as a result of a certain conception of mental states, which was first articulated in the Second of Descartes' *Meditations*.[1] So long as this conception was taken for granted, self-knowledge seemed also, in a sense, taken for granted, as being something built into our very conception of mental states. It was knowledge of others—indeed, the very idea of minded others—that was troublesome.

What was the 'problem of other minds', and what did it owe to the Cartesian conception?

In that work, it is said,[2] Descartes had made it seem natural that our mental terms get their meaning from our relating them to our own experiences. If we understand what it is to have a pain, say, or a belief, from our own case, a question arises as to whether such a perspective on them will even allow our talk of others having pains and beliefs to make sense. This perspective is said to be a strictly first person perspective. The idea that these terms ('pain', 'belief') get their meaning from our own case is meant to emphasize that we have an irreducibly *subjective* conception of pain and belief; and though Descartes, as I said, did propose such a conception of mentality in his 'Second Meditation', he also went on to compromise it somewhat in the later Meditations by talking of the mental as a substance and, therefore, as an objective thing. Husserl since then had restored the fully uncompromising Cartesian position, without its confused contamination with the idea of a substance. In a more recent revivalist trend, Thomas Nagel has been its most ardent advocate, with a growing number of followers who think of the position as valorously addressing a problem, which others have insouciantly brushed aside and which they describe, with that charming phrase, as 'the hard problem'.

But quite apart from shedding Descartes' own compromise, notice that there is a distinction here of some importance. The problem of other minds, which grew out of what I am calling Descartes' assumption about what is a natural way to conceive mental states, is not merely an epistemological problem. It is a problem about meaning. It is not merely the problem of how we know whether others have mental states; it is a problem of whether talk of others' mental states even so much as makes sense. The assumption that gives rise to this more fundamental problem does not surface in Descartes till the 'Second Meditation'. If we work with just the assumptions of the 'First Meditation', where our knowledge of the external world is put into doubt, the problem would be a less distinctive one, just a special case of the question, how do we know that there is anything external to us?[3] It is only with the 'Second Meditation' where we are told how mental states are to be conceived, that the issues gather an urgency that is echoed in our more recent concerns about the meaning and reference of mental terms, and we are led without too much strain to read a hidden philosophy of language into what were initially presented (in the 'First Meditation') as merely epistemological subjects.[4]

The difference between the assumptions that do and that do not give rise to the distinctive problem of other minds can be found in non-Cartesian settings as well. The stricter versions of phenomenalism, as, for example, in the early writings of A. J. Ayer, where all things in the empirical domain that are not themselves sense-data are *logical constructs* out of (and not just entities inferred from) sense-data, also give rise to the distinctive problem of other minds. This doctrine allows one to retain the intelligibility of our concept of material objects by reducing them to one's own sense-data, but it is not clear that it allows one to find intelligible the idea of another *mind* since all we have to work with are our own sense-data and logical constructs out of them. It is not obvious that once we give up the idea of material objects as logical constructs out of sense-data for inferred entities from them, as Ayer's later writings did, that the distinctive problem emerges with the same vividness or the same excruciating difficulty.[5]

Getting back to Descartes, and to our question, in a little more detail: what is it to have this strictly subjective conception of the meaning of mental terms, and why is it exactly that its implications are said to constitute a 'problem' for the minds of others? The routine story, told in contemporary terms but under the (by now) abusive historical label 'Cartesian', is roughly this: On the subjectivist assumption, I know what 'pain' means from my own case. Others may have taught me the word in circumstances that as far as they were concerned they could see only as outward signs of my being in pain, but it was I who actually gave the word the meaning that it from then on had for me, and I did so via something like a private ostensive definition, perhaps saying to myself (in Wittgenstein's dramatization), "*This* is what the word stands for." Now that I know from my own case what the word means, I can attribute pain to others, even though I only have the outward signs of their pain to go by—that is to say, even though I have no access to that which makes my attributions to them true or false.

It may seem that the story is better suited to terms describing pains and other phenomenal states, where the assumption of subjectivity is more apt, but not to terms describing intentional states such as beliefs. But the structure holds here as well. To the possessor of intentionality, when he attends to his states, they *seem* representational. This appearance of intentionality is exactly what is lost, or so the first personal conception will insist, when one gives any other treatment than a first personal treatment of intentionality—for instance, to mention those in our own times, a causal-theoretic or even a functionalist treatment of it. These accounts of intentionality, even when they are internalist[6] and Cartesian in the '*First* Meditation' sense—as many versions of functionalism certainly are—are primarily objectivist or third personal in their mode of defining the terms involved. When they are internalist, they are only so in making the mind independent of anything in the external world, which in the 'First Meditation' has been doubted away. But this internalism of mind is not yet a subjectivism about the mind. It could well be given a functionalist and therefore quite objectivist account. The genuinely subjectivist conception of intentionality of the '*Second* Meditation' alone retains the *appearance* of intentionality *to oneself* because it alone permits the primary description of intentionality to be as one finds it in one's own attendings to one's states. From this subjectivist perspective, when I try to grasp what someone *else* believes, how someone else is conceiving something—say, conceiving that one-day cricket matches are amusing to watch—I make an effort at entertaining the thought myself—even if it is alien to my own conceptions—and then project it in just the way that we had suggested earlier in the case of pain. Of course this does not mimic the first personal view of pain perfectly, but there is the basic shared commitment to the first personal-cum-projective ideal here as well.

In effect, it was Wittgenstein who first saw in any detail the importance of this thoroughly first personal assumption that lay behind the 'problem' of other minds when he emphasized that it was only if one thought of the mental states as *logically* private (as in the 'Second Meditation' and in the early Ayer formulations) that the distinctive problem arises. It was he who first argued that any strategy that left that assumption in place and tried to *solve* the problem of other minds could only be misunderstanding the problem and the assumption about meaning from which it issued. There simply could be no *solution* to the problem. He tried to show how the so-called 'argument from analogy', which lay philosophically behind these projective exercises I have mentioned, did not so much as address the problem, since it could at best establish a conception of mind for others that was wholly different from the one defined by the first personal mode.[7] And it was he who proposed the alternative strategy, not of solution but of dissolution, the strategy of questioning the first personal assumption itself, and indeed brought against it what is perhaps the only serious available *argument* to this day.

Since I am merely setting up the historical backdrop for how self-knowledge came to be discussed in recent philosophy, I do not have to take up the question of whether Wittgenstein's argument and criticism were effective.[8] Whether or not his argument carries the day, his instinct that the first personal assumption must be given up and that mental states must be conceived in some alternative way has been highly influential among philosophers who succeeded him.

The most general description of the alternative is that mental terms get their meaning (at least partly) due to a special connection[9] that holds between the states they describe and the publicly observable behavior of individuals who possess those states. The idea of such a special connection in Wittgenstein's own hands was not intended as a commitment to behaviorism at all. Wittgenstein himself described the special connection as 'criterial', and by this he intended to mark (among a number of other things) that behavior did not exhaust the meaning of mental terms; and this makes clear that what he had in mind was not consistent with behaviorism, as it is usually understood. The fact that he also never demanded that the relevant behavior should be described in non-intentional terms makes that clear as well. However, the notion of 'criteria', for quite other reasons that are irrelevant for present concerns, has attracted much controversy. Hence, for the present purpose of merely highlighting the shift from the first to the third person perspective in the characterization of mental terms, it is not important for us to retain all the details of the notion of a 'criterial' connection as it is found in Wittgenstein. What is important about it for our purposes is that it shifts the emphasis generally to a third person conception of mental states. When described as generally as that, a diversity of philosophers and psychologists (including both behaviorists and non-behaviorists) such as Watson, Skinner, Ryle, Quine, Davidson, and a substantial infantry marching under the banner of functionalism may all be said to have embraced this conception.[10]

However philosophically problematic the first person assumption for conceiving mental states may have been, the fact that it seemed natural should make us worry that simply reversing to a third person mode of defining mental terms would raise various difficulties of its own.[11]

3. Much motivation for the contemporary discussions of self-knowledge as a philosophical issue begins right here. For, with this reversal of direction, it would now seem that when we know our own mental states, we do so on the basis of our behavior—which is, on the face of it, highly counterintuitive. It is counterintuitive not because it denies what seems to be the case, denies that we seem to know our own thoughts without inferring them from anything, to know them quite *directly,* as it were. (I will raise a question later as to whether, in the end, 'directly' is the right description for what we want to say here.) After all, one could deny something that seems to us to be the case quite justifiably, so long as we have a satisfactory explanation of why things seem to us that way. But *given the shift in direction* as we have described it, one has no explanatory resource for this but to say that it seeming more direct in our own case is due to the fact that we have a closer and more constant acquaintance with our own behavior. That is indeed counterintuitive. The appearance of greater directness in our own case would surely survive if one were to have as constant and close an acquaintance with the behavior of another. I might know someone's personality and character and standing dispositions and commitments extremely well as a result of such acquaintance, but it would still seem obvious that there is a difference in kind between the way I know her intentional states and the way I know the ordinary cases of what I believe and desire.

(A longish and important aside: I say 'ordinary' cases because there is no doubt that we do sometimes come to know our states of mind[12] by inference from our behavior. For instance, that certainly holds for the self-knowledge acquired in psychoanalysis and other such disciplinary regimes. Here we often scrutinize our behavior [even sometimes behavior going back to our childhood] and through the disciplines of the regime infer what we may or must or do have in mind. I will eventually [in Appendix I] say much more about such highly inferential and other cognitive forms of self-knowledge and, while doing so, make clear exactly what is meant by calling them all extra-

or non-ordinary cases of self-knowledge. For now, I will simply register that it seems quite the wrong extrapolation to erect what goes on in these cases of self-knowledge into a doctrine about the nature of self-knowledge.)

So something like a dilemma has emerged: if one accepts the Cartesian assumption of subjectivity regarding the nature of mental states (and the meaning of mental terms), one has an insuperable problem of other minds, and if one rejects that assumption and adopts a more third person perspective on mental states, that leads—at first sight, anyway—to counterintuitive consequences for our knowledge of our own minds.

Gilbert Ryle[13] was so fearful of the Cartesian idea that (out of a zealous sense of almost ideological disapproval) he embraced the counterintuitive consequence for self-knowledge that comes from adopting the third personal alternative to how we should conceive of mental states. For instance, he says that "[t]he sorts of things that I can find out about myself are the same as the sorts of things that I can find out about other people *and the methods of finding them out are much the same*" (p. 155, my emphasis). But Wittgenstein himself never embraced such a view. I say this, but will pursue it no further. Though I have used him as an expository instrument in this stage-setting phase of my discussion, the discussion of the issue of self-knowledge itself will now leave Wittgenstein's own views on the subject behind, since I am not entirely confident—as no person should be—of what they are in detail; and even those who by the tone of their writing manifestly seem to be confident succeed in doing nothing but invite the contempt of others who are just as confident that they have not even a vestigial understanding of what was *really* meant by the master. All I want to stress in citing him just here is that it is not compulsory, after having rejected the first person conception of mental states, to go on to say, as Ryle does, that self-knowledge is gained just as knowledge of others is, by inference from behavior. And much of recent discussion of the subject is an exploration of what alternative there is to Ryle's view, once we have found our way past the Cartesian view. That is the starting point for us, and the succeeding chapters of this book will embark on just such an exploration.

4. But before we start, we should ask: have we dismissed Ryle too quickly by simply asserting that it is too counterintuitive that we know

our own states of mind by inferring them from our behavior? Some
recent work in cognitive psychology has suggested precisely that. In
her extensively reviewed article "How We Know Our Minds,"[14] Alison
Gopnik supports the inferential view and argues that all efforts to
deny that knowledge of our own mental states is inferential in this
way and to claim for it something more direct instead are based, first,
on a faulty idea of what mental states are and, second, on a faulty
idea of what is involved in such inferences. Some philosophers have
found her claims broadly convincing,[15] and it is worth pausing to consider if these sophistications of the Rylean idea do much to remove
our initial sense of its counterintuitiveness.

Gopnik argues on the basis of certain developmental data that to
have a mind is really to have a theory of mind, and she frankly accepts
for this view the label 'the theory theory' of mind. The idea is that
we come to be minded when we begin to get a full grip on mental
terms, and in getting a grip on mental terms, we get a grip on something highly theoretical: we get a grip on these terms within a network
of related such terms, all of which form a theory of the mind and its
explanatory potential. On such a picture, a grip on mental terms is
not supposed to be any different from what it takes to be wielding
the terms of the theories of natural science. This, she thinks, makes
any judgment that deploys a mental term (or the concept it expresses)
dependent on its evidential and theoretical links; and so she describes
these judgments about mentality as being based on *inferences* from
these other items with which they are theoretically and evidentially
linked (or presumably, inferences from other judgments about those
linked items). And finally she insists that these inferences are the basis
of judgments about mentality, whether the judgment attributes mentality to another or *to oneself,* since it cannot be that the theoretical
nature of the judgment vanishes when the judgment applies to oneself
and appears only when it is applied to another. So once we appreciate
the 'theory theory' of mind, we cannot but restore the symmetry between self-belief and belief about others.

To the question, How come we seem to have so strong an impression that when it is self-belief, these judgments, in the ordinary cases,
are not inferentially based on evidence and theoretical connections
but are much more direct? she responds by reminding us that it seems
to us just the same when we make theoretical judgments in natural

science, if we have fully internalized a scientific theory. So just as it may seem to a physicist in confident grip of a theory she has internalized that she is directly perceiving the movement of an electron when she views the tracks in a cloud chamber, so also we theorists of the mind (on this view we are all psychologists and—unlike physicists—need no other training to gain this confident theoretical grip than the one we get up till about the age of four in a normal upbringing) make effortless perceptual judgments about our own beliefs, desires, and so on.

Inference from one's own behavior is the basis of judgment about ourselves, Ryle said. Though Gopnik is careful to distance herself from this simple version of the claim that self-knowledge is inferential, it is her entire brief that the explicit acknowledgment of the 'theory theory' of mind will allow a more refined inferential picture, which can avoid the feeling of counterintuitiveness in Ryle's suggestion while at the same time retaining its real strength: the denial that there is anything epistemologically direct about our self-knowledge. As mentioned, there are two main parts to the view. First, mental terms (or concepts) are theoretical, thus inducing a theoretically mediated and inferential epistemology wherever they are used in judgment; and second, the appearance of a difference in their use in first and third person judgment is explained by the fact that the theory within which these terms are embedded is highly internalized by those making the *first* person judgments.

To repeat: What underlies Gopnik's refinements of Ryle is a commitment to the idea that knowledge of our own states of mind is a result of a kind of perception or a result of something highly analogous to perception. The comparison explicitly given by her is that we know our own minds in a way akin to a seasoned physicist who simply *sees* the electron in the tracks in the cloud chamber. This perceptual aspect is supposed to give the impression of directness, but it is only an impression. The perceptual aspect does implicitly involve an inferential aspect, an aspect present in the role played by the internalized background theory from which the inference, in part, flows. But because (and when) the background theory is so well internalized, the inference is effortless, it is quite natural to say that she simply *perceives the electron in the tracks.* With just the same effortlessness, we are said to simply *perceive our own mental states in our own behavior,* given our internalized mastery of a certain theory after a certain stage of normal cognitive psychological development, plus our utter familiarity with ourselves.

Now, here is a curious thing. And given Ryle's allergy to Descartes, a paradoxical one. This underlying perceptual aspect of Gopnik's view, which adds an explicit theoretical dimension to the simpler Rylean picture, in fact shares one important strand with the way Descartes himself thought of self-knowledge. Descartes, among other aspects of his conception of self-knowledge, did think of self-knowledge as a kind of inner perception. The other aspects of his view, which I will discuss immediately below, did much to make the notion of perception here very different from perception of the external world and therefore did much to say what makes self-knowledge a very special and unique kind of knowledge; and Gopnik certainly has nothing in her view to echo these other aspects. But the fact is that a core of her view and of Descartes' is quite similar in that the analogy with perception is taken quite seriously by both. Descartes says, for instance, "I manifestly know that nothing can be *perceived* more easily and more evidently than my own mind" (p. 69, my emphasis).

We had said something earlier about Descartes' subjectivist or first personal conception of mental states, which gave rise to the problem of other minds, reactions to which, in turn, gave rise to a problem about self-knowledge. But we have not said anything about what he himself took self-knowledge of mental states to be, so it is time to give a very brief exposition of that.

It is a familiar point that the special character of self-knowledge is set on a new path by Descartes, a path not much trodden these days but all the same constantly and anxiously visible as a thing to avoid on the maps on which other paths are plotted. There are three broad features in his view of our awareness of our own mental states, the first two of which make it very different from our awareness of the external world or of anything else. First, his view makes self-knowledge or self-awareness play a definitional (or what philosophers like to call) *constitutive* role in the very idea of what it is knowledge of, i.e., in the very idea of a mental state. Second, it makes self-knowledge *infallible*. And third, it makes self-knowledge a form of infallible (inner) *perception* of one's mental states.

Gopnik, like Ryle (despite the refinements she visits upon him), is at pains to deny the special character of self-knowledge in anything more than a superficial sense, as well as to deny the first two features of Descartes' view since it is these that make self-knowledge special, make it unlike knowledge of others and of the rest of the world around us. But, as we saw, she is quite as committed as Descartes to the third feature since it is that feature that self-knowledge shares with various other forms of knowledge. It is not that anyone making a denial of the special character of self-knowledge is bound to embrace this third feature. One could make the denial by stating as Ryle does that self-knowledge, like knowledge of others, involves an inference from behavior and leave it there, without any mention of perception. But anyone keen on making that denial (at least initially) plausible is bound to embrace it, since it is this feature that allows one to show why it *seems* to us that there is no inference involved in knowing our own minds because perception at least generally *seems* to proceed without inference. Ryle left the inferential view of self-knowledge unprotected. By pointing out that the inferences involved require an *internalized* mastery of a theory of mind, Gopnik introduced the analogy with the *perception* of theoretical phenomena, thereby adding to Ryle.[16] This perceptual analogy shares something central with Descartes, even as the claim that it is the perception of something *theoretical* is intended to have the effect of subtracting from Descartes, the first two of the three features that characterize his view.

It is because Descartes actually does claim that self-knowledge is perceptual, and because he is also keen to say that self-knowledge is special, that he has to add the two other features that preempt the possibility of conceiving the perception involved in self-knowledge (as Gopnik does) as having an inferential element.

For obviously sound reasons, not all the features that Descartes thought to be essential to self-knowledge are found acceptable today. Ever since the explicit acknowledgment of the sort of phenomena that Freud and other psychologists (not to mention novelists and playwrights before him) have so long and so urgently brought to our attention, no one is prepared to take seriously the second feature—infallibility—of his account.

But this gives rise to a deep problem. Without infallibility, the third feature is hard to reconcile with the first. Without infallibility, the idea of self-knowledge as inner perception of one's mental states seems to have nothing distinctive and takes on too much the character of perception of the external world, and then it's hard to see how one can think of self-knowledge as also having a constitutive or definitional role, since perception does not seem to play that role with the external world. In fact, it is precisely because so much of our knowledge of the external world is perceptual that we think of that world as having a certain independence, as being what it is whether or not we had perceptions of it and whether or not we had the capacity to perceive it. *The idea that our intentional states are not in the same way independent of our capacities for self-knowledge is what defines the idea of the constitutive role of self-knowledge,* defines the idea that it is constitutive of the intentional states it is knowledge of. Let that stand for the moment as the briefest, initial characterization of what is meant by a 'constitutive' conception of self-knowledge. (Much more will be said about it later in this chapter and developed over the course of the whole book.) Because this notion of 'constitutive' turns on a notion of dependence that is defined by contrast with the *in*dependence of external objects from our perception of them, the constitutive conception of self-knowledge stands *opposed* to a perceptual conception of self-knowledge. That is to say, though there may be all sorts of things that would make inner perception of one's own states of mind special and different from the perception of outer objects and facts, it had better not be that one of these things is that it is constitutive. For it is hard to see that anything would actually remain of what we would count as a genuinely perceptual model for self-knowledge if what is special about self-knowledge is that it has a definitional and constitutive role for the mental states it is knowledge of.

But now, if we are convinced by this and shed the idea that self-knowledge is constitutive, then there is just as deep a problem on the other side. If self-knowledge does not have *either* infallibility *or* a constitutive role (if it has neither of Descartes' first two features), then whatever it is that makes for the special character of self-knowledge will not be all that special. It will be too much like ordinary perception.

I have dwelt on these semi-historical points because they are still in a most interesting way with us. For if I am right in this conceptual mapping, the most interesting doctrinal issue on the subject of self-knowledge remains fairly closely tied to the Cartesian elements, even as we are anxious to avoid the particular complexion these elements have in Descartes' own full and integrated picture of them.[17] *That issue is this:* Given the widespread and wise discarding of the first feature (infallibility), and given the intolerable tension we have just noticed between the two remaining features—between the perceptual model and the constitutive ideal—*only one of them* can serve in any account of self-knowledge. So which one should it be, and how shall we think of it in a non-Cartesian setting? This is the fundamental disjunction that will be with us for many pages to come.

To choose the constitutive ideal would be to opt for the view that self-knowledge is special, and if we can detach it from the Cartesian setting of infallibility, it may aspire to some plausibility. It may be a hard and challenging task, though, to think of how self-knowledge may be constitutive in the sense we have defined it above, without resorting to some notion of infallibility. That challenge will be with us till the very end of the book, and I will address it explicitly then, once a great deal of apparatus and argument is presented in the central chapters.

To choose the perceptual model would be to deny that self-knowledge is special, and it would be relatively easy to think of the perceptual view in a non-Cartesian setting. Gopnik has already told us how to do so. She has told us that if we shed the first two of Descartes' features, and if we understand certain developmental data, we must view self-knowledge as both inferential and perceptual, just as we view the knowledge of any theoretical phenomena in the world outside.

As said earlier, there are two parts to her argument. The first is that the inferential view is forced on us because what we know when we know our own mental states is something highly theoretical. Second, the perceptual view is forced on us because it shows why it *seems* to us that our knowledge of our own mental states is direct and non-inferential, but like perception of any theoretical phenomena, what seems so is not actually so since it is induced by the fact that the inferential basis (the theory involved) is a highly internalized theory in the background.

Let us, then, briefly evaluate this view critically. An instructive worry can be raised about each part of her argument.

First, suppose we accept Gopnik's explanation of her developmental data and say with her that mental vocabulary is highly theoretical and refers to theoretical phenomena. Why should something theoretical in this sense force something about epistemology? Why should it force an inferential basis for knowledge and judgment about that theoretical thing? That is, why should judgment that is highly conceptualized (because what the judgment is about is highly theoretical), just by that fact, necessarily be thought of as a product of an inference? Is there not some conflation here between an essentially semantic claim (the holistic embedding in theory of certain terms or concepts) and an epistemological claim (the inferential basis for making judgments with those terms or concepts)? I will return to this question in a moment.

Second, how is the claim that we know our own minds in a way that physical theorists perceive something theoretical about the world (via inferences issuing from evidence, plus a highly internalized background theory) supposed to explain what it is intended by Gopnik to explain, viz., that it seems to us that we know our own minds more directly than we know the minds of others? Gopnik, given her view, has no resources other than to say: we know others' mental states in the way that a *novice* physical theorist *without* a fully internalized grip on a background theory knows something theoretical about the world, whereas we know our own minds in the manner of the more seasoned theorist. But then her view seems to have shed none of the counterintuitiveness of Ryle's view, which has it that we know our own minds better and with a sense of greater directness because we have a closer and more constant acquaintance with the sorts of things from which it is inferred.

The first of these questions puts into doubt that the argument she gives really gets her the conclusion she wants, the conclusion that our knowledge of ourselves is not in essence different from other kinds of knowledge; and the second question raises a doubt about whether, even given her conclusion, she is able to plausibly explain why it seems to us that there is an essential difference between them.

The first question can be put differently. Take the constitutive view of self-knowledge that is opposed, in the fundamental disjunction we posed above, to the perceptual/inferential view, which she favors. Let us, for the sake of argument, assume that the constitutive view is right and that therefore—given the disjunction we posed—the perceptual/

inferential view is wrong. To say that the constitutive view is right has the following important consequence: our very notion of a mental state requires that mental states lack an independence from our capacity for knowing that we have them. In other words, our mental states lack the independence from our knowledge of them that facts or objects in the external world have from our capacity to have knowledge of *them*. Now, another way to put our first question is, *why should mental states, so understood, not be thoroughly theoretical?* Gopnik gives no argument to suggest that this is not possible. And if that is so, she gives no reason to promote her view, which proceeds from the theoretical nature of mental states to the claim that they must be inferentially and perceptually known by those who have them. The developmental data that drives her to assume the theoretical nature of mentality (by showing that children acquire full mentality by acquiring a theory) does nothing to promote her conclusion. The constitutive account need not fall afoul of any such data. It can simply say that whatever developmental stages are undergone before a child arrives at this stage, *what the child arrives at* (mental states such as beliefs and desires) are governed by the constitutive ideal.

And the second question raises for her a question that was raised equally against Ryle. We want to be able to say, despite his view and her refinements upon it, that the distinction we make between knowing our own minds and knowing others' minds survives the fact that we may on occasion have a very close and constant acquaintance with the behavior of another. Speaking specifically to Gopnik, the point is that even if we on occasion knew others' behavior so well that our knowing their minds is now no longer analogous with the novice scientist but with the seasoned one, we still want to retain the distinction between the way we know others' minds and the way we know our own minds. Given *her* explanations of the seeming directness of self-knowledge, we should not retain the distinction in this occasional circumstance. This seems most implausible and simply seems to be an assertion of her theory against a clear intuition. At this point the theory seems to have become an ideology.

We will make progress in setting up our dialectic for the rest of this book's argument if we diagnose our failure to be convinced by Gopnik's critique.

Part of the trouble is with the word 'direct' when it is applied to

self-knowledge. Gopnik, by making 'direct' self-knowledge the target
of her critique, does not quite take in what exactly she is supposed
to be opposing when she opposes the views she does. What makes
self-knowledge special and different from other forms of knowledge,
we have said, is that what it is knowledge of—viz., (first-order) intentional states—lack a certain independence from the self-knowledge of
them. They lack an independence from the (second-order) states that
go into self-knowledge. This is what (following others) I have called
the 'constitutive' view, the view that self-knowledge *constitutes* intentional states. One, of course, needs to say much more about what is
meant by 'dependence' and 'constitutive', and I will do so just a little
further below. But even before one does that, the point remains that
it is not clear that this feature that makes for the special character of
self-knowledge is best described with the rhetoric of terms such as
'direct'. Such a rhetoric leaves one with the impression that intentional states are no more dependent on their possessors' knowledge
of them than the objects and facts in the external world are dependent on our perceptual knowledge of them. That is to say, they
are not dependent in any interesting philosophical sense. 'Directness'
in knowing need not convey any notion of the relevant conceptual
dependence since something that is directly known can still be something that has a distinct and independent status from the states of
knowing it.

By stressing that it is directness that she opposes, Gopnik goes away
with the impression that she has repudiated the views in question by
offering the analogy with something that she says *seems* direct but *is
not*, i.e., perception of theoretical phenomena when the theory involved is highly internalized. Even if she is right in saying that views
committed to directness of the knowledge are repudiated by this
strategy, the strategy is powerless against what should really be the
target of her attack—constitutive accounts of self-knowledge, as I have
(admittedly very briefly) characterized them. It is no surprise, then,
that the two questions we have raised for her satisfy us that her critique is not convincing. She can provide no answer to the (first) question (why should constitutive accounts of the self-knowledge of intentional states not survive a view of intentional states that sees them as
highly theoretical phenomena?), since the idea of a conceptual dependence of intentional states on the self-knowledge of them is not

defeated by the fact that intentional states are highly theoretical. And she can provide no satisfactory answer to the (second) question (why does knowledge of our own intentional states seem different from knowledge of others?) because she has no resources to provide it except to say (lamely, as Ryle does) that it *seems* direct only because the theoretical knowledge involved is more familiar to us when our own states are the objects of the knowledge.

Quite apart from these two difficulties, which are bad enough for Gopnik, there is another question that confronts inferentialist views of self-knowledge generally. It is a question that is so fundamental that it arises equally for inferentialist views of our knowledge of *other* minds. In fact, it was first raised explicitly for such views by John McDowell, when he argued against certain interpretations of Wittgenstein's notion of 'criteria'.[18] Putting aside the quarrels about how to interpret that notion in Wittgenstein, the far-reaching upshot of his argument for our own subject is this.

It is McDowell's plausible claim that it is not really possible to describe the behavioral basis for our inference about another person's mental state in terms that are so neutral that genuine and successful inference to her mental state can be made without knowledge of the mental state in question being already presupposed in our knowledge of the allegedly 'inferential' behavioral base. If the behavioral basis of the inference was described in terms so neutral that it did not presuppose knowledge of the mental state that was supposed to be inferred, then it is not clear that the inference can actually even be made. To use McDowell's metaphor, if the behavioral basis was not described in mentalistic language (say, intentional vocabulary, since we are focusing on intentional states), then one would have to think of behavior as some kind of 'outer husk' for an inner intentional life, and that would be to fail to see behavior as *expressive* of our intentional states; and without seeing it as expressive of intentional states, it is not clear what kind of leap an inference would have to be to our intentional states and whether behavior, so described, would even yield inferences to determinate conclusions about another's mental states.

Since Gopnik in her discussion of mental states never considers this question, she is nowhere explicit about what she has in mind as the right descriptions for the behavioral base upon which an inference to another's intentional states is built. Were Gopnik to consider this objection, she might take the view that the behavior is not intentionally described and would perhaps add that all that talk of a *theory* of mind and its mastery is intended to try and make this leap more intelligible. But if McDowell is right, it is not at all obvious that it does or can do so. It is not obvious that we can get determinate inferences to something as rich as intentional states if all that we had to go on as an inferential base is behavior, non-intentionally described, that is to say, behavior, 'behavioristically' described as the movement of limbs, utterance of sounds (as opposed to meaningful words), etc. As he argues, behavior with such impoverished descriptions will simply not be able to rule out any of a number of inferences to quite bizarre mental states, such as those that Kripke mentions in setting up his 'deviant' rules that all equally fit a person's meaningful behavior.[19] In order to effectively make determinate and correct inferences, therefore, one would have to see the behavioral basis of inference not in these impoverished terms but as itself intentionally described, and that would mean already seeing it as expressive of the mental state in question. "Inference" would then be the wrong term to describe such transitions. So McDowell suggests that in the case of our knowledge of other minds we directly *perceive* the mental states *in* another person's intentional behavior, i.e., behavior that we would have properly described in intentional vocabulary. And so, finally, the argument implies that the inferential view simply collapses with the perceptual view of other minds.

Now, if this is right about our knowledge of other minds, *there should be an exactly similar line of argument that is right for inferential views of self-knowledge as well.*[20] The behavioral basis of our self-knowledge of intentional states must see our behavior as expressing our intentional states, if the inference is to go through, and to do so is to presuppose knowledge of the intentional state that is to be inferred. So it seems that here too the inferentialist view will collapse with the perceptual view and that there is no genuine inference going on. Thus Gopnik gets it wrong when she suggests that the perceptual element is just the phenomenological sign of a very rapid inference due to the internalization of a background theory.

Ryle himself, oddly enough, was very clear—as clear and explicit as anyone could be—that the inferential basis for conclusions about another's or one's own mental states was behavior *intentionally* described. So in this one important respect, he shared some of McDowell's commitments. (That is why presumably there is no effort on his part to locate self-knowledge in a highly theoretical view of intentional states, as Gopnik does.) But in that case, if McDowell is right, then knowledge of our own intentionally described behavior presupposes our knowledge of the mental states that are supposed to be inferred. This is because that behavior gets its intentional descriptions from the intentional states it *expresses* and that rationalize it.

Once we have this insight of McDowell's firmly in place, then the only way to read Ryle, when he argues for a *symmetry* between self-knowledge and our knowledge of other minds, is that the symmetry consists in the fact that we perceive mental states in behavior (intentionally described) whether others' or our own. That we should perceive our *behavior* first in order to perceive our own mental states in our behavior (i.e., that we should not perceive our intentional states independent of our behavior but only in our intentionally described behavior) will capture for him now the *in*directness he wanted for self-knowledge of our intentional states. So with McDowell's point in place, the Rylean view is that self-knowledge is not a matter of inner scanning but, rather, is a matter of outer scanning of behavior and *seeing* the mental states *therein*.

But now the earlier doubt we had expressed (the one outlined in the second of the questions I raised for Gopnik above) will resurface even for such a revised Rylean position. This is the doubt that the only explanation that Ryle, given his views, has for why knowledge of our own states of mind *seems* more sure and quite different from knowledge of another's states of mind is an extremely counterintuitive one. For this revised Rylean position, the explanation will just be to lamely say that we *see* a lot more of our own behavior than we see the behavior of others. It is very counterintuitive that this is the only important difference there is between knowledge of our own states of mind and knowledge of others' states of mind. Revising Ryle in these perceptualist directions to cope with this line of critique inspired by McDowell, therefore, does nothing to remove this general counterintuitiveness of views like his (whether interpreted as perceptual or inferential) that stress that knowledge of our mental states must go via (perception of or inference from) our behavior. If there is to be

a perceptualist view of self-knowledge that is going to avoid such counterintuitiveness, it will have to think of the perception of our intentional states as not involving perception of our behavior at all (not
even intentionally described behavior). Such a perceptualist view will
be quite different from the revised Rylean view we have been discussing, and I will present it below in Section 5. It will have none of
the counterintuitiveness of Ryle's or Gopnik's position and will provide for the most plausible opponent against the constitutive view. In
fact, it will be the persistent foil for the constitutive account of self-
knowledge throughout the book.

With that said, it is time to leave both Ryle and Gopnik. But it is
worth recording before we leave them that in the end it has turned
out that in a curious way McDowell's kind of argument helps us see
that, for all her attempts at sophisticating Ryle, which seemed at first
to make his sort of position more plausible, it was *he* who had something more right than Gopnik did (viz., that our behavior that is
supposed to be the basis of our knowledge of our mental states is
intentionally described behavior) even if, by the lights of the constitutive theorist, he did not have it right at all because his position
continued to have very counterintuitive consequences on the subject
of self-knowledge.

The question arises as to whether all these difficulties that we have
accumulated for Gopnik's and Ryle's views give us sufficient reason
to give up on non-constitutive views of self-knowledge altogether. To
think so would be highly premature.

What these considerations from McDowell have made clear is that
however we interpret Ryle and Gopnik, however much we sophisticate
and revise inferentialist views by bringing them closer to or collapsing
them with versions of the perceptualist view, they all suffer from one
major flaw: they are all driven by the urge, as Ryle made clear, to
repudiate the claim to any inner directness of self-knowledge. In
Gopnik's case, it took the form of repudiating the claim by insisting
that there was inference present even despite the phenomenological
directness of self-knowledge. In the revised Ryle case, inference was
altogether abandoned under pressure from considerations from Mc-
Dowell, so it took the form of insisting that one perceived one's intentional states in one's behavior and not directly, independent of
one's behavior.

Given the fact that this was the major flaw in these views, then if there is to be any sympathetic way left of presenting non-constitutive views of self-knowledge, one must be looking to non-constitutive views that *embrace* directness of self-knowledge rather than make such directness the target of their critique, as Ryle and Gopnik do. If there are such non-constitutive views, they will not have to face the problem that the non-constitutive views of both Ryle and Gopnik faced and to which they were forced to give counterintuitive responses, viz., the problem of having to say why it is that self-knowledge seems direct but is not. If, unlike Gopnik and Ryle, the non-constitutive views thought of self-knowledge as direct in the first place, they would face no such problem. And moreover, unlike Gopnik and Ryle, they would be clear-eyed about what it is they were supposed to be opposing—*not* views of self-knowledge that made self-knowledge of intentional states *direct* but views of self-knowledge that made self-knowledge *constitutive* of intentional states, i.e., views that made intentional states conceptually dependent in a crucial sense on our self-knowledge of them. This is progress because, as I said earlier, the rhetoric of 'directness', so common in the way that the constitutive view is often described, actually fails to characterize the constitutive view's real commitments. With the critique of Gopnik behind us, we can diagnose this failure as arising from the fact that too often those who oppose the constitutive view (Gopnik, before her Ryle, and even the revised Ryle that we sketched above) took themselves (and still take themselves) to be standing up for an indirectness in self-knowledge, in doing so. It would be shallow on the part of the constitutive theorist to accept that the debate with his opponent should be formulated in these terms of directness versus indirectness. Even those constitutive theorists who are manifestly not shallow sometimes carelessly slip into this formulation and distract from the deeper issues at stake. And I think that only the kind of critique of Gopnik we have been providing brings out the need to be clearheaded about the issues at stake and to reformulate the debate in less misleading terms.

The non-constitutive view that I now turn to no longer understands itself as opposing a directness in self-knowledge but, rather, tries to capture for self-knowledge the directness it thinks it possesses. Its opposition to constitutive accounts therefore is now over issues that are much more faithful to what is really at stake; viz., however direct self-knowledge may be, if it is to be constitutive of intentional states, it is not due to any directness (which after all can be a property of perception, sparely conceived) but is due to a conceptual dependence of intentional states on self-knowledge.

5. In order to locate and sympathetically motivate such a non-constitutive view, let us establish first the obvious disanalogies that exist between perception (in general) and self-knowledge, then formulate a perceptual model of self-knowledge that avoids the disanalogous elements.

The perceptual paradigm would be too obviously inappropriate for self-knowledge of intentionality if it was demanded of it that it should always preserve an analogue to the idea of some minimal cognition—even if it was direct and non-inferential—on the part of an agent that, in *external* perception, is captured by such expressions of hers as "I saw," "I looked," or most generally, "I checked" (which seems better because it allows us to include in perceptual knowledge, knowledge of such things as the position of one's limbs). There are no analogues to 'looking', 'seeing', 'checking' in the ordinary cases of our knowledge of our own mental states. If I believe that I believe that my mother lives in India, I don't usually come to do so by conducting some inner checking of my mind to see whether it contains the belief that my mother lives in India. This much perhaps is obvious.[21]

It might be thought that just pointing out that these analogies are missing is not enough to undermine the perceptual paradigm for self-knowledge because looking, seeing, etc., are not present in much knowledge of the external world either. For instance, I may know that there is no elephant in my closet without looking, seeing, or checking on whether there is one. But the fact is that a fair amount of perceptual and inferential knowledge (and knowledge by testimony, which is also knowledge by cognition of a sort that is missing in ordinary self-knowledge)[22] is a necessary *basis* for knowing (without perception) that there is no elephant in my closet—not merely knowledge of the size of the closet but also knowledge of the size of elephants, where they tend to go and not go, and so on. The realm of non-perceptual knowledge of the external world is based on such a store of perceptual (and other sorts of cognitively acquired) knowledge. But in the realm of self-knowledge, there is no analogy with such a store of cognitively acquired self-knowledge on which it is based. All it seems to be parasitic on is the possession of intentional states and a conception of what intentional states are. No more specific store of knowledge is required as a basis for self-knowledge. Of course, if I know that I believe there is no elephant in this closet, that bit of self-knowledge of the first-order belief *presupposes* that I have the store of knowledge that the first-order belief is based on. But the point is that the self-knowledge is not *based* on that knowledge in the way that the first-order state is.

So, to repeat: there are no analogies in self-knowledge with cognitive acts such as looking, seeing, having read about, and being told of by expert testimony that provide a basis for the knowing, as they do with other forms of knowledge.[23]

What, then, could possibly be left of the claim to a *perceptual* model of self-knowledge if it contains nothing analogous to these things in perception of the external world? Should we say nothing is left of it and see that as a reason for adopting the constitutive view? No. By looking to a perceptual model that depends not at all on any analogy with these cognitive activities, we will have identified a perceptual account that does not have the shortcomings we found in Gopnik and that will pose a much more interesting and worthy challenge to the constitutive view over the next few chapters.

There is a limitingly spare version of the inner perceptual account of self-knowledge, which was perhaps first suggested in David Armstrong's[24] early work and which makes explanatory appeal to *only* a *causal* mechanism. The account says that it is a causal mechanism that takes one from a mental state, let's say an intentional state, such as a desire that p, to a belief that one has the desire that p. It does not put any weight on any kind of cognitive activity (analogues to "checking," "seeing," etc.), and therefore, I suppose, one should not feel particularly motivated to call it a '*cognitive*' mechanism. (We should perhaps move more carefully with this terminological suggestion here, since so much of '*cognitive*' science sees itself as dealing with purely and merely causal mechanisms, and in fact cognitive science can be viewed as the conceptual and empirical sophistications of the general ideas to be found in such early philosophers as David Armstrong, whom we have just cited as the founder of this spare and limiting view. If cognitive science posits such causal mechanisms, it might seem odd to withhold the term 'cognitive' mechanisms in describing them. Perhaps the right and careful thing to say is not that there are no 'cognitive' mechanisms involved in this view, but rather that there are no 'perceptual' mechanisms involved.)

But to say that there are no perceptual mechanisms involved should not give the wrong impression that this cannot, after all, be a spare version of a *perceptual* model. Despite there being no perceptual mechanisms, what it shares with the perceptual model is a very crucial similarity that allows for the intended contrast and disjunction with the constitutive view. The point of similarity is that since it is a causal mechanism that is doing the central explanatory work, even if unaccompanied by the 'perceptual' or 'cognitive' trappings, there will be a certain *independence* of the first-order mental states from the second-order states about them. That is to say, since it is a causal mechanism that connects the desire that p with the belief that one has the desire that p, the first-order desire has a certain independence from the second-order belief about it, which is precisely what is being denied by the constitutive view.

This sort of position, though non-constitutive, is conspicuously different from Gopnik's. By downplaying the analogies with perceptual activities such as seeing, it has no echo of her claim that self-knowledge is like the perception by a scientist of highly theoretical phenomena. It has no echo, as a result, of the inferential element that she shares with Ryle. In fact, this spare version of the perceptual view can claim to have captured all the *directness* that our intuitions tell us is possessed by self-knowledge and that is missing in other kinds of knowledge. It can capture the very intuition about directness that Gopnik is claiming to be false in all respects except a superficially phenomenological one.

This is how it does that: Knowledge of others and the world lacks the directness of knowledge of our own states of mind because it is overlain by perceptual activity such as seeing and looking, activity that can, as Gopnik would like us to believe, be highly inferential, at least implicitly. Causal mechanisms are central to both inner and outer knowledge. The difference is that in outer knowledge one is caused to believe that the world is thus and so, or that one's friend believes something or other, or even that one's limbs or torso are in such and such position, *by* looking, hearing, checking, etc. In knowledge of one's inner (mental) states, one is, in the ordinary cases, directly caused to have the belief that one believes or desires something or other, *without* having to look, see, etc. This is precisely the directness that Gopnik cannot (and does not want to) capture, since she believes self-knowledge is not direct. It is because she did not want to capture this directness that she was stuck with the problem of having to account for what *seems* like a greater directness in self-knowledge. And in addressing this problem she, like Ryle, was forced to give counter-intuitive responses that appeal to our greater acquaintance with our own behavior. If we find it too obvious and intuitive that the special nature of self-knowledge exists even in cases where our acquaintance with others might be as close and constant as of ourselves, her view is put to an immediate disadvantage. No such disadvantage attaches to this much more spare perceptual view that does not repudiate the genuine directness of self-knowledge. Therefore, it does not have to make a distinction between self-knowledge seeming direct but not being direct. It *is* direct, on this view. Its directness depends on a purely causal relation, with no overt perceptual or other cognitive activity and therefore no covert inferential activity.

Despite the disanalogies and differences with external perception, I will continue to call this view the 'perceptual' view of self-knowledge. To acknowledge these differences, I may sometimes qualify it by calling it the 'spare' perceptual view, or the 'limiting' case of the perceptual view; or I might sometimes call it the 'causal-perceptual' view. Since I do think that it has something crucially in common with the perceptual view when it is contrasted with the constitutive view in our basic disjunction, I may sometimes slip and fail to add these qualifiers, without feeling as if I've done great violence to the view. By continuing with this perceptualist terminology, what I want to stress is that though by Gopnik's and Ryle's lights (lights, which want to rule out self-knowledge as being direct and non-inferential) this view might have disappointingly succumbed to the idea that there *is* something very distinct and special about self-knowledge, by the lights of the constitutive theorist it has disappointingly succumbed to the *denial* of the special character of self-knowledge in just the way that the perceptual view does. Despite not sharing a lot (the failed analogies above), what it does share with the perception of the external world (i.e., the explanatory causal mechanisms) is enough to spoil any real and interesting claim to a distinctive and special nature for self-knowledge. Thus the governing disjunction—only one of the two models, perceptual or constitutive, can be right—continues to dominate what follows in the book, and I will say more to justify seeing things disjunctively in this way as the discussion proceeds in later chapters.

From now on, I will allow the spare version of the perceptual model to specifically stand in for the general perceptual disjunct in our disjunction. It is the most plausible version of the perceptual model, as we have seen, because no questions of the sort we raised for Gopnik's or the revised Rylean perceptual account arise for it. It captures a great deal of what seems special about self-knowledge, even if not enough by the constitutive theorist's lights. This, not Gopnik's, will have to be the view that the constitutive theorist must show to be false, if she is to carry the day.

6. The time has come to take a stand on this disjunction. I count myself as embracing one of the disjuncts, count myself as a constitutive theorist. Though it is a minority view among philosophers of mind and epistemologists, I am in quite numerous company. To mention those I have read with much instruction: Davidson, Shoemaker, Wright, McDowell, Burge, Goldman, Peacocke, and Descartes himself. Descartes of course stands apart in this company, since all of us oppose his idea of what makes self-knowledge constitutive of mental states. Since we are all in broad agreement about which disjunct we favor and the fact that it must take a non-Cartesian form, my disagreements with the other constitutive theorists, where they occur, are bound to be more subtle than the disagreements already registered earlier against Descartes, and of course they are bound also to be more subtle than the disagreements with the many philosophers who take the perceptualist view in one or another form, whom all of us named above oppose.

In the rest of the book, I will be making a case for the constitutive view. The primary focus will be on that philosophical task, and I will only occasionally distract myself from the task to provide commentary on others and say how my case differs from other cases that have been made toward the same end.

We have said a fair amount to characterize what the perceptual theorists say, but we have said little by way of initial exposition of the position of the constitutive theorists, except to cite their position as one disjunct in what was presented as a fundamental disjunction in how to think about self-knowledge. We did say that if self-knowledge is constitutive of what it is knowledge of, if it is constitutive of mental states, then mental states lack a certain kind of independence from our knowledge of them. What sort of independence is it that they lack?

Given the governing disjunction, we can confidently say this much. What they lack is precisely the independence possessed by the things *of* which we have perceptual knowledge, *from* that perceptual knowledge, i.e., the independence from perceptual knowledge that objects and facts in the external world possess. (I am assuming throughout that something akin to Berkeleyan idealism, which would dispossess objects in the external world of such independence, is a false doctrine. I will not say anything to argue for this assumption, since I can take for granted that there is broad agreement on this among philosophers today. I should add that the quite other form of idealism— Kant's transcendental idealism—is perfectly compatible with the view of self-knowledge and its contrast with perceptual knowledge that is claimed by the constitutive theorist. It is only Berkeleyan idealism that would raise questions for the contrast. Kant will be discussed in Chapter 4.)

We need to say something more positive about this non-independence than that it is of a sort that is not possessed by the objects and facts of the external world.

The non-independence of mental states from our knowledge of them is a result of two phenomena, or what might be better to call two presumptions. Both presumptions are sometimes described by the single label 'first person authority', but that is very misleading. We will need two labels to mark them.

To begin with, there is the presumption that since our beliefs or judgments about our own states of mind are not relying on our senses, they cannot go wrong in the way that our beliefs, which are so reliant, do sometimes go wrong. Most constitutive theorists today think that this presumption is merely that, a presumption. It is not a claim about the infallibility of beliefs about our own states of mind. The point is that *even as a presumption* it does not hold for perceptual knowledge

of the external world. Not even the most uncritically generous de-
ployers of the principle of charity would say that there is a presumption that our beliefs about the external world are true. (Of course
perception of the mid-sized external environment in the immediate
vicinity *is* remarkably often true, and glaring cases of illusion and
delusion here are rare, so the idea of there being no presumption at
least for this limited region has to be carefully handled.) There will
be a good deal of detailed discussion later about the differences between perception and self-knowledge. For now, let's just say that the
fact that knowledge of the world is, in the standard case, based on
casual and perceptual mechanisms (which could fail us) makes the
idea of such a presumption holding for such knowledge untenable.
For just that reason, such a presumption can be said to hold for self-
knowledge that is not based on any such mechanisms. It would be
natural to call the presumption we've been discussing the presumption of 'authority'. That we have epistemological 'authority' over our
states of mind is a good way to describe the idea that it is presumed
that when or if we believe that we have a state of mind, say, a desire
or belief, we are right. No other person has such epistemological
authority over our states of mind. And that is why it is often called
'first person' authority. The presumption of authority, then, can be
formulated as a conditional. I will call it (A).

> (A). It is a presumption that: if S believes that she desires (believes)
> that p, then she desires (believes) that p.

There is also a quite different phenomenon that makes for the non-
independence we mentioned, a quite different presumption. This is
not the presumption that our beliefs about our own states of mind
are true, but rather the presumption that if there is a state of mind,
then its possessor will believe that it is there. This too contrasts with
perceptual knowledge of the external world; in fact, it does so even
more starkly than what we called 'authority'. Surely we are not even
slightly tempted to say, in the name of charity or anything else, that
if there is a fact or object in the external world, then there is a presumption that a perceiver will know that it is there. To repeat a point
we had elaborated earlier, we are not tempted to say this because in
perceptual knowledge of the external world the agent has to do something or (more passively) be doing something—looking or seeing,

etc. Knowledge of the external world is in ordinary cases the result of such *cognitive achievement* (as philosophers call it), which if the agent does not do or have happen to her, then she will not form the belief that there is some fact or object in the world. In self-knowledge there is, in the ordinary case, no such cognitive activity nor any analogue to it, which is required to believe that one has some mental state. (I have said earlier that my use of the expression 'ordinary cases' is intended to allow for exceptions, and I will say much in Appendix I to accommodate them within the constitutive picture of self-knowledge.) This presumption, then, is a result of the fact that beliefs about our mental states come with the mental states. To put it as I have in various papers over the years, it comes, as it were, 'for free', without any cognition. (Please note quickly an important caveat here, which can avoid much elementary confusion. In saying this, one is not saying that beliefs about our own thoughts are not cognitive states. That is, one is not saying that they are not truth-value bearing. Rather, one is saying that they are truth-value bearing or cognitive states that are not a result of cognition. So no one should go away with the impression that what is being suggested here is a non-cognitive conception of mentality and its self-knowledge on a par with non-cognitive theories of value, etc.) 'Transparency' is a good traditional philosophical term to describe the phenomenon being captured by this presumption. Our mental states are transparent to us; we have knowledge of them without having to make any cognitive effort. It too, then, can be put down in the form of a conditional, a conditional going in the other direction from the one for authority: I will call it (T).

(T). It is a presumption that: if S desires (believes) that p, then S believes that she desires (believes) that p.

Summing up: These two presumptions formulated as two conditionals make for the non-independence of mental states from self-knowledge of them, and *that* is the special character of self-knowledge. Special, because no such presumptions hold for any other kind of knowledge, in particular, not for the kind of knowledge we have set up as a contrast in our disjunction, i.e., perceptual knowledge. To claim authority for our perceptual beliefs about the external world and transparency for facts or objects in the external world is simply false because of the fact that perceptual mechanisms are involved there. These mechanisms might fail, so there is no presumption of authority. These mechanisms might not be switched on, so there is no presumption of transparency. Hence facts or objects in the external world are independent of our beliefs about them in a way that our mental states are not independent of our beliefs about *them*.

So it looks, prima facie. Much needs to be said to redeem this initial contrast in detail if it is to get its full philosophical argument.

I will be arguing over the next many chapters that there is *a sense* in which these conditionals are true, and I will be specifying what exact sense that is and why and how that sense captures our intuitions about the special nature of self-knowledge in a satisfying way. In the rest of this chapter, I will not be arguing for the truth of these conditionals. I will only be spelling out a little more fully, though still in a preliminary way, why the conditionals—if true—capture what the constitutive view of self-knowledge is, by contrast with the spare perceptual view of self-knowledge.

A few qualificatory points should be noted right away regarding these conditionals, before I spell that out.

For one thing, they only establish that (in the case of transparency) one has second-order beliefs about the presence of first-order intentional states, when they are present, and that (in the case of authority) since the relevant first-order intentional states *are* present, these second-order beliefs that they are present are therefore *true*. But our subject is self-*knowledge*, not merely true self-belief. Knowledge consists of more than true belief, as the general wisdom says, so what more needs to be said to establish that the conditional for authority reaches up all the way from true self-belief to self-*knowledge?* This question can and will only be answered much later, after we have made the full case for the conditional (A) for authority. It will be answered in Chapter 5.

Also, many philosophers (McDowell and Burge, for instance) who take the constitutive view and claim that self-knowledge is special and wholly unlike other forms of knowledge such as knowledge by perception and inference, nevertheless, make no commitments to the radical and controversial-seeming theses that I have formulated in the conditionals. Why, then, am I pinning the constitutive view so closely on these conditionals? I suppose I can only answer this question by saying, "Wait and see," but I will add right now that the point of the reading I will be giving these conditionals over the next few chapters is to remove the obviously controversial and radical impressions they might suggest at first sight, before such a reading is given. Philosophers like McDowell and Burge may of course disagree with the reading, but then that is where the controversy will lie, rather than in the fact that the conditionals seem to be saying something too radical *at first sight*.

Finally, since these conditionals explicitly mention second-order beliefs, they will be true only of creatures capable of second-order belief. Assuming that (non-human) animals and human babies lack the capacity for second-order beliefs, they fall outside the scope of the subject of self-knowledge. But if self-knowledge is constitutive of intentional states themselves, then there is a sense in which these animals lack intentional states too. None of this is intended to promote the view that animals lack 'intentional' states in any sense of the term whatsoever. They lack them only in the sense that is demarcated by the constitutive claims. If there is another sense of the term, and there surely is one (perhaps more than one), which is in widespread use, they will not be the focus of our discussion, though from time to time it will be necessary to keep the distinct uses of the term in mind in order to see the scope and applicability of the book's claims about self-knowledge. The entire issue about whether animals possess intentional states has caused vexed disputation among philosophers, but I intend to resolve these disputes amicably in the word. Keeping a watchful eye on the distinct senses of the word 'intentional' should keep the dispute at arm's length. The claims about self-knowledge I make will be claims restricted to creatures who have the capacity for second-order beliefs, the capacity for beliefs about intentional states such as first-order beliefs and desires, and therefore restricted to creatures who have the *concept* of an intentional state. This means that the sense of 'intentional' states itself will be restricted to one sense of that term, and what that is will emerge much more fully only later (in Chapters 5 and 6). For now, it is enough to say that it is a sense of the term that does not seem to apply to animals in any clear and uncontroversial way. The restriction is relevant not only to the question of animals and the intentionality they possess but also to the kind of self-knowledge that the book focuses on, the relatively full and articulable forms of it rather than the vaguer forms of awareness that we all possess of our states of mind, such as, say, of our fears and anxieties. We often call such states 'unconscious', but that is not because a state of this kind, a fear, say, is something we have *no* awareness of whatsoever. It may even pervade our consciousness and experience of the world, and if it pervades our experience, it must in some sense be in our awareness. Still, as I say when I discuss this particular example more fully in Appendix I on unconscious states, there is no reason to think that such forms of awareness spoil the kinds of philosophical claims I want to make within my restriction.

I will repeat these points about the relevance of my restriction in two or three places again in the course of the book because they are important points, and it would be unfortunate to have the general line of argument in the book go missing for those who feel somehow that the intentionality that non-human animals possess or the vaguer form of self-knowledge human beings have is not being taken seriously enough. One does not have to fail to take them seriously in order to present the general line of argument in the book, nor does it undermine that line of argument to have its relevance restricted in these ways.

There are two further clarifications that need to be made about this.

One: Some might feel that in restricting the discussion to intentional states in this specific sense, in restricting ourselves to intentionality possessed by creatures capable of second-order beliefs, perhaps we are taking the interesting or controversial element out of the constitutive view of self-knowledge. Or perhaps that we are arguing in a circle. But that is clearly wrong. It cannot be uninteresting or uncontroversial because most philosophers think that our knowledge of our own 'intentional states' (even when that term is understood in the restricted sense that does not apply to non-human animals) is to be understood on some version of the inner perceptual model rather than the constitutive model. And it cannot be circular because surely these philosophers are not denying a trivial and circularly arrived at conclusion. They are taking themselves to argue for a perceptualist account against a view that sees serious disanalogies between self-knowledge and perception. The charge that the disanalogies simply are a circular consequence of restricting our focus to non-human animals quite fails to see the subtle and difficult issues on which this disagreement turns. What is true—though it would be a comical exaggeration to describe this truth as amounting to a 'circularity'—is that we cannot see what is special about the nature of self-knowledge without seeing a lot into the nature of intentionality as it is found in creatures such as human beings. In general, the interest and the controversy in restricting oneself to intentionality in the specific sense that human beings alone seem to have will be exactly the interest and the controversy we may find in Descartes' own ambitions. By restricting ourselves in this way, we will hope to realize something that is an essentially Cartesian ambition, but along non-Cartesian lines. *This is the ambition of claiming that if we get clear on the nature of self-knowledge, we will have become clear on a great deal else; we would have become clear on the nature of human mentality.* Of course, Descartes did this in terms of a notion of mentality and self-knowledge that turned on a narrow notion of the first person point of view and of consciousness, which we have been discussing as having given rise to the problem of other minds, something he then went on to deny to non-human animals, whom he was quite prepared to treat in essentially third personal terms as automata. Even if we disagree with his particular way of realizing his ambition, we can retain the ambition and try to realize it by trying to show something quite different, viz., that a proper understanding of self-knowledge in terms of the notion of agency and of value and of the first person point of view (where that point of view is understood in much broader terms than in Descartes, understood in terms of the exercise of agency and value in deliberation and action) will reveal a quite different conception of the human mind—a conception more plausibly denied to non-human animals. The point of the book's argument is that to see self-knowledge as revelatory of all this, and as a fallout of all this, is *necessarily* to see it in terms that are quite unlike as it is seen in the perceptual model.

Two: Others might feel that these conditionals and the constitutive view are so startlingly controversial in the first place that restricting the discussion of self-knowledge so that animals without the capacity for second-order beliefs are excluded does nothing to make it more plausible. After all, creatures with the capacity for second-order beliefs have all sorts of first-order intentional states that they have no self-knowledge of, such as unconscious or tacit or various kinds of dispositional states.[25] This will be addressed in detail in the course of the book. By the end of the book, the conditionals for transparency and authority will be given a reading that will have something to say regarding all such phenomena.

To go back now to the two conditionals and elaborate a bit more on why they capture what is intended by the constitutive view, notice that if they were true, there would be something of a *rule*-like quality connecting our own intentional states with our beliefs about them—just the quality missing in the relation between facts or objects in the external world and our perceptual beliefs about them. Thus, if the perceptual view of self-knowledge were to be true, it is just this quality that would go missing between our intentional states and our beliefs about them. If it were true, then even if one were the sort of creature who has the capacity for higher-order beliefs, there is *no* sense in which if one has the desire that p, one must (as if by a rule) believe that one desires that p, and vice versa. The perceptual view of self-knowledge, in the spare version we are discussing, posits a causal mechanism that connects first-order intentional states with second-order beliefs about them. Because the perceptual view, however spare, has the causal mechanism central to its explanation in a way that is just missing in the constitutive view, its account of why the epistemology of self-knowledge seems intuitively different and special in some way can at best be a reliabilist and inductivist account. It can at best be an account that says such things as: the causal mechanism is in fact reliable (even more reliable than our perceptual mechanisms); we have in the past tended to give the right answer to questions about what we believe or desire (even more often than to questions about what is in the perceptible world external to us); and so on. For the constitutive theorists who also want to account for the special character of self-knowledge, these remarks are poignantly insufficient.

Since it is a causal mechanism, which is central to the perceptual account, it is the kind of thing that, however reliable, *could* break down—just as our perceptual mechanisms could fail us on occasion—and so there would be *no* relevant sense in which one could think of there being this sort of necessary, rule-like tie between the embedded belief and the higher-order belief. (I will use the expression 'embedded belief' for those first-order beliefs that are picked out by the embedded clauses of a statement reporting a second-order belief.)

There might be a temptation to breezily dismiss the contrast I am insisting on between the perceptual and constitutive accounts by saying something like this: The initial perceptual account due to Gopnik *does* contrast with the constitutive account, but the sparer account due to Armstrong is too spare, and it does *not*. It does not because it requires merely a causal mechanism, and that is too spare to provide the contrast. A merely causal mechanism, without any perceptual or cognitive activity, is too *un*controversial. No account, not even the constitutive account, should deny the existence of some such underlying causal mechanism linking first-order intentional states and second-order beliefs about them. If first- and second-order states are different states, which they surely are, then some causal link must be connecting them when we have self-knowledge, even if self-knowledge is constitutive of mental states.

This temptation issues from a missing of the point. The missed point has already been made. I will risk the tedium of repeating it. Even in its spare version, the perceptual account provides for a deep contrast with the constitutive account because as accounts of self-knowledge, they offer explanations, and these explanations are very different. It is part of the constitutive theorist's brief that even if there were an underlying causal mechanism, whatever role that mechanism plays, it cannot play the sort of explanatory role that would disallow one from saying the following: that there is *a sense* in which there can be *no* breakdown in the connection that is expressed by saying that if someone desired that p, then he believes that he desires that p, and vice versa. What makes her a constitutive theorist is precisely such a claim that there is no breakdown, and what makes an Armstrong-like position proximate to the perceptual account despite its sparer appeal to a purely causal mechanism is minimally, but also precisely, a denial of such a claim. My aspiration is to provide such a reading for the conditionals over the rest of the book, that they will reveal the sense in which there can be *no* breakdown. (I will take up the question of the compatibility or incompatibility of the constitutive and the causal accounts again in Chapters 3, 4, and 5.)

Once this point is clear, scruple demands that some terminological revisions be reasserted so as to avoid a continuing use of misleading terms, of which I myself have been guilty in the early sections of this chapter. Since the constitutive theorist denies even the minimal causal claim as providing the explanation of self-knowledge, that suggests that even the standard ways of describing what the constitutive theorist takes to be special about self-knowledge should be different from how I have myself (following others) been putting it so far. It should not be put in terms of self-knowledge being more 'direct' than other forms of knowledge. We have already seen how Gopnik failed to see the real point of what she was arguing against because of this misleading vocabulary. After all, the spare perceptual account, which is a non-constitutive account, *does* capture in some sense the directness of self-knowledge. So the constitutive view is not about the greater directness of self-knowledge at all, and one should drop the word 'direct' in describing it. To describe things by saying that, on the constitutive view, self-knowledge is more 'direct' than perception suggests that it has something *minimal in common* with perception that is doing the explanation (some mechanism, a causal one) and that operates without any inferential or evidential or cognitive mediation of the sort that Gopnik was proposing. But this minimal explanatory element is *also* being denied by the constitutive view. For such a view, it's not the same sort of thing, only more direct. It's not the same thing at all. (See the end of note 16 for the discussion of a related terminological point.)

This also suggests that it is misleading to use the term 'introspection' as it is often used by philosophers (by Armstrong, for instance)—as a neutral term intended to be synonymous with 'self-knowledge' in general and intended to describe therefore a kind of knowledge about which we are giving different theories, the perceptual and the constitutive. The verb 'to introspect' suggests a kind of cognition (analogous with perception, perhaps, at any rate involving some causal activity) that tilts the usage in favor of the perceptualist against the constitutive theorist.

The point is not that knowledge of our own states of mind is come by via something more direct than other knowledges; it is not come by via anything at all. As I have been putting it in earlier papers I've written, it comes with the states of minds themselves, for 'free', as it were. In the ordinary case, second-order beliefs are not acquired by anything at all; they are 'just there', along with the first-order intentional states. The idea of 'its just being there' is radically different from the idea of 'directness' because it puts a conceptual distance between the constitutive view and any view that merely makes the self-knowing agent merely inarticulate or unaware of her cognitive activities. It's not that a self-knowing agent is giving the right answers about what her intentional states are (just as the chicken-sexer is giving the right answers) on the basis of a minimally causal and therefore cognitive mechanism, only that she cannot articulate what it is. Nor is it that (because there is no looking, seeing, or checking) she is just unaware of such a minimal causal mechanism. It's much more radical than these views because the causal mechanism, even if it exists, is simply irrelevant to explaining the second-order beliefs. These beliefs just come with the first-order intentional states; and given that they do, it follows trivially that the second-order beliefs may be presumed to be true since all they require to be true is that there be the first-order intentional states that they are about.

The perceptualist might wonder: Why does one need anything stronger than the spare perceptual account? Why should one follow this book's project of seeking something more than a spare causal-perceptual link between first-order intentional states and second-order beliefs about them? Why should one seek something like a rule-like link? To this there really are two related answers, the first stronger and less conditional than the second.

The first answer is simply that we *do have* these more rule-like links because we are certain kinds of creatures, endowed with agency and with a capacity to exercise norms and values, which are capacities for things that are not reducible in any sense to a purely causal picture of the human mind and action. And the second answer is that these rule-like links capture what intuitions we may have to begin with about what is special about self-knowledge, intuitions about authority and transparency, which the perceptual view cannot capture. One may of course, on considered philosophical grounds, want to deny the intuitions of first person authority and transparency, but that does not spoil the more cautiously made claim that to the extent that one has the intuitions, we need something over and above the perceptual view to account for them.

The conditionals I have formulated are intended to capture the idea of a rule-like link by saying that the second-order beliefs come with the first-order intentional states. If they really do so, then it would follow that whenever there is a first-order intentional state, there is a second-order belief about them, and vice versa. And if there is no explanatory causal link between the first- and second-order states, then there is nothing to break down; so it is not really possible to say that a first-order state could exist without the second-order belief about it, on the grounds that there might be such breakdowns. Similarly, again because causal relations and explanations are not to the point, it is not really possible to say that a second-order belief could be false on the ground that the first-order intentional state it was about was not in this particular case the cause of the second-order belief, that it did not exist at all, and that something else was the cause of the second-order belief. So what the conditionals claim is precisely a sort of necessary tie between first and second order, what I called a 'rule-like' quality. But—and this is a demand of great significance—there is a major constraint on how the constitutive theorist can uphold these conditionals in our times. The trick, in our times, when Descartes is treated as something of a leper, is to show how this view does not get to be the view it is because it has retained the feature of infallibility as one finds it in his conception of self-knowledge.

In order to pull off that trick, one has to be clear about what is meant by 'Cartesian infallibility'. Protestations against Cartesian infallibility are so apt because they point to phenomena that Descartes never really even considered, phenomena of a kind that were presented by Freud in a very articulated and general theoretical framework but that are found also in much more ordinary and less theoretically imbued cases of apparent failures of self-knowledge. There are two broad kinds of apparent failures of this sort.

There seem to be lots of such cases when we have intentional states of which we lack self-knowledge. That is one kind of failing, the lack of transparency of some of our first-order intentional states. This can happen sometimes when there is self-deception. Someone has a certain desire, say, and because it would be too uncomfortable to believe that he has it, he fails to have this second-order belief, due to standard forms of repression of the first-order state. These are the interesting cases of failure of transparency, ones studied in psychoanalysis and of great general interest to the psychologist and the moralist among us. There are also any number of much more mundane failures of transparency, where there is no self-deception involved, where there need be no motivated repressing of the first-order state, no blocking of the second-order belief because of the discomfort that the self-knowledge will bring. Rather, we may simply fail to know many of our intentional states because we are too deep for ourselves, where 'deep' is not intended as a bit of eulogy.

Apart from transparency, there are—on the face of it, anyway—many cases of failure of authority as well. These are cases where we believe that we have a certain intentional state when we do not. This too can happen when we are self-deceived. Someone may deceive himself into believing that he has a certain first-order intentional state because that is what he is comfortable believing about himself.

Failures of both these sorts are widespread and widely acknowledged. What remains of the constitutive view, then? Didn't I say that the constitutive view claims that there are *no* breakdowns in the link between first-order intentional states and the second-order beliefs that amount to self-knowledge of them? Don't these failures show that the conditionals that capture the constitutive view's main claim have serious exceptions, and doesn't that in turn show that there must be some breakdowns of those links? These questions are vital to the proceedings that follow in the rest of the book. Clearly, to acknowledge these failures of self-knowledge, to acknowledge fallibility, leaves one with a huge challenge, the challenge of giving a *non*-Cartesian account of the constitutive ideal.

The challenge can only be met by carefully distinguishing what is right and what is wrong in Descartes.

Descartes was not wrong to insist that self-knowledge of our mental states was constitutive of mental states. That is, he was not wrong to insist that mental states lack a certain independence from our self-knowledge of them, an independence that external objects have from our knowledge of *them*.

But he made two enormous mistakes despite this insightful insistence. First, he showed great insouciance by not registering the fact that we seem to have a lot of lapses in self-knowledge of the sort we have just mentioned. To insist that intentional states lack an independence from our self-knowledge of them is prima facie a very awkward thing to insist on, once we register these failures. He never had a sense of this awkwardness. Our task will therefore have to be to somehow reconcile the insistence with the failures, i.e., to give such a reading to the dependence that mental states have on our self-

knowledge of them, that the failures of self-knowledge are accommodated without threatening the dependence. That requires doing a
special kind of philosophical work; it requires taking the very idea of
mentality in a philosophical direction, which is simply missing in Descartes. The second huge mistake on his part was to think of self-
knowledge as a kind of inner perception. I have already said how hard
it is to square this element with his own constitutive view of self-
knowledge, unless you simply assert that inner perception is infallible,
something Descartes is able to do *precisely because* of the insouciance
that I have recorded as his first mistake. And the kind of work needed
to correct his first mistake, i.e., the direction in which one has to take
the very nature of mentality in order to deal with the apparent failures
of self-knowledge once one does acknowledge those failures, is made
quite impossible if one thinks of self-knowledge as a form of inner
perception.

Once one sheds the perceptual element, one is able to appeal to
quite different sorts of things than infallibility of inner perception to
account for the constitutive element in Descartes. One can (and I
will) appeal to considerations about agency and normativity, which
will show that the link between first-order intentional states and
second-order beliefs about them is indeed exceptionless and without
breakdown. In other words, *one will have the counterpart to what was
sought in Descartes mistakenly by infallibility of inner perception.* The reason
why we are nevertheless not infalliblists is that we *will have acknowledged
a prima facie problem that, in his insouciance, he did not acknowledge;* i.e.,
we will not have ignored the Freudian and other more general sorts
of phenomena that we tend to count as failures of self-knowledge.
And we will show how those acknowledged phenomena relate to considerations of agency and normativity that affect the very nature of
mental states, and once we do that, we will be able to *accommodate* the
phenomena as being unthreatening to the idea of an exceptionless
link between first-order intentional states and second-order beliefs
about them, which is essential to the constitutive view.

In essence, then, the task of this book can be seen as one of keeping
what is creative and insightful in Descartes and then, by avoiding his
extraordinary and glaring mistakes, grounding and developing that
insight at length in quite non-Cartesian directions. At the risk of
taxing endurance, I will say again that to do that one must first, even

as we insist on his constitutive ideal, do the non-Cartesian thing of registering at the outset that we seem to often fail to have self-knowledge of our intentional states. We must then read the constitutive ideal in such a way that the dependence it marks—of our intentional states on our self-knowledge of them—is compatible with these failures of self-knowledge of intentional states. And since we have seen the constitutive ideal and the dependence it marks out to consist of two different phenomena, we have to give such a non-Cartesian reading of both transparency *and* authority. The conditional for each will have to be given a reading that accommodates what we, unlike Descartes, are registering at the very outset as lapses of self-knowledge.

These lapses of self-knowledge, lapses in transparency and authority, show the bare conditionals to be false. To protect the conditionals from that, I had at this early stage formulated them as presumptions rather than as bare assertions. One can presume something is true, and it could still be a good presumption even if what is presumed is not always the case. What makes self-knowledge special is the fact that these two presumptions (each formulated as a conditional) hold, and no corresponding presumptions hold for other kinds of knowledge. The challenge, then, is to give ourselves *the right* to make these presumptions here (where we, unlike Descartes, acknowledge fallibility), when we cannot with any right make them anywhere else (where there is *also* fallibility).

To meet this challenge requires, as I said, to give a reading to the conditionals that takes the very nature of human intentionality in a direction that has no place in Descartes' thinking. This will mean first situating it in a normative conception of agency (Chapter 2), then teasing out of that the radically normative nature of intentionality itself (Chapter 4). In doing so, in correcting for the mistakes in Descartes—enormous as they are—along these lines, one would have shown that Descartes was right not only about the constitutive view of self-knowledge but also about his great general integrating idea that such a view of self-knowledge *revealed something very deep about the nature of the human mind itself.* It would just be very different from his own specific understanding of the nature of the human mind, much more revealing of its essential links with normativity and agency than anything found in his work. Thus the constitutive ideal of self-knowledge is not merely of self-standing interest. One is not simply distinguishing the rule-like links, the essential dependence of intentional states on self-knowledge of them, as an isolated interest. With Descartes, one is claiming for them a revelatory status about much else besides.

With the broad agenda now stated in very summary form, let me raise the challenge I have so far raised in a Cartesian context, in another way, so as to prepare us for the theme of the next chapter. The special character of self-knowledge, what distinguishes it from knowledge by perception (and inference), has sometimes been characterized by philosophers as an *asymmetry* with knowledge of others. Crudely put in summary form, the asymmetry is: in order to know what others think—taking what they think to be a special case of what there is in the external world—we have to perceive their behavior (or infer from their behavior), and we do not have to do anything of the sort to know what we ourselves think.[26] P. F. Strawson,[27] in a famous discussion of the subject, remarked that this asymmetry was an essential feature of the very idea of creatures with minds, the very idea of what he, introducing a term of art, called 'persons'. Only 'persons' are the sorts of subjects that possess states of mind that are characterized by this asymmetry, whereby another knew them in a way that one oneself did not.

The remark—and, in particular, the label 'persons'—is highly suggestive, but Strawson himself does not at all see the suggestion that I will tease out of it in the remaining chapters. In fact, as it stands in Strawson, the remark is not very helpful because he nowhere elaborated what it is about persons that accounted for the asymmetry. Without the elaboration, the remark seems to come off as a superior form of intellectual laziness. It seems to simply announce or label what is needed rather than provide it. If this is all that the constitutive view amounts to, it seems to have no other effect than one of saying: since self-knowledge does not, except at the margins, seem perceptual nor inferential, and since there are no other paradigms for knowledge (at any rate, none that are relevant to self-knowledge) than perception and inference, let us announce that self-knowledge, unlike knowledge of others, is unique in being neither. Any constitutive theory has to do the work required to remove this air of stipulation in

Strawson's perfectly correct remark. The challenge in this book, then, is to make that remark less arbitrary and less stipulative. To meet the challenge, I will address, over the next four chapters, the deeply integrated relations that self-knowledge bears to the nature of agency, of intentionality, and of value.

✤ ✤ ✤

TWO

The Conceptual Basis for Transparency I

A Normative Conception of Agency

1. MY BOOK'S TITLE mimics the title of an essay by Strawson[1] that has abidingly changed the shape and direction of philosophical discussions of freedom of the will. Instructed by that essay, I will try to add a particular context and an explanatory twist to another, only seemingly distant Strawsonian theme, the theme of this book as I have sketched it so far, the special character of self-knowledge of our mental states, in particular, our intentional states such as beliefs and desires.

At the end of the last chapter, the special character of self-knowledge was described as it often has been by philosophers, in terms of an asymmetry between our knowledge of our own mental states and our knowledge of the external world, including others' mental states. I also pointed out there that Strawson, in a quite different work,[2] had said that this asymmetry was a defining feature of what he, with deliberate technicality, called 'persons'. This, as I said, did nothing to *account* for the asymmetry but simply stipulated it as being intrinsic to this concept of a person; and so I set it up as one task of this book that his suggestion might be redeemable if it was somehow made less stipulative.

Here is one way we might proceed with this task. Strawson's claim is stipulative because he nowhere elaborates what it is about 'persons' that lay underneath this asymmetry in the epistemology of mind. This chapter will try and make that elaboration, and it will do so by situating Strawson's stipulative claim in the much wider context of his

46

own subsequent discussion of responsibility and freedom, a context that, in his own mind, is quite independent of the asymmetry in question. The context is wider because it is not just one where 'person' is brought in as a term of art to label a specific epistemological point about a certain asymmetry but one in which the concept of a person is our more ordinary and everyday practical concept, where freedom and responsibility are also at stake. So a way of describing the task is to say that my elaboration will emerge in the passage from 'persons' to persons—that is to say, in the passage from Strawson's own technical term to his own conception of the non-technical, ordinary understanding of persons. The stipulative and labeling claim that it is only 'persons' of whom the asymmetry holds occurs in the work *Individuals*. The discussion of persons as the site of our notions of freedom and agency is the subject of the remarkably innovative essay just cited, "Freedom and Resentment." It hardly matters that Strawson himself did not see the link between his seemingly separate concerns. If we can make the link, the elaboration we are seeking can be made. So I will argue.

A note of caution: Will this elaboration amount to an 'explanation' of the asymmetry, an explanation of why self-knowledge has a special character? I don't know. I would know if I was clear about what hostages I would be handing over by saying so. The term 'explanation' (like the term 'argument') seems mandatory to many philosophers when they think about their subject—you are not doing the subject, or you are making it cheap (that is to say, easy) if you are not providing such things as 'explanations' and 'arguments' for our key notions and claims. To many philosophers but not to all. To some others (quietists, often invoking Wittgenstein's metaphilosophy, as if there was one such thing), the term 'explanation' rings loud and jarring bells of a false expectation of what it is the business of philosophy to do, one that inevitably leads to false theories to which no ordinary person would ever subscribe.

Once the elaboration I have in mind to give is on these pages, it should become clear that my own view is that if one means something rather specific by explanation, then the quietists would have a point, and I have not given an explanation; but if not, then the elaboration might well be counted as an explanation of the asymmetry. I will return to this matter once the elaboration *is* on the pages; but until then I refuse to be made watchful about the matter and will freely use the word 'explanation' without sensitivity to this somewhat paltering dispute. The reader will have to wait till the very last page or two of the book to decide whether 'explanation' is the appropriate description for what is offered in the book.

The present chapter is wholly devoted to a subject seemingly afar from the subject of self-knowledge, the subject of freedom and responsibility, but that is the underlying basis for the 'explanation' of the special character of self-knowledge provided in the rest of the book. It underlies it at quite deep levels, and these levels will continue to be plumbed all the way until the late chapters of the book. The plan is roughly this: first, as we have already done in the last chapter, to divide the special character of self-knowledge into two properties, transparency and authority. Then, after an initial presentation in this chapter of a normative conception of agency based on Strawsonian ideas, one-half (transparency) of the special character of self-self-knowledge will be shown to have a conceptual basis in Chapter 3. A longish thread of argument is then unreeled in Chapter 4, which introduces the idea of the *point of view* of agency, a first person point of view, and this leads eventually to a much fuller development late in Chapter 5 (in Section 4, in particular) of the present chapter's initial presentation of the normative notion of agency. This flowering of the fully normative nature of agency is based not only on such an idea of a first person point of view but also, as a result of it, on a very specific normative notion of intentionality (presented in Sections 1–3 of Chapter 5) and its capacity to make a 'causal' difference (of a very non-standard kind) to the world, through our doings. The passage of the book's discussion of agency is, therefore, looped—with the normative conception of agency as initially presented in this chapter implying the notions of a first person point of view and a very specifically normative notion of intentionality with a highly non-standard causal efficacy, and it is these notions themselves that will *complete* the normative picture of agency, first presented here. Once all this is in place, and only then, will we be able to show that the second half of the special character of self-knowledge (authority) has a conceptual basis. But all that is far ahead.

2. The traditional problem of freedom and responsibility lay in asking: how are freedom and responsibility possible in a world gov-

erned by causality?[3] And the various answers in the tradition are as familiar to us as is anything we have learned in philosophy. Let me, all the same, just so as to set the stage, walk with you through the main causeway here.

The subject's history first offered up two opposing answers. The one claimed that freedom was indeed an illusion, since all events, including human actions, are governed by causes. The other claimed that freedom of action was a real thing, and questioned the universal sway of causality by conceiving human action or, at any rate, the sources of human action (in the 'will' or the 'self') to be—as they used to say—'contra-causal'. Both these positions, despite their starkly opposed conclusions, shared a common assumption, which is actually what made it necessary for them to oppose each other. This was the assumption that human responsibility was incompatible with universal causality.

It was Hume perhaps who first systematically tried to finesse the entire dispute by questioning this shared assumption of these opposed positions. He denied that causality *in itself* was any threat to freedom and responsibility. Rather, he thought it was a particular property of *some* causes that held the threat. This was the property of being a *coercive* cause. Coercive or compulsive causes undermined freedom but not causality in itself. So since it was only *some* causes, causes with a particular property, that thwarted freedom, causality *in general* was perfectly compatible with it.[4]

This compatibilist idea in this schematic form was an attractive one, but it was markedly incomplete. A hard question that was bound to be posed by the incompatibilist to this compatibilist position is: since you admit that all events, including human actions, are caused, by what criterion do you decide that only some of these causes threaten freedom and others do not? Which ones have the threatening property of coercion, and how can you tell them from those that do not? Hume really gave no answer to this vital question and seemed never to have been too perturbed by it. Nor were his many successors into this position, such as, for example, A. J. Ayer.[5] They gave examples and left it to our intuitions. Thus, for instance, we may say that someone who was made by brute physical force to do x was coercively caused to do it. We may perhaps say that someone who was encouraged by a gun being held to his head and told to do x was also coerced into doing x. Intuitions may begin to slip here, but some may even want to say that someone who was encouraged to do x by a large financial bribe in the circumstance of extreme poverty (and when, for example, his child desperately needed money for medical aid) was coerced into doing x. We can go on adding to this sort of list, pumping our intuitions, which may slip around in the margins here and there, but still the point emerges as intuitively clear as to what is coercive. By contrast with the actions on this list, another list may cite only those actions that are caused by a person's beliefs and desires and intentions without any of these sorts of intuitively coercive properties, actions such as your going to a friend's place for dinner last night, picking up this book to read, making a philosophical point in a seminar, and so on.

However, our demanding incompatibilist may be quite unmoved by these intuitively drawn laundry lists. *What about* the items on the one list make them coercive, she will persist, and what about the ones on the other make them non-coercive? What philosophical point or criterion underlies our intuitions? Without having an answer to this (what about?) question, we have no right to say that the actions caused by the causes on the latter list are free actions and those by the causes on the former list are not, since, after all, both sets of actions are determined by causes.

An initial thought might be that the 'what about?' question is answered by offering the following criterion: what makes the coercive causes coercive and the non-coercive ones non-coercive is that they flow from external and internal sources, respectively. But this is easily shown to be wrong since we may and do say that someone who had a constant waking urge to smoke or drink or steal had internal rather than external causes that were coercive.

And no other criterion comes obviously to mind.

3. I don't think any satisfactory answer was given by the tradition of this subject to this demanding incompatibilist's "what about?" question, and one only began to surface with the relatively late appearance of Strawson's essay "Freedom and Resentment." Though Strawson does not raise the question I have, his essay all the same provides a more or less satisfying answer to it. I will be bending the exposition of his paper only just a bit to make it address the question I have posed and to give exactly the answer to it that I want.

After a slightly reconstructed exposition of his view in this section, Section 4 will present a modification of Strawson's view along more radically normative lines. Sections 5 and 6 will then consider objections to Strawson's overall redirection of the subject of freedom and to my own modification of his view.

Strawson can be read as saying that no answer to the question about what makes a cause coercive can be had by staring at the cause itself. Causes don't wear their coerciveness on their sleeves. We can only say that they were coercive by looking to our evaluative responses to the actions, which are caused by those causes.

Let us take, as an example, some action of some agent that is manifestly and uncontroversially injurious to another. Now, Strawson says, if our responses to these actions harbor evaluative reactive attitudes such as resentment or indignation (for actions that are not harmful but beneficial, the relevant reactions would have to be ones like moral admiration), then that is a sign that the actions are free, and the causes that caused them are non-coercive. If our responses to it are excusing or indifferent, ignoring their obvious harmfulness, then that is a sign that the actions are unfree, perhaps brought about by coercive causes.[6] Hence the main and innovative point he makes here is that coerciveness in cause, and therefore the very ideas of freedom and responsibility are not things that we can come to grips with independently of noticing our own evaluative responses to the actions involved. The whole question of freedom and responsibility is not a purely metaphysical theme, independent of our reactive evaluative attitudes.

That the attitudes are *evaluative* reactions is a point of some importance, though Strawson himself does not draw explicit attention to its importance. What Strawson is really implicitly saying is that the distinction between free and unfree actions, and between the causes on the two laundry lists that respectively cause them, itself rests on decisions we make based on *normative* considerations that we bring to them, rather than in the nature of the causes themselves. So, in a way, *it almost seems* as if Strawson proposes a reversal of the direction from which we should approach the question of freedom and responsibility. The traditional direction was to go from saying something about the causes (that they were coercive or non-coercive) to inferring something about the actions that they caused (that they were free or unfree), and then finally, on that basis, in turn, evaluating actions (as praiseworthy and blameworthy or not so). The reversed direction is to notice our evaluative reactions to the actions, whether they are ones of praise and blame, resentment and admiration (or not), and from that impute freedom (or not) to the actions, and non-coerciveness (or not) to their causes.

His sort of compatibilist gives up on the idea that freedom of the will is a metaphysical idea because he no longer thinks of it as an idea that gets its substance and point exclusively from a metaphysical basis in a specially non-coercive and innocuous conception of causality. Rather, the idea of such a conception of causality is itself derivative of, is itself a fallout from, normative considerations that justify our reading responsibility and freedom into the actions they cause.

There are many extremely important properties to be noted and then kept in mind about these reactive attitudes of evaluation.

First, they could of course be directed toward ourselves, as much as toward others. When they are toward ourselves, the attitudes are such things as guilt, remorse, and pride.

Second, evaluative attitudes of this kind can have a varied texture. They can be more or less bland. When bland, they amount to mere criticism (whether of others or of ourselves), mere judgments that something is wrong; when less bland and more emotively ridden, they will be states such as resentment and shame.

Third, the attitudes can target not only actions but also our intentional states of mind. We can react with criticism, resentment, or shame not only to what others or we ourselves do but to what others or we believe and desire.

Fourth, we can have these reactive attitudes (presumably usually in their more bland forms) to intentional states or actions that result out of failures of logical and practical inference as well as (presumably usually in their more emotive forms) to our failures of moral character.

Fifth, these attitudes, though they need not by any means always do so, can and do often get translated into institutional practices such as punishment, and that is historically very much an *intrinsic* part of the concept of freedom and responsibility.

All these properties are of great importance, and I will take them for granted throughout the book, without constantly reminding the reader that they hold true of this general category of evaluative attitudes that I will (following Strawson) refer to as "the reactive attitudes."

But the deep underlying structural point behind this entire set of claims is that it is this normative turn alone, invoking these attitudes with these properties, that can answer the insistent demand of the incompatibilist that I mentioned above, who is not satisfied with the pre-Strawsonian version of compatibilism. Without such a turn, we have the two laundry lists but no grounding for our cherished distinction between freedom and its lack. Without such a turn, we have no answer to the incompatibilist's 'What about?' question.

I was careful to say a little while ago that '*it almost seems*' as if Strawson is reversing the direction of the tradition. This reticence was prompted by the fact that to some it will seem clearly too brash to think that it is quite like that. The tradition has it that we *first* decide whether there is a coercive or non-coercive cause of some action, then decide on its basis whether an action is free or unfree, and then finally decide on that basis whether to blame/praise/resent/admire the action or to excuse/ignore it. The brash reversal of the tradition would have it that we look at these last first, i.e., look at the reactive attitudes first, then conclude on their basis whether the action is free or unfree and coercively or non-coercively caused.

But perhaps the point should be put more cautiously than the talk of 'reversal' suggests. The reversal suggests that at the start the concept of coercive and non-coercive causes is playing no role at all; only the reactive attitudes are the focus, and conclusions are arrived at about the nature of the cause on the basis of the reactions to the actions they have caused. The more cautious thing to say instead would be this: It's not so much that the relevance of a non-coercive causality is playing *no* role in our understanding of responsibility at the start; it's rather that there is no understanding the idea of non-coercive causality at the start if one *leaves out* our normative responses to the actions caused non-coercively. There is no understanding it in strictly metaphysical and non-normative terms, as traditional discussions assumed. On this cautious understanding, the effect of Strawson's point would be to say that at the start we look to the kind of reactive attitudes we have to the same actions when they are caused by causes on one laundry list and when they are caused by causes on the other laundry list (thereby bringing in the causes in at the start); and *in doing so* we class one of the lists as coercive and the other as non-coercive. So the incautious statement of the view says that the direction is reversed in the sense that one has a *full understanding* of the evaluations of resentment or admiration toward actions *independently* of the metaphysical description that the actions are non-coercively caused, with the latter being explained entirely in terms of the former. That is wrong. The right and more cautious view that I myself take says that the non-coercive nature of the causes and the reactive attitudes are *both* relevant and necessary for responsibility, and they are both inseparably caught up with each other. There is no recognizing one class of reactive attitudes as opposed to the other (blaming, say, versus excusing) without recognizing them as reactive attitudes to actions caused by one class of cause rather than another. The two recognitions come in tandem.

It would be a misunderstanding of my position, therefore, to think that it reads Strawson as allowing us to "bypass" metaphysics and metaphysical questions (a charge recently leveled against my reading of Strawson by John McDowell, about which I say more later in this chapter).[7] Rather, the position seeks to provide a norm-based *metaphysics* of agency and norm-based answers to *nothing less than* metaphysical questions about agency.

The plain historical fact is that traditional discussions thought that freedom of action was *all in place* without the normative element of the reactive attitudes, simply on the basis of the non-coerciveness of the causes of those actions; and once in place, *it* justified the *attitudes* of evaluation; whereas the truth is, if Strawson is right, that it is not in place at all (nor is the non-coerciveness of the cause) independent of those attitudes. So, to stress again, the idea need not be expressed by saying that the traditional direction of explanation should be *reversed* but by saying that neither direction of explanation is satisfactory since each imagines that it can leave something vitally necessary out of the explanans. To reverse the direction would be to imagine that we can have the idea of the relevant reactive attitudes that account for freedom of action without any mention of non-coercive causation. That will seem to many to be just as wrong as it is to imagine—with the tradition—that one can have the idea of a non-coercive cause without any mention of the idea of the reactive attitudes. Neither position is feasible. So Strawson's main point, cautiously put, is just this last one, of the unfeasibility of the tradition.

Even qualified with caution, it is a point of great consequence. Properly understood (an understanding that Strawson himself does not make quite explicit and sometimes seems even implicitly to resist), it shows nothing less than this: *To leave the reactive attitudes out, in one's account of freedom, would be to commit a generalized and rarefied version of the naturalistic fallacy.*

How does it quite show this? The short answer, of course, is that to leave out the reactive attitudes is to leave out the normative element, to see a normative notion as non-normative, whether or not one sees it exactly as a natural property. But it is worth spelling out the longer answer, for that brings out the full normative implications of Strawson's redirection of the subject. Since those implications will be crucial to my own smaller and more parasitic efforts at redirecting my own subject of self-knowledge, I will spend some time on this.

4. The reactive attitudes are, on the face of it, curiously unprincipled phenomena. They are often emotive, and more important, we often have them helplessly. The very name suggests that. By themselves, therefore, they are not quite fit to be placed on the high mantle of normativity as we think of it—as we find it in deductive rationality, say, or in the stern imperatives of morality. I had a cat once that used to urinate on my favorite volumes of poetry, and I resented her for it. My wife sometimes resents her untuned piano. These reactions come helplessly.

We should ask, given these reactive attitudes, must we count cats and pianos as free and responsible? For all we have said about Strawson so far, the view requires that we must ask this. But, on the other hand, it is obvious that we cannot ask it but rhetorically.

That being so, there is a generalizing question, a question that the stubborn incompatibilist is poised to raise. If we are so sure that we cannot with appropriateness blame cats and pianos, that raises the specter of the ideological psychiatrist (for example, the one whose ideology gets to be a monstrous statist institution in Burgess's—and Kubrick's—*A Clockwork Orange*), who asks: But why, then, should we blame and resent people who are just as much the subject of causal influence and inner dispositions? Why don't we treat them too as merely to be modified wherever possible by drill, training, technology, medication, whatever it takes? The technology may be more or less material (it could, say, be straightforwardly medical, or it could be the cultivation of habits), and when less material, it could be more or less caring, more or less harsh (it could, say, be on a psychiatrist's couch or in the regimes of an incarceration), but in no case would it involve blame and resentment and indignation. This ideological psychiatrist's response is one that finds us altogether too judgmental of each other in the face of the fact that we are all causally determined by our psychologies and biologies and chemistries to behave as we do. It asks that we replace such reactive judgment with one of material and immaterial technologies of improvement, much as we might with pianos and cats.

The point, drawing this generalizing lesson from our qualms about resenting cats and pianos, is really one that is being made by an *incompatibilist* to Strawson's version of compatibilism. The incompatibilist, in general, is skeptical of *any* move to distinguish between some causes as coercive and others as not, saying that all causes threaten freedom. Thus, she will oppose Hume, but she will oppose Strawson as well. She (rightly, I say) expresses this skepticism against Hume by demanding that they tell her the philosophical ground for the difference between the two kinds of cause. That was the "What about?" question, she posed. Strawson responded to this (rightly, I say) by offering such a ground in terms of our reactive attitudes. But she will be skeptical of this too if we cannot justify our qualms about our reactive attitudes toward cats and pianos. She will ask, How then can we justify our reactive attitudes toward people since they, just like cats and pianos, are also caused by their own dispositions to do what they do? So unless we can manage to say something about how we might justify the one as targets of these attitudes and justify not having the other as targets, we will have no answer to such an incompatibilist. Hence, this still persistent incompatibilist, invoking the psychiatric ideologue, forces us to say not merely that freedom requires the reactive attitudes but that it requires *justifiable* reactive attitudes.

(I should add as an aside that by 'ideologue' I don't mean to be tendentious and convey an abusive or dismissive attitude toward someone who holds this position. It is a position, after all, that forces a point on us that is very instructive and a position toward which I am saying that one must have a considered response. I merely mean someone who wants to write large and make comprehensive a point that, for others, holds only in particular cases.)

In a word, such an incompatibilist forces a Strawsonian position to dig toward a deeper normative grounding of its own account of freedom.

Strawson himself does not say very much about this, and there is a real question as to whether what he does say is adequate. In fact, he tends to say the sort of thing that suggests that he does not quite see the deep normativist insight in his own overall position.

One thing he says is that it is 'inappropriate' to blame and resent creatures that are incapable of reason, whether it is because they are so by intrinsic nature (cats, pianos, very young children)[8] or by disease and degeneration, as with some adult human beings (those with a damaged brain, say, or in very advanced senility). This does not answer our incompatibilist, who demands to know by what criterion these are being singled out as inappropriate targets for the reactive attitudes since normal and healthy human beings are no less caused to do what they do than brain-damaged people or cats and pianos; for such an incompatibilist, if we fail to provide such a criterion, we should look for medical improvement or cure of one kind or another (pharmacological or psychiatric) for *all* human beings when they need it, rather than constantly judging them (and ourselves) with blame and criticism and expending inappropriate reactive emotional energy on them (and ourselves) with such attitudes as resentment and indignation (guilt and shame).

At this point, Strawson's tendency is to simply dig his heels in and say this is impossible, this is to cease to be what we are, since it is defining of us in some way (transcendental?) that we respond to each other and ourselves with reactive attitudes. Here is the sort of thing he says.

Finally, to the further question whether it should not be *rational*, given a general conviction of the truth of determinism, so to change our world that in it all these attitudes were wholly suspended, I must answer, as before, that one who presses this question has wholly failed to grasp the import of the preceding answer, the nature of human commitment that is here involved: it is *useless* to ask whether it would not be rational for us to do what it is not *in our nature* to (be able to) do. (p. 18)

(The emphases are his. For my purposes and interest, I would emphasize all of what follows the colon.) He also says on that page: "Our natural human commitment to ordinary interpersonal attitudes ... is part of the general framework of human life, not something that can come up for review."

This style of response is familiar from other areas in Strawson's philosophy. He has tended to a similar response elsewhere, where something basic about us was put into philosophical question. For instance, his response to the philosopher driven by modern science (Strawson, no doubt, thinks of her as an ideologue too akin to the psychiatric ideologue), who wondered why our ontology should not be one of sub-atomic particles, was that that is just not how we are; we simply do come to the world with a conceptual scheme in which middle-sized objects in the environment are fundamental, and this is not a perspective we can shed and remain what we are. A descriptive metaphysician (unlike a revisionary one) does no more than describe such basically (transcendentally?) grounded facts about us and our conceptual scheme. These (transcendental?) truths are ground-floor philosophical descriptions; they are *analytically* true of us. (Strawson is keen to disavow that the term 'transcendental' carries much more meaning than 'analytical', since that would promote a form of idealism and an intolerably strange sort of psychology that in Kant especially emerged with all sorts of non-standard faculties.) A similar attitude seems to govern how he thinks of our reactive attitudes. To ask that we give up those attitudes, in the face of pressure from the psychiatry-driven ideologue, would be to be revisionist in just the way that philosophy would be wrong to demand of us. It is revisionary metaphysics, outsize in ambition, whereas philosophy's task is a more modestly descriptive one.

Now, it is perhaps quite right to say that we would in some important sense cease to be what we are if we ceased to have reactive attitudes to one another. If Strawson is right (as I am suggesting he is) about the claim that freedom and responsible agency cannot be understood without the reactive attitudes being in place, then we would cease to be agents if we ceased to have the reactive attitudes. So if agency is fundamental to the way we conceive of ourselves, then we would indeed be changing the subject to something else than ourselves if we imagined that we could aspire to what the psychiatry-driven ideologue urges. But the question is not whether or not we would in some sense be giving up something fundamental about us. Let us admit that it would be. The real question is, can it be a satisfactory resting point in thinking of why we do not give up being agents by giving up the reactive attitudes to simply say that we do not give them up because "this is how we are"?

It might have been a satisfactory resting point if we could not even *coherently conceive* that we could give up having the reactive attitudes. But there is no such conceptual difficulty in conceiving it.

We can begin to think of it by imagining a sort of creeping disenchantment with the point of blaming and praising and generally judging evaluatively. What's the point, we might ask, of blaming a cat who urinates on books? Then we might move on to ask, what's the point of blaming an addict who does something harmful to gain money to feed his addiction? Then, what's the point of blaming someone who was offered and accepted money if he did something harmful when he desperately needed money to restore the health of his child? And then, what's the point of blaming someone who was persuaded by a very convincing sounding argument to do something harmful? We could continue on, citing any cause that influences and determines harmful actions. The strategy here would be like any sort of creeping skepticism, such as the one, for example, about the external world—starting with specific perceptual illusions, moving on to dreams, and so on, to comprehensive illusion, in a story familiar to us. Here, as there, the idea is: if you can imagine it in one case, there is no conceptual bar to extending it to all others. Remember, we are not talking of whether it is reasonable to so extend it, or the reasonableness of imagining it for any particular case, only of whether it is conceivable. No skeptic claims that it is reasonable to doubt in the most ordinary, everyday circumstances that he is seeing his hand or the furniture in the house, only that it is not inconceivable. So also with imagining the giving up of our reactive attitudes in any of the cases mentioned—each one is conceivable even if not reasonable, so perhaps all are conceivable.

The creeping strategy is not the only strategy by which the conclusion is imaginable. What we are being asked to imagine is that we cease to praise and blame and therefore, by Strawson's lights, cease to be agents and see each other as agents. That is *a kind of* suicide. We can certainly talk intelligibly of and imagine biological suicide and do so often. Why, then, should talk of a less physical form of agential suicide be deemed unintelligible? It is to see oneself as a creature to whom nothing matters. Perhaps we can see ourselves as only gratifying sensations but not caring for thinking or doing things that are right or wrong, nothing that involves the exercise of norms of rationality, theoretical or practical, and the accompanying attitudes of criticism, when they are violated. My students call it a sort of pervasive or comprehensive "vegging out," a slight shift from the late 1960s rhetoric ("mellowing out"). More ceremoniously, in a philosophical book, we might call it a form of 'normative suicide' or 'rational suicide' or, as I just put it, 'agential suicide'. 'Normative' or 'rational' or 'agential', rather than biological, suicide is of course a more rarefied form of the phenomenon, but it could come just as much from the despair of alienation, as biological suicide often does, and it could come just as much from an ideological zeal (e.g., as in the psychiatric ideal), as biological suicide is sometimes known to do (e.g., as in the Waco episode).[9]

It may seem very challenging to actually imagine a subject who has simply by will ceased to make basic normative judgments in both the theoretical and practical domains. How can he get through the day, one might wonder? What sort of superlative act of will is this, which kicks the ladder of all willing away from under one? I actually don't see the difficulty here as acutely as some might, but, in any case, it does no harm to the point I am making to allow that this is unimaginable. Nothing in what I am claiming is overturned if someone can only commit normative suicide *by* committing biological suicide (or by some other means, such as a drastic use of drugs). So long as it is clear that the reason why he or she commits biological suicide in such a case is *in order to* altogether cease normative and rational judgment, the idea of normative suicide and biological suicide are conceptually distinct.

If normative or rational suicide is conceptually distinct in this way, the question can arise: 'Why should we not commit normative suicide?' That is a question that does not arise for Strawson since he thinks it is not a matter of whether we should or should not. It's simply not how we are. We would not do it because we could not do it. Philosophy, properly practiced, is supposed to make that clear to us. Here, I think, something important goes missing because of Strawson's complacence, because of his refusal to countenance these fundamental, if extreme and unreasonable, possibilities. What goes missing is a real understanding of what exactly it is that sustains us as agents. The idea that agency, our sense of wielding norms and exercising attitudes of reaction toward ourselves and others, is so basic to us that the question about whether we might surrender it in a fit of alienation ('nothing matters') or zealous psychiatric aspiration ('we are all creatures of mere natural disposition and should be treated, not blamed') is not something that philosophy could possibly rule from being coherently imaginable without being Nelson-like about some fundamental kinds of despair and zeal. These things are not *easily* imaginable, but they are perfectly intelligible, however extreme and unlikely, and they cannot be stipulated away in the name of a 'descriptive metaphysics'. If so, the question, 'What makes us continue to be agents?' is one that cannot be answered merely by a defining and 'transcendental' description of what we naturally *are*. It must issue from something else. But what would this be? What could it possibly be?

The mind flinches at the task of finding something *else* that sustains our agency, and it is worth exploring why. What *more* fundamental thing could possibly explain something so fundamental as agency itself? The question itself seems to expose the difficulty of answering it.

There are actually two sources of difficulty.

The first is the product of an expectation that anything that explains must be more fundamental than what is explained. As I said, the mind boggles at the task of trying to find anything more fundamental than agency itself. And second, to find something more fundamental upon which agency is founded would in some broad sense of the term be 'reductive' of agency, and that is another thing that perhaps puts Strawson off from even trying. Agency is not to be thought of as reducible in this broad sense if it is basic to what we are. Both these inhibiting difficulties are based on sound instincts. There is nothing more fundamental than agency that explains agency, and therefore, there is no broadly reductive ground of agency.

So it should be admitted that these difficulties are real ones. But one should, all the same, wonder how and why we allowed ourselves to get into the difficulties in the first place.

The initial misstep was to have the *wrong expectation* of what must explain why we continue with our agency, why we continue with our sense of norm and value and our reactive attitudes. If it were to be something *more* fundamental than what is to be explained, these two sources of difficulty would present themselves; but why should we expect that it would be something more basic and general than our norms and values themselves? It seems like a prejudice about what constitutes an explanation in this region of thought to insist that it must. And armed with that prejudice, Strawson's own resting point seems quite natural and sage. But without the prejudice, things might open up. The idea that if we do not find an explanation that is more general than agency itself, we are stuck with a stipulating definition of what we are that rules out 'rational' or 'normative' suicide as intelligible is to impoverish the options. And it is this impoverished conception of the options that has restricted Strawson's vision of where his own initial normativist insight leads him.

To look for something less basic than agency to answer the question, what sustains us as agents against creeping psychiatric zeal, or thoroughgoing alienation, and therefore against rational and normative suicide, is a task well worth pursuing. It is the task of providing a non-reductive picture of agency. How do we go about it? The answer is obvious. To look for something less basic is to look for something *within* our agency, not for something outside it, that will explain it. And if agency is an evaluative notion, as Strawson rightly points out, if it consists in our own evaluative reactions toward each other and ourselves, then an answer to our question would have to be that it is from *within our own values and evaluations* that we can find a reason not to commit normative and rational suicide.

Notice something interestingly familiar here. The task is to justify agency by appealing to further values. These values would *have to be* more specific than the value of agency itself. "Why do you want to be an agent?" cannot be a question answered by pointing to some value that is even more general than agency, because the question, if Strawson is right about what agency is in the first place, *is the same* as the question, "*Why do you want to exercise values?*"—that is, why do you want to make judgments of value such as those expressed in the reactive attitudes? What the mind really boggles at, then, is the idea of an appeal to a more general value in answering the question "Which value or values justify one's wanting to be creatures that have and exercise values?" In other words, "Which values justify valuing?" can obviously be answered only by appealing to a value *more specific* than what it is supposed to justify. What is familiar here is a recognizable feature that we have encountered before in the doctrine of coherentism. If only beliefs can justify beliefs (the doctrine's main claim), then it is bound to be the case that the most general beliefs will sometimes be justified by more specific beliefs in order to avoid an intolerable regress. The situation is no different with values than it is with beliefs. It is no different once we give up on finding an answer to a question about what sustains us as agents, as normative creatures, by looking outside of agency and norm itself. Coherentism sees no shame in answering this by appeal to some more specific value than the value of agency and the value of being normative creatures, itself.

What are these further more specific values that sustain our agency, i.e., sustain our valuing? Being quite specific values, they could be highly varied, depending on the evaluative tastes of the person concerned. Thus a Lytton Strachey might value agency (or value valuing, if Strawson is right to integrate agency with value) on the specific ground that it is only as an agent and an evaluator that he can live a Moorean life of appreciation of art and friendship; a Leonard Woolf might value agency on the quite different specific ground that it is only as an agent that he can carry out the Russellian mission of bringing about social good; and a John Maynard Keynes may value agency because of a combined adherence to both these specific sets of values. To pursue any of these specific values, we have to be agents and cannot do without the evaluative reactive attitudes. We cannot enjoy a novel by Huxley or a painting by Duncan Grant as an aesthetic experience without the exercise of evaluative reactions, nor can we have the full exchanges with others that constitute friendship without them. Nor indeed can we oppose the war-mongering policies of a national government or give advice to the Treasury to promote public good, without the exercise of our evaluative reactions. All these activities would fail to survive, or at any rate would survive in some unintended, unrecognizable, grotesquely transformed versions, if the psychiatry-driven incompatibilist's vision held of them. To the extent that we value these activities and want to pursue them, we have a justification for being evaluative creatures, since only by being so could we pursue activities of this kind.

Nothing less than this kind of appeal to specific values would suffice to silence the incompatibilist who thinks we should suspend our evaluative reactive attitudes *altogether.* Something less might silence the philosopher who *only* asks for a justification for why we should not have the reactive attitudes to cats or to rationally incapacitated human beings. To her we can say something more general than the appeal to these specific values. We can perhaps say that, in some extended sense of fairness and justice, it is unfair and unjust to cats and rationally incapacitated human beings to resent them in the way we do normal human adults.[10] But this sort of response is useless against the more ideological objection of the incompatibilist who wants to learn a *generalizing* lesson from the case of the cat and the incapacitated human being. This ideological objection demands not a justification for why we should not have the reactive attitudes toward such subjects; rather, the objection allows that we should not have it toward them, then adds that since all other subjects (normal human adults included) are just as much caused to do what they do as these other subjects, we need to be told why we should not suspend the reactive attitudes altogether. No appeal to justice or fairness can speak to the point of this question. Only the sort of appeal to more specific values I made in the last paragraph addresses its point.

It is not as if Strawson does not at least implicitly consider at all the general direction of modification and extension of his view that is being proposed here. He does (implicitly in some of the things he says) consider a possible appeal to further values to ground the reactive attitudes, and rejects it. What he looks at is the proposal that we should justify the possession and the retention of the reactive attitudes (despite determinist pressure) by invoking the *utility* of doing so—as he puts it, by invoking their "efficacy in regulating our behavior in socially desirable ways. They [the reactive attitudes] are represented solely as instruments of policy, as methods of individual treatment and social control" (p. 21). And he finds this utilitarian picture painted for us here abhorrent, as producing in us a kind of "recoil" and "shock" because "it is painted in a style appropriate to a situation envisaged as wholly dominated by an objectivity of attitude. The only operative notions invoked in this picture are such as those of policy, treatment, control" (p. 21). He does not deny that there is an *element* of utility in our practices of condemnation and praise, but he very sensibly does not think that it can be made into a *general* justifier of these things. As he says,

> On the contrary, savage or civilized, we have some belief in the utility of . . . condemnation. But the social utility . . . is not in question. What is in question is that to speak in terms of social utility alone is to leave out something vital. . . . The vital thing can be restored only by attending to the complicated attitudes and feelings which form an essential part of the moral life as we know it, and which is quite opposed to the objectivity of attitude. (p. 22)

One way to put the point of all these excellent remarks is that the reactive attitudes are *expressive* of our own normative responses to people, and this aspect cannot be overturned or reduced or converted to some objectivist understanding of our reactive attitudes by a general justification of them in terms of the *utility* of having such attitudes.

Such a justification actually would have the opposite effect from justifying the reactive attitudes as we understand them to be, for the justification would ultimately feed into precisely the outlook being recommended by the psychiatrically driven incompatibilist ideologue. The deepest point about that ideologue is that he is encouraging us to have the objectivity of attitude toward ourselves and others from which Strawson has just asked us to recoil. It is true that the ideologue recommends this objectivity of attitude by recommending that we *give up* our reactive attitudes. However, what he has in mind by the reactive attitudes when he asks us to give them up is a notion of reactive attitudes that *thwarts* the objectivity of attitude, *not* one that promotes it. What he is asking us to give up is precisely the attitudes in the form that Strawson thinks is essential to us because they *express our sense of norms*. If the attitudes, on the other hand, were to be seen not as such expressions of our normative sense, not as the unreduced things that Strawson sees them, but instead as reduced to an *instrument of utility*, as sophisticated forms of providing control or cure, and as part of a general medical and objective attitude toward ourselves, the psychiatric ideologue would have *no* objection to the reactive at-

titudes, since his deepest point is that that is what the objective attitude toward ourselves as seen by an incompatibilist determinism rationally requires.[11]

So Strawson's instinct here is very sound. But what he subsequently
fails to see is that he *can* have the unreduced form of the reactive
attitudes, where they are not justified by their utility, without plonking
them down as a defining condition of our nature, as persons. He
could, if he were prepared to extend his vision of things just a bit,
see them as justified by further values, in the way proposed above,
where nothing is introduced to reduce them from the expressions of
our own values and normative responses to others and to ourselves.
The appeal to specific further values of the kind I proposed earlier
(rather than an appeal to utility) in no way encourages an objectivity
of attitude of the kind that leaves out the expression of our normative
selves. What the proposal, in fact, provides is a fuller picture of what
is implied by the turn that Strawson himself gave to the subject.

In this fuller picture, *both* an internalism *and* a coherentism characterize a rigorously Strawsonian answer to the demanding incompatibilist. These are closely related features but separable. Here, to
recapitulate, is how they are related: To answer her, we must show the
psychiatric ideologue to be wrong, and to do that we must justify why
we should continue to be agents and not commit agential suicide, i.e.,
normative or rational suicide. *Internalism* comes with the realization
that there is no answer that appeals to something outside of agency
itself. That would, in some broad sense, be reductive of agency. What,
then, is it to give an answer internal to agency? The crucial point is
this: Agency in Strawson's picture is marked and defined by the exercise of *evaluative* reactions. So the question, Why should we remain
agents; why should we not commit agential suicide? is no different
from the question, Why should we continue to have and exercise
values at all; why should we not cease making evaluative judgments
and having evaluative reactive attitudes? Now, if this question is to be
answered *within* agency, if it is to be answered by considerations internal to agency, and agency itself is marked and defined by the exercise of evaluative judgments, then that must mean that we must cite
further value judgments in order to say why we should continue to
make value judgments at all. But an answer that cites further values
in order to answer the question, Why should we have and exercise

values at all? will have to appeal to specific values to justify a more general one and therefore to mimic in the realm of value the sort of justificatory picture that characterizes *coherentism* in the realm of belief. That is the straightforward sense in which the internalism is related to coherentism.

This fully Strawsonian picture of freedom and agency is more radically evaluative than the one Strawson himself presents. He stops at the fact that we have reactive evaluative attitudes. To say that the fact that we have them is sustained by *further values* that justify having them is to go further in the same direction he has taken us than he himself does. It goes further in the same direction by bringing out that there is no resting point for values other than values themselves and therefore by bringing out, in turn, the radical irreducibility of values. Even though it was he who introduced the normative component in the first place by pointing out that in traditional compatibilism Hume rested too early against the incompatibilist (by resting with the idea of a non-coercive cause instead of bringing in the evaluative reactive attitudes), he himself then also rests prematurely by failing to see what really sustains our evaluative reactive attitudes themselves. There *is no* resting point in the realm of values. That is part of what it is to think of values as irreducible. *To think Strawson's insight through to its logical end is to see that to refuse to reduce agency is to refuse to reduce values,* i.e., to refuse to think that we may dig deeper than values to ground evaluation. (This integration of agency with value is the first of the integrations in this book, and from the point of view of the book's aims, it is of far-reaching importance, as we shall see.) So even if we were to say with Strawson against the incompatibilist (who, heady with the psychiatrist's vision, asks us to give up our reactive attitudes), "Sorry, but this is how we are," it will not just be, as it is for him, because of some definition of what it is to be 'us' (persons, human beings), abandoning which will change the subject from philosophical anthropology to something else. Rather, if this is how we indeed are, *it is because of certain values and goals we embrace,* and it is *they* that sustain the subject of persons and of philosophical anthropology. It is further values that justify our continuing to be evaluators, reacting evaluatively to others and ourselves, in other words, that justify our being agents.[12]

I must stress again that this departure from Strawson is not intended to "bypass" metaphysical puzzlement about agency. It is not meant to respond to the incompatibilist, who wants us to abandon the reactive attitudes on the basis of his metaphysical puzzlement, with evaluative reasons for not doing so that make no mention of the metaphysical elements (the allegedly deterministic and agency-threatening nature of all causes) that define his position. On the contrary, these evaluative reasons will try and show why our values tell us that we ought to count some of the causes (and not others) that bring about our doings as relevant to agency and responsibility. This is, therefore, not at all to finesse metaphysical considerations of causality; it is only to ground those considerations in values.

The full development of this normative conception of agency will only surface by the end of Section 4 of Chapter 5, by which time we will have made explicit the nature of the causes that our values will count as non-coercive (i.e., the nature of our beliefs and desires) and what sort of causal relations beliefs and desires have with our free actions. Only then will we have a full understanding of what is meant by a non-coercive cause that allows for freedom and agency. By then we would have added quite radically to Strawson's initial and innovative essay on the subject. But I wanted to register that even now we have departed from Strawson with this one crucial modification I have presented, and I am doing so because the departure will be vital in later chapters, first to show why we cannot think of self-knowledge along perceptualist lines, then to show (see Appendix I) that self-knowledge is itself a value commitment.

5. These last points have been made by way of modification (extension, really) of Strawson's own view of agency and freedom. But, of course, there is no reason to think that most philosophers share my sympathy for the initial Strawsonian view of freedom, let alone my modification of it. To fortify my general sympathy for this overall Strawsonian redirection of the subject, some more sensitivity should be shown to the doubts of those who have a natural and traditional resistance to it. So, in this section, I will try and raise objections from their point of view and respond to them.

I assumed pretty much from the beginning that Strawson's innovative twist on the subject opened up genuine and convincing possibilities for compatibilism, possibilities that seemed to be unavailable to the traditional (Humean) compatibilist who had failed to produce any serious response to a persistent sort of incompatibilist. The persistence of the incompatibilist consisted in asking what it is about a cause that makes it coercive or non-coercive, a distinction that was essential to the traditional compatibilist. Strawson's innovative turn consisted in saying quite frankly that there could be no response to such an incompatibilist if all we had to go on were the intrinsic properties of the causes themselves. One could not leave out our own evaluative responses to the actions caused by those causes from the basis that would allow us to count a cause as coercive or non-coercive. I claimed that this turn transformed what was, until Strawson, a purely metaphysical notion of freedom to a normative one (and I then went on to offer a modification of Strawson to show exactly how far this initially normative position would go if it was taken to where it logically led). But in all this, I had assumed without too much argument that this turn was a turn in the right direction. Someone who was a more traditional metaphysician about the whole subject of freedom might protest that not enough effort was made to explore *non-normative* responses on behalf of the compatibilist against the persistent incompatibilist. This is something to which I will return, once I say more about the subject of self-knowledge in the next chapter, but I need to say something about it here as well.

A non-normative response, resisting Strawson's turn, would have to rely on some criterion for picking out coercive from non-coercive causes. The standard analyses of freedom that have accepted a traditional version of compatibilism have mostly looked to how we might attribute to an agent a certain ability, an ability to have done otherwise than she did on any particular occasion. Applying that analysis, the criterion would have to be that if we could have done otherwise than we did, we were caused to do what we did by a non-coercive cause. This well-known analysis of freedom in general has had much critical discussion in the philosophical literature. Serious questions have been raised about whether notions of 'could have done otherwise' can provide a necessary condition of freedom and equally serious questions about whether it can provide a sufficient condition. There is also the much-discussed difficulty about whether these abilities would have to go implausibly many further steps back (i.e., Do we need to say that we have to have the ability to have *chosen* other than what we did if we are to have *done* other than what we did? And then, in turn, the ability to choose to choose other than we chose? . . .). But in the dialectic of this chapter, there is actually a more basic question than these other difficulties, and that is whether the nagging incompatibilist could possibly be satisfied by such an analysis, asking of this too: *what about* an action (given that all actions are caused) tells us that we could have done otherwise than that action, and what about it tells us that we could not have done otherwise? In other words, the very thing that makes for the difficulty of distinguishing between coercive and non-coercive causes simply carries over to distinguishing when we could not have and when we could have done otherwise. The idea of 'could have done otherwise'—however sophisticated our analyses of the idea may turn out to be—does not get us much further than the idea of a non-coercive cause. Presumably the occasions on which actions were caused by the very causes on the list of non-coercive causes would be the occasions on which we think we could have done otherwise. And presumably occasions on which actions were caused by the very causes on the list of coercive causes would be the occasions on which we think we could not have done otherwise. Our nagging incompatibilist, therefore, is bound to press on with the same sort of question for the idea of 'could have done otherwise' as she did with 'non-coercive cause', and she is bound to press on this way with *any* further effort at solution in this traditional and more purely metaphysical direction, until we come around to the normative element toward which Strawson has made us turn.

When the incompatibilist is viewed this way, Strawson's compatibilist achievement can be seen to be even greater. What the Strawsonian turn does is give us a way of saying not just which actions are free, and not just which causes are non-coercive (thereby making the actions that they cause free), but also when we 'could have done otherwise' (thereby making the causes of the free actions non-coercive).

I can see that this will only cause mounting irritation and frustration in the metaphysician in this subject. The protest to be made is an obvious one, and it would go as follows:

Once you take the Strawsonian turn, nothing we provide by way of a non-normative answer to the persistent incompatibilist's "What about?" question regarding what makes a non-coercive cause non-coercive will do. This is obvious from the response just given to the answer that appeals to the "could have done otherwise" analysis of freedom. But we don't have to take the Strawsonian turn. Why should one be bullied by this incompatibilist? She is supposed to have asked this devastating "What about?" question. But the difficulty posed by this question is no difficulty at all unless one *already* has an expectation that the intuitive answers given by Hume are unsatisfactory in a *very particular way*. It is perfectly clear that a gun being held to a person's head causes an action of his in a way that is different from the way in which his own unforced belief and desire might cause it. The incompatibilist only gets away with her nagging question because she *presupposes* that there is something deeply and irreducibly normative about freedom and agency, and that is the only reason why she finds the more purely metaphysical compatibilist accounts of agency wanting. She does nothing to argue for the presupposition itself. So why not reject this presupposition and rest content with the more traditional accounts.

This frustrated voice should be heeded and soothed.

One thing that is quite acute about the line of protest is that it correctly notices that Strawson builds up his non-traditional compatibilist position *not* by immediately answering and therefore *defeating* our persistent incompatibilist but by granting her *a victory*, at least in the short run, and then defeating her in the long run. The protest therefore voices a frustration about why we are listening to her persistence in the first place, since it is based on an unargued presupposition in which the decks are stacked because it is taken for granted that nothing short of a normative criterion for distinguishing the coercive from the non-coercive causes will satisfy, thereby ensuring a short-run victory for the incompatibilist, even if a long-run recuperation of compatibilism via a *normativist* notion of freedom.

The first thing to understand, therefore, is that this persistent incompatibilist has a quite different strategy than the *traditional* incompatibilist against whom the traditional Humean compatibilist had formulated his compatibilism. The traditional incompatibilist was pretty much everyone who ever wrote about freedom before compatibilism was formulated as a doctrine by Hume and others. Innocent of the possibility of compatibilism, everyone believed either that freedom was a real thing or that universal causality held. Whether they believed in freedom or in universal causality, they were incompatibilists because they assumed that at most one (and at least one) of these claims was true. So what the traditional incompatibilist demanded of anyone who believed in freedom was that he also believe that the sway of causality was occasionally halted by exceptions. Freedom, before compatibilism, had to be 'contra-causal', to put it in the terms that were once in currency. That is all that traditional incompatibilism demanded. And it won its victory each time anyone formulated a 'contra-causal' account of freedom.

All that must necessarily change once compatibilism came into view as occupying a space in the conceptual possibilities on the subject. Now incompatibilism had to be reformulated with it in mind. Now victory against those who believed in freedom was not to be had *only* whenever someone was persuaded to deny the comprehensive sway of causality. How, then, could it still gain a victory against the *compatibilist* who believed in freedom? Shouldn't one conclude that incompatibilism could *not* gain a victory if freedom was made possible via a compatibilism? That is certainly how it would seem if Humean compatibilism were true.

But unlike with Hume's, with Strawson's compatibilism things are not quite that simple. Strawson only successfully makes his compatibilist claims by *changing the subject*. He grants to the traditional incompatibilist that she is invincible by a purely metaphysical strategy such as Hume's. This is the short-term victory that is granted. So long as one thinks of freedom in purely metaphysical terms, there is no defeating her. That is victory enough for the incompatibilist. She has gotten compatibilism to have its way only by first granting this concession to incompatibilism.

So what is interesting is that it is only with post-Strawsonian hindsight that we can now redescribe the incompatibilist as someone who presupposes that freedom can only be established if it is seen as a normative and not purely metaphysical notion. It is Strawson who confers on the incompatibilist whom he opposes the strategy (which is being resisted by the frustrated protest of the traditional compatibilist we are discussing), the strategy of saying: Nothing you compatibilists say by way of answer to the 'What about?' question will satisfy unless you bring in normative considerations as Strawson does. You compatibilists can only have your way if you change the subject from my metaphysical subject to a normative one.

Should we allow him to do this, or should we reject the strategy as being based on a false presupposition, as the protest suggests, and stick with the traditional compatibilism?

I don't know if there is an *argument* exactly, but I think that there are non-arbitrary considerations that do support the new-fangled incompatibilist strategy of demanding that we change the subject in order to gain our belief in freedom and that therefore also support Strawson's compatibilist notion of freedom based on such a change of subject.

These considerations lie in the fact that the notion of free agency, *our* notion of free agency, cannot, except by very artificial philosophical engineering, be seen as separable from the notion of responsibility; and the notion of responsibility, in turn, is inseparable from our *practices* of praise and blame, punishment and reward. Strawson, throughout his essay, takes these connections for granted. So far in my exposition of him, I have not really differentiated all these interconnected elements in a detailed way, and it would be useful to do so now.

The reactive attitudes are brought in by him to tell us what underlies and justifies these *practices* surrounding responsibility, which are *identified* with our notion of freedom.[13] To take this *identification* for granted is to view the nagging question posed by the incompatibilist as saying something quite specific. That question was, "What about a certain cause, what about a cause that falls in one laundry list of causes (the intuitive list of so-called uncoercive causes, we listed above) distinguishes it from a cause that falls in another laundry list (the intuitive list of coercive causes)?" So far in my exposition, I had said that this question is a question about when an action is *free and not free.* But really it is taken for granted throughout by Strawson that this question gains its point from a concern about the nature of freedom, understood in the specific way I've just mentioned, as *identified* with responsibility and its practices. The question has no point, or only has an idle point, if it is not driven by this identification. This is absolutely essential to his picture of agency. If he is right about this, the incompatibilist's question, in effect, is asking, "What about a cause that falls in one laundry list of causes of actions makes an action caused by it *fit for praise or blame, punishment or reward,* and what about a cause in another laundry list of causes of actions makes an action caused by it unfit to include within these practices?"[14] For him, this question is not in substance different from (that is what is meant by saying that it is identified with) the question, "What about such a cause makes an action caused by it, *free or unfree?*"

It is to any answer to *this* question that he thinks the evaluative reactive attitudes are indispensable. It is our evaluative reactive attitudes of resentment and indignation that underlie and justify our responsibility-reflecting *practices* of blame and punishment and the reactive evaluative attitudes of admiration and regard that underlie and justify our responsibility-reflecting practices of praise and reward. And since all of these responsibility-reflecting practices, justified in this way by these reactive evaluative attitudes, are *identified* with freedom and agency, the reactive evaluative attitudes underlie our notions of freedom and agency as well, making these radically normative notions.

It should now be clear how my earlier exposition of Strawson was a little too brisk and left a crucial element out, crucial because it helps us see how we might respond to the protest voiced against him, which we are considering in this section. It has emerged now that there are at least *three* distinct but mutually supporting elements in his compatibilist account of free agency, which reconciles freedom with universal causality: (1) the evaluative reactive attitudes, (2) the practices surrounding our notion of responsibility, and (3) the property of noncoerciveness in the causes of actions. In my earlier exposition, I had not really mentioned (2) explicitly as a separate element at all. I had assimilated it crudely and casually with (1), the evaluative reactive attitudes. I had simply said that he claimed (1) was necessary if we were to see our actions as free and to see their causes as having (3). But the more explicit exposition requires one to say that finding actions to be free *is* to see (2) as having an essential role to play. Free actions emerge as free because of all three elements together, which relate as follows: (1) is relevant to saying what makes our actions appropriate targets for (2), and when the actions are appropriate in this way, the causes that bring about these actions have properly been identified as having (3). That is, it is because we have evaluative *reactive attitudes* to actions that are caused by *non*-coercive causes that these actions are appropriate targets for the *practices* integral to responsibility, practices such as punishment, reward, blame, and praise. It is this full and proper situating of these causes that finally puts us in the position of having answered the nagging question and said what it is about these causes that puts them in the list of non-coercive causes rather than the coercive ones. With all this in place, those lists are no longer merely intuitively drawn laundry lists, and the compatibilist has been able to finally define free actions in terms of non-coercive causes.

What (2) adds to the picture is the fact that the very notion of agency and freedom being analyzed is *identified* with a set of practices, *evaluative* practices surrounding responsibility, the practice of blaming and praising, punishing and rewarding. Once so identified, the point of absolutely crucial importance emerges clearly: *nothing can account for the notion of agency and freedom that is not also evaluative and normative, at least not without committing something like the naturalistic fallacy.* And something normative, such as the evaluative reactive attitudes, will be able to account for it or at the very least (if my modification, and extension, is called for) will be a first crucial step in accounting for it.

To claim this identification between free agency, on the one hand, and responsibility with all its practices, on the other, is to claim that our notion of freedom is not even identified properly if these practices are ignored. It is not as if there is a well-defined and self-standing picture of freedom, which when it is present as a property of some actions we can *then* see those actions as the sorts of things to which these practices surrounding responsibility are relevant. If that were so, then the protest we are considering would have more of a point than it does.

The protest would then run as follows. Since freedom is to be defined and identified *without* mention of the notion of responsibility and the normative practices around responsibility, we may say what about the cause of a free action makes it non-coercive without introducing the additional normative element (the reactive attitudes and the values that support and justify them). Once we have established that an action is free because caused non-coercively, as the traditional compatibilists always claimed, we can then go on to take up—as a *subsequent* bit of philosophy—the question of responsibility and its practices. Free actions are indeed the sorts of things to which those practices are relevant, but we must have a notion of free action fully defined and cleared up before the normative question of these practices of praising and blaming, punishing and rewarding, so much as gets on the map. Freedom is *a prior* and necessary condition for responsibility and its practices; it is not to be *identified* with responsibility, and so it needs prior definition in non-normative terms. The traditional compatibilist always offered that and was only tyrannized into thinking that what she offered was not satisfactory by a nagging incompatibilist who presupposed that only a normative way of distinguishing non-coercive causes was going to satisfy. *What made the incompatibilist get away with this presupposition was precisely the Strawsonian identification of freedom with certain of our evaluative practices surrounding responsibility.* But without that identification, the nagging question can be seen to be just what it is, a misguided tyranny.

Does this protest really convince? Are freedom and responsibility really separable in this way? Is there a notion of freedom prior and independent of the idea that we praise and blame people, punish and reward them? These are questions that are bound to divide philosophers. The fact is that a great deal of philosophical energy expended on the subject of freedom in the past proceeded as if there was no intrinsic connection between the two notions. Though the terms 'freedom' and 'responsibility' were often used interchangeably, or at any rate in very close association, the actual accounts and analyses of freedom gave no real normative description of it. Before compatibilism, the idea of contra-causal sources of action in the will and in the self made no mention of anything normative. After compatibilism, conditional analyses of freedom seemed to philosophers to be the most attractive way of defining freedom within determinism, and here too the idea that we were free if we could have done otherwise than we did was never really assumed to have a normative ground. Even more recently there have been efforts to tie freedom to a notion of cause that implies none of the nomological implications that are found in Hume and his legacy in the philosophy of science. In all these accounts and analyses, therefore, though it was often unthinkingly claimed that it was freedom *and responsibility* that were being analyzed, it is obvious that all that was really being analyzed was a notion of freedom that had nothing to do with our finding people responsible *in the way we do,* in our *practices,* by praising them and blaming them, rewarding them and punishing them. Why is this obvious?

Because how could something that gave analyses of causality but made no mention of anything normative in the analysis of freedom analyze or establish a normatively understood analysandum?

Let us assume for the moment that one or another of these analyses or accounts was convincing. What would that show? All that one could establish by positing contra-causal features, or by purely conditional analyses, is an abstract notion of freedom. What relevance did this notion of freedom, so established, have for our practices? None at all. Let's take one of the accounts, the analysis in terms of notions such as 'could have done otherwise'. Perhaps an action is free in this abstract sense if one could have done otherwise than one did, and perhaps there is a clear, coherent, and unitary notion of 'could have done otherwise'—which I very much doubt. Even if there were, why should it show that we may now regard that action as free in the quite different sense of being a product of *responsible* agency, i.e., the sort of thing that can be justifiably blamed or praised, punished or rewarded? It could not possibly show this because what is established when it is established to be free (in the initial sense) is something highly abstract, which has no connection with these other evaluative institutions and practices.

This objection may not move the traditional compatibilist who is protesting the Strawsonian turn. He may simply be indifferent to the fact that the notion of freedom and agency will not also deliver up all sorts of relevance to our practices. "Philosophy ought not to be contaminated by our practices at all levels," he will say. "There is a corner in philosophy for pure metaphysics."

Be that as it may, there is a question that will never go away: Why should we care for the deliverances of such a detached metaphysics? Why should we care for a notion of freedom that has nothing to do with our practices? The answer will presumably be: we will care for it because, quite apart from our interest in our practices regarding responsibility, we are also interested in freedom as a metaphysical abstraction.

Let that be so. Were it even so, what it shows is that we care about *two different things* when we care about freedom. There is no need for Strawson to assume a strict pragmatist line here and deny the more metaphysical interests, saying that something that has nothing to do with our practices has no interest for philosophy. Strawson does not need to claim that all philosophy must be relevant to our practices. All he needs to point out is that we will now need *another* notion of freedom that *is* relevant to our practices. And this other notion of freedom will need to have a normative grounding because the practices involved are manifestly normative ones. Perhaps this notion will not be quite the same as Strawson's. Perhaps it will make no appeal to a grounding in the reactive attitudes, as he does. But if it is sensitive to the question, How does it relate to our practice of blame and praise, punishment and reward? it will still have to have *some* normative element grounding it, even if not quite Strawson's version of that element. And in that case, it would still be bootless to work with a non-normative criterion of what makes a cause non-coercive.

That is the general and implicit, if not specific and explicit, point of Strawson's redirection of the subject. In all this he is indeed changing the original subject of freedom as it was standardly discussed. But it is a well-motivated change that begins with our most entrenched practices that define our notion of responsibility. Even if there are other more purely metaphysical notions of freedom that have nothing to do with this notion, the fact is that there is *this* notion and *it is not going to go away*. And it is this notion that I will be exploiting in my account of self-knowledge. I will return to some of these issues in the next chapter and again in Section 4 of Chapter 5, where the normative notion of agency presented here along Strawsonian lines is given its fullest development. In the latter discussion, I will give a much fuller account of what is meant by saying, with Hume, that our beliefs and desires (as opposed to all the other sorts of causes in the world) are non-coercive causes. To do so, I will have to first show how thoroughly non-naturalist we will have to be about beliefs and desires, treating them as normative states in a very specific sense. The sense in which beliefs and desires 'causally' relate to our actions will then be seen as amounting to a non-coercive form of 'causation'. In order to show any of this, I will have to develop at length the idea of a first person point of view—indeed, a duality of point of view or perspectives (first person and third person), which has radical consequences for a variety of naturalist ideas, including the naturalist idea of supervenience and the naturalist idea of causation.

What, then, has been shown so far if the full development comes much later? What I have tried to show in this chapter is that however exactly the idea of a non-coercive cause is fully developed later, so long as it is developed in terms that fail to situate it in a normative setting, it will not establish agency. How to fully reconcile normativity and causality will be presented later, but that we cannot even so much as speak relevantly about freedom and the practices of responsibility that surround it and define it without bringing in the normativity of the reactive attitudes and the values that justify the reactive attitudes has already been secured in this chapter.

Strawson's great innovation was to show that someone who protests in the following familiar way is failing to see the point of what is indeed a fallacy, the naturalistic fallacy:

> Since all events including human actions are caused, and causes compel their effects, we are not in the slightest bit convinced by your *evaluative* justification of our practices surrounding responsibility and the reactive attitudes that support them. Why should citing further values we possess and that you cite in your justification move us in the face of this metaphysical difficulty of the compelling nature of causes?

John McDowell[15] makes this sort of protest of my use of Strawson, saying that the philosopher in the grip of a metaphysical puzzlement about freedom will be quite right to protest that I illicitly "bypass" metaphysics in my response to a metaphysical puzzlement. McDowell thinks, rather, that it is only when we show that beliefs and desires do not fall within a naturalistic picture, and when we show that the explanations they provide of human behavior cites causes with no nomological implications and therefore no compelling deterministic force, that we will have given the right (metaphysical) solution to the metaphysical puzzlement of freedom.

I will say much more about some of the gaps in McDowell's discussion of causality and freedom in Section 4 of Chapter 5, but I don't have to wait till then to point out right here that what McDowell misses is Strawson's *identifying* the very idea of freedom with the practices surrounding responsibility. Once that identification has been made and once we acknowledge the obvious fact that those practices are evaluative practices, no non-evaluative grounding of the practices in a purely metaphysical solution is possible without committing a form of naturalistic fallacy. And were we to think that there is a highly abstract notion of freedom, which is independent of the practices of blame and punishment surrounding responsibility, then, as I said earlier, we have two notions of freedom, and we are still stuck with the problem of dealing with the notion that *is* tied to those practices. For such a notion, no purely metaphysical solution can avoid committing such a fallacy. That is, at bottom, the Strawsonian position, and I insist that it would be a tendentious characterization, in fact, just a plain *mis*-characterization, of this position to think that it 'bypasses' metaphysics in dealing with a metaphysical puzzlement. It only says that the resolution of the puzzlement cannot (without committing the naturalistic fallacy) avoid bringing in the evaluative reactive attitudes and the values that justify them in order to ground the evaluative practices of punishment and blame surrounding responsibility, which define this notion of freedom. To put it in Hume's terms, why some metaphysical items (causes of one kind, the nature of which is to be elaborated fully in Section 4 of Chapter 5) allow for freedom of our actions and other metaphysical items (causes of another kind) do not is a question that cannot be addressed without saying that our *values* see one, and not the other, as relevant to our practices of blame and punishment of the actions caused by the one and not the other. In other words, neither Strawson nor I repudiate metaphysics; we just insist on a value-based metaphysics because our metaphysical notion of freedom itself is not independent of our evaluative practices of blame and punishment that surround the notion of responsibility.

I have pledged that I myself will do (in Section 4 of Chapter 5) what McDowell thinks needs doing in order to address the puzzlement about freedom, viz., show the special way in which beliefs and desires *cause* our actions. But it would be to miss the point of what is being said here in this chapter if one thought that the evaluative basis of this metaphysics of freedom as provided by the Strawsonian position will be made redundant or irrelevant when I show later what goes into the *causality* by which beliefs and desires make a difference to the world via our actions. McDowell seems to think that once this sort of thing is shown, we can have a metaphysical resolution to a metaphysical puzzlement, and so the Strawsonian strategy is irrelevant to the puzzlement. I repeat that this is to miss the point that nothing non-evaluative *could* make the Strawsonian position redundant or irrelevant, since Strawson *identifies* the puzzlement as *being* a puzzlement about something that is *evaluative*—viz., what justifies our *evaluative* practices of blame and punishment surrounding responsibility that mark our notion of agency and freedom? Metaphysics and value are not distinct for Strawson. They are not distinct when identifying what the problem of freedom is, and therefore they cannot be distinct in any solution we might summon for the problem.

6. Now that Strawson's own position has been given full dress by making clear his point that freedom is to be identified with certain practices, let me return and say just a word about how exactly to understand the *modification* of his position made in Section 4 and how to respond to some immediate objections to that modification.

My modification extended his conception of what exactly it is that makes the practices surrounding responsibility so entrenched. Strawson argued that what makes our practices entrenched is that under- lying and justifying them are not claims about their utility, but rather our reactive attitudes that express our normative and moral selves and that define and make us what we are. I have claimed that coming to a full understanding of what makes our practices so entrenched cannot stop at pointing to the fact of the reactive attitudes as a de- fining condition of us, it requires further evaluative justification for having the reactive attitudes, further evaluative justification that once again cannot appeal to the utility of those attitudes (since, as Strawson points out, that would be to cease to see them as expressive of our normative selves), but rather can appeal to a variety of specific values that we could only pursue if we were the sorts of creatures who had the reactive attitudes. In making this claim, with purposes to be pur- sued in later chapters on self-knowledge, I have tried to bring out how thorough and far going the normative character of agency is. It is as far going as to suggest that if one did not go as far as is being proposed, if one stopped before this point in justifying our practices of blame and praise, punishment and reward, then a version of the naturalistic fallacy was being committed. To stop short of the appeal to further values, after all, is to think that something evaluative (our reactive attitudes) can have a justification that is not based on values themselves, that they have their ground in some natural fact about us. Of course it is our nature to be evaluative creatures; but that nature is sustained to be so by values themselves, not by some aspect of nature that is not itself evaluatively conceived, not some ground floor natural fact about us that digs deeper and outside of values to sustain them and provide a basis for them. To think of values as naturalistically irreducible is to think that no deeper or external basis of this kind exists for value. Strawson, unlike Hume, sees the point that value is of the essence in our understanding of agency; but then he does not get enough beyond Hume, in the passages we have quoted from him, when he does not find an evaluative basis for our evaluative reactions, simply citing them as part of a naturalistic description of the sort of creatures we are.

Let me close by addressing two questions that are bound to have arisen in the minds of readers by the modification I have made to Strawson.

First is an objection from the threat of relativism that comes from this modification. If it is *values* that justify these evaluative practices that surround responsibility and thereby ground freedom and agency, does this not raise the specter of a relativism regarding when we are free agents? Should there be different cultural responses as to whether the practices are justified or not? Would not the attribution of freedom be variable, depending on the responses? Or, for that matter, should the responses within a culture change over time, wouldn't one be forced to say that what was once free is no longer so?

The response to this anxiety will depend entirely on how one conceives of the realm of values.

If one thinks that values are subject to a kind of relativity that is missing in the realm of facts as studied by natural science, then there will no doubt be this possibility of relativism about agency. But that will just be the consequence of viewing agency in essentially evaluative terms. Once it is so viewed, if evaluation is regarded in relativistic terms, so obviously must agency and freedom. It does not seem any more urgent to protect agency from relativism than it is to protect values from it.

However, it is not, in any case, obvious that one should take a relativistic attitude toward values. Many philosophers do not, and I share their confidence in this stand. There are, of course, all sorts of subtleties that distinguish the realm of values from the realm of naturalistically characterized facts, even within a broad anti-relativism about both, and those distinctions need not be denied. The parity between values and facts nevertheless goes far enough to make this anxiety about relativism seem quite exaggerated.

I have said that justification of our evaluative practices surrounding responsibility turns on further background values we possess. There is no more reason to conclude from this that we are stuck in some wholesale relativism about freedom and responsibility than there is to conclude that we are stuck in some wholesale relativism about scientific judgments because we need to justify them, and justifications differ in different theoretical frameworks, which characterize the observational data in different terms.[16] Moreover, in both cases, at any given time, we justify our scientific conclusions and our evaluative practices from the point of view of our best current background doctrine or our best current background set of values, respectively. And of course what is deemed justified as a scientific conclusion at one time may be turned over for what is deemed justified at a later time, just as much as that can happen with the justifications of evaluative practices of blaming and punishing. None of this *forces* any relativism in science, and there is no need to assume that it does so in the case of values. At any rate, to jump to conclusions that one is stuck with a crippling relativism if one takes the Strawsonian account in the direction I have is quite unwarrantedly asymmetrical. I don't want to deny that a philosopher *already committed* to relativism about values (as opposed to science) will want to take an evaluative notion of freedom to be relativistic, but then such a philosopher will not present this conclusion as crippling or as an anxiety. I do, however, want to say that I am not such a philosopher. And I do not, in any case, think that there is *any more* anxiety created for the subject of agency by my modification of Strawson than there exists in the realm of science, as a result of such things as the denial of the analytic-synthetic distinction or the theory ladenness of observation or indeed the fact that we judge truth and justify theoretical conclusions by the lights of our best current background doctrine, there being no other lights.

No doubt the anxiety about relativism regarding what counts as free, which I have just raised for the modified Strawsonian view, will arise again, in later chapters, for what counts as self-knowledge. This is natural because I will be arguing that self-knowledge is a fallout of the modified Strawsonian view of agency. So if freedom depends on such reactive evaluative responses, and self-knowledge rides on a notion of freedom that depends on those responses, then if there is an anxiety about relativism regarding such a notion of freedom, there is bound to be a similar anxiety regarding the notion of self-knowledge that rides on it. Rather than repeat the response to that derivative anxiety about relativism in later chapters, let me say here that the response just made applies without remainder to that anxiety as well.

Second, there is bound to be an objection that there is something unscientific in the anti-naturalism about values expressed in my modification of Strawson. I have argued that it is a fallacy to think that evaluative reactive attitudes should not get further evaluative justification but be thought of as ultimately reducible to natural facts about us. I have also said that Hume's earlier claim that a non-normatively understood notion of an uncoercive cause should ground our evaluative practices of responsibility commits the same fallacy. All this is bound to produce the familiar response that there is a whiff here of something unscientific. Let me close the chapter with some (no doubt also) familiar remarks that that is not intended.

It cannot be unscientific to insist that not all themes—themes such as agency or freedom and value, for instance—are scientific themes. Just to give one example, Noam Chomsky, a scientist if ever there was one among philosophers, has argued that semantic themes, specifically some having to do with the lexicon, are not scientific themes. One does not have to agree with him on this particular judgment (though I myself do) in order to see the general point I am stressing, that not all themes are scientific themes.

Moreover, to insist that agency and value are not scientific themes is not in any way to deny the importance that a great deal of science, and our understanding of the nature that science studies, has *for* agency and value. Understanding the nature that science studies, including our own place in it as central nervous systems, greatly enhances our understanding of agency and value, even if we do not equate these latter with elements in nature that science studies. What is more, the very concepts of agency and value would not be the concepts they are if the facts of nature, as science studies them, were very different from what they are. In other words, perhaps we could not be the evaluative creatures we are if our nature (as natural science studies it) were very different from what it is. We can, and should, acknowledge such a dependency of the domain of value and agency upon that of nature, even if we deny other forms of dependency, identity, and reduction. All one is insisting on, in insisting on this autonomy for agency and the evaluative elements that define it, is that evaluative concepts, the concepts that go into the reactive attitudes that Strawson stresses, are not concepts we can properly employ by meeting standards of propriety that are formulated exclusively in terms of nature as science studies it. They are properly employed by meeting standards of propriety that are formulated (at least partly) in their own *further evaluative terms*. Thus the coherentism about value, which we have already stressed in our own modifications of Strawson.

All this may puzzle someone. If it is claimed that one is not unscientific when one insists that there are themes out there that do not get scientific coverage, what is it to be unscientific?

The answer is obvious. It is unscientific to give unscientific responses to the themes that *are* within the coverage of science (a creationist answer to the theme of the origins of life, for instance).

And so, what then are the criteria by which we decide which themes do or do not fall within the coverage of science? It is not clear that such criteria can be stated in a general way in advance of a consideration of the specific contours of a theme as it surfaces in given contexts of discussion. This chapter provided just such a contextual discussion of the contours of the subject of agency, causal determination, and their compatibility. I have, following and extending Strawson, tried to show that there is a certain sense in which there seems to be no way in which a certain set of practices can be justified if one looks to facts and concepts that fall purely within the realm of nature and the sciences that study them. Those practices and their justification in values are essential to the way we understand one notion, if not all notions of freedom and agency;[17] and that is the context in which one may claim to have identified a theme that itself falls outside of the sway of naturalistic reduction. Even the theme or question, what biochemical nature and origin must a creature and species have in order to be the kind of creature and species that has such evaluative practices? is a theme that falls within the coverage of science. It is a theme regarding certain capacities and what endows some creatures with them. All that is being denied is that the *justification* of the evaluative practices is something that falls within that coverage, since it appeals to further values and not to any element that is within the purview of natural science. To think otherwise is to betray an ambition that is outsize in just the way that we should be inclined to call a fallacy.

The naturalistic fallacy, then, is not what it is sometimes confusedly thought to be, one of taking values themselves to be facts. Values may indeed be facts—of course, a special kind of fact—and valuing some thing may indeed be a cognitive state such as having a special kind of belief about those facts, about what is valuable. I take no stand right here (though I do in Chapter 5) on whether or not that is so, but what is clear is that if one thought it is so, it is not to commit what was intended by the term 'naturalistic fallacy'. The fallacy is, rather, to think that we can dig deeper into the nature of values and see that they are wholly accountable by, that they have their basis in, something that is wholly non-evaluative—in other words, to think that evaluative concepts have in their criteria of correct application no mention of conditions that are themselves described evaluatively. As I said earlier, the idea of such a fallacy need not deny a general sort of dependency that values may have on the facts that nature studies. The question of what exact sort of dependency values have on what is not evaluative is not something with which we need be concerned in this chapter. I will take it up again in Chapter 5 in some detail. Though this too is a subject that has exercised philosophers greatly, it would make no difference to what I have said so far. So long as the dependency is weak enough that it does not amount to a denial of my own claims of the irreducibility of agency and the reactive attitudes, I need take no immediate stand on what it does amount to. If it is stronger than that, it does fall within the sorts of naturalism that I am opposing as a fallacy in the context of this specific discussion of agency; and those who claim that stronger thing for it would have to make their case by responding to the specific sort of claim I am making in the specific context of justifying our practices and our reactive attitudes.

The reader should also be cautioned about terminology on this score to avoid a simple misunderstanding. My talk of naturalism and naturalist here and throughout the book is intended only to mark out a doctrine and a philosopher who thinks that all the facts or properties there are, are the facts that are countenanced by the natural sciences. I will be saying things from time to time to oppose such a philosopher. But this opposition is not targeting any broadly conceived naturalism, that countenances evaluative facts and properties as being part of nature.[18]

These last remarks, making and responding to the charge of an unscientific anti-naturalism in the irreducibly normative conception of agency I have presented in this chapter, cover ground that is, no doubt, familiar from ongoing debates about naturalism.[19] I will say something much less familiar on the subject when I raise the topic again in Chapter 5, when the other integrations I have in mind to make are in place.

The next chapter is intended to see through the relevance of such a normative conception of agency for the subject of self-knowledge, in particular, that property of self-knowledge that we have called 'transparency'. After that, in Chapters 4 and 5, the implications of the normative notion of agency presented so far are gradually developed. In particular, it is shown that the normative conception of agency presented so far (viz., that we are subjects whose doings are the justifiable objects of the reactive attitudes) implies, indeed consists in, possessing intentional states, which must be conceived in thoroughly normative terms and which must be seen as making a difference to the world via our doings in a very specific sense that does not entail causal and dispositional notions, standardly understood. All of that will be necessary to put in place before we can establish authority. But the tasks are a little more straightforward for establishing transparency, which comes first.

❖   ❖   ❖

The Conceptual Basis for Transparency II

Evaluation, Agency, and the Irrelevance of Cause

1. THERE WAS THE thesis (Chapter 1) that self-knowledge had a special character, which is expressed in two conditionals that reflect two presumptions. There was the pledge (Chapter 1) that these conditionals would be established as true in a very specific sense, if not all senses. There was the elaboration (Chapter 2) of a notion of agency in normative terms.

The time has come now to redeem the pledge made in the first chapter in terms of the elaboration of agency made in the second, thereby establishing the thesis of the special character of self-knowledge.

In this chapter, only the conditional capturing transparency will be addressed. The conditional for authority, which is more controversial and requires a consideration of a wider range of issues, will be discussed over the next two chapters. In both cases, the idea will be to read and expound the conditionals and show them to be true in a specific sense, i.e., a sense sanctioned by the very specific normative conception of agency just sketched, for the first conditional (transparency), and by a very specific way of thinking of the normative nature of intentionality to be sketched in Chapter 5, for the second conditional (authority).

This section will present a very summary recapitulation of the main thesis and its surrounding philosophical (non-historical) points from Chapter 1. Section 2 will present the gist of the use being made of the content of Chapter 2 in an argument for one-half (transparency) of the main philosophical thesis about self-knowledge. Section 3 will elaborate and consolidate the argument and the thesis by responding to certain objections. Section 4 will present the rewritten conditional for transparency and its chief radical implication. Section 5 will further elaborate and defend the main thesis by responding to objections whose point is to make it less radical and interesting.

Here again are the two conditionals.

(T) It is a presumption that: if S desires (believes) that p, then S believes that she desires (believes) that p.

(A) It is a presumption that: if S believes that she desires (believes) that p, then she desires (believes) that p.

The conditionals are regarding two properties, transparency and authority, respectively. The former is a property of first-order intentional states. They are transparent to their possessors; i.e., whenever they exist, they are accompanied by the second-order belief that they exist. The latter is a property of these second-order beliefs about the first-order intentional states.[1] They are authoritative; i.e., whenever they exist, the first-order intentional states they are about also exist.

These two properties capture the special character of self-knowledge because no other kind of knowledge has these properties. Only our knowledge of our own intentional states has them. Knowledge of the external world or of others does not have these properties because (1) unlike our own intentional states, others' intentional states and objects in the external world are not such that when they exist, they are always presumed to be accompanied by our beliefs that they exist, and because (2) unlike our beliefs about our own intentional states, our beliefs about others' intentional states and about objects in the external world are not such that whenever we have them, it is presumed that those states and objects exist.

Since the special character of self-knowledge was defined in terms of this contrast with knowledge of the world and others, it seemed right to describe it also in terms of a matching contrast with perceptual knowledge. Knowledge of the world and others paradigmatically involves looking, seeing, hearing things in the world, including what others have to do and say—in general, a testimony of the senses. (Even the testimony of others that the world is thus and so involves hearing what they have to say.) Testimony of the senses, or any inner cognitive analogue of the senses, is precisely what is *not* involved in the ordinary and paradigmatic cases of self-knowledge.

Even the minimal underlying *causal* element in perceptual knowledge, the causal link between what is known and the knowing of it, is not involved in any essential way in what explains our self-knowledge. The causal link between a fact or object in the external world and our belief about it is indeed an essential minimal element in explaining our perceptual knowledge of the external world. But it will be claimed that even if there is such a causal link between our intentional states and our beliefs about these states, it plays no essential role in accounting for the ordinary cases of our self-knowledge of those intentional states. So not even in this minimal sense is self-knowledge like perceptual knowledge (of the world and others). And that is why the properties of transparency and authority presumptively hold of it and not of perceptual knowledge. If causal links were what was relevant to accounting for self-knowledge, transparency and authority would not hold, and therefore self-knowledge would not be special among knowledges. Causal links can always break down since they owe to (causal) mechanisms that could break down. This would disrupt transparency because intentional states may, in that case, not cause the second-order beliefs about them. Also, if causal links are relevant, then there can be non-standard causal links. This would disrupt authority because, in that case, second-order beliefs about intentional states could be caused by links to things other than the intentional states they are about. It is because causal links are present in perceptual knowledge that these properties cannot be presumed to hold of perceptual knowledge. Since causal links have no explanatory role in self-knowledge, there is no bar to presuming that these properties hold in self-knowledge.

To presume these properties as expressed in the two conditionals is to assert a rule-like quality of the relation between intentional states and our beliefs about them, precisely the quality missing in the explanatory relations (causal) between objects or facts in the external world and our beliefs about them. And the rule-like quality of these relations between first-order intentional states and second-order beliefs about them is what made for the idea that our account of self-knowledge was constitutive rather than perceptual. Our second-order beliefs about our intentional states are constitutive of the very idea of intentional states, which they would not be if the explanatory work was being done by any causal relations (if they existed) between our intentional states and our beliefs about them. In perceptual knowledge, by contrast, our beliefs about the external world are lacking this constitutive status vis-à-vis the objects or facts in the external world they are about. And this is because the explanatory work *is* being done by the causal relations and the causal-perceptual mechanisms linking those objects or facts with our beliefs about them. Facts or objects in the world thus have a sort of independence from our beliefs about them, which this constitutive, rule-like relation shows to be lacking for our intentional states from our beliefs about them.

The task we had set ourselves was to explain why the presumptions expressed in the conditionals held for self-knowledge and not for any other knowledge or, to put it differently, to show what about self-knowledge gave us the right to say that it was quite unlike perceptual knowledge in the respects just summarized.

I am being careful throughout to say that what needs explaining are 'presumptions'. Conditionals (T) and (A) were formulated not as strictly holding but holding merely as presumptions. This was forced on one because if they were formulated strictly and not merely as presumptions, the conditionals would be false. So formulated, there would seem to be many exceptions to the conditionals in the form of failures of transparency and authority. On the face of it, self-deception and other less interesting phenomena suggest that there are intentional states unaccompanied by second-order beliefs about them and that there are second-order beliefs about intentional states that are unaccompanied by the first-order intentional states they are about. No formulation of the conditionals, obviously, can ignore this apparent fact, once we have abjured Cartesian ideas of infallibility. It must accommodate the apparent fact of the exceptions. The presumptive formulation of the conditionals provided that accommodation since a presumption may remain true, even when a corresponding strict assertion is made false by the exceptions.

However, after the mission of the present chapter is completed, we need no longer continue to see the conditional for transparency as a presumption, for otherwise we would not have made any progress, since what we want and have pledged is to '*explain*' (or some cognate of that) the presumption that the conditional expresses. The same

will be true of the presumption and conditional for authority, once
we complete our consideration of that in Chapter 5. So, in this
chapter, a non-arbitrary way must be found to rewrite the conditional
for transparency so that it does not merely assert a presumption. The
'explanation' offered here will have the effect of such a rewriting.

The fact of the exceptions that the presumptive formulation was
supposed to acknowledge does not, however, vanish as a result of the
rewriting. The exceptions are accommodated in the rewritten conditional too. The notion of agency elaborated in the last chapter will
be crucial to the way in which the conditional is reformulated to accommodate the fact of the exceptions. It will enter as a proviso, under
which the conditional holds, and the presence of the proviso is intended at once to provide the explanation of the presumption while
accommodating the exceptions that the initial presumptive formulation acknowledged. The reformulated conditional, given the proviso,
will be *strictly* true and not true merely as a presumption. Thus, the
presence of the proviso will both provide the explanation of why we
may presume authority and transparency and also acknowledge the
fact of the exceptions by claiming that whenever there is an exception,
the proviso *does not* hold. Since the conditionals are true only when
the proviso holds, this accommodates the exceptions.[2]

These abstract-sounding claims and intentions should emerge as
quite concrete and intuitive, once spelled out in an argument.

Let's now take the conclusions of the last chapter and visit them
upon the conditional for transparency.

2. The question is: whence our conviction of transparency?

Might it not be that there is no transparency? Given the fact that
our intentional states, whether or not as result of our own motivations,
sometimes get to be too submerged for us to be aware of them, what
gives us the right to presume transparency as a property of these
states? Why don't we rather assume that there is simply a pretty reliable (but not wholly unfailing) causal mechanism that mostly (but
not exceptionlessly) links our intentional states with our states of
awareness of them, thereby accounting for the *impression* of transparency and also at the same time accounting for the failure of awareness
when that happens? That would be to assimilate intentional states to
states and objects in the external world and see them as lacking transparency.

Perhaps we should do that, but to the extent that the conviction of transparency seems to have survived among philosophers for so long as a genuine property that we intuitively take to hold (uniquely) of our own mental states and *not* of states in the external world, one ought to at least diagnose whence the conviction before we dismiss it as illusory. If the diagnosis is a good one, in the sense that the considerations it appeals to are independently convincing, it might instruct us to stick with the conviction as being philosophically grounded and not merely intuitive.

To the extent that independently convincing reasons have been given in the last chapter for a notion of agency to be a normative notion, should such a notion of agency now provide a diagnosis of where it is that our intuitive conviction of transparency comes from, then that intuitive conviction would seem to have a philosophical ground lying beneath it. To provide that diagnosis is the immediate preoccupation of this section.

Here, then, is the opening shot in providing it.

It is a conspicuous fact about the notion of agency (given its familiar and close connection to notions of responsibility and freedom, and understood in the evaluative terms in which we elaborated it in the last chapter) that it takes for granted self-knowledge. Actions do not *justifiably* (in the terms mentioned in the last chapter) get counted as responsible if the actor does not know that she has acted in that way. Let's put this point about responsibility more fully and explicitly in the modified Strawsonian terms of the last chapter. Let's also work, for the sake of convenience, with the negative attitudes mentioned by Strawson, resentment and indignation and the practices they support such as blame or punishment. The claim, then, is that these attitudes and practices are not justifiable when they target actions that are not self-known by the agents who perform them. And from this emerges another related point. These actions are not justifiable targets of such attitudes or practices, not only when the actions themselves are not self-known to the agent but also if the intentional states that rationalize the actions are not self-known.

If this is, in first approximation, right, then we can say that to the extent that intentional states fall within the region of responsibility, that is, to the extent that they are tied to responsible action, then there must be self-knowledge of them. In other words, transparency of intentional states is established so long as the intentional states have such ties to responsible action. The ties in question are fairly straight-forward and familiar. Intentional states rationalize intentional action. They provide the lights by which an action gets to be seen as rational, by which it gets to be made sense of. And so if an intentional state actually or potentially[3] does this for some action, and that action or potential action, if it is in turn viewed as responsible in the normative sense elaborated in the last chapter, then we can say that the intentional state that rationalizes it or would rationalize it must be self-known by the actor concerned.

That is the opening shot, as I said, to be refined and qualified in various ways.

Here is another way of making the point. It is a good bit more roundabout, but traversing the longer route will be instructive and revealing.

For an intentional state to be self-known, it will, among other things, have to be accompanied by a second-order belief on the part of its possessor, the belief that she possesses that intentional state. One task in explaining self-knowledge is to explain what underlies this, what makes for this accompaniment. Let me first put out some terminology. For the sake of convenience, let's call the first-order intentional state an 'embedded' intentional state, since it is the object of a second order belief. (This is an abbreviation, of course, because the more correct and longer description of it is that it is the intentional state captured by the embedded clause of a statement reporting a second-order belief about the intentional state.) We can correspondingly call the second-order belief about it the 'embedding' belief. So if X believes that he believes that London is the capital of England, then his *belief that London is the capital of England* is the embedded state. I call such a first-order state an 'embedded' state rather than a 'transparent' state because it is a *neutral* description of first-order intentional states that are accompanied by second-order beliefs about them. Since I am saving terms like 'transparency' and 'authority' as descriptions of properties that are claimed by a very specific view of self-knowledge, the constitutive view, I don't want to beg the question in favor of this constitutive view, against the causal-perceptual view, by calling such states 'transparent' at this stage. The causal-perceptualist view will explain embedded beliefs quite differently from how they will be explained by the constitutive view.

And the question is, which is the better explanation? The constitutive view sees the embedded states as satisfying the presumptive property that I have called 'transparency' and that is captured in a conditional that reflects the presumption. But the causal-perceptual view will not see them as transparent. It will see the embedded state's relation to the embedding state in terms that are *essentially the same* as it sees the relations between facts in the external world and perceptual beliefs about them. That is, see the relation as the product of a causal mechanism, only perhaps a more reliable mechanism than is perhaps involved in the case of perceptual beliefs about the external world—thus the (false) *impression* of transparency. To see them that way means that since facts in the external world are *not* transparent (i.e., since one cannot presume that if there is a fact in the external world, then we believe that it is there), *neither* is a first-order intentional state. Therefore, calling 'embedded' states 'transparent' right at the outset would be to assume (at the outset) what has to be shown, viz., that such a perceptualist view gives the wrong explanation.

With all this terminology in place, a good question can be raised. All 'embedded' intentional states have a recognizable status. And the good question is, what is that status? In other words, what sort of animal is the intentional state picked out by the emphasized expression in the next sentence? She believes that *she desires (or believes, etc.) that p.* I think that the right answer to this question will help us say a little bit more about what makes for the transparency of intentional states.

It is tempting to answer the question by saying simply that these are the states that we call 'conscious' intentional states. But that, though true, would not be an illuminating answer. This is because for many philosophers[4] the idea of a conscious state is to be analyzed in terms of being the object of a second-order belief, and that does not get us further than where we started. And if we reject this analysis of a conscious state for some other analysis of it—say, a more phenomenological analysis—then it is doubtful that the description "conscious" always correctly characterizes the embedded intentional states we are interested in. After all, embedded intentional states may not always, may not even very often, have any phenomenology that marks them out. For one thing, as I will stress immediately below again, embedded states need not necessarily even be occurrent states, and they certainly do not have to be in the forefront of one's mind in deliberation or be the object of one's attentive gaze or be explicitly self-ascribed or generally in any way be experienced by us in explicit terms of phenomenological awareness. When they are not any of these things, they do not, by any means, lose their 'embedded' status and become '*un*embedded'.

Thus, calling the embedded intentional state 'conscious' gives us *either* the wrong answer to our question *or* no more than a label for what we want an answer to, since it gives no illumination. How, then, shall we characterize the kind of state it is, if the characterization "conscious" won't do?

It is here that the excursus about agency in the last chapter impresses with its relevance. The proposal I have been working up to in what I called the 'opening shot' is this: the kind of intentional state that is picked out by the embedded clause in a second-order belief ascription is one that (along with other such intentional states) rationalizes or potentially rationalizes actions that can be the objects of justifiable reactive attitudes. That is to say, it rationalizes actions that are, in the modified Strawsonian picture of responsibility sketched in the last chapter, free and responsible actions.

The point becomes vivid if we contrast this kind of intentional state with intentional states that are *not* 'embedded' states. Compare them, that is, with intentional states that are not accompanied by second-order beliefs about them. All states standardly described in ordinary talk as well as in psychoanalytical talk as "unconscious" mental states are examples of unembedded states.[5] These unembedded intentional states are precisely ones that, when they rationalize actions (if that is what they do),[6] do *not* rationalize actions that are the objects of internally justifiable reactive attitudes, blame and punishment, etc. I will be saying a lot more further below about why these unembedded states and the actions they rationalize are not the objects of justifiable reactive attitudes. (I will also be saying a lot more much later—in Chapter 5—about what I say passingly in the important anticipatory note 6, viz., that talk of 'rationalizing' may in the end turn out to be entirely inappropriate for these unembedded states.)

But notice an important point about the opening shot: in saying that the unembedded states are not the object of such responses, one is *not* saying that only the states that are in some sense in the forefront of one's mind in very explicit and conscious deliberation are embedded. Some accounts of transparency and the special nature of self-knowledge restrict their focus initially (and even eventually) to conscious states in this very narrow, occurrent sense, a sort of phenomenon usually captured in present-tense first person self-ascriptions. On the notion of transparency provided by the opening shot, no such initial or eventual restriction is necessary. By the nature of the considerations that the opening shot appeals to (considerations of agency), its coverage of intentional states is much wider, and its goal is more ambitious. It is by no means restricted to occurrent states, self-ascribed in the present. It applies to any intentional state—occurrent or standing—that is the justifiable object of the reactive attitudes or that rationalizes or potentially rationalizes actions that are the objects of such attitudes. Thus the strategy of this book's effort to characterize what is special about self-knowledge is not to find some '*basic* case' of self-*ascription* and then extend it more generally to all cases of self-knowledge.[7]

The point is worth pressing, for it quite intuitively captures our ordinary understanding of the notion of self-knowledge. In ordinary speech, one would see nothing wrong in saying that I knew fifteen minutes ago that I believed that one-day cricket is an abomination. But fifteen minutes ago I was not thinking of my beliefs about cricket, nor was I thinking about cricket. I was thinking intensely about philosophy. Yet, fifteen minutes ago, I *did* believe that one-day cricket is an abomination, and I *did* believe that I believe that one-day cricket is an abomination. The account given here of self-knowledge and transparency covers beliefs such as the one about cricket because that belief can be the object of justifiable reactive attitudes, as are the actions that it might have rationalized. The contrast between such embedded states and unembedded states is therefore not at all the contrast of occurrent versus standing states. It is, rather, the contrast of states that are or rationalize actions that are the objects of justifiable reactive attitudes versus states that are *not* and rationalize actions that are *not* the objects of such attitudes.

We do routinely make a distinction, of course, between occurrent versus standing states, states that are 'conscious' in the sense of being in the forefront of one's mind in explicit deliberation versus states that are not so. But that is not the ordinary and intuitive contrast between intentional states that are self-known and intentional states that are not. The ordinary and intuitive contrast, rather, is with states that, even when not occurrent, one expresses in assent on prompting without much effort ("Do you believe that New Delhi is the capital of India?" "Yes." "Do you believe that one-day cricket is an abomination?" "Yes.") versus states that one does not so express in such assent, states for which assent may require a great deal of cognitive self-inquiry, and of which psychoanalysis, for instance, makes quite a lucrative meal, though of course the kind of inquiry needed is not restricted to psychoanalytical cognitive self-inquiry. (Thus compare the previous questions and assenting answers about the beliefs about New Delhi or cricket to the classic question, "Do you believe that your father was hostile toward you? to which, if there are assenting answers, they are, in the classic understanding, often supposed to be at the end of much cognitive effort and vast expenditures of money to an analyst.) This contrast is the intuitive contrast between self-known and unself-known intentional states, and it is the contrast that the considerations of agency invoked in my opening shot are intended to illuminate. It is because this contrast does not coincide with the contrast between standing and occurrent at all that self-known states may be both standing (as the belief about cricket is) and occurrent. Transparency, in the opening shot, is intended therefore to hold of a much larger class of intentional states than those ascribed in first-person, present-tense, explicit self-ascriptions.

Two important asides regarding this opening shot before it is defended and elaborated.

I have been talking of rationalizing 'actions'. I mean to use the term as broadly as possible. I mean to include among actions such things as the conclusions we come to in a bit of theoretical reasoning. Or, for that matter, conclusions we come to in practical reasoning, since for many—unlike Aristotle—it is not actions that are the conclusions of practical reasoning but a judgment of what is the best action to perform. I intend by 'action' to include all such conclusions as well. So my claim above should read more fully and explicitly as saying that the status of embedded intentional states is that they are the ones that rationalize or potentially rationalize actions *or conclusions (of deliberation),* which can be the justifiable targets of our practices and reactive attitudes that characterize our normative notion of agency. From now on, I will not distinguish conclusions from actions but simply include them among actions.

There is also a further point, a quite different one. We have reactive attitudes, and justifiable reactive attitudes, not just to actions and conclusions of this sort but also directly toward intentional states themselves. We may thus justifiably react to someone's or our own belief or desire by calling or thinking it illogical or otherwise irrational or immoral. In these cases, the overall point being made applies more *directly* to intentional states themselves and does not just apply to them indirectly via the actions and conclusions they rationalize. So the opening shot, most fully stated, says that an embedded intentional state is a rationalizer or potential rationalizer of an action or conclusion that is the target of justifiable reactive attitudes, or it is *itself* a direct target or potentially direct target of justifiable reactive attitudes.

More needs to be said if this opening shot is to fully convince. But notice, even without that, it at least says something that could be illuminating (if it were fully convincing) by providing an answer to our good question about what kind of animal the embedded intentional state is. It says much more than is said by calling it a 'conscious state', which illuminates nothing since all it does is label the embedded intentional state, without giving any analysis of what sort of state it is. It purports to give that analysis by making deep connections between states of this kind and our notion of agency and all the normative elements that that notion brings with it. *The property of transparency resides in these connections.* What these connections show is that intentional states that go into *agential* mental life and behavior, that is to say, intentional states that go into mental life and behavior that is or can be the justifiable target of our reactive attitudes, are necessarily self-known. Self-knowledge is a necessary condition for agency; and intentionality as it figures in agency therefore must be transparent.

3. To elaborate some of the details of this opening move and to make it more convincing and more nuanced, one must deal with some obvious objections. These objections therefore are raised and answered here not only because it is responsible to be sensitive to

objections to one's position and defend it against objections but because the responses will reveal a great deal of the substance and fine points of the position being defended.

Objection 1.

The most obvious, though not the most difficult and fundamental, objection flows from doubts someone might have about how I have moved from saying that self-knowledge of one's *actions* is a necessary condition for the reactive attitudes toward those actions to be justifiable to saying that self-knowledge of one's *intentional states* (which rationalize the actions) is a necessary condition for justifiable reactive attitudes toward those actions. To say the first might be all right, but by what argument do I extend the point to demanding self-knowledge of intentional states?

The answer lies in the nature of rationalizing. To rationalize an action (to make sense of it) is to see it as rational by the lights of intentional states of the actor. It is by now a well-known feature of such making sense that the action gets to be described the way it does get described only because the intentional states that rationalize it are the ones they are. That is to say, the way we specify the intentional states (the propositions we use to say what their contents are) also makes a difference to how we describe the action being rationalized. One might begin with some description of the action to be rationalized, and then when one finds the intentional states that rationalize them, we *re*describe the action as making sense by their lights. Thus we might begin by saying that someone lifted a glass of some substance and drained it, then redescribe that action as his quenching his thirst by drinking a glass of water because he desired that his thirst be quenched and believed that drinking the glass of water would quench his thirst. The belief and desire, once identified, recast the action as they make sense of it. What this familiar point shows is that any justifiable reactive attitude we have toward the action is toward the recast or redescribed action. Actions are resented or admired, praised or blamed and punished, only under descriptions, and which descriptions they are praised and blamed under turns on which intentional states we have appealed to in making sense of them. Thus, any necessary condition we lay down for justifiable reactive attitudes and practices toward the actions carry over, as a matter of conceptual analysis (the one just provided), to the intentional states themselves.

I had said earlier that I included among actions such things as judgments that we come to in the conclusions of theoretical (and practical reasoning), judgments such as that Socrates is mortal, say, when one has judged that Socrates is a man and that all men are mortal (or judgments such as that I should drink that glass of water, having judged that I am thirsty and that drinking that glass of water would quench my thirst). The point just made applies to these actions and the states that rationalize them as well. With such actions, the point just made ensures that if self-knowledge is a necessary condition for reactive attitudes toward such conclusions as that Socrates is mortal or that one ought to drink a glass of water (e.g., a reactive attitude such as, "Good thinking"), then that establishes self-knowledge not just of the conclusions but of the intentional states on the basis of which they are made and that make sense of the conclusion.

Thus, the extension of the point about self-knowledge from self-knowledge of actions to self-knowledge of intentional states is natural and proper and hardly controversial, once we understand what rationalizing is.

Objection 2.

But even if that is uncontroversial, the more fundamental, indeed the most fundamental objection to the view being taken here of what grounds transparency, is: are we really only justified in having reactive attitudes to actions that are self-known? True, if we demand that an action or conclusion must be self-known in order to have justifiable reactive attitudes toward it, we may extend that to saying that even the intentional states that rationalize that action must be self-known. But why *in the first place* demand that the *action* must be self-known in order to have justifiable reactive attitudes? After all, don't we often praise and blame and even punish those who commit actions that are harmful, even if the actors are not aware of what they have done? This happens ubiquitously in everyday reactions and in the practice of the law. Why, then, this demand of self-knowledge that seems to be so often at odds with everyday as well as legal practice? Are we straining too much and distorting the constraints on what justifies our reactive attitudes (which are in fact much less demanding than we are proposing) just so as to establish our point about the transparency of our intentional states? This objection has a very deep-going point to make, and it needs a careful and elaborate discussion and response. It raises detailed questions about issues of mens rea and the law while at the same time having implications about how we are to understand the more abstract issue under discussion of relation between action and intentional states and self-knowledge.

There is no denying the fact that the objection brings to our attention. We, and the law as well, often blame and punish those who commit actions that are not self-known to the actors concerned. The question is: does this fact overturn what we have been saying? Is the blame and punishment justifiable? This question, by itself, has an answer that too cannot be denied. Yes, we do indeed take ourselves to be justified in blame and punishment in these cases—and are right to do so.

So the real question is not, are we justified in our reactions and legal practices? but, what exactly is it that these justified reactions and practices are justifiably *targeting*? What are the justified evaluative reactive attitudes reactions to?

I submit that these cases (despite the common talk with which we praise and blame, talk that targets the actions themselves) are not cases of justifiably holding culpable the act of doing something done unknowingly but rather cases of being culpable for *not knowing* that one has done that thing. There is no justification for blaming an action under a certain description that the agent does not recognize as a description of her action, as she intended it and thinks of it. Of course, if the action was injurious or harmful, we moralists do talk as if that action was culpable. (And the objection is right in saying that even the law sometimes talks that way.) But our blame is only *justified* if the blame is redescribed as targeting the agent's failing to know what she is doing, rather than blaming the doing, under that description, which the agent does not even recognize.

Thus when we say, "Ignorance is no excuse," strictly speaking that ought not to be interpreted as saying, "We will hold culpable the action you are ignorant of having committed"; rather, it is to be interpreted as what the law calls "culpable *ignorance*." It is the ignorance or lack of self-knowledge that is culpable, not the action under that description.

(A point of terminology: The distinction being made here is not the familiar distinction between blaming an action and blaming the agent. It is perhaps odd to talk of blaming actions at all. We blame agents. But what do we blame them *for* in these cases? is the question: for his act or for his ignorance of having done that act? That is the relevant distinction. From now on when I ask what the target of the blame is and speak as if it is the act that might be blamed or the ignorance, it will just be shorthand for this longer and more correct version that it is agents who are blamed *for* an act or *for* their ignorance of having done that act.)

And notice one important thing. To take this view that it is the ignorance that is culpable is in *no way to ignore* the fact that it is a harmful action that has been done, nor is it to ignore the fact that blame or punishment has to take into account the harmfulness of the actions as well. Blame does not merely address the fact of ignorance just because it targets the ignorance. The full description of the object of our blame is: the lack of self-knowledge *of having done that harmful action*. It may be quite a distinct question as to whether or not we should *in general* blame a lack of self-knowledge. That would depend on whether it is *in general* a good thing to have self-knowledge, whether we place a *general* value on having self-knowledge. That is a subject that will surface in Appendix I. In the present context, the point being stressed is that the blame for the lack of self-knowledge is not this general sort of blame, detachable altogether from the harmful action that the agent concerned lacks self-knowledge of.

A clear sign of this is that the *extent* of our blame or punishment for not knowing we have done some harmful thing often tends to track *how* harmful the action concerned is. There is nothing peculiar or inconsistent about the idea that in these cases, even though we blame someone not for what they did but for not knowing what they were doing, we blame them more or punish them more severely if what they don't know about is an action of theirs that was more, rather than less, serious in the injury it caused. There is nothing inconsistent in this because it is *still* the case that the blame is not for *doing* that harmful thing but for *not knowing* that one has done that harmful thing. Culpability (when it is justifiably attributed) attaches to the ignorance, but the harmfulness of the actions *of* which someone is ignorant is all the same addressed because the extent of one's culpability is (justifiably) assigned, depending on the extent of the harmfulness of the action that is not self-known.

Thus the point that needs to be understood is that in such a case of culpable ignorance of a certain action, say, x, what is culpable is neither the lack of self-knowledge by itself nor the 'action x' by itself but rather the following: "ignorance-of-action-x." The hyphens in describing the target of blame are thus crucial. So if the extent of culpability is greater for ignorance of action x rather than ignorance of action y (because x causes greater injury than action y), the comparative judgments of culpability are always expressed *with the hyphens in place*. Thus, the formula must always be, "Ignorance-of-action-x is more culpable than ignorance-of-action-y." The actions and the ignorance are not to be decoupled from each other and become independent objects of assessment. In these cases under consideration, we do blame the ignorance, not the action, but the actions are relevant to the blame in the sense that the blame is always for ignorance of the action in question, as is evident in the fact that it often makes a difference to the extent of the blame. There is nothing odd about having it both ways, in this way. It is no more odd to say that the importance of blaming the ignorance is compatible with stressing also that the ignorance is always ignorance *of* an injurious act (and is not decouplable from the injurious act that one is ignorant of) than it is odd to say that the importance of intention in criminal law is compatible with stressing also that the intention in question is always intention *to have done the injurious act* (and it cannot be divorced from the act that was intended). If this last were odd, that would imply that we would have to find intentions to do harmful acts liable, *whether or not one did the act;* but that is clearly an undesirable implication. In fact, a monstrously tyrannical one. Hardly anyone in the world would not be liable if we went around holding harmful intentions liable whether or not what was intended was done. And there would hardly be any reason not to hold thoughts liable quite generally, once we started extending liability to intentions that are not acted upon—a nightmarish vision of criminal law. Part of the point of stressing intention and self-knowledge (and mens rea, generally) is to rule out strict liability for harmful actions. But at the same time we don't want to err in the other direction; we don't want it to be the case that we are blaming just the intention to do harm and the self-knowingness. Rather, we are (to put it awkwardly with hyphens) blaming the intentional-action and the self-known-action. And so that carries over to the culpability of the *lack* of self-knowledge too. We blame someone for his or her own ignorance-of-the-harmful-act.

But there is bound to be a skeptical interlocutor who will want to resist the initial conclusion I have drawn in the first place, the conclusion that, in such cases, it is the ignorance of the harmful act that is culpable rather than the act. And he will want to invoke the philosophical significance of our *ordinary talk* on this matter. In ordinary speech, we do not talk the way my proposal regarding the target of blame does. In ordinary talk, we say of harmful actions that are not self-known that they are wrong, and we think of ourselves as being justified in saying so. So my reformulation is quite unnecessary, a bit of revisionist philosophizing, the interlocutor will say.

Just to be clear about what the dispute is: The question before us is not whether or not ignorance or lack of self-knowledge is something that can be invoked as an excuse. Both parties to the dispute are agreed that it can be. And let us say both parties have very good reasons for being agreed on this. (What those reasons are will emerge just a little later below.) So there is no *general* denial on either side's part of the importance of ignorance as sometimes providing an excusing condition. The issue therefore is not one of strict liability versus the importance of such things as requiring self-knowledge (or requiring intention or mens rea, more generally)[8] in order to find someone liable. Both parties agree *as a generality* that self-knowledge is required for blame and punishment. Rather, the issue is about how to understand those *specific and special* cases in which it is judged that ignorance of what one has done is *not* going to be allowed as an excusing condition, those *special* cases where the moral or judicial response is: "ignorance is no excuse." (I am trying to avoid the terms 'negligence' and negligence amounting to 'recklessness', which is the standard legal terminology in which such cases are presented because those terms tend to be associated with all sorts of other issues by legal scholars, and I want to pare things down to the core philosophical issues here without these distractions.)

So suppose someone does x, an act that is universally perceived to be an injurious or harmful act. The actor invokes his ignorance of the fact that it is x that he did. He understands what he has done under some other description than x, but it is under the description x that the act is injurious. The moral and legal judgment on this is that the appeal to ignorance in this specific case is not excusing.

About everything so far, *both parties to the dispute are completely agreed.*

And now the ordinary and (apparently) legal *formulaic* understanding of the case is this: "The actor is to be blamed (and punished) for the injurious act x, and we will not allow ignorance as an excuse, in this case."

My claim is that this very set of agreed-upon facts should be described differently. The blame should be formulated instead as: "The actor is to be blamed for being ignorant of having done the injurious act x."

That is the dispute. I am insisting that the judgment "Ignorance is no excuse," when made of specific cases such as this, implies that such cases should be described as cases of 'culpable ignorance' of the relevant injurious acts. My interlocutor (both the man on the street and the surface talk of the law) are inclined, rather, to shun talk of 'culpable ignorance' and stick with talk of not merely an injurious act but a *culpable act,* whose culpability is not mitigated by the actor's ignorance of it.

Why do I insist on this revisionist understanding of the agreed-upon facts? That is to say, why do I want to revise the ordinary and legal understanding of the agreed-upon facts? What turns on this arcane-sounding dispute?

The dispute may be subtle, but it is not at all arcane. Nothing less than the following depends on taking the revisionist line I am proposing in these special cases. When the ordinary and legal understanding does not take the revisionist line I am proposing *in these special cases,* it is in fact backsliding from whatever rationale one (that is to say, everyone, all parties to the dispute) had for demanding *in general* such things as mens rea and the self-knowledge requirement in the first place. (I repeat: both parties to this dispute are one on the fact that in general—in criminal law at least—strict liability is not in play and that in general there is a mens rea requirement whether in the form of demanding intent or demanding self-knowledge.) This point is of such absolutely fundamental importance that I will immediately repeat it so as to have had it vivid in mind. *If one does not take the revisionist line on what the target of blame and punishment is in the cases where self-knowledge is missing, we will lose our rationale for having any commitment to self-knowledge (and mens rea) in the law, in the first place.* Since my interlocutor agrees with me that we need that commitment, he must cease to disagree with me on the revisionist understanding of the target of blame and punishment in the unself-known cases. This needs to be extensively argued.

So let's ask the underlying question: What is the rationale for, in general, repudiating strict liability and for requiring intent or self-knowledge in our understanding of wrongdoing? There is of course a long story here and, in many ways, a familiar one. The story is very much related to the entire Strawsonian picture of agency, i.e., whereby blame and punishment are tied closely to viewing those blamed and punished as *agents.* The short version of the story is that the requirement of self-knowledge in our understanding of wrong-doing reflects our view that there is something deeply wrong with the justifications of blame and punishment in the strict liability picture.

Usually the justifications in the strict liability picture are purely con-sequentialist ones. (There could be other justifications such as the ones that surface in discussions of the crime and punishment of Oe-dipus's incest in Ancient Greece—perhaps the purest case of not re-quiring self-knowledge—justifications in terms that address only the pollution brought into the world by injurious and harmful or taboo action. But I am assuming that these ways of conceiving of punish-ment do not move the modern, liberal mind, indeed do not move the modern mind, liberal or not.) Consequentialist justifications of pun-ishment make no requirement of self-knowledge because an act may have harmful consequences whether or not it is self-known and in-tended, and preventing it in the future, and deterring others from doing it, is all that the consequentialist is concerned with as a ground for punishing acts that have such harmful consequences. Why do our values shun such an understanding of punishment? Because, at its worst, it cannot rule out scapegoating, and even if we (somewhat ar-bitrarily) add to consequentialism about punishment the demand that some injurious act actually *be done,* for punishment to be justified consequentially (thereby ruling out scapegoating), this addition would do nothing to allay our qualms about the justification itself. The qualm would remain: a world in which there is only a conse-quentialist basis for blame and punishment of injurious action would be a world in which we would not have any place for respect for individuals and their autonomy. So to the extent that we value those things, such a world would be repugnant to us.

The only ideal of respect for individuals that consequentialism acknowledges is restricted to the avoidance of an individual's suffering, but it has no place for the stronger ideals of respect that we demand in terms of autonomy. It is even doubtful that such a world would satisfy our valuing of privacy, though, in the case of privacy, one has to be a little careful in formulating the point; i.e., though it is true that a purely consequentialist picture would have no place for respect of privacy, the insistence on mens rea, on intention and self-knowledge, would not be *sufficient* as an argument for the right of privacy, either. But it is nevertheless the case that if one did demand self-knowledge and intention, one would allow for the basic respect for the individual and his autonomy, which are things *upon which one could then build further demands* that would then *be* sufficient to argue for privacy.

Apart from the fact that it would fall afoul of our values of autonomy, respect for the individual, privacy, etc., there is another important theoretical reason to shun the consequentialist picture and insist on the self-knowledge requirement: a world in which one did not demand that a wrongdoer know what he had done would be a world in which one could not really in any sense that is relevant or important to the question of blame and punishment distinguish between someone who acts out of compulsion and someone who acts out of ignorance. Both would be just as subject to blame and punishment. Yet it seems that we do distinguish between cases of ignorance and cases of compulsion in the sense that we think that some of the time (though not all times, of course) ignorance is avoidable and within an agent's capacity and control (to avoid), which ex hypothesi compulsion is not. The whole point is that one is a pathology of some kind, but the other is not, and a differential treatment is therefore warranted but might not be allowed in such a world. And the blindness to the importance of this distinction might make one suspect (though there may not be a quick argument for this) that in such a world there may even be a danger of a slide to equating punishment and blame with pure manipulation and management, as in a purely medical understanding of punishment. At any rate, there may not be such a great distance between punishment in the purely consequentialist world and such a "Clockwork Orange" world. So, as I said, it is to the extent that we possess values that find such worlds repugnant that we demand in our justifications of blame and punishment the necessary conditions of self-knowledge, intention, etc.[9]

(There is a widespread temptation to think that a "rule" utilitarian version of consequentialism might have the resources to bring back in notions of respect for individuals and autonomy, etc., that are ushered out only when the focus is on an "act" utilitarian version of consequentialism. But for reasons I cannot present here in detail, I think that that temptation is quite wrong. Roughly speaking, the reasons are that when push comes to shove, when hard cases arise, rule utilitarianism has no way of avoiding a collapse into act utilitarianism, if it is to be a version of utilitarianism at all, and so the notion that such resources are available to it is an illusion. This should not in the end be surprising, since rational motivation attaches primarily to acts.)

These, then, are our rough reasons for laying down a *general* self-knowledge (and intention) requirement in criminal law, which we may then put aside in the *specific* sorts of cases we are considering, cases that the law would often describe in terms of 'negligence' or negligence amounting to 'recklessness'. And my overall claim is that unless we revise and reformulate our understanding of what is going on in these specific cases where we put aside the general demand for self-knowledge, *as I do rather than as my interlocutor in this dispute does*, we will be abandoning the very thing that these reasons point to— our commitment to certain values of respect for the individual and his autonomy, privacy, etc. Recall that my interlocutor understands these cases as follows: it is the *act that is to be blamed* in these cases, and ignorance of the act will not deflect one from blaming *the act*. This forces one into the consequentialist justification of punishment in general (or, as said earlier, some more obviously outdated justification as one might find in Ancient Greece). If one asked my interlocutor, "What are your *general* grounds for punishing injurious acts if you take the view you do about what punishment and blame target in the *special* cases of injurious acts that are not self-known?" there is no other answer to be had but a consequentialist one. But my interlocutor is *not* a consequentialist. As I said repeatedly, he and I are *agreed* that strict liability is not in play in criminal law, and self-knowledge and intent are necessary for blame and punishment, and we are also (let us say) broadly agreed on which cases are to be excused because they fail to fulfill the self-knowledge or intention requirement and which are not. It's just that his understanding of *specifically* the latter kind of case, the case that is not excused, breaches what presumably *underlies* and prompts his own *general* commitment to shunning strict liability and to placing the self-knowledge and intention requirements on blame and punishment. What underlie it are values about autonomy, respect, perhaps privacy, and in general perhaps the ideal that in punishment one engages with people rather than manages and manipulates them. It is these values that are under threat within a purely consequentialist justification for blame and punishment. And in formulating the *special* cases under consideration as he does, my interlocutor allows himself to fall into a position that leaves no scope to justify punishment except in terms that threaten these values that his own *general* position is, by implication, committed to.

Of course, a world in which these values of respect, autonomy, and privacy are fulfilled will be a world in which appeal to consequentialist values of deterrence and reform may still be made, but it will not be a world in which consequential*ism* is erected into a general ideology regarding wrongdoing and its blame and punishment.[10] In this world, if 'deterrence' and 'reform' of criminals are introduced as considerations, it will be in a piecemeal way, for this or that punishment, often to make clear that nothing retributive is intended by punishment. But such a selective place for consequentialist consideration is perfectly compatible with a general commitment to the other fundamental values mentioned that framework this world. When we say we are committed to these non-consequentialist values, then our general view of punishment is that it must be viewed as engaging with rational *agents* and not merely managing and manipulating them. The institution of punishment expresses in a general way our willingness for such *engagement* with wrongdoers, and it often does so by seeing the institution as expressive of our Strawsonian responses of outrage, resentment, indignation, etc. Within that general picture, we may often want in a local way to appeal to various values, including the ones stressed by consequentialism, such as deterrence, etc. But to do so will, as I said, be part of an attitude of *engagement* with wrongdoers. It will not be a result of a comprehensive doctrinal commitment to consequentialism in which engagement with rational subjects deserving of respect and autonomy is passed over for *managing* individuals in order to increase happiness and reduce suffering. This localist way of bringing in consequentialist values will take the 'ism' out of consequentialism; it will only be a reflection of the fact that *various* values can be in play in our *engaged* responses to wrongdoing (i.e., our treating wrongdoers as agents), even often consequentialist values.

There is no paradox here, or if it is a paradox, it is one that crops up interestingly also for doctrines much more extreme than consequentialism. Take, for example, the fact that ever since Spinoza and most dramatically since Freud it is widely and correctly thought that when we sometimes adopt a third person and spectator's angle on ourselves and try to understand our motives and desires and passions in an objective and impersonal mode, the knowledge we thereby gain is liberating—it increases our agency and our freedom. But then if one erects this thought into a *general and comprehensive ideology*, it results in exactly the opposite outcome—the *eradication* of agency and freedom. A *purely* third person angle on ourselves (as one finds in the perceptual view of self-knowledge, for instance) is exactly a negation of agency because agency consists precisely in the exercise of the *first* person point of view. (Please note as an aside that the use of the expression 'first person point of view' here to capture something about the agent's perspective is very different from the way in which it was being used in Section 2 of Chapter 1 to present the Cartesian view of the meaning of mental terms. This idea of a first person point of view will play a very large role in the book's argument over the next few chapters.)

So the crucial point is this: *the very thing* that when writ small can be salutary and liberating and increasing of agency when writ large is repugnant and destructive of agency. This mildly paradoxical situation is just the same when it comes to understanding wrongdoing. We may in local and piecemeal ways ('writ small') appeal to deterrence and reform in our punishment of wrongdoing, and doing so is salutary because it shows, among other things, how primitive and unattractive retributive ways of thinking of punishment are. But if we erect this appeal into a comprehensive *conception* of the punishment of wrong-doing ('writ large'), it is far from salutary because it threatens our commitments to some of our deepest values, such as respect, autonomy, and privacy.

The trouble is that if one does not formulate one's understanding of the cases of blame and punishment for un-self-known wrongdoing under consideration in this section (the ones sometimes described as 'negligence' by the law) along the lines I am insisting on, we *are* forced into a consequentialist *conception* of the punishment of wrong-doing, and we cannot then lay claim to the other values of autonomy, respect, etc., to which *both* I and my interlocutor are committed. Hence my interlocutor is backsliding from this commitment by not taking my revised understanding of how to describe and deal with these special cases.

If that is right, we have responded effectively to the objection against revising our ordinary talk of what is targeted in blame and punishment when self-knowledge is missing. Though, as the objection rightly points out, we do talk as if we blame and punish and resent harmful actions that are not self-known to the agent, this talk is loose talk. We cannot justify such blame and punishment when it has these targets. That does not mean we do not justifiably blame or punish the agent in question. We do. But when we do so *justifiably,* the blame and punishment really target the lack of self-knowledge of the harmful thing the agent has done and not directly the action itself.

This stress on 'justifiably' makes clear the connection between this point and my modification of Strawson in the last chapter, where agency and freedom were grounded not merely in the reactive evaluative attitudes but in *justifiable* reactive evaluative attitudes. It is this modified notion of Strawsonian notion of agency that has been in play in my response to the objection, and it is this notion that I have invoked more generally in my opening shot to forge a conceptual tie between self-knowledge and agency. With the objection answered, we may be reassured that what was presented as an opening shot has now been consolidated into a sound conclusion.

Before we are entirely reassured with the conclusion, a couple of somewhat less deep and fundamental objections should be addressed.

Objection 3.

There is an obvious complication in my position that needs to be made explicit. On the face of it, I have claimed two seemingly inconsistent things. *First*, if X is justifiably blamed for something, this presupposes that X knows what he is blamed for. And *second*, we may justifiably blame X when he is self-deceived (or generally self-ignorant) for not knowing his own thoughts. This might seem to imply that if X is to be blamed for a particular case of lack of self-knowledge, he must know that he does not know some thought of his. But that cannot be right, of course. Blame for lack of self-knowledge is an exception to the first claim.

Why? Because in this case it is blame for the lack of a specific case of self-knowledge, so knowledge of the lack of self-knowledge cannot be presupposed in the blaming. It is incoherent to say that someone knows that he does not know some particular truth. Someone's knowing that he does not know that p is not possible without him knowing that p. That is to say, one cannot say that someone knows that he does not know that snow is white without refuting the claim that he does not know that snow is white. Of course, one can know *in a general way* that there is something in a region of one's thoughts and intentions that one does not know. That is presumably what prompts us sometimes to go to analysts or to other ways by which we cognitively inquire into our own submerged or suppressed thoughts. In such cases, one perhaps says to oneself or one's analyst says to one: there is *something or other* in my (your) psyche that I am not (you are not) quite aware of, and let's try and find out what it is. But of any *particular* thought of ours we could not coherently be said to know that we do not know *it*. Incoherent in the way that self-refuting propositions are incoherent. Thus to insist that our first claim's demand (that justifiable reactive attitudes require that there is self-knowledge) apply when we have a justifiable reactive attitude to someone's culpable ignorance of his motives and other intentional states is to insist on something impossible. The self-refutation ensures that it is impossible to meet the demand when applied to *blame for lack of self-knowledge itself*.

So the demand in the first claim is perhaps better phrased as follows: Justifiable reactive attitudes toward some target presuppose self-knowledge of the targeted state *unless there is an impossibility theorem regarding the self-knowability of the targeted state*. That impossibility is what has just been demonstrated when the target of justifiable reactive attitudes is itself a lack of self-knowledge.

I have been arguing that a certain sort of exception, which I myself noticed, to a certain sort of theoretical demand that I have made does not refute the demand and its plausibility. It is not unprincipled to say that a certain theoretical demand has exceptions when it is clear that the exceptions occur *only* when there is a *demonstrable* impossibility in applying the demand. Moreover—and this point is crucial—the theoretical consideration or motivation for imposing the demand in the first place is in no way compromised by the sort of consideration (the demonstrated impossibility due to self-refutation) involved in allowing the exception to the demand. The theoretical motivation for *the demand* is one that connects responsibility and liability with self-knowledge by saying that our values do not justify the reactive attitudes that target actions and states of mind that are not self-known; by contrast, the consideration and motivation that forces *the exception to the demand* is a quasi-logical point about self-refutation. This latter does not overturn in any way the theoretical motivation, just stated, for the demand. We are in no way less convinced of that theoretical motivation as a result of acknowledging that there will be exceptions due to these quasi-logical considerations. These latter are irrelevant to the motivations that prompted one to place the theoretical demand.

That last consideration should establish the sort of counter-example being considered as arcane and non-destructive of the main point being made. But to the reader who is unmoved by it, who simply digs his heels in and says, "A counter-example is a counter-example and that's the end of it," one could reply, without compromising anything in the deeper point being made, that the point applies restrictedly. That is to say, the point about the deep links between responsibility and self-knowledge applies to all cases but the case in which responsibility is regarding a lack of self-knowledge itself. The grounds and motivations for making the link (and which I have presented in the discussion over the last many pages) are all in place. Those grounds and motivations are not tainted or made irrelevant by restricting the link in this way. The principle behind the link, once it is understood, is not made any less a principle, and the link is not made any the more arbitrary, by restricting its application in this way.

To conclude: in formulating this objection, I had said that there may be an inconsistency in my two claims: (1) that justifiable reactive attitudes presuppose self-knowledge of what they target and (2) that we have justifiable reactive attitudes toward (culpable) lack of self-knowledge. The points I have been making, however, show that, for perfectly principled reasons, when it comes to (2)—i.e., when it comes to justifiable blame for lack of self-knowledge, (1) lapses as a demand. So there is no inconsistency in the two claims.

Objection 4.

Another objection worries about the scope for an indefinite regress of higher-order beliefs, which may be implied by the account of transparency being given. If an intentional state is constituted by the second-order belief that carries the self-knowledge of it, shouldn't the fact that the second-order belief is an intentional state require that there be a third-order belief? And so forth?

The worry is not a deep one. What grounds the view that intentional states are constituted by self-knowledge carried in second-order beliefs about them is the notion of responsible agency specified in very specific normative terms. On this view, it is only if the intentional state has links with agency, if it rationalizes actions that are the justifiable objects of evaluative reactive attitudes, that this question of a higher-order constitutive belief enters. That beliefs of the nth order should be rationalizing actions that are the targets of our justifiable reactive attitudes is questionable. Perhaps clever people will devise intelligible examples of how beliefs of higher and higher order may rationalize actions. If so, to the extent that the examples are comprehensible and gripping as genuinely involving agency in this way, we *will* be highly motivated—for all the reasons given so far—to require that there be beliefs of one level higher to account for the requisite self-knowledge of those at the immediately lower order. So there is no need to be embarrassed by the climb to higher orders *if* the rationalizing and the agential element is intelligibly present in each case. Not only would it not be embarrassing, but there will actually be a conviction that it is *required.* There is no crippling infinite regress. The regress goes, with no crippling effect, just as far as the view requires—to the point where agency (normatively understood along modified Strawsonian lines) is recognizably in play. And it *must* go that far.

Objection 5.

An objection may be raised about how I have been talking rather simply and crudely of cases of total lack of self-knowledge of one's actions and the states of mind that rationalize them. It is indeed true that I have been conveniently focusing only on those cases of self-deception in which the agent has *no* self-knowledge at all of a certain intentional state. But, it will be objected, self-deception is a highly variegated phenomenon and often involves a sort of half-knowledge of the very intentional states that one has deceived oneself about, echoing what was said of King Lear—"he hath ever but slenderly known himself." In response, I must simply admit this and admit that to give an analysis of such cases is a subtle philosophical business, but there is no point in embarking on that now. This book is not a book about self-deception. These more subtle cases of partial knowledge involved in self-deception would not force me to revise any point of principle in the account of self-knowledge I am setting out to give. It may force me to add nuance to the account, but the direction of nuance should be pretty obvious, showing perhaps that blame and the reactive attitudes may have to be thought of as less all or nothing than I have presented them so far, if the requirement that they be toward self-known states and acts is fulfilled (or not fulfilled) only partially sometimes, as in these subtler cases. Nothing in the more subtle cases would spoil the general explanatory connection being made between self-knowledge and agency. These cases would just make the connection more qualified and more sensitive to the empirical complexities surrounding self-knowledge and its absence. The connection remains, only now it remains in the form that: *to the extent* (whatever extent that may be, partial or complete) that one thinks that self-knowledge is present, *to that extent* only is it justifiable to have the reactive attitudes that define agency. So there may be degrees of self-knowledge that calibrate with degrees of blame. Granting degrees of self-knowledge does not overturn anything being said here so long as the calibration with normative considerations of blame and the reactive attitudes is not lost sight of.[11]

Objection 6.

Finally, it might be objected that in my appeal to agency (understood in terms of the reactive attitudes) in our understanding of self-knowledge I have not paid attention to the relevance of some widely noticed asymmetries between the pro reactive attitudes and the con reactive attitudes, between praise and blame, between resentment and admiration. I have said of cases where we find ourselves blaming (resenting) someone for an unself-known harmful action that we cannot really justifiably blame (or resent) the action itself that is not self-known, though we can justifiably blame (resent) the lack of self-knowledge of a harmful action. Thus the harmful action gets blamed not directly but only derivatively or secondarily, via the blame for the lack of self-knowledge of it. But what should be said of cases where we find ourselves *praising* (admiring) someone for unself-known beneficial actions? It would be more than odd—it would be absurd—to say that here too the praise (admiration) is justifiable when it targets the lack of self-knowledge of the beneficial action. That is simply not so. If there is to be any justifiable praise at all, it is directly for the beneficial action itself. This is clearly an asymmetry. And the asymmetry is built into the difference between praise and blame.[12]

My response is to entirely concede the point made in this objection and to say that it is blame, not praise, that is the primary focus of the point I am making. Blame is the sort of practice that needs more care in our understanding of its justificatory conditions, in a way that is simply not demanded by the practice of praise. And similar differences hold for the reactive attitudes that respectively lie behind these practices. It makes a bigger difference to blame than praise; its consequences are more important, and so we have to be more watchful in what we say about its justification and about what its targets are.

These asymmetries are reflected at two levels in the way I have proposed to deal with our responses to unself-known actions. There is, first, the point that in the case of praising actions of this sort I can easily and amicably accommodate the praise by distinguishing between a notion of praise where self-knowledge of what is being praised is a prerequisite of the praise and another notion of praise where we simply praise the action quite independently of considerations of self-knowledge. (There would be an analogy here with praising an action that was done intentionally and praising the action independently of such considerations as whether or not it was intended.) Both ways of praising may seem quite justified. But in the case of blame, I am not making any such distinction between different notions of blame. I am, rather, denying that there is any justification for blaming an action that is not self-known. Things simply cannot be resolved amicably by saying that there are two quite different notions of blame if (unlike as in the case of praise) one notion of blame is never justified. So that is one level at which the asymmetry crops up in the way I deal with our responses to unself-known actions. It also emerges more straightforwardly at another level in the fact that lack of self-knowledge is itself prima facie blameworthy, but it is not praiseworthy. So it's not surprising that I can be more relaxed about praising the action that is not self-known. There is no question of praising the lack of self-knowledge of it, so if praise is forthcoming, its target is bound to be the action. However, as I will argue in Appendix I, lack of self-knowledge is *prima facie* blameworthy *in itself,* and so there is a natural target for blame when actions are not self-known, other than the actions themselves. These asymmetries between praise and blame should all be admitted. They leave intact (even as they add nuance to it) the fundamental point I am making by which I connect a normative notion of agency with self-knowledge. What I say about blame (even if I cannot always say it about praise) is quite enough to make and preserve that fundamental point.

4. All these objections have been objections to my way of establishing transparency—establishing it by saying that self-knowledge of one's intentional states is a necessary condition for agency. Assuming the objections answered, how exactly does transparency get established in this way? Transparency, so far in our dialectic, had been the *presumption* that if someone has an intentional state, then she knows that she has it. That it is *merely* a presumption is forced on one by the fact of exceptions to transparency. The pledge was that we would 'explain' the presumption and thereby rewrite the conditional for transparency without any mention of a presumption.

The 'explanation' being offered is that whenever responsible agency is in the offing, transparency exists *without* exception. If responsible agency is not in the offing, if justifiable blame, punishment, resentment are not apt, then self-knowledge need not be present either. The exceptions to transparency are those intentional states that are unaccompanied by second-order beliefs that we have them. But those are precisely the intentional states that, when they rationalize our behavior (if that is what they do), rationalize behavior that is *not* the target of justifiable reactive attitudes. And these are also intentional states that are not themselves the target of justifiable reactive attitudes. We may be justified in having reactive attitudes toward the fact that these intentional states are unaccompanied by second-order beliefs about them; i.e., we may be justified in having reactive attitudes toward the lack of self-knowledge of them. The ignorance is culpable but not the intentional states themselves nor the actions that they bring about.

If this is right, then there is a perfect fit in one direction between the absence of the accompanying second-order beliefs and the absence of responsibility. Whenever the former is missing, the latter is absent too (though obviously not vice versa, since there may be more conditions that are necessary for responsibility than self-knowledge). Self-knowledge being a necessary condition for responsibility, there are *no exceptions* in this direction. So if we can find a way of bringing in the element of responsibility into the conditional about transparency, then the conditional need not be seen as a presumption at all. The presumption was there to allow for exceptions. But there are no exceptions if responsibility is built into the conditional. So let's simply rewrite the conditional by dropping the presumptive element and adding the element of agency. We can do so by adding a proviso that explicitly mentions agency. That proviso will then accommodate the exceptions that the notion of presumption was intended to handle in the initial conditional. It will handle them in the sense that when there are exceptions, the proviso will fail to hold. It is the conditional with the proviso holding, however, that is true, and true without exception, and that therefore captures transparency, i.e., that captures one-half of the special character of self-knowledge.

Fully (re)written out, the conditional would read: *To the extent that an intentional state is part of a rationalization (or potential rationalization)*[13] *of an action or conclusion, which is or can be the object of justifiable reactive attitudes, or to the extent that an intentional state itself is or can be the object of justifiable reactive attitudes, then that intentional state is known to its possessor.* More abbreviatedly, for the sake of convenience, let the rewritten conditional for transparency be:

(T). Given agency, if S desires (believes) that p, then S believes that she desires (believes) that p.

As is visible, the proviso "Given agency" does a great deal of summarizing. The reader should not lose sight of this fact that (T) here is shorthand for the longer and fuller conditional I have emphasized in the previous paragraph because no claim to transparency is being made, no claim to self-knowledge as a necessary condition for agency is being made, if agency is not thought of in the normative terms we gave it in the last chapter. The proviso in the fully written out conditional specifies all the elements of normativity that go into the notion of agency. It is quite possible that if we were unconvinced by the analysis of agency in the last chapter, we would also be unconvinced by the argument for transparency in this one. There may well be other notions of agency, more purely metaphysical ones, that do not presuppose self-knowledge of intentional states. It is only a notion of agency in terms of justifiable reactive attitudes (the modified Strawsonian one) that establishes transparency. This point is vital in demonstrating that self-knowledge is not a perceptual epistemological notion.

5. To demonstrate why it is vital, consider a position—and, at first sight, it seems like a thoroughly reasonable and natural position to take—that does not quarrel with the conceptual connections I have been trying to make between self-knowledge and a normative notion of agency but instead is skeptical about the claim advanced on the basis of those connections, viz., that the perceptual view is shown to be wrong by the connections.

Since Chapter 1, I have been pitting the perceptual view against the constitutive view, and indeed I have been defining the constitutive view in (the negative) terms of its contrast with the perceptual view. But now, in light of the positive elaboration of the constitutive view in terms of the conditionals, this means that the point of the conditionals is to contrast with and contest the point of the perceptual model of self-knowledge. We have so far only established the conditional for transparency, one-half of the constitutive ideal. But even with that partial constitutive account in place, the skepticism I am raising about my own anti-perceptualist stance can be stated quite succinctly. It will be instructive to state it and respond to it, because it will reveal some of the detailed force of the constitutive account (partially) established so far.

Why, it might be asked, am I so keen to put a distance and claim a contrast between the perceptual view of self-knowledge and the constitutive view, which singles out self-knowledge as having a special character? The point of this contrast might seem particularly unconvincing to many if by the 'perceptual' view of self-knowledge is meant something as spare and minimal as what I called the 'causal-perceptual' view, which acknowledged that there was no analogue to such things as 'looking', 'seeing', or 'checking' in self-knowledge.

The skeptical thought here is roughly this. All that I have shown in this chapter, by establishing the transparency conditional along the lines I did, is that there is a *conceptual setting* for self-knowledge of our intentional states in considerations of agency. Given this conceptual setting, there is a *conceptual* connection (of the sort the conditional indicates) between an intentional state and its possessor's belief that she has it. This may be a very important thing to have established, but it does not show that self-knowledge (or, at any rate, true self-belief)[14] is not in every case *also* a product of a *causal* mechanism that connects the intentional state with the possessor's belief that she has it. Why may we not grant that self-knowledge has conceptual links with agency and *yet also* insist on it being a product of such a mechanism? What about the conceptual links spoils the idea that there is such a causal, reliabilist, and sparely perceptual account of self-knowledge? Can't we combine the two accounts by saying that the constitutive account's point about the links with agency provide a *constraint* on any understanding we might come to have of the nature of our self-knowledge? But it is the perceptual account that tells us *how* we come to have self-knowledge, by positing a causal mechanism. If so, the intolerance shown toward the perceptual account is excessive and unnecessary, even if the transparency conditional is true and the constitutive account is (partially) in place. The reasonable position is to be ecumenical and see both views as compatible.

Here is the general direction of answer to these questions.

Any causal-perceptual account worth its name (taking perception of the external world as a paradigm, even if we drop the demand that it should involve analogues to cognitive activity such as "looking", etc.), must allow that there can be a breakdown in the causal-perceptual mechanism, however reliable it is. But as I've argued—*so long as the agency condition as expressed in the proviso of the rewritten conditional for transparency is fulfilled*—there is *no* possibility of a breakdown in the connection between intentional states and beliefs about them, in the way that there is between external objects and our perceptual experiences and beliefs about them.

Now, there is a temptation to respond to this by saying that to the extent that I have granted exceptions *at all,* i.e., to the extent that I have allowed that there is self-deception, etc., I *have* allowed for breakdowns akin to those that occur in causal mechanisms. So why am I insisting on the incompatibility between my constitutive thesis and the causal-perceptual account? Thus the temptation is to ask: why might it not be that the breakdowns of the causal mechanisms occur whenever there are these exceptions to self-knowledge, exceptions that I have allowed by saying that their occurrence is signaled by the failure of the proviso to hold? Why might it not be that the condition of agency expressed in the proviso fails to hold in just those cases where there is a breakdown in the causal mechanism? Both the perceptualist view's and the constitutive view's way of handling the exceptions can thus be seen to calibrate.

The temptation, however, is based on a confusion. It fails to notice a very conspicuous failure of fit between the two accounts, which makes the idea of this calibration an absurdity. The (partial) constitutive thesis established so far turns on a conditional, and as such, even though it allows for self-deception and fallibility, it does not allow *(given the fact that the conditionals are governed by a proviso laying down conditions of responsible agency)* for breakdowns in the connection between the first-order and second-order beliefs mentioned in the conditional. That proviso lays down a condition that mentions a particular notion of agency, one that has been given a radically normative (rather than the traditionally more purely metaphysical) analysis in Chapter 2. In other words, since my version of the constitutive thesis (unlike others in the recent literature on self-knowledge—such as, say, Crispin Wright's[15]—which also explore such conditionals) owes to a conditional that is governed by a proviso that specifies a condition that is thoroughly *normative,* the conditional itself necessarily falls outside the scope of anything that is relevant to the operations of a *causal* mechanism.

Why is that?

Because the operations (and breakdowns) of causal mechanisms are blind to normative considerations of responsible agency. This point is of the utmost importance to my claim that self-knowledge is constitutive of intentional states and that it is therefore not to be thought of along causal-perceptualist lines. Causal mechanisms of the kind that are involved in perception simply do not operate and break down, with an eye to whether such normatively characterized conditions of responsible agency have obtained. Recall that the notion of agency depended on there being justifiable reactive or self-reactive attitudes of the sort that I characterized in my modified Strawsonian analysis. The idea that a causal mechanism is sensitive to facts about whether there is such a justifiable reactive attitude present or potentially present (or not present) before it is operative (or fails to be operative) is absurd.

And it won't do to say what I have already argued against at length in Chapter 2; viz., "Yes, the causal mechanism cannot track whether or not an evaluative condition holds. That is true. But it should, in any case, be the other way round. The evaluative condition of the proviso, i.e., the justifiability of the practices surrounding responsibility and of the reactive attitudes, should be tracking the causal mechanism's operations and breakdowns!" It won't do to say this because, as discussed in Chapter 2 when criticizing and modifying Strawson, to say it is to commit something like a naturalistic fallacy. Whether or not an evaluative attitude is justified cannot turn on considerations that *leave out* other evaluative attitudes (values) we have. So if the causal mechanisms' being operative or inoperative are seen as relevant to whether evaluations are justified or not, *it is only because our other values tell us to see them as relevant.* In the realm of values, it is values all the way down. It isn't as if something *non*-evaluative like the operations or failures of causal mechanisms underlie values. That is why the proviso mentions an evaluative or normative condition regarding justifiable reactive attitudes, the normative condition that grounds agency. And that is why there is a failure of fit between the two chief claims of the two accounts of self-knowledge—the claim that, given conditions of responsible agency, there is a connection between first-order intentional states and second-order beliefs about them and the claim that there is a causal mechanism that makes a connection between first-order intentional states and second-order beliefs about them. To say there is such a failure of fit is just to underscore that even if all (non-Cartesian) parties allow for exceptions to self-knowledge, the big difference is that there cannot be a breakdown of the connection posited by the former claim while there can be a breakdown of the connection posited by the latter claim.

Therefore, the explanation of the fact of someone's believing that she has an intentional state whenever she has it by the claim (1) that there is a causal mechanism whereby the latter reliably causes the former and the explanation of the same fact by the claim (2) that it is a fallout of the notion of agency in which intentional states (and the actions they rationalize) are implicated are not merely two essentially *different* explanations. They are also *incompatible* explanations. It is quite confused to say that (2) provides a sort of *constraint* and then (1) tells you *how* self-knowledge is achieved, since the causal mechanism posited by (1) could not possibly be sensitive to the sort of normative constraint posited by (2).

The skeptical and ecumenical position, which I am repudiating, may appeal to the following analogy to press its case.

> You say that a subject knows her states of mind when the states of mind or the actions they rationalize are good targets for justifiable attitudes of evaluation. We similarly might say that a knife has a sharp edge when it is good for cutting. But having a sharp edge is a non-normatively characterized fact about the knife entailed by its normatively characterized property of cutting well. So why can't the self-knowledge also be seen as a non-normatively characterized fact (a fact elaborated in terms of a causal mechanism connecting first-and second-orders states) about a subject whose intentional states or the actions they rationalize are the justifiable target of the evaluative attitudes?

The analogy is imperfect because the normative property of cutting well is not normative in the sense that the deliverances of human agency are normative. The normative property in the former case lacks the irreducible distance from the non-normative facts, which raise all the questions I have been raising about how causal mechanisms cannot be expected to be in sync with the justifiable evaluative attitudes. In Chapter 5, I will present what I am calling this irreducible distance in terms of G. E. Moore's open question argument in tandem with a Fregean notion of sense, terms that do not apply to the case of knives cutting well and the non-normative facts that they entail. But even without that elaboration, it is quite intuitive to say right here that there is no sweat in admitting that a sharp edge constitutes, in some sense, the normative property of a knife's cutting well because it is such a low-grade sense of normativity that is involved. It is precisely because the normativity is of a higher grade in the cases where the issue of self-knowledge arises that we are given serious pause in saying that the working of causal mechanisms and their breakdowns are in perfect sync with the deliverances of the normative judgments involved. Pressing such an analogy cannot make the case for the ecumenical position because the ecumenical position was supposed to be fully on board with the thoroughly normative nature of agency and self-knowledge's part in it. Its ecumenism tried to reconcile the causal mechanism with an acknowledgment of such a *high-grade* normativity. The analogy uses the term 'normative' very schematically when it says that knives that cut well are normatively characterized in the same sense that is relevant to the justifiable blaming and resenting of subject's intentional states and actions. By doing so, it downgrades the normativity in the latter case and therefore abandons the aspirations of the ecumenical position that wishes to reconcile the idea of causal accounts of self-knowledge with a full acknowledgment of the high-grade normativity invoked in the account of self-knowledge being presented in this chapter.

Any effort to make the constitutive account of self-knowledge (in my version of it) and the causal-perceptual account of self-knowledge compatible must therefore rely on a misunderstanding of the former account as it has been developed in this chapter. It is possible that the calibration and compatibility pursued by our skeptic would have been more convincing if one were working with a more 'metaphysical' and less normative conception of agency; but that was precisely what was put aside in Chapter 2. That is why the argument for self-knowledge as being constitutive that is on offer here is thoroughly dependent on the specifically normative conclusions about agency argued for at length in Chapter 2. Someone who rejected that conclusion and the idea that agency turned on the question of justifiable reactive attitudes—for instance, the sort of philosopher who makes the protest considered in Section 5 of the last chapter, by questioning the appropriateness of the reactive attitudes themselves on the grounds of a metaphysical puzzlement about causality and its universal sway—will not be convinced at all by the account of self-knowledge on offer. Therefore, the special character of self-knowledge (in the aspect of transparency being considered in this chapter) and the normative notion of agency form an *integrated* ideal. It will become clear by Chapter 5 that there is much more integration involved than just this. The special character of self-knowledge (in the aspect of authority) will be integrated not just with agency and with value but also with intentionality as it integrates with agency and value, in a way that will be elaborated over the next two chapters.

Notice that I am not saying something as strong as that the constitutive view on offer rules out that there are or can be causal relations between first-order intentional states and second-order beliefs about them. No stand on (nor much interest in) that question is taken here. It is only being denied that causal relations of this kind, even where they do exist, provide the explanation of self-knowledge. *In a world in which there are no such causal relations between first-order intentional states and second-order beliefs about them (perhaps our world, perhaps another), and in which there is agency, understood as I claim it must be, there will still be self-knowledge,* there will still be the rule-like link between intentional states and second-order beliefs about them, which the conditional for transparency (partially) captures.

So if someone insisted that there is a causal relation between first- and second-order states for each case of self-knowledge of our states of mind, there is no particular reason for me to deny it. I would only ask that it be noticed that these causal links would have to mirror, would have to keep faith with, the transparency conditional regarding self-knowledge, as I have formulated it. Presumably this would mean that a causal mechanism that linked the states that realize the intentional states of first and second order cannot be any ordinary sort of causal mechanism such as those found in ordinary perceptual knowledge of the external world (which do *not* have to keep faith with any analogous conditionals reflecting any transparency of objects or facts in the external world or reflecting any authoritative knowledge regarding them). Rather, the relations of cause would necessarily have to be embedded in what was presumably something like a *part-whole* relational system, which would echo in the functional (causal) characterization of underlying physical realizations the impossibility of breakdown in the connection between "I desire (believe) that p" and "I believe that I desire (believe) that p."

Perhaps such causal relations do exist, but it is a matter of some (principled) indifference to me. I cannot possibly rule them out, but I can point out that to insist on them is to demand of causal mechanisms a sort of sensitivity to normatively governed phenomena that our present understanding of ordinary causality does not have the conceptual resources to include. Perhaps in the fullness of time, with enough theoretical change in the physical and psychological sciences, our notion of cause will itself change enough to make this inclusion. After all, over the centuries, theoretical change has brought about changes in the notion of matter to include all sorts of things that it did not in earlier times. I suppose it would be foolish to rule out such possibilities for change in our notion of causality. But even to concede this is to speak with some reserve about what we might fruitfully say at present. So if the reader has noticed a lack of interest on my part in these philosophical claims insisting on causal relations between the first- and second-order states involved in self-knowledge, it is not because of a casualness about the theoretical urges that motivate them but because of a studied reluctance to overlook the tallness of the order that it would place on causality, as we presently understand it—not to mention the fact that even if in the eventuality that we do have this more accommodating notion of cause, we would *still* have to be convinced that it has enough in common with our present notion of cause before we can be sure that we have not simply acquired a quite different notion, one that is not a notion of cause at all. (I will say more about the relations between causality and normativity in a different context—the context of the causality that links a normative notion of intentional states with our actions—in Chapter 5, Section 4.)

All that I have been saying is by way of explaining an indifference on my part to contemporary metaphysical preoccupations about the relevance of causal relations in regions where, for reasons of principle, they at least *seem* not to have an explanatory place. What I am not indifferent to is the claim not only that causal relations do exist but also that they provide the explanation of our self-knowledge. If the 'explanation' I am presenting is available wherever there is agency, whether or not the causal relations are present, then no explanations from the causal relations are either expected or sought. If the constitutive claim is right, the notion of cause in our ordinary sense, in the sense we find holding between the facts of the external world and our perceptions of those facts, provides no explanations of self-knowledge at all.

(I should add as a quick aside here that it will not do for someone to agree with the argument I have just given and to concede to me that I am right to insist that there is no compatibility between the *causal-perceptual* account and the constitutive account I have offered but not to concede that an *inferential* account of self-knowledge is incompatible with my constitutive account of it. Since, as we saw in Chapter 1, constitutive views define themselves by contrast not just with perceptual but also with inferential views, this may seem to be a problem for me. Thus, someone might ask, "Why can't it be that all the links between a normative notion of agency and self-knowledge that my constitutive account insists on are quite correct, but much of the time we do have inferential self-knowledge of our intentional states?" "Here," it will be said, "all my points about the blindness of causal mechanisms to normative considerations are irrelevant, since it is inference, not cause, that is doing the work that is compatible with the agential considerations." The reason I can be quick in my response to this line of resistance is that in Section 4 of Chapter 1 I had already shown—applying McDowell's criticisms of certain criterial accounts of our knowledge of other minds—why it is that inferential views of self-knowledge must presuppose, depend on, and therefore eventually just collapse with the causal-perceptual view of self-knowledge against which I have just offered criticisms, and which criticisms this line of resistance begins by conceding. I will not repeat that argument here.)

Though I have said as sharply as I can why the two accounts (constitutive and causal-perceptual) of self-knowledge are incompatible, and why one simply has to let go of the idea that it is a causal mechanism between first-order intentional states and second-order beliefs about them that explains our self-knowledge, it is not easy within our current philosophical frameworks to really let go of it.

Here is another path of resistance. Unlike the skepticism just discussed, this path does not simply say, you have not shown why we cannot have both accounts; it actually tries to motivate the compatibility between the two accounts by saying why the causal-perceptualist view, or some such view over and above the (partial) constitutive view I have presented, is absolutely necessary.

The argument in this chapter has turned on the claim that a subject must have self-knowledge of the states of mind that are involved in her responsible agency. But since to count as a responsible agent means nothing other than that a subject is interpretable as one, and a subject won't be interpretable as one if she lacks self-knowledge, that shows that we have to have *a prior and independent* grip on her self-knowledge, one that does *not* rely on the notion of what goes into responsible agency itself. And the spare causal-perceptual account is there precisely to explain that *independently grasped* notion of self-knowledge. Thus the constitutive thesis, when it is defined *in contrast* with the causal-perceptual account, is overlooking its own prior credentials.

One can put this path of resistance slightly differently and more directly. Since, in my argument, I myself have insisted that self-knowledge is a necessary condition for responsibility and agency, I should be giving an account of self-knowledge independent of the notion of agency, on the *general grounds* that one must have a full understanding of what a necessary condition is, independent of and prior to understanding what it is a necessary condition for, and how it gets to be a necessary condition for it. But I have precisely not given an account of self-knowledge independent of agency. On the contrary, I have rested my account of self-knowledge entirely on the notion of agency, seeing it as a fallout of agency, seeing agency as providing a vital proviso in my conditionals about self-knowledge. That is a foul. If I had played fair, if I had given an account of self-knowledge independent of the notion of agency, I would (or could), then, have appealed to the causal-perceptual considerations to provide such an account, precisely the considerations from which I have been so keen to distance myself. The point is not that I was wrong to say that self-knowledge is a necessary condition for agency. That link may be impeccable. Rather, I was wrong in failing to see that that very link requires that I had to fully account for self-knowledge prior to and independent of considerations of agency, and that could only be done (or best be done) by the causal and perceptual considerations I have eschewed.

So once again, the moral is supposed to be that I am right to link agency with self-knowledge, but a proper understanding of the relations between agency and self-knowledge should lead me to see how they merely provide a conceptual setting, a mere constraint on an account of self-knowledge. The actual account should be one that appeals to a causal mechanism.

But notice what an extraordinary principle is being invoked by this path of resistance, the principle that if something is a necessary condition for something else, one *must* have an account of *it* that is independent of what it is a necessary condition *for*. We sometimes perhaps do have such an account. But why must we? The principle makes a quite extraordinarily strong demand, stronger than anything justified by philosophy. A great number of very satisfying philosophical analyses would be called unilluminating by such a principle, and there is every reason to think that the deliverances of such analyses are on far surer ground than this principle that threatens them. Just one example should bring this out, though I don't doubt that others can be given.

In a subtle and widely accepted analysis of the concept of meaning, Grice proposed various forms of complicated, nested intentional states that were necessary for someone to mean something by an utterance.[16] So, repeating the exact terms of the objection being made to me above, suppose someone says of such an analysis of meaning: since to count as meaning something by an utterance is nothing but to be interpretable as having these complicated Gricean intentional states, we must have an account of intentional states independent of meaning. Or to put it in the more direct way, again as above, if it is a necessary condition for meaning something by an utterance that one has those intentional states, then we must give an account of the idea of such intentional states prior to and independent of the notion of meaning. But the fact is that it is not at all clear that we *can* have an account of intentional states (complicated ones of the kind Grice invokes) independently of the notion of language and meaning. Perhaps we can give some such independent analysis of a much more primitive notion of propositional attitudes ('proto-intentionality', as it is called, the intentional states that animals who lack language and meaning are often said to have) than the sort of states Grice specifies. There is no reason for me here or for Grice to have denied that there is such a more elementary notion. But the complicated and nested intentional states actually offered in his analysis are precisely not extricable in this way from what it is that they analyze and provide necessary conditions for—meaning. Nothing about this inextricability puts into doubt that these can serve (and serve illuminatingly) as a necessary condition for meaning. The situation is quite analogous with how self-knowledge is a necessary condition for agency, as presented in this chapter. In both cases, there are looped interrelations between the analysandum and the analysans.

The point I am making here echoes my earlier point made in Chapter 2, repudiating the claim that if free agency is a necessary condition for our evaluative practices such as praise and blame and punishment and our evaluative reactive attitudes that underlie them, we must at least have a non-evaluative account of this necessary condition. As I said there, the only reason why freedom can be seen as a necessary condition for our evaluative practices and attitudes is that it is our *values* that justify our seeing it as such. Thus its role as necessary condition is not uncontaminated by the sort of evaluative notions that it is a necessary condition for. These interdependencies and inextricabilities of analysandum and analysans, of a necessary condition and what it is a condition for, are built into a great deal of philosophical analysis without detracting from the illumination it provides. It would only detract from it if one took the quite extraordinarily narrowing view that the *only* form of illumination lay in providing for some sort of reductive analysis. Since (in this book) reduction is not being sought (putting aside the question for now as to whether it is even possible), the underlying general principle being invoked to plot a path of resistance to my claim about the incompatibility between the causal-perceptual and the constitutive accounts is not a principle that we are bound to respect.

For centuries philosophy had pursued its theoretical goals and implicitly its conceptual analyses of a range of notions in epistemology and other areas without any obvious commitment to *reductive* analyses—until the British empiricists who sought to ground various concepts or 'ideas' (such as those of 'material object', 'causality', 'self', 'meaning', etc.) in terms of a notion of 'simple' experiential, qualitative, or phenomenal states. No doubt, there were some exceptions to this freely non-reductive pursuit before the empiricists—perhaps Ockham's analysis of language, and a few others—but these were exceptions to the rule. The idea that *either* there are stipulative definitions that are unhelpfully circular *or* there are reductions is a somewhat late and tyrannical shrinking of the options for philosophy. There is a great deal of philosophical analysis that is non-reductive and yet is by no means stipulative or trivial but in fact greatly surprises and startles by forging links between concepts hitherto viewed as having no tight mutually illuminating connections. Present proof of this lies in the fact that Strawson's remarks on the special and constitutive nature of the asymmetry about self-knowledge, with which we closed Chapter 1, have links with *his own* normative twist, given to the notion of freedom, which we developed in Chapter 2—links of which he himself seems to have been quite unsuspecting. It takes a lot of philosophical spadework to unearth such links, and as we shall see by the end of the book, there are more links to be forged between these already linked notions of self-knowledge and freedom and yet others. Not only is it narrowing to dismiss these links as unilluminatingly circular just because they are not reductive; there is some tension in both dismissing them in this way and *also* claiming that the constitutive view that invokes these links harbors an unnecessarily controversial denial of the perceptual model of self-knowledge. To say in the same breath that a view is unilluminatingly, circularly true *and* controversial is to be a quite unprincipled critic of the view.

Returning to the analogy between the account being given here of self-knowledge and Grice's account of meaning, it is true that there have been philosophers who *have* taken up Grice's work with a view to providing reductive analyses of meaning—by analyzing intentional states themselves in purely causal and functionalist and (sometimes even, eventually) physicalist terms.[17] So analyzed, the intentional states that go into a Gricean account of meaning will have the effect of canceling the feature of his account that I am invoking as an analogy: the feature of a looped interrelation between the analysandum and the analysans. But there is no evidence whatsoever that Grice himself had this agenda when he analyzed the notion of meaning. Of course, one may have all sorts of further agendas once one grasps his analysis of meaning. And the reductive agenda is one of them. But it is a *further* agenda that uses a quite different conception of intentional states from the one Grice deployed.

If the analogy with Grice is sound, the incompatibility between the perceptual account and the constitutive account withstands the efforts to undermine it by placing the unreasonable demand (we have been discussing) on the constitutive account. The incompatibility withstands here because the constitutive account can reject the general demand that a grasp of the necessary condition for something must be spelled out in terms prior to and independent of all considerations having to do with what it is a necessary condition for. Grice does not honor that demand in his illuminating account of meaning, and in general it is a demand that is quite uncompulsory. Without having to meet that demand, there is no need to give an account of something that is a necessary condition for agency (self-knowledge) in terms that are prior and independent of considerations of agency. One can, as the constitutive view does, account for it as a fallout of a normative notion of agency, without any need to resort to causal mechanisms that are more than usually reliable.

The need to find the two accounts compatible is thus not well motivated. The constitutive account, one-half of whose force has now been elaborated, presents a property of intentional states, which explains our self-knowledge in terms that make the explanatory claims of the perceptual account unnecessary. It is a property that owes conceptually to a notion of agency, understood in thoroughgoing normative terms. That debt is specified in the proviso of the conditional. With the proviso in place, the conditional holds without exception, and it does so not as a *contingency* of great remarkableness. It does so because now there is a *rule-like* connection between intentional states and second-order beliefs about them, quite different from the reliable causal link posited by the perceptual model. It is this rule-like link rather than the remarkable reliability of a causal link that transparency consists in and that the considerations mentioned in the proviso in the conditional make possible.

Of course, there are exceptions to self-knowledge. But all those exceptions are viewed as a manifestation of the failure of the proviso to hold. They are not viewed as presenting exceptions to the conditional, *with the proviso in place*. We promised ourselves a result that approximated one aspect of an intuition of Descartes' without it actually being a Cartesian result. That promise has been redeemed, at least for transparency. The Cartesian view, which has no place for the proviso and the considerations it brings to bear, makes a claim to transparency (to exceptionless self-awareness of intentional states) that comes off as an impertinence, an utterly implausible claim, manifestly refuted by the fact of these exceptions. But with the considerations specified by the proviso held steadily in place, the exceptionless truth of the conditional captures that core intuition of transparency without any implausibility whatever, since the fact of the exceptions is now in place as well.

In closing this chapter on the element of transparency character-

istic uniquely only of self-knowledge among all knowledges, there is
a terminological point worth noticing, if only because it quite possibly
points to something important and more than merely terminological.
Throughout this discussion, I have not invoked the rhetoric of 'justification' or (to use a more current term) 'entitlement' when talking
of self-ascription or second-order beliefs. I have not said, as is often
said, that a normative notion of agency 'entitles' us to our second-
order beliefs or that our self-ascriptions are justified by such a notion.
Nor have I said that, given the fact of a normative notion of agency
within which our intentional states are situated, our intentional states
'entitle' us to our second-order beliefs about them or our self-
ascriptions of them. Why is this fairly widespread and current form of
epistemological description being avoided?

It is not that there is something wholesale wrong with such forms
of description. The worry, rather, is that one might be misled by it.
What the account of transparency, i.e., what the fully specified conditional for transparency presented in this chapter, really claims is
that we *have* self-knowledge whenever our intentional states are in the
realm of agency. We *must* have it whenever the proviso specifying the
condition of agency is fulfilled. Now, someone might want to say that
what that account shows is that when agency is in place in this way,
our intentional states *entitle* us to our second-order beliefs about them.
This would be all right if it is not intended to give the impression that
there is a kind of *transition* or *movement* from the first-order intentional
state to the second-order belief, or self-ascription, with all of the tem-
poral element that brings in. One way to put this point is to say that
the way in which the account invokes agency to deliver self-knowledge
is not so much that it sets up a *dynamic* relation between first-order
intentional states and second-order beliefs about them but rather that
it reveals that there is a sort of *part-whole* relation between them. Once
one grasps the role of agency in self-knowledge, one's intentional
states are to be seen *as* self-known; i.e., it has to be *presupposed* that
they *are* self-known. Intentional states come with the awareness that
the second-order belief is supposed to capture. 'Part-whole' does seem
a better description of it because it does not mislead us into thinking
that there might be serious transitions from one to the other in time,
in the way that the talk of 'entitlement' does.

Crispin Wright[18] in various papers has claimed that if there is no inference or observation involved in the gaining of self-knowledge, then there is no substantial epistemology at all to self-knowledge. In itself (that is to say, all by itself) that may be a bit too swift. Christopher Peacocke,[19] for instance, denies Wright's conclusion, even though he grants that inference and observation are not to the point. And he thinks that we may correctly say that our conscious first-order intentional states give us *'reason'* to believe that we have them, give us reason to self-ascribe them. What seems right, and what makes it seem as if Wright's conclusion is the sort of thing that one might jump to too swiftly, is that whether or not there is or is not a substantial epistemology of self-knowledge will depend on what detailed account one gives of self-knowledge after having said that an inferential and observational account is not satisfactory. The long excursus on agency was intended in part (the transparency, not the authority, part) to give an account that supports Wright's conclusion. It does so because it allows one to present an account in which the relation between the first- and second-order state in self-knowledge is not best seen as a dynamic transition. How does this square with Peacocke's own way of describing the relation?

As Peacocke knows very well, at least on the face of it, the 'reasons' view is not a promising view. Reasons are usually thought of as the sorts of things that issue from the propositional content of intentional states. Thus when we say that someone's belief that all men are mortal and her belief that Socrates is a man gave her a reason to believe that Socrates is mortal, we are saying that the propositional contents of the first two beliefs are the rational basis for the third. But clearly the propositional content of the belief that all men are mortal is not, in that sense, a reason for her belief that she believes that all men are mortal.

What, then, could possibly tempt one to say that first-order intentional states provide reasons for the second-order beliefs about them? If the difficulty is that it is not the propositional content of the first-order state that provides the reason for the second-order belief about it, perhaps what is meant is that it is the intentional *state* (with that content) that provides it. (This is in any case something that someone might think necessary since the sort of reason that a belief-state would provide may be quite different from what a desire-state would provide; i.e., it may be a reason for a quite different conclusion than the conclusion that a desire-state would provide, since one would provide reason for the conclusion that one had a belief and the other that one had a desire.) But this would be unpromising too. If I needed to know that I was in the state of believing that Socrates is mortal in order to have a reason for believing that I believed that Socrates is mortal, the latter belief could not count as a new bit of knowledge at all since it is already contained in knowing that I was in the state of believing that Socrates is mortal. Thus it would offer no informative account of self-knowledge of the sort we are seeking to say that first-order states provide one with a reason, in this sense, for the second-order beliefs about them.

But perhaps in raising both these difficulties for the idea that there is a reasons-based account, I am assuming wrongly that to have a reason one must be reason*ing* from one state to another. That is to say, perhaps I am assuming wrongly that in order to say that a first-order intentional state is a reason for believing that one has it, its possessor must be reason*ing* from the first (or the possession of the first) to arrive at the second. Perhaps it provides a *reason without any reasoning* being involved.

If reasoning *were* involved in the way a reason was provided by the first-order intentional state for a second-order belief about it, then presumably that would be an *inferentialist* account of self-knowledge. I have already criticized the idea that self-knowledge is a matter of inference in my comments on Ryle's views on self-knowledge and also on Gopnik's more perceptualist version of Ryle's account. Of course the kind of inference *they* were proposing is quite different from what we are presently discussing. Ryle proposed an inference *from one's behavior* to one's second-order beliefs about one's intentional states. Gopnik sophisticated this view by introducing into her explanation of our second-order beliefs the sort of inference involved in the perception of highly theoretical phenomena, which she takes our first-order intentional states to be. These proposals are very different from the idea that our first-order states *themselves* provide the basis (a non-perceptual basis) for inferring our beliefs that we have them. That is why the criticisms of Gopnik and Ryle were very different from the two difficulties I just raised about this inferentialist reasons-based approach. The present two difficulties are simply about the notion of validity that would allow it as a sound inference. The inference, as I said, could not be from the propositional content of the first-order intentional states to the beliefs about them. And if this means we must look for an inference in which the subject must be sensitive not just to the propositional content but also to the first-order intentional *state* of which it is a content (a belief, or a desire), that would amount to saying that it is an inference of the sort "I believe that p, therefore I believe that p," which, as I said, is manifestly uninformative and un-illuminating as an explanation. That is why perhaps we must look instead to interpret the reasons approach as not involving itself in any idea of inference at all. Peacocke himself is very clear that he thinks that a first-order intentional state provides a reason for the second-order belief about it, but he is equally clear that he rejects an infer-entialist account of self-knowledge. He explicitly says that we should not be tyrannized by the threefold disjunction: "Observation, Infer-ence, or Nothing." He thinks a *fourth* option is "Reasons." But if it is to be reasons and yet not be inferential, he must mean Reasons *without* Reason*ing*. He admits, indeed asserts, that as a result this fourth option, though different from the 'Nothing' option of a wholly insubstantial epistemology, nevertheless commits itself only to a very minimal substantial epistemology, nothing as substantial as the Infer-ence and Observation options.

I think something like this 'reasons without reasoning' view, which is gaining currency in recent discussions, may be fine, but it must be properly understood, since there is much scope here for being misled. Current ways of describing the phenomena under discussion has it that the first-order state '*entitles*' us (another way of saying it gives us 'reason') to self-ascribe it or form beliefs about its existence, at the second-order. Even if we allow these ways of talking, and I am not particularly keen to eradicate such a way of talking, one has to be very careful that we don't spoil the special quality of self-knowledge among other knowledges when we allow it. Why might such a way of talking spoil that special quality? Because we say things *just like it* in other forms of knowledge, precisely those forms of knowledge that we want to make self-knowledge stand apart from, in insisting on its special quality.

For instance, it might and has been plausibly claimed (by Peacocke himself, following McDowell),[20] with a number of suitable details put in, that the fact that there is a table in front of me 'gives me reason', 'entitles me', to believe that there is a table in front of me, or that my experience of a table in front of me prima facie 'gives me reason', 'entitles' me, to believe that there is a table in front of me. In such instances of perceptual knowledge, these ways of talking do clearly suggest that there is some minimal substantial epistemology, even if there is no inference or reasoning involved. Though there is no reasoning, there are reasons. Thus in the domain of perceptual knowledge, this way of talking of 'entitlement' and 'being given reasons' is entirely appropriate because it quite properly captures a sense of *dynamic transition* of warrant from one (facts in the world or experiences of things being thus and so) to the other (perceptual beliefs about the world). *But that is precisely what is missing* in the agential account of self-knowledge, at least in the agential account that I have offered, invoking what is presupposed by a Strawsonian conception of agency, suitably modified. So to the extent that these ways of talking ('entitlement', 'reasons') capture or convey such a form of transition, I have shied away from it. To the extent that it conveys a transition of that kind, it would undermine what has been established as special about self-knowledge in this chapter to then go on to say that our intentional states give us 'reason to believe' or 'entitle us to believe' that we have them.

All these remarks have been made by way of clarification of what is and is not implied by the transparency conditional for which I have argued so far. Now that it has been argued for and fortified by clarifications as well as responses to a number of fundamental objections over the last many sections, let me repeat the abbreviated version of the rewritten form of the conditional, with its crucial proviso and without any longer its presumptive characterization. It is,

(T). Given agency, if S desires (believes) that p, then S believes that she desires (believes) that p.

For the unabbreviated version, which spells out all the details of the normative notion of agency that go into the proviso ("Given agency"), please return to the end of Section 4 above.

As I said, this conditional with this proviso is now true without exceptions. The exceptions, fully acknowledged unlike as with Descartes, have been addressed by the substantial bit of philosophizing regarding agency done in this chapter and the last, and that has allowed us to put the proviso down, thereby to accommodate the exceptions. The conditional therefore captures one-half of what makes self-knowledge special, and as promised, it does so in a non-Cartesian setting.

We must now turn to the conditional for authority. That is a longer story that reaches out to two large presuppositions and implications of the normative notion of agency: the first-person point of view and the real underlying sources of the irreducibly normative nature of intentionality. These will be themes of the next two chapters, at the end of which it is hoped that the conditional for authority will also find its proper ground.

✦ ✦ ✦

FOUR

The Conceptual Basis for Authority I

Agency, Intentionality, and the First Person Point of View

1. THE TASK OF establishing the conditional for authority requires us first to achieve two large and related prior tasks. *One,* to show that agency is a necessary condition for thought or intentionality. (I will use these two terms 'thought' and 'intentionality' interchangeably in this context.) That is the subject of Section 3 onward, in this chapter. In the course of making out that claim, the significance of the first person point of view will emerge for all of the book's themes, and its significance will be developed over the next chapter as well. And *two,* to show that intentionality is a normative notion in the quite specific sense that intentional states are themselves normative states. The two claims are closely enough related and indeed interdependent enough that the full argument for each (and the overall argument for the truth of the authority conditional) will not be complete till the end of Chapter 5.

2. Before any of this is undertaken, I want, in this section, to show at length that though it may *seem* otherwise, there is nothing obviously implausible in thinking that authority holds. At first sight, it may appear obviously implausible because there seem to be so many exceptions to authority, coming from self-deception and other such phenomena. And so, at first, it may seem that the very idea that our second-order beliefs are always true is a holdover from Cartesian infallibilist thinking about the mind. But I would like to show that there is a way of thinking about authority that does not fail to acknowledge

the fairly widespread phenomena of self-deception that Cartesian stipulations about the mind are supposed to have left unacknowledged, nor does it *require us* to see the acknowledged phenomena as providing exceptions to authority. I say cautiously that this way of thinking does not 'require' us to see the seeming exceptions as exceptions. That is all that I will be able to show in this section. It is not until the two tasks mentioned above are done that I will be able to show the less cautious and more ambitious thing: not only are we not required to see the exceptions as threatening the conditional, but we have full and legitimate grounds for not doing so. That is, I will be able to show not merely that it does not require us to see them as falsifying the conditional for authority but that it is actually *better* not to see them as falsifying it because that fits in better with the right way to think of intentionality and its relations to norms and to agency.

The conditional for authority, as stated in Chapter 1, says this.

(A). It is a presumption that: if S believes that she desires (believes) that p, then she desires (believes) that p.

As with transparency, the conditional is initially expressed as a presumption: here too the task is to explain the presumption and thereby rewrite the conditional without the presumption.

As explained in Chapter 1, the conditional is initially formulated as only a presumption in order to acknowledge that there are exceptions to the conditional, in order to acknowledge what Cartesian infallibilism has failed to acknowledge. (If p is only a presumption, then qua presumption it can still be true even if p turns out, on occasion, to be false.) Without the presumptive formulation, the conditional would seem to express a glaring falsehood. The most ordinary cases of self-deception will seem to falsify it. It happens repeatedly that someone who is self-deceived believes that he desires (or believes) something, but does not seem to desire (or believe) it at all. He has deceived himself into thinking he does, perhaps, as I said in Chapter 1, because he is more comfortable believing that he desires or believes that thing than not believing it. One hardly need spell out the scenario. It is all too familiar.

So these cases do not falsify the presumption. But I am now claiming that there is a way of thinking about authority whereby it is not required of us that we see these cases as falsifying the conditional, even when it is not merely a presumption. How may one establish this claim?

Perhaps as follows?

The conditional asserts that second-order beliefs are always true. Now, standard evidence for having second-order beliefs about intentional states is found in *avowals* of first-order intentional states on the part of the agent. If someone *says*, "I desire (believe) that p," that is standard evidence that he has the second-order belief that he has the desire (belief) that p. But this means a person who has a second-order belief that he has some intentional state is assumed to be genuine and sincere in his avowals of that intentional state. Otherwise, the avowals would not count as evidence for the existence of second-order beliefs. The sincerity and genuineness of the avowal and the existence of the second-order belief go hand in hand. Therefore, it is taken for granted of an agent to whom a second-order belief is attributed on the basis of avowals on his part that in making the avowals he is not lying or merely sounding off.[1] And now the question is, can we be so sure that if there is self-deception on his part, the agent in question is really sincere in his avowals? Might it not be that what really goes on when cases of self-deception seem to show that second-order beliefs are false is that they, rather, show that the initial assumption that there was a sincere avowal is put into question? Or what amounts to the same thing, what it really shows is that we were wrong to have the impression that there was a second-order belief present in the first place. So, it might be thought, it is not as if self-deception shows that second-order beliefs are not true. It only shows that there exists no second-order belief where we thought one existed. And since the conditional only makes a claim about the truth of the second-order *beliefs*, it remains unharmed by these cases of self-deception. They are not really exceptions to the conditional.

But this move is clearly too quick. It generalizes illicitly. No doubt this *sometimes* happens. Self-deception does sometimes have the effect of canceling the sincerity of an avowal and, therefore, does not leave in place a second-order belief at all. But it would be to quite misrepresent the psychology of self-deceived agents to say that this is what *always* happens, that *all* cases of self-deception of the sort we are considering show us to be under an illusion that there is a second-order belief present on the part of the agent. It is often the case that an agent quite *sincerely* avows an intentional state and, therefore, can be truly said to *have* a second-order belief but is self-deceived in the way we have been discussing. Very often, nothing in the self-deception shows that *we* are mistaken in taking his avowals to be sincere or mistaken in attributing a second-order belief. All the signs of sincerity may be there in the avowal. What those signs are is something we can take up in a further discussion, of course, but there is no reason to assume that among those signs must be the fact that the person should not be self-deceived about the first-order intentional state he is avowing. That would be sheer stipulation. Thus, it is not ruled out yet that what the self-deception shows is that *he* is mistaken in thinking that he has a certain first-order intentional state. To deny this by always treating it as a case of a wrongly attributed second-order belief or an insincere avowal is to artificially strain to save the conditional despite ordinary seeming facts about the psychology of self-deception.

This effort at establishing authority, in the face of self-deception, therefore, fails. All the same, it teaches us an important, if obvious, lesson. It is instructive insofar as it points out the obvious connection between sincerity of avowal and the possession of second-order belief—these two things stand or fall together. However, it fails because it is wrong to think that there are no cases of both self-deception *and* sincerity of avowal.

I want to now pursue another strategy for showing that authority is not threatened by these cases of self-deception, one that does not try to deny that the agent's avowals are sincere or to deny that his second-order beliefs are genuinely present. It grants that there are second-order beliefs in these cases but concludes even so that self-deception does not falsify the second-order beliefs. And it claims that this is so because when one believes that one believes (or desires) that p, and one is self-deceived, it is *not* that one *lacks* the first-order belief (or desire) that p, and therefore it is *not* that the second-order belief is *false*, it is rather that one *has another* first-order belief (or desire) that is in some sense *inconsistent* with the belief or (desire) that p (let's say, taking the clearest case, not-p).

If the second-order belief is not false even in a case of self-deception, then this strategy has provided a way of viewing self-deception such that it leaves authority intact. As I said, all I am claiming for this strategy is that it shows that *it is not required* of us

that we see the relevant cases of self-deception as providing exceptions to the conditional for authority. By itself, the strategy does not
(yet) *justify* seeing these cases of self-deception as unthreatening to
authority and the conditional that expresses it.

But even though seeing them this way is not yet justified, there is
nothing *obviously wrong* in seeing them this way. The strategy cannot,
for instance, simply be faulted on the grounds that because it attributes *blatantly* inconsistent first-order intentional states to an agent
(just in order to save an agent's authority), it is in violation of the
most elementary principle of charity that forbids one to attribute *blatantly* inconsistent beliefs to an agent. Attribution of blatant inconsistencies fall afoul of charity when there are no explanations given of
why the inconsistencies exist. But when there are explanations for why
there is an inconsistency, there is nothing uncharitable about attributing it. Sometimes the explanation is that one of the inconsistent
beliefs (let us take the example of beliefs rather than desires, to keep
things simple) is not something that the subject is aware of. At other
times, a subject may be (severally) aware of two inconsistent beliefs
but has not brought them together, having compartmentalized them
and their surrounding implications. And so on. In the case of self-
deception, there will always be some such explanations of the inconsistency invoked by my strategy for saving authority.

In cases of self-deception, it is perhaps most often (though not
necessarily always) the former explanation that is in play. Assuming
it is in play, my strategy can admit that though it would be uncharitable to say of someone that she has inconsistent beliefs if she is *aware*
of, has self-knowledge of, both the beliefs involved in the inconsistency, in fact both of the inconsistent pair of beliefs in our example
are *not* self-known—in particular, the belief that not-p, mentioned
above, is not self-known to the agent. And if that is so, there is *no* lack
of charity involved in attributing inconsistent beliefs in this way to
save authority, since lack of charity only holds in cases of blatant inconsistencies, where there are no extenuating explanations of them
in terms of lack of self-knowledge of one of the inconsistent beliefs
or in some other terms. (At the end of the next chapter, I will have
the conceptual apparatus to describe the inconsistency quite differently from how I have just described it, to describe it in quite other
terms than as 'the inconsistency between the self-known belief that p

and the unself-known *belief* that not-p'. When I do so, there will open up quite other ways of dealing with the question of charity and lack of charity in attributions of irrationality.)

This has all been presented a little abstractly. To put it less abstractly, let's take a standard sort of case of self-deception. Suppose someone has the following second-order belief: she believes that she believes that her health is fine. But let's suppose that her behavior suggests to others around her that she is full of anxiety about her health. Let's suppose that she does not recognize her behavior as being anxious in these ways, but any analyst or even friend can tell that it is so. One view to take of this sort of familiar case is that her second-order belief is simply false. It is the simpler view, and it is wrong. The right view is more complicated: her second-order belief is true, which means she has the first-order belief that her health is fine, but she also has another belief that she is not aware of, the belief that she is sick. So authority (a property of *second-order* beliefs) is not unsettled by the phenomenon of self-deception; rather, self-knowledge is missing regarding one of the two inconsistent *first-order* beliefs (i.e., it is missing of the belief that not-p; in our example, it is missing of the belief that she is sick). Perhaps she has suppressed her belief that she is sick because it discomforts her to think of herself as sick, perhaps because she does not want to be bothered with it in her busy life, and so on. If this is right, then allowing for self-deception clearly does not undermine the conditional regarding *authority*. And, as said above, we have saved it from being undermined without any lack of charity in the attribution of inconsistent beliefs to the agent, since lack of charity in inconsistent attribution only holds if (among other things) the person is aware of both inconsistent beliefs. In the example above, we have even offered specific possible explanations for the lack of awareness of one of the pair of beliefs in the inconsistency, so there is nothing uncharitable about finding her inconsistent.

Of course, there is an immediate and obvious point regarding this strategy that we have already registered. To save the authority conditional by this strategy, one is being forced to say that self-knowledge does *not* hold for the first-order intentional states that are inconsistent with the first-order intentional states that are 'embedded' in the second-order beliefs, whose authority is saved. This strategy saves authority of second-order beliefs about first-order intentional states by insisting that in cases of self-deception these ('embedded' and sincerely avowed) first-order states are indeed always present, and therefore the second-order belief is always true—it's just that in each such case there is always another first-order intentional state that is inconsistent with the 'embedded' (or avowed) first-order state and that is *not self-known* to its possessor.

The question must now arise whether this only shows that we are saving authority by jeopardizing transparency. Are we by this strategy saving one conditional only by undermining the other? The answer to this question is no. The transparency conditional, as we presented it by the end of the last chapter's discussion, had a proviso that must be met. The point of the proviso is to acknowledge that there are exceptions to self-knowledge, that self-knowledge may go missing for many of our first-order intentional states. All we need to point out is that these intentional states that are not self-known to their possessors are not the kinds of states toward which we can have justifiable reactive attitudes, nor can we have justifiable reactive attitudes to any actions or conclusions that the agent comes to or might come to on their basis. They are not in the realm of responsible agency. Once this is pointed out, these intentional states fall within the ken of the rewritten conditional for transparency, since the proviso of that rewritten condition does not hold. Admitting lack of self-knowledge for them, therefore, brings no surprises. It leaves all our claims about transparency and the conditional that expresses it perfectly intact.

Here, then, is what we have shown thus far. To the extent that it has been established that an avowal of an intentional state is sincere and, therefore, that a second-order belief really exists, then (even in the cases of self-deception) so must the intentional state it is about really exist, thus making the second-order belief true. Of course, an agent can make insincere avowals. But what that shows is that we don't really have a second-order belief since sincere avowals and second-order beliefs stand or fall together. And if there are no second-order beliefs, then the subject of authority is not yet on the table, since authority is a claim about the truth of second-order *beliefs*, not the truth of insincere avowals. But if and when authority *is* on the table, self-deception *need not* be seen as overturning it. Second-order beliefs need not be seen as having any role in a psychological economy without the presence of the first-order beliefs they are about.

As with my efforts to save transparency, a basic and important objection to this strategy for saving authority must be addressed at some length, not only to show that it is defensible but also to bring out what underlies this way of thinking of authority in some of its detail.
Objection.

The objection is about how I will extend my strategy (for reconciling authority with self-deception) from the *positively* formulated first-order intentional states, which I have considered above, to *negatively* formulated ones. On the face of it, my strategy does not seem to carry over to them, and if it in fact does not, that might prove the entire strategy a failure.

What is this difficulty, exactly? I have formulated my strategy to save authority in the face of self-deception with regard to the following sorts of second-order beliefs: X believes that *she believes that p.* (I will once again restrict myself to beliefs among 'embedded' first-order intentional states and ignore desires, for the sake of abbreviation.) I have not looked at second-order beliefs of the following sort: X believes that *she does not believe that p.* The latter sort, unlike the former, is what I am calling 'negatively formulated'. The embedded clause is negatively formulated in the sense that it expresses that there is a *lack* of belief, rather than a belief. The second-order belief is thus about the lack of belief. And the worry is that in these cases my strategy to save authority is unworkable.

Let's repeat the strategy, so as to have clear what the worry is in detail. Its claim is that self-deception does not imply that a second-order belief is false; it leaves the second-order belief as true. Thus authority remains in place. This means that it allows that there exists the first-order belief. It allows that there exists the belief that p. And the strategy accounts for the self-deception by saying that what self-deception really implies is that there is another first-order belief that is inconsistent with the belief that p, say, the belief that not-p.

The worry being raised about this strategy is that it will not work when the second-order belief is of the form: X believes that she does not believe that p. Here is why. In these cases one cannot simply say what one said earlier, that the second-order belief remains true because the first-order belief exists despite self-deception. In these cases, there is, in the first place, *no* first-order belief. The second-order belief is about the *absence* of a first-order belief. If I were to glibly try and apply my strategy here, I would get an intolerable result. I would have to say (just as I said about the other positively formulated cases) that the second-order belief is true, and all that self-deception shows is that there is another belief that is *inconsistent* with what is expressed in the embedded clause of the second-order belief. If the second-order belief is true, then X does not believe that p. But if self-deception shows what my strategy says it shows (i.e., an inconsistency), then it follows that X is also attributed the belief that p. That is the inconsistency that my strategy would have to claim is generated by self-deception in such negatively formulated cases. But this latter inconsistency is intolerable since it makes the *attributer* inconsistent.

In the other positively formulated cases, it was X the attributee who is inconsistent. If the attributer says (as he does in the positively formulated cases), "X believes that p and X believes that not-p," he is attributing an inconsistency to X. However, if he says (as he is forced to say, if one blithely applies the same strategy in the negatively formulated cases), "X believes that she does not believe that p, and X believes that she does believe that p," he is *himself* being inconsistent. Here is why. If he attributes that inconsistency to X *and he assumes authority* (which he must do in order to be attributing *both* of the embedded states he does to X in the face of X's self-deception), then it is *he* who will believe the following: it is not the case that X believes that p *and* X believes that p. In other words, if he believes in authority, then he must believe that X really does have the embedded states that his second-order beliefs are about. Now, for him to be inconsistent in this way, as I said, is intolerable in a way that it is not intolerable for him to attribute an inconsistency to X.

Why is the one inconsistency intolerable and the other not? Because the examples are set up to be dealing with self-deceived attribut*ees*. X, in the example above, is known to be self-deceived. That is the point of the example. But there is no parallel thing that holds of the attributor. There is no reason therefore to say of the attributor that he lacks self-knowledge of one of his inconsistent beliefs; in general, there is presumably no reason to say that he is self-deceived at all. He is not suppressing one of his beliefs because of some discomfort he feels in having them or for any other reason. Those are only considerations that apply (ex hypothesi) to X but not to the person attributing beliefs to X. And it is because X is not aware of one of the two of her beliefs that are inconsistent that makes the attribution of the inconsistency to her tolerable. As I said earlier, it happens often that we are inconsistent when we lack self-knowledge of one-half of the inconsistent pair of beliefs. No elementary principle of charity is violated in attributing an inconsistency if it is also made clear that there is lack of awareness of this sort. But since, as we have just said, unlike as with X, in the case of the attributor there is presumably no such lack of awareness of one of the inconsistent beliefs he is supposed to have, an elementary principle of charity *is* violated when he is said to be inconsistent. The inconsistency in this case would therefore indeed be intolerable. And that is the intolerable consequence of my applying my strategy to the negatively formulated cases.

If we have no response to this difficulty, the strategy might seem doomed, and therefore authority might seem to be in jeopardy since it would have been shown that whenever there is self-deception, it is not to be a property of the second-order beliefs involving the negatively formulated cases.

It will turn out, by the time we are at the end of the next chapter (see the long note 44 in Chapter 5), that there is nothing in the way I conceive of intentionality that requires or motivates one to say that our first-person authority over our intentional states should hold of the negatively formulated cases. That is to say, once the fully and specifically normative nature of beliefs and desires is made clear, and once the argument for our authority over such states is presented, there will be no compulsion felt to have the negatively formulated cases behave just like the positively formulated ones. The argument for authority will turn on the fact that the conditions under which second-order beliefs exist are the very same conditions under which the first-order intentional states they are about exist. Such an argument depends on the existence of the first-order states and therefore will not apply when no such states exist. It will not apply, therefore, to second-order beliefs that have negatively formulated embedded clauses. There is an admissible asymmetry between authority as it applies to the positive and the negative cases. All this cannot be presented now since the fully and specifically normative nature of intentional states required to present it has to be motivated and argued for first.

But quite apart from the fact that a proper appreciation of the nature of intentional states makes for this admissible asymmetry in how we think of authority, it is a matter of some real doubt whether the difficulty that is being raised about the negatively formulated cases is threatening to authority at all. In other words, even if we don't take the specifically normative view of intentionality that I will argue for in the next chapter, authority may very well hold symmetrically for these two sorts of cases, and there may be no need to admit the asymmetry. Since this is a subject of intrinsic interest, and since it is always an interesting challenge to argue for a more, rather than less, strong claim (in this case, for a symmetry rather than an admissible asymmetry), I will spend some time doing so now. This strong claim, if true, will add further support to the conclusion that is being pursued in this chapter that far from being obvious that authority is falsified by the fact of self-deception, it is very hard to make the case that authority needs to be given up as a result of self-deception. Even if it is only in the next chapter that we are given the philosophical ground for deciding how extensive authority is (for deciding the question whether or not we have grounds for claiming authority even over the negatively formulated cases), in this chapter it is still worth establishing just how difficult it is to show that we *need ever* think of authority as being less than fully extensive.

The response to this difficulty regarding the negatively formulated cases must begin by first pointing out that the very form in which it is raised presupposes that my strategy for saving authority in the face of self-deception is *half* right. It *grants* that my strategy works for the *positively* formulated cases and then denies that that strategy is *extendable* to the negatively formulated ones.

Let's, then, see what it is exactly that goes on in the negatively formulated cases. We have an agent, X, the attributee, who is attributed the belief that she does not believe that p. I repeat: the problem, according to the objection, is supposed to lie entirely in the fact that the embedded clause expresses a negatively formulated content for the second-order belief. It does not arise for any positively formulated contents. So it follows that if one could show that the negatively formulated contents in all these very cases had *a positive reformulation,* the problem would go away. I will try and show that.

Now, let's first ask: what, in general, could it mean to say of someone that she does not believe that p? What would have to hold true of X for us to attribute such a negatively formulated state of mind to her that is being reported in the embedded belief in the case under discussion? Any, and only, one of three things. (1) It could mean that X has considered the matter of whether or not p is true and denies that p is true. Under such a circumstance, one can say of her that she does not believe that p.(2) Or it could mean that she has considered whether or not p is true and has decided that on the present information available to her she has not made up her mind whether or not p is true. In such a circumstance too, it would be quite true to say of her that she does not believe that p.(3) Or finally, it could mean that she has never considered the matter of p; the question has never arisen in her mind in any way. Under such a circumstance, we can also say of her that she does not believe that p.

These *exhaust* the general sorts of truth-conditions of statements like "X does not believe that p." There simply are no other general sorts of condition than these three under which the negatively formulated embedded clause could be attributed to her. Therefore, it is also only under one or another of these three conditions that the second-order belief that she does not believe that p is true.

I—in my defense of authority even in the face of self-deception— am saying that a second-order belief is always true. So, if I am right, the second-order belief with the negatively formulated embedded clause must be true in all three of these circumstances in which the embedded clause is rightly deployed.

Notice that of these three circumstances under which such a second-order belief is true, circumstance (1) is very clearly such that one could just as easily attribute to her (without any loss or shift of meaning) a *positively* formulated embedded clause in the true second-order belief. Under condition (1), we could just as easily say of her: "She believes that she believes that not-p." This is no longer the difficulty-inducing negatively formulated case: "She believes that she does not believe that p." Remember, the criterion for being a 'negatively' formulated attribution is that it is an attribution of an *absence* of a belief. By this criterion, to say that someone believes that not-p is to present a positively formulated case, since it is not attributing the absence of belief.

Take, now, circumstance (2). Here too we can attribute a positively formulated embedded clause in the second-order belief, though it takes more work to show why. The second-order belief "She believes that p is undecidable by her on the present evidence" actually does, at first sight, seem to register something negative at the first-order level, viz., that she has not decided whether p on the basis of the evidence so far. "She believes that she has not decided . . ." is a lot like "She believes that she does not believe. . . ." Both register an absence of belief or, more generally, an absence of an intentional state of mind. If so, shouldn't this raise the problem of the attributer being inconsistent when he deals with the self-deceptive cases in the way I am suggesting they should be treated?

This is not obvious at all.

We first have to emphasize that these are all cases of second-order beliefs *in the face of self-deception*. This is a crucial and unignorable aspect of the cases involved. We are not just interested in any second-order beliefs with negatively formulated embedded clauses. For any difficulty to be raised about authority, we have to consider only those cases that are accompanied by self-deception. So, let us work with an example of self-deception for cases in circumstance (2). Take a juror who, out of some prejudice, has made up his mind to vote that the defendant is guilty, but his self-image is one of great fair-mindedness and impartiality, so he manages to suppress his prejudice from his own conscious states of mind. As a result, he has deceived himself into thinking that he has not made up his mind on the evidence that he has so far. In other words, he is in *denial* about the fact that he has made up his mind. So when the attributer says that the juror's first-order state of mind is that he has not decided on the matter of p (the matter of the defendant's guilt), he is also at the same time conveying this: he is fair-minded and impartial regarding the matter of whether p. That is what the *second-order belief in the face of self-deception* is conveying. It is conveying that the juror believes that he is fair-minded. The agent is affirming his fair-mindedness on the matter inasmuch as he is in denial about his prejudice. The affirming is just the other side of the denial. There is no other way to understand the example. And all examples of second-order belief regarding absence of belief in the face of self-deception are cases of denial/affirmation of this kind. Thus all such cases involve the following four ingredients: a first-order state of mind; a second-order belief about this first-order state of mind; self-deception about another first-order state that amounts to a denial of that state; and finally, the ingredient that the agent in his second-order beliefs (and avowals) is really affirming to himself (and others) his fair-mindedness and open-mindedness.

Now, if all this is clear, a question arises, what exactly is his state of mind at the first order that the second-order belief is a belief about? Suppose, as is being claimed, his second-order beliefs are authoritative about his first-order states of mind. What are they authoritative about? How should we characterize a state of mind that conveys indecisiveness about the matter of p or not-p (in this case, the defendant's guilt or innocence) but that is, at the same time, being affirmed as his fair-mindedness or open-mindedness about the matter of p or not-p. The only way to characterize this affirmation is in terms of the juror's being in a state of mind of *suspense between p and not-p* until evidence weighs in. "Being in suspense between p and not-p" is a *positively formulated* description in the sense that it describes an *existent* state of mind of the juror. It is not *just* registering an *absence* of a decision. When one is affirming that one is open-minded, the idea of not having decided *is the idea* of being in a state of suspense between p and not-p.

It is not necessarily being suggested that in all cases when an attributer says of an agent that "X does not believe that p" under circumstance (2), where the agent is undecided, that it *must* be understood in positive terms of the agent *possessing* a state of mind that he is in suspense about whether p or not-p. It is only being suggested that such cases *when they are also accompanied by self-deception* (and those are the cases that are under discussion because those are the cases that prima facie threaten authority) necessarily contain all the four ingredients mentioned above. And one of those four elements is the crucial element of affirmation of one's open-mindedness between the alternatives; and it is *this* that forces upon us the idea that the attributee in these cases does not merely lack a first-order state of mind but *has* a first-order state of mind, properly described as being in suspense between the alternatives. "X believes that she is in suspense between p and not-p," then, is the positive reformulation of this case, a positive reformulation of the, at first sight, negatively formulated, "X believes that she has not decided between p and not-p." If that is so, then the self-deception can be handled just like with the other positively formulated cases, and the inconsistency involved is the agent's (the attributee's) and not the attributers. (As I said earlier, that my strategy works for positively formulated cases has been granted by the objection right at the outset.)

Only circumstance (3) remains. It poses some initial difficulty as well.

Circumstance (3) is when the agent in question has never considered the matter of p. And we are once again pondering the nature of the authority of (the negatively formulated second-order belief) "X believes that she does not believe that p" under this circumstance. If X has never considered whether p, if the question of p has never come up in her psychology, then were she to have the relevant second-order belief, its representation, it seems, would *have* to retain this negatively formulated embedded clause marking an absence of a belief. There does not seem to be any recasting of it in positive terms. And so the problem for my strategy being raised by this objection (viz., that the attributer ends up with an inconsistency, not the attributee) seems to be unavoidable in this sort of case.

Here a point pressed by Gareth Evans offers the beginnings of a response to the objection.[2]

This case depends on the fact that the question of p has never crossed the subject's mind. That is the circumstance under which it is true that she does not believe that p. But we are not just considering the condition under which the subject does not believe that p. We are considering also her second-order belief; i.e., we are considering that *she believes that* she does not believe that p. Now, we know that if someone assents or dissents to a question about whether she believes that p, she is expressing a second-order belief. And Evans pointed out that if you ask someone whether or not she believes that p, *she does not scan her interior* to find out if she does or does not. *Rather, she considers the matter of p; she considers whether p.* If you ask someone whether she believes that it's raining, says Evans, she does not scan her mind to see whether she believes it or not; she looks out of the window to see whether it's raining. So: if one way of attributing the second-order belief to someone ("She believes that she does not believe that p") is to ask her whether she believes that p; and if Evans is right that when so asked, she *considers the matter of p itself rather than gazes inward into her repository of beliefs,* then the problem being posed for me by this objection disappears. The problem was supposed to be that positive reformulations of the negatively formulated 'embedded' beliefs couldn't be given when the question of p has never crossed the subject's mind. But if Evans is right, her second-order belief, if attributed to her on the basis of her response to a query about what she believes, *would* involve the question of p having crossed her mind. It would involve her having considered the matter of p. So circumstance (3), the one and only condition under which the positive reformulations of the negative formulations are blocked, *can never really obtain.*

What is to be admitted is that Evans did not consider the negatively formulated cases we are considering, and so a question arises whether his point is very well suited for such cases, however insightful it is for the positively formulated cases. We need to say therefore how to apply his point to the negatively formulated cases, especially under our condition (3), i.e., when the question of p has never crossed one's mind.

The worry might be this: When asked whether I believe that p, if the question of p has never so much as crossed my mind, I would likely answer: "I have never considered the matter of p," and my questioner could then conclude by inference that I don't believe that p (which just is the negatively formulated case). If so, this is a case when it would be correctly said of me that I don't believe that p, and as my answer to the question shows, I have not done what Evans says always happens when answering the question, viz., that I consider the matter of p.

But Evans's point should be able to handle this worry since it is surely the case that when I give that answer to the question, I give an answer that is *explicitly* a report *about the past.* But the question is about what I *currently* believe. If we look only at what is explicitly stated in the answer, we don't really have an answer to the question. Therefore, we must conclude that by giving that answer, though I am saying that I have never considered the matter in the past, *I am not merely saying that.* I am *implicitly* also saying something about what is being asked, i.e., my current beliefs on the matter. I am also conveying (implicitly) that right now I do not have any particular view on the matter of p because of never having considered it in the past; and now that the question has been raised about what I currently think of the matter, there is nothing in my immediate, present considering of the matter to give me sufficient reason or evidence to decide. That alone provides an answer to the question being asked. Without this element, the question remains unanswered. So, in effect, the answer *does implicitly* express a positively formulated belief of a kind that is roughly like the one we have already discussed regarding condition (2) about how the subject cannot decide on the basis of his current evidence. It is just that, unlike as in (2), where the conclusion that the matter is not decidable on the present evidence is made as a result of a lot of deliberation upon the evidence, in this case the conclusion is arrived at without any detailed consideration but rather as a result of a very hasty consideration at the time of the question being raised. The point is that all the considerations that we mentioned in dealing with (2) apply here too, and they can both get *positive* formulations. So (3), which is supposed to be a case of the subject not having considered the matter, is not really such a case at all if the Evansian point holds. There are no such cases as (3).

It might be complained that by invoking Evans in the first place we have loaded things in our favor by insisting on attributing the second-order belief (X believes that she does not believe that p) on the basis of a prompted response by X to a question, as Evans's own example does. "Once you see the second-order belief as expressed in a certain response to a question," the complaint says, "then you are viewing the subject as considering the matter, even if the deliverance of the considering is that you have not considered it sufficiently to come to a decided view of the matter. What do you say of the case of second-order beliefs that one does not believe that p, where there is *no* prompting with a question involved?" But this complaint is seeing undue significance in the fact that a question is posed to the subject. Even if there is no question asked to the subject, presumably there is a difference between (1) a subject who does not believe that p and *has* the second-order belief that he does not believe that p and (2) a subject who does not believe that p but does not have that second-order belief. And presumably the difference is that in (1) *something has occasioned* the second-order belief. In some sense she has raised the question *for herself*, even if no one else has.

I conclude, then, that no real threat comes from circumstance (3) where the subject who believes that he does not believe that p has never considered the matter. The negatively formulated case poses no problem here either, because, as has just been shown, these cases cannot be taken at face value. There really are no such cases. They are all in fact cases of the matter having been considered, and they too have a positive reformulation, roughly of the sort that we handled when we handled (2) above. Since my objector admits that positive reformulations are not objectionable, that settles this case as well.

That concludes my treatment of negatively formulated second-order beliefs in circumstances (1), (2), and (3).

Thus, for *all* cases, positively and negatively formulated, under *all* circumstances, whenever someone has a second-order belief and is self-deceived, one never *has* to say that the second-order belief is false: one can, if one wants, take up my strategy and say the agent has another first-order belief that is inconsistent with the first-order belief that his second-order belief is about. Authority thus may be seen as surviving self-deception, at least in the weak and modest sense I had promised to deliver: it is not *required* that we view self-deception as providing any exceptions or any threat to the truth of the authority conditional. And so, as I said at the beginning of this section, there is nothing obviously wrong in saying that authority is exceptionless even if we, unlike the Cartesian infallibilist, acknowledge that there are many cases of self-deception.

3. It remains now to provide an argument for the more ambitious claim that we would actually be better off embracing the strategy we have adopted and viewing the authority conditional as being true, despite the fact that there are so many cases of self-deception. The argument will turn, as I said at the beginning of this chapter, on two large and closely related claims, which will be pursued over the rest of this chapter and all of the next. To set the stage for the argument, let us set up a question for authority that parallels a question we posed for transparency in the last chapter.

One starting point for our discussion of transparency was the question: What are the nature and status of *'embedded'* intentional states? That is, what are the nature and status of the first-order intentional states that are accompanied by second-order beliefs about them? This is a good question to raise when the subject is transparency because transparency is a property of first-order intentional states. Our answer to this question was roughly that they are not most helpfully described as being 'conscious' states; they are more helpfully described as being the sorts of states that are the potential objects of justifiable reactive attitudes, i.e., the sorts of states, if Strawson's analysis is right, that are caught up in agency.

Now, as a starting point for a discussion of authority, therefore, a parallel question to raise would be: what are the nature and status of *'embedding'* or second-order beliefs? This is a good question when the subject is authority because authority is a property of second-order beliefs.

When our subject was transparency and we posed the corresponding question about 'embedd*ed*' beliefs, the answer of the causal-perceptual model we were opposing was that there was a causal mechanism that linked the 'embedded' intentional state with the accompanying second-order belief. That is what made them 'embedded'. And since, on this model, it was to be *denied* that 'embedded' intentional states possess the property of transparency, something had to be said to account for the *appearance* of transparency. And it was said that the fact that it was a highly *reliable* casual mechanism accounted for that appearance. We, on behalf of the constitutive model, said something quite different, eschewing all explanatory appeal to causal mechanisms and appealing instead to considerations of agency, showing thereby that transparency was not merely an appearance but a real property of 'embedded' beliefs.

Now, when the subject is authority, and we pose the corresponding question about what the status and nature of 'embedd*ing*' beliefs are, the causal-perceptual model we are opposing will have to provide an answer that is again going to account for the *appearance* of authority, since it wants to deny that authority is a property of second-order beliefs. Being a *causal* view, it will have to account for it by appealing to some considerations that attach to the causes of second-order beliefs. And presumably the answer will be something like this: though second-order beliefs *may* have all sorts of causes, as a *matter of fact* the *usual and canonical* cause of the second-order belief is the first-order intentional state it is about. This is not the *unique* cause, of course. That will be admitted. Just as when the subject was 'embedd*ed*' beliefs, it was correspondingly admitted that even reliable mechanisms *sometimes* break down. But even if it is not the unique cause, the first-order intentional state it is about is very routinely the cause of a second-order belief. This accounts for why we think (falsely) that second-order beliefs are authoritative. The appearance of authority comes from the routine expectation of the truth of second-order beliefs, an expectation produced by the presence of the first-order beliefs that *routinely cause* them. Since we, on behalf of the constitutive view, want to say that authority is not merely an appearance but a real property of second-order beliefs, we have to say something quite different, appealing to quite different considerations than (routine) *causes*.

So, to repeat, we are concerned to answer a question about the nature and status of 'embedding' or second-order beliefs such that they may be said to really—not apparently—have the property we call 'authority'.

And here is where we are headed with this question over the rest of this chapter and the next.

To answer this question, one needs to look at the conditions under which second-order beliefs, *in general,* are present. I will be arguing that the considerations we appeal to in laying down these conditions are considerations of agency rather than of a routine or canonical cause, and that is partly because agency is *also* a condition for the first-order intentional states that 'embedding' or second-order beliefs are about. That will be the focus of the rest of this chapter. Once this is established and its implications are understood, a very specifically normative notion of intentional states emerges, and that notion is the focus of the next chapter. The relevance of this notion of intentional states to authority is that it turns out that the conditions for any *particular* second-order belief are the very same as the conditions for the particular intentional state it is about. If, therefore, the second-order belief exists, so must the first-order intentional state it is about. In other words, the authority conditional is true.

The reader should be warned once again that what I have just stated here so briefly in the last paragraph about where we are headed will be explored by a relatively complicated dialectic all the way till the end of the next chapter, introducing various bits of conceptual apparatus and argument that I have not mentioned in this brief summary.

4. It was argued in Chapter 3 that self-knowledge is necessary for agency, as agency is spelled out in Chapter 2. This amounts to saying that agency is sufficient for self-knowledge. If you cannot have agency

without self-knowledge, then if you have agency, that suffices to establish that there is self-knowledge.

But the question now is: even if it suffices for self-knowledge, is
agency also *necessary* for self-knowledge? Could someone grant all that
has been said so far and take the view that there would be self-
knowledge of intentional states even if we were not agents, or more
cautiously, that there would be self-knowledge of intentional states
even in a subject who was not an agent in the sense involving responsibility as I spelled that out in Strawsonian terms in Chapter 2? This
is a very hard and fundamental question.

If we gave an affirmative answer to this question, something other
than agency would have to be the basis of an account of the subject's
self-knowledge, and the causal-perceptual account that I have been
resisting could step in and account for such self-knowledge. (Or perhaps even some non-perceptual, constitutive view very different from
mine, could step in and account for it.)

I will argue for a negative answer to this question; i.e., I will argue
for the thesis that a subject who is not an agent does not have self-
knowledge of intentional states; and the argument will turn on a negative answer to a *more fundamental question:* can a subject who is not
an agent have thought or intentionality?

However, I should add as an aside that even if the reader were not
carried by my arguments for these two negative conclusions, it would
at least be clear what is at stake in the questions just raised. What is
at stake is the exact nature of the link between agency and self-
knowledge. Even if turns out that it is not convincingly established
that subjects without agency lack intentionality and self-knowledge of
intentionality, and even if it turns out therefore that a causal-
perceptual account of self-knowledge is the right account of self-
knowledge in such subjects, what remains in place is the more qualified conclusion that it is *only* when we do not require agency as a
necessary condition of intentionality, and of self-knowledge, that the
causal-perceptual account can emerge as plausible. This more qualified conclusion will remain even if the two negative claims mentioned
above do not carry conviction.

Here, however, is how I have allowed myself to think toward the
(unqualified) negative claims.

Imagine, *if you can,* a subject that is completely passive. If it helps, think of Oblomov, the eponymous hero of Ivan Goncharov's novel,[3] and then exaggerate him superlatively. For much, but not all, of the novel, Oblomov simply lies in bed, and in a marvelous description of him, Goncharov says that he "grows cold before he grows any enthusiasm of the will." In our exaggeration of this character's passivity, let's see instead a subject who is *altogether* passive and who has *always* been so, and let's see the source of the passivity as being *philosophical.* What would this source be? It is not as if Oblomov, in being wholly passive, necessarily lacks movement or behavior. It is very likely that he lacks movement and behavior (and Goncharov's protagonist's passivity *is* portrayed by the fact that he does not actually come out from under the blanket in bed). But nothing in our thought-experiment requires him to lack movement or behavior, since he could have his movements and his behavior happen to him. His passivity has its source rather in the lack of a certain *point of view,* what Kant thought of as the point of view of agency.

For such an Oblomov, as he conceives of things, the future is just like the past. As far as he is concerned, he cannot make any difference to it. Why then would he *act*? If that is how he thinks of the future, how does he think of the world? How does he perceive it? Well, if passivity is his problem, then he sees the world as offering him no opportunities for *action,* nor as making any normative demands on him whatsoever. The evaluative aspects of the world are simply unavailable to him because those are precisely aspects that spur our subjectivity to action. But he takes himself to be an object; he thinks of himself as he thinks of any *other* and, as any *other* thinks of him, from the third person point of view. And he thinks of the world and the future in just that way too, in thoroughly disengaged terms, wholly detached, not as a place and a time to which he can make a difference. He is best described as the subject who is object. So, really, the right thing to say about this Oblomov is that he lacks the '*first* person point of view'. He may even use the words 'I' and 'me' instead of referring to himself as Oblomov, but he *never* uses those words from *the point of view of an agent, in the first person mode.* Rather, he always uses them as if he is talking of another, in the *third* person mode, as when someone says, "I had such and such happen to me" or "Such and such will happen to me."

Before I say anything else, I should make a point of caution about

my use of the term 'first person point of view.' Since it is a widely
used bit of philosophical terminology, it is best to be clear about what
is and is not intended by it. Often, talk of the 'first person point of
view' in recent philosophy is intended to convey the specially qualitative and experiential and felt quality of our phenomenological
states, such as pain, for example. But I will not be focusing on the
first person point of view understood as a phenomenological point of
view. The sense I have in mind by the use of the expression is not the
phenomenological but the rational point of view, the point of view
not so much of the undergoer of sensory experience but of the rational deliberator. Not only are these two quite different notions of
'a point of view', but there is good reason to think that not all conceivable subjects who have the one have the other. Perhaps this is less
controversial in the case of subjects such as non-human animals who
have a phenomenological point of view but lack the capacities for
rational deliberation. But as Carol Rovane has argued,[4] there are
strong reasons to think that there could in principle be deliberatively
rational subjects ('persons' is the term of her interest) who are individuated in such a way that their rational points of view altogether
fail to coincide with any phenomenological points of view. A corporation (i.e., a group or corporate person), incorporating many human
beings, on the one hand, and multiple personalities within a human
being, on the other, may in principle have rational points of view but
no *correspondingly individuated* phenomenological point of view. By
'not correspondingly individuated' Rovane has in mind the following.
The corporation has no phenomenological point of view, only its
compositional elements (individual human beings) have it. Yet the
corporation can have a rational and deliberative point of view. So also,
two (or more) multiples (alters, as they are some times called) might
not each have separate phenomenological points of view; they might
all partake in the phenomenological point of view of their larger host,
an individual human being. Yet each multiple can have a deliberative,
rational point of view. If her claim is right, it provides proof that the
rational point of view is not to be conflated a priori with a phenomenological point of view. It is conceptually possible that the 'first
person' qua deliberator may not be the 'first person' qua undergoer
of sensory experience, as the possibility of these diverging individua-

tions makes clear. The use of the term 'point of view' in the following discussion will be restricted to the rational, deliberative sense and not the phenomenological one.

But things are not entirely sorted out terminologically by saying that. Someone may claim that a subject like Oblomov who is supposed to be entirely passive can have such a first person point of view as I am interested in. They might argue that Oblomov can surely reveal a sort of rational sensitivity. He can *undergo* changes of mind (of intentional states or thoughts) as a result of incoming states of information from his senses. I may have a thought and then, as a result of undergoing some perception, have a quite different thought, one that is even inconsistent with the first thought; but I would remain rational if I just ceased to have the first thought. This is a sort of processing that the passivity of an Oblomov would not find beyond him. Such a change among thoughts (the coming to have of a thought, the ceasing to have of a previous thought) as a result of perception is a process that he could uncontroversially be said to *undergo,* despite his lack of agency (as agency was defined in Chapter 2). And many would find themselves saying that this all surely happens within a point of view— after all, things are being processed as his mind changes, and he remains rational during changes of mind.

I don't see any reason to think that a point of view is involved in such processing. It's the sort of thing that occurs in automata, and that is enough reason to think that the term 'point of view' is not apt. So, just to clarify usage, by the term 'first person point of view', as I have introduced it in this context, I mean something that contains processes much more 'deliberative' than such processing. The sort of change of mind that we have just discussed is quite different from a change of mind in which rational deliberation is involved and that a purely passive subject cannot undertake. If it is not already obvious, I will return to this issue soon and spell out what exactly I take to be involved in deliberation that is missing from such processing and that is such that it requires a point of view. But for now, I just wanted to be clear that by the lights of what I will mean by the term 'point of view' Oblomov (and, for that matter, rational automata) lacks a first person point of view, and indeed he lacks any point of view. That is to say, someone who is said to have *nothing* but a third person point

of view like Oblomov is not really imaginable as having a point of
view at all because he is not imaginable as having thought. He is not
an agent.

This does not mean, of course, that agents *cannot* have a third
person point of view on the world and on themselves. When they have
a third person perspective on the world, they will not see it as making
normative demands on them, but rather will see it in disengaged ways,
as, for instance, when a natural scientist describes it or a social scientist predicts the behavior of populations or even of individuals. And
we all can and do, in our amateurish ways, play the social scientist
every day and often take such a disengaged view of the world and of
ourselves. When we have a third person perspective on ourselves, we
will speak in predictive modes and say things like, "Knowing myself,
I know I will not be able to resist. . . ." But the scientist who describes
the world in disengaged ways and such a person who predicts his own
behavior are (unlike Oblomov) *doing* the describing and predicting,
and so they (unlike Oblomov) are agents. Even so, they are doing
these things *from* a third person point of view and not from the point
of view of agency. To describe the world from the point of view of
agency is not to see it as a natural or social scientist does but is to see
it as something that offers or demands actions on our part, to see it
as laden with value and opportunity for action. To think of ourselves
in an agential rather than a third personal mode is to ask not what
we will do in the predictive sense but what we should or ought to do
or think. In Section 4 of the next chapter I will have much more to
say about the great significance of this duality of first and third person
ways of thinking that agents like us can have on the world and ourselves. But the point I am making here is only that, unlike Oblomov,
we are agents who are talking and thinking even when we sometimes
(actually, quite often) do *not* talk and think of the world and ourselves
from the point of view of agency, but rather do so from a detached
third person point of view. So, for instance, in that remark I just cited,
in which the subject takes a third person point of view on himself,
"I" in its first occurrence of it ("I know . . .) is expressed in an agential
and first personal mode. It is the second occurrence of "I" in that
remark ("I will not be able to. . . .") that is used in the third person
mode. What Oblomov lacks, as I have set things up, is the expressive
use of "I" in the first person mode. Why is it that Oblomov is different

from us in this crucial respect? Because, as I have set things up, he has *no thoughts at all* that do not assail him. He is *comprehensively* passive.

This very last point, of course, subverts my entire ask that we imagine such a figure as Oblomov. I intended that. In order to even set up the Oblomov case for consideration, I have, with some awkwardness, in fact barely coherently, been saying two quite different things in my rhetoric about this character: *first*, that he lacks a first person point of view; and *second*, that he lacks a point of view at all. To say the first could suggest that he, by contrast, has a third person point of view. (In fact, I as much as said this about him when I said that he thinks of himself as he thinks of another.) To say the second suggests something more radical. And this vacillation between these two quite different rhetorics on my part in describing Oblomov has its source in the fact that there is something odd about my asking that such a subject as Oblomov be imagined. By the lights of my own claims about Oblomov, the effort to imagine such a subject should be defeated. That is exactly so. In this chapter, it is really *from the defeat* that I want to draw my lessons and claims. That is why I was careful to begin by saying, "Imagine, *if you can*, a subject such as Oblomov."

What I have asked is that we imagine a subject who is superlatively passive, and I have defined this comprehensive passivity in terms of his *thinking* of himself from a third person point of view, *thinking* of himself entirely as he thinks of another, *thinking* that all of the future is just like the past, *thinking* that he cannot make any difference to the future whatsoever. That element of 'thinking' is the defeating element, the element that makes it impossible to imagine what is being asked, for one question that immediately arises is: Is it even so much as possible to regard such a subject as thinking these things at all, as thinking *anything* at all? Can it really have thoughts if it is comprehensively passive?

The point is this. If he is being imagined to be entirely passive, he cannot *think* anything, since he does not *do* anything at all. That much simply follows, ex hypothesi, from what is being asked to be imagined. So what could possibly remain of the idea that he has thoughts if he cannot think them? It must be that if he has thoughts at all, they simply *happen to* him. Since he cannot think them, they must *assail* him. And the question is: Is that a coherent idea? Or is it a requirement on being a thinker that one's thoughts at least some of the time (and in fact, a good deal of the time) be active? Can it be said of a subject who has *all* his thoughts merely assail him that it is really *thoughts* that assail him?

My own answer to this last question is: "No." (In this, I believe, I am following Kant, and I will return to Kant in just a moment.) And of course, when I say Oblomov lacks thoughts because he is passive, or when I say that someone who has all his 'thoughts' assail him cannot really be said to have thoughts, I don't at all mean to suggest that we, that agents, do not have many of our thoughts assail us. It's not that someone who has thoughts cannot have thoughts assail him, only that no subject can have thoughts who has *all* his 'thoughts' assail him.

What is it to say 'no' to this question about whether Oblomov has thoughts? Let's initially (in the next section) approach the question just a little historically, before moving on to a more purely conceptual treatment of the question.

5. It is very much part of Wittgenstein's overall picture of mind that the Oblomov of my thought-experiment should not be counted as a thinker at all. But in Wittgenstein there is a less and a more deep-going set of considerations to make this case, and it is the latter that are closely linked to the more Kantian position, which I think emerges from the overall argument from agency that I have been trying to give for the nature of self-knowledge.

In this chapter I will mention only the less-deep strand of considerations.

Wittgenstein[5] would not allow that we attribute mental dispositions to our Oblomov, who is in no way active at all, for to do so would be in a familiar Cartesian way to sever the 'criterial' links between (inner) thought and (outer) action. Such a severance in our times would usually amount to a view of mental dispositions that is reductive or bordering in relevant ways on the reductive. It would be the modern kin of Cartesian internalism, where the internalism of the mind is fortified now, if not by a reduction, then by something less strong like supervenience. In other words, mental dispositions, if they are not identical in some strong sense with physical states of the brain, at least stand in relevantly weaker dependency relations to physical states of the brain. On such a view, there need be no outward signs for the possession of mental dispositions, even if there usually are such outward signs. They are present in a subject, whether or not the outward signs of behavior are present, so long as the right overall configuration of physical states of the brain is present. On such a view, a subject (even a completely passive subject) with identical neurophysiological states as another (say, an active subject) has the same mental dispositions as the other, even if there can be no reductive type-type identities established between the dispositions and the brains' states. There is no bar, therefore, to thinking of Oblomov as having thoughts, so long as his brain states are appropriately configured. He (like other imagined subjects in recent philosophical literature such as brains in vats) has a mind, has intentional states; he is full of *potential* behavior. On such a view, if Oblomov were to produce behavior (if the brain in a vat were to be put into a body and released into an environment of the sort we inhabit), the potential of his already existing mind would be fully actualized.[6] So, Oblomov is fully minded.

To turn one's back on such a view of mental dispositions would be to require of them that they be defined in terms of outward signs of behavior, precisely what would disallow Oblomov from having thoughts since behavior in the ordinary sense is precisely what he lacks.[7]

I will come to the quite different and second and deeper strand of considerations in Wittgenstein in the next chapter after saying something in this one about what I take to be an essentially Kantian response to the question of whether Oblomov has thoughts. To keep continuity with how I have elaborated Wittgenstein's first set of considerations, let me make the Kantian point, again in terms of dispositions—though, as will emerge in the next chapter, after the second set of considerations in Wittgenstein has been introduced, dispositions, in the standard sense, are not to the point at all.

There are two philosophical positions one can have on mental dispositions, generally. Taking up some terminology in Kant (which he does not apply to intentionality), one can call them the 'transcendental realist' and the 'transcendental idealist' versions of mental dispositions. I am going to make a claim in favor of the second of these positions, and I will be reconstructing it a little freely here, putting together things Kant says in the third section of his *Groundwork of the Metaphysics of Morals*[8] with the general philosophical claims of the *Critique of Pure Reason*.[9] I do, however, believe that, had Kant explicitly taken up questions of intentionality, this position would be a natural fallout of things implicitly to be found in these very basic texts I have mentioned.

What are these two different positions one can take on mental dispositions?

In our own times, to insist that intentional states are *real* states is to say that they are not merely the instrumental attributions of an 'intentional *stance*'. One standard story regarding such a stance is that we take it and make these instrumental attributions for the sake of convenience because we are at present in a position of epistemic weakness regarding the physical bases of our minds and our behavior. Until we know more about that physical basis, as a stopgap measure, we can make sense of human behavior by attributing these intentional states. Being stopgap, and mere forms of convenience, we do not make any commitments as to the reality of intentional states, in making these attributions. In fact, when we emerge out of our epistemic weakness, we may not need the convenience of these attributions any more and may eliminate them. Or we may still continue with the stance if we have purposes that are fulfilled by these instruments. But they would have no reality except as instruments for these purposes. So, in summary, goes a familiar story about the distinction between realism and instrumentalism.

Let us put aside instrumentalism and assume that attributions of intentional states are made with realist commitments. That still leaves things entirely open on another much more interesting front. Of such real states, it is possible to say two quite different things. One may say that they are dispositions, which are constituted by what Kant, in the third section of the *Groundwork,* called 'the perspective of freedom' and agency. Or one may say that they are dispositions that are *there anyway,* independent of this perspective, and what the perspective of agency brings to them at best is a sort of switch of activation.

These two quite different positions on these states, I am claiming, correspond to what might properly be thought of as a transcendental idealist and a transcendental realist position on them, respectively.

If one took the *latter* position, then Oblomov could certainly be said to have thoughts. The phrase 'there anyway' (ever since Bernard Williams's use of it to describe Descartes' 'absolute conception of reality')[10] familiarly captures a kind of 'metaphysical realism', as we call it now, and what Kant called 'transcendental realism'; and when the doctrine is applied to mental dispositions, it is quite possible to see Oblomov as having these dispositions, which though they might need activation by the perspective of agency, which he lacks, they are nevertheless *there*. They are there, *anyway*. They are there *independent of this perspective*.

However, if we took the *former* of the two positions on intentional states, it is precisely because he lacks the perspective of agency that he would lack thoughts. The term 'transcendental idealism' is therefore a particularly suitable label for this position. The reason why Oblomov lacks thoughts when thoughts are viewed from the former position is precisely because thoughts are not there anyway, independent of the perspective of agency, which he lacks. The perspective of agency, according to this position, is not simply a switch that activates dispositions already present; rather, it constitutes the dispositions.

The Kantian doctrinal categories apply neatly here because of the deep analogy that surfaces in the idea that for a Kant who did bring together the claims of the third section of the *Groundwork* and the general claims of the First *Critique*, it would be no more correct to say that Oblomov had thoughts without the perspective of agency than it would be to say that someone had objective experience independently of having and applying the concept of, say, cause. So, on this view, unlike the instrumentalist picture, thoughts are indeed really there; but, unlike as in transcendental realism, they are not there anyway, such that those who possess the perspective of agency bring that perspective to them as a bit of bonus or extra. To say this would be as wrong, for Kant, as it would be to say that objective experience is there anyway, and we bring as an extra element to the elements of objective experience the idea of causal connections between them. Neither thought nor objective experience is there anyway, in these ways. Once we bring together the two texts, we can see that it was Kant who thus first brought to shape and to our attention a profoundly integrated and refined realist position in which freedom constitutes the very possibility of thought, just as causality (among other things) constitutes the very possibility of objective judgment in thought.

It is this transcendental idealism about thoughts that agrees with the conclusion of Wittgenstein's first set of considerations mentioned above, i.e., the conclusion of disallowing thoughts to Oblomov. But it brings to the disallowance something far more interesting and more underlying than those considerations, something far more interesting than the usual Wittgensteinian drill about how the demands of the publicness of thought requires an outward manifestation of it, which would be missing in Oblomov since he does not produce *actions*. It brings the idea of *a point of view* of agency, *a first person point* of view, which is essential to intentionality, an idea that does not surface at all in all the business about public criteria for mental states.

Kant himself is fairly explicit about the claim that freedom is a necessary condition for the having of thoughts and not just for actions, that it pervades judgment in the realm of the theoretical ('speculative', to use his term) as well as the practical. In the *Groundwork*, he says,

> I say now: every being that cannot act otherwise than under the idea of freedom is just because of that really free in a practical respect, that is, all laws that are inseparably bound up with freedom hold for him just as if his will had been validly pronounced free also in itself and in theoretical philosophy. . . . Now, one cannot possibly think of a reason that would consciously receive direction from any other quarter with respect to its judgments, since the subject would then attribute the determination of his judgment not to his reason but to his impulse. Reason must regard itself as the author of its principles independently of alien influences. (*Groundwork*, 4:448)

Hence, it is not just actions but *judgment* itself, whether theoretical or practical, that is to say, thought itself, that has, as Kant says in the passage, to be conceived "under the idea of freedom" (which elsewhere in the *Groundwork* he calls the 'perspective of agency' or 'the first person point of view'). In the *Critique of Practical Reason*, he is again explicit about the claim that freedom governs in this way not just practical but speculative reason.

> Accordingly, considerations of this kind which are once more directed to the concept of freedom in the practical use of pure reason, must

not be regarded as an interpolation serving only to fill up the gaps in the critical system of speculative reason (for this is for its own purpose complete), or like props and buttresses which in a hastily constructed building are often added afterwards; but as true members which make the connexion of the system plain, and show us concepts, here presented as real, which there could only be presented problematically. This remark applies especially to the concept of freedom, respecting which one cannot but observe with surprise that so many boast of being able to understand it quite well and to explain its possibility, while they regard it only psychologically, whereas if they had studied in a transcendental point of view, they must have recognized that it is not only indispensable as a problematic concept, in the complete use of speculative reason.[11]

If these passages establish that Kant thought freedom is necessary for thought, then we would be right to say that a Kantian position would deny not just outward actions to Oblomov (which are in any case denied to him, ex hypothesi) but *thoughts* to him too, since he lacks the perspective of freedom; and it would do so on a ground that is quite different from Wittgenstein's ground, which cites the publicness of thought.

Before leaving Kant, I should say at least four important things, partly by way of clarification of my own position and partly by way of scholarly scruple, in case the scholar of Kant misunderstands the point of, and the level at which I am, invoking him as an ally.

First: It must be noticed (and it is noticeable in this last passage where he says the concept is "indispensable" but also "problematical") that Kant talks of the '*idea* of freedom', whereas he talks about 'cause' as a '*concept*' (of the understanding); and in his elaborate framework for these things, he distinguishes between ideas and concepts, with a view to saying that the latter can be derived by 'deductions' of various kinds, whereas no proofs of this sort are available for ideas, which must be presupposed without proof if the concepts are to so much as apply. And so when I said above that, for Kant, our Oblomov would no more have thoughts without the perspective of agency than someone would have objective experience of the world without the concept of cause, I was seeing freedom and cause as being on a par, as both being constitutive in exactly the same way of intentionality and of objective experience of the world, respectively. I am happy to grant that in saying this I am not sticking to the letter of Kant's finer distinctions within his framework, and conflating where he would have distinguished, saying both are constitutive, whereas he would have said only the concepts are constitutive and 'ideas' are presupposed in some other way. But, even so, I think at a more general level of description, if we put aside Kant's finer distinctions, there is a common claim about both freedom and cause that I am drawing on, and that is that they are both necessary conditions (even if of different sorts in Kant's elaborate framework), necessary conditions in the one case of intentionality and in the other of objective experience of the world.[12]

Second: I should stress that though I will be using this point in Kant about agency being a necessary condition for thought to advance a constitutive view of self-knowledge against a perceptualist view of it, Kant himself does not draw any such conclusions about self-knowledge. Indeed, alas, he does not even hold a constitutive view of self-knowledge. It's not merely that he is silent on the subject of self-knowledge of intentionality, merely failing to see the point that I will be claiming. It is more surprisingly disappointing than that, since he actually makes remarks on self-knowledge that run counter to the point that he could, and should, have drawn from his own excellent views on freedom's relation to thought. In his explicit remarks about self-knowledge, he makes no effort at all to link his views of agency with self-knowledge and seems to assume throughout that self-knowledge is a product of what he calls 'inner sense', a product of inner perception. However, unlike Descartes, more like Gopnik, he seems to think that inference is involved; and unlike both of them, he thinks that such inner perception is pervasively fallible, and there is not even a *seeming* presence of direct access. He seems in general to be too thoroughly impressed by the phenomenon of self-deception to think that there is something to be said nevertheless about first person authority and transparency, which issues from his own ideas about agency and reason as governing mentality. These remarks are most evident in works that fall under the heading of 'anthropology'. As Allen Wood makes clear in his fine study of Kant's texts on moral philosophy and other neighboring disciplines,[13] Kant here is most impressed by the very phenomena that moved Nietzsche and Freud. In his work *Lectures on Anthropology,* cited by Wood, Kant says regarding self-knowledge that, in this area, we "play with obscure representations and have an interest, when loved or unloved objects are before our imagination, in putting them into the shadows." And Wood concludes that that for him "most of our mental life . . . is unaccompanied by consciousness; and if we ever learn about them at all, we must do so through inference."[14] So Kant's relevance to my argument is strictly limited, and though it would be very interesting to stay and diagnose what in his overall thinking prevented him from concluding from his views on freedom and reason that self-knowledge is not paradigmatically a matter of inner sense or inference, I will not do so now, since this discussion of Kant was not really introduced with the intention of providing a scholarly treatment.

Third: Though I think the passages from Kant I have cited are very congenial to my reading of him, I don't want to be too ambitious in the parallels I am drawing. I don't deny that for Kant the idea and indeed the problem of freedom (even though it has a practical importance, as he repeatedly stresses) is more metaphysical than the modified Strawsonian one I am stressing, which is inseparable from the reactive attitudes. So there are real differences to be noted, and that is why, if I haven't already said so, I should say that the position I am taking is better described as Kantian than as Kant's. But to repeat: what I think is most interesting and crucial for my purposes— and it is the reason for my invoking Kant at all—is that despite the differences I have noted, thinking of freedom as a necessary condition for thought allows one to embrace a transcendental idealist position on the nature of intentionality quite akin to his general transcendental idealism about the world and our knowledge of it. As is well known, for Kant such a position is intended in a general way to stand opposed both to various forms of idealism (what we today more generally call 'anti-realism') and to transcendental realism (what we today call 'metaphysical realism'). Applying this position to the realm of thought or of the intentional in particular (something Kant never did) and to put it in our own contemporary terms, one can then say: to be a transcendental idealist about intentionality is to avoid saying, on the one hand, that it is merely a deliverance of a sort of stance we take toward subjects with complex behavior (some combination of anti-realism and instrumentalism) and, on the other hand, that it is reducible to or supervenient on the internal physical states of such subjects, and therefore, as I put it, 'anyway, there' (metaphysical or transcendental realism). There are many today who would like to avoid both instrumentalism and metaphysical realism about the mind and to occupy a quite different space. And it is my claim that they will have a basis for the position they want to occupy if they appeal to the necessary links between freedom and thought in the way I am proposing. In fact, I cannot think of another really convincing basis. Hence, if one did not think those links existed, the honest thing to do might well be to admit that the debate between the metaphysical realist and the anti-realist would exhaust the alternatives. It's not obvious that those today who don't want these to exhaust the alternatives and who wish to occupy that intermediate space have realized at all that *this* is what is at stake. The usual talk of publicness issuing from Wittgenstein and other such ploys familiar in the philosophical literature simply will not be enough to provide for the tenancy of that space.

Fourth, and finally: There is scope here for a confusion that it would be good to avoid. I have claimed that transcendental idealism holds not just of the perceptible world, as Kant claimed, but of thoughts as well. Neither is 'anyway there', independent of their respective 'constitutive' conditions (in the case of thoughts, the perspective of freedom; in the case of the perceptible world, cause and the other 'categories of the understanding'). But in Chapter 1, I had also declared the purpose of establishing the further claim that our thoughts are not independent of our beliefs about them, while *denying* that this is so of facts or objects in the world and our beliefs about *them*. This lack of independence of our thoughts from our beliefs about them is what I am calling the 'constitutive' thesis about self-knowledge. These two claims, the initial one and the further one, are perfectly compatible. Just because facts or objects in the world are independent of our beliefs about them (in the way that our thoughts are not independent of our beliefs about *them*) does not mean that the world is also independent of the more abstractly conceived thing that Kant called 'the understanding'. Transcendental idealism is a more abstract and more general constitutive doctrine than anything I have to say about self-knowledge. And it is *within* the general doctrine of transcendental idealism, which holds of *both* the world *and* of thoughts, that there is a *further* thesis that I claim holds *only* of thoughts but *not* of the world. And this further thesis is what I am calling the constitutive thesis about self-knowledge. The crucial point of interest that has been argued from Chapter 2 onward is this: freedom, which is the constitutive condition for thoughts, unlike cause and the other categories of the understanding that are the constitutive condition of the perceptible world, contains within it *the basis* for the *further* constitutive thesis relating thoughts to self-knowledge. I say 'contains within it', but it is clear that it takes a lot of philosophy to bring it out, all the philosophy from Chapter 2 on, as I said.

6. Having said something historical about why it is that a passive subject without agency lacks thought, we are in a position to try and strengthen the point conceptually.

I have said that Oblomov lacks the point of view of agency or the first person point of view. And I have defined this notion of a first person point of view, not in terms of phenomenology but in terms of evaluative and rational deliberation. Hence we must ask, what is it about the deliberative, evaluative, rational point of view that makes it clear that Oblomov does not have that point of view, and therefore does not have any point of view or any thought at all, and what does that, in turn, have to do with the theme of self-knowledge as it has been presented in the book so far?

There is, as I said, a temptation (against which I have urged resistance) to say that since there might be sightings of something like rationality in Oblomov, we should therefore conclude that he has thoughts, a point of view, and indeed a first person point of view.

What is the seeming relevance of these sightings of rationality to the theme of self-knowledge?

Let us for a little longer continue to imagine, or pretend to coherently imagine, despite the points made above, that Oblomov has thoughts assailing him. Let us further imagine that his thoughts have the property of rationality. (Once you imagine that he has thoughts, there is no bar to imagining he has rational thoughts, thoughts that meet the codifications of rationality, whether deductive, inductive, etc.)

This exercise is important because philosophers might think (and have thought) that if a subject's thoughts have the property of ration-

ality, then he or she has self-knowledge. Sydney Shoemaker, for instance, a constitutive theorist about self-knowledge, as opposed to a
perceptualist account, as I am, says that "believing that one believes
that p can be just believing that p plus having a certain level of rationality and intelligence."[15] There is nothing I disagree with in this.
But everything turns not only on what level of rationality is intended
but on what *underlies* that level of rationality.

So, on this exercise, let's then imagine that Oblomov has the following trio of thoughts assail him: first, the thought that all men are
mortal, then the thought that Socrates is a man, and then the thought
that Socrates is mortal. And let's imagine that he has many other such
trios of thoughts assail him. Given this, it would seem right to say that
he and his thoughts are rational, but in fact, if we are to keep faith
with the fact that he is completely passive, it would be more exactly
right to say that the thoughts that assail him *exemplify* rationality. Now,
if this is the manner in which he is rational, is it also plausible to say
that his rationality is sufficient to establish that he has self-knowledge
of his thoughts? If the picture of self-knowledge I have been arguing
for so far is right, it is not plausible. I will arrive at the explanation
for why it is not plausible by continuing with this exercise just a little
longer.

Perhaps we should be more tempted to say that his rationality by
itself establishes that he has self-knowledge of his thoughts if he has
the following quartet of thoughts assail him: first, the thought that all
men are mortal, then the thought that Socrates is a man, then the
thought that Socrates is not mortal, and then the thought that Socrates is mortal. And let's imagine that he has other such quartets of
thoughts assail him from time to time. Now here we will want to talk
of his irrationality as well as his rationality, or more strictly (respecting
again his passivity) that he exemplifies irrationality in the third
thought, and then with the fourth thought in these quartets, he exemplifies rationality. One might think, to use Shoemaker's expression, that the 'level of rationality' here is pretty high. After all, it is
not merely that the set of beliefs exemplify rationality (as in the trio),
but there is also a *revision* of belief from the third to the fourth belief,
which is in accord with norms of rationality. But, on my picture of
self-knowledge, here too he lacks self-knowledge. Why? Remember
that here too this level of rationality is only properly described as
being 'exemplified' by him. On my picture, any claim that he has self-

knowledge must turn on the fact that he has (or potentially has) a reactive attitude, a critical reaction to his third thought, and then comes as a result to his fourth thought as a matter of such critical deliberation. (I should add—significantly—that it equally turns on whether *others* have *justifiable* reactive attitudes to his third thought. More on the significance of that later.) If this quartet of thoughts merely assails him, then the third thought does not get discarded because of any critical reactive attitude he has toward it or (as discussed in Chapter 2) that others *justifiably* have toward it. (I am assuming here, as throughout, that critical reactive attitudes toward bad logical reasoning is a special—and 'bland', as I called it—case of reactive attitudes generally.) In fact, Oblomov did not even bring his first three thoughts together to be able to see and react by thinking that they are irrational, since he *does* no thinking *or* bringing together, being passive.

Indeed, for that very reason (i.e., the absence of reactive attitudes toward his thoughts), one should say that he would lack self-knowledge even if the following duet of thoughts assail him: first, the thought that all men are mortal, then the thought that he believes that all men are mortal. And we should say that for all other such duets of thoughts that might assail him. Of course, this last claim is a facetious exaggeration. The right thing to say is that, on my picture, it is a complete mystery what role there *could* be for the second in these duets of thoughts in a totally passive subject.

Let us explore this last point a little.

What, in general, is the role of second-order beliefs in a psychological economy? This question can be approached in various ways. One approach would be to say that the role of second-order beliefs about first-order intentional states bears some structural similarity to the role that the first-order intentional states have vis-à-vis actions.[16] Thus, if as is widely held a first-order desire or belief has the role of standing in certain relations to our actions, then in looking for a structurally similar role for second-order beliefs about our-first order intentional states, we should be looking for actions to which they are similarly related. But given that they are *second*-order beliefs and not first-order intentional states, clearly these would have to be actions that are directed not to things in the world but rather to first-order intentional states. Which actions are these?

Perhaps the most common actions we visit, not upon the world but upon our first-order intentional states, are revisions of them. Let's take revision of a first-order belief as an example. The first thing to notice is that it is by no means the case that all revisions of beliefs require any role to be played by second-order belief. Some changes of belief take the following form. One has a belief. New information comes in (through perception, through testimony) that is inconsistent with the belief, and so one simply moves to a second belief and sheds the first. This sort of processing is done by us ubiquitously. One comes to campus with the belief that the departmental administrative staff is in the office, one notices (or one is told by another colleague) that the door to the office is locked, and one revises the belief. No mention has been made at all of second-order beliefs about any first-order beliefs. Change in the latter has occurred without any role given to any second-order belief. It is revisions of belief of this kind that lead philosophers to say, in what may be a plausibly special use of the term, that it is 'beliefs' that animals have since such 'brute' changes of mind, such processing, coming from basic sensitivity to incoming states of information and the evidence they provide, are something that routinely occur in animals.[17] And I take it that the fact that we ascribe such revisions of belief to animals is sufficient reason to deny that second-order beliefs are involved in such 'brute' revision.

(It is worth taking a moment for a sermon-like aside, putting in a quick reminder here of something that was said emphatically at the outset, viz., that nothing in this book disallows the notion of intentionality or rationality as applying to little children and animals. Just as Shoemaker did in the remark I cited above, I too am merely focusing on the kinds of full-blown and sophisticated forms of these notions that apply to creatures capable of *self-knowledge in a sense over and above awareness of the world.* Is any question being begged here by this restricted focus? Is one trivializing the account of self-knowledge by focusing on these higher levels of intentionality, rationality, etc.? Since the kind of 'constitutive' view of self-knowledge being presented in the book is controversial and often said to be wrong *even within this restricted focus,* it could not possibly be conveniently begging any questions to have imposed this restricted focus, and therefore it could not possibly be to say something trivially true by imposing it. Something can't be wrong or controversial and be trivially true at the same time. The fact is that the restricted focus is demanded by the nature of the book's primary theme: the nature of self-knowledge that involves second-order beliefs, which animals do not possess. Such a notion of self-knowledge is intuitively said by many to have certain properties that make it special among knowledges. And I claim that these intuitions are not appearances to be explained away; these properties—of transparency and authority—are real, and they are to be accounted for by noticing the deep conceptual links that self-knowledge has to notions of agency and value. As a result of this focus, there will be, throughout the rest of the book, a certain basic contrast set up between full-blown intentionality and mere dispositionality of the kind that Oblomov is imagined to have. That contrast will reflect the restricted focus that the reader is being alerted to and therefore should not be thought of as denying intermediate conceptions of intentionality, agency, rationality, and awareness of the world, of the sort that animals and very young children may also be said to possess. If those intermediate notions *do not* and only their high-level, rich, full-blown counterparts *do* account for the special nature of self-knowledge, that does not trivialize things at all. It shows that a certain family of concepts at a certain high level of richness and sophistication is essential to understanding the special nature of self-knowledge at a sophisticated level that goes beyond low-level forms of awareness of the world. Indeed, it is the book's whole point to *integrate* the notions of value, agency, intentionality, and self-knowledge at this higher level and this richer understanding of these notions. That the notion of self-knowledge and its unusual status among knowledges cannot be understood except as they stand integrated with other such notions is a substantial and illuminating claim. And those who feel denied something because this integration only takes place at high levels of the characterization of the notions involved in the integration should not allow this feeling to confuse them into thinking that the substance and illumination provided by the integration are somehow fake.)

To pick up the thread before the parentheses, the question remains: if these sorts of revision of belief are not the sorts of actions upon first-order intentional states to which second-order beliefs have a relevance, to *which* sorts of revision of belief *do* they have relevance? Perhaps by this stage of the book, the answer is obvious. They are relevant to revisions of belief that are not brute but are revisions of belief that are *mediated by reactive attitudes of criticism that we might have toward our first-order beliefs.* So if a revision of belief takes place not 'brutely', as I have been describing in these cases, not simply as a case of moving from one belief to another because of new information but, rather, as a result of one deliberating (however rapidly and inexplicitly) and finding some first-order belief of ours *wrong*—whether for theoretical or practical and moral or any other reason—and therefore discarding it for another, then t*hat* normative element is the hallmark of a genuine role for second-order belief.

This normative element of revision mediated by the reactive attitudes is precisely what is *not* involved with Oblomov's assailed 'thoughts', *not even in his quartet of 'thoughts' mentioned above,* where the transition from the third assailed 'thought' to the fourth assailed 'thought' is quite brute—it is not mediated by any reactive attitude exercised against the third 'thought'. That is why one may not describe the transitions in terms of moving from an irrational to a rational thought but, rather, in terms of a transition from an assailing 'thought' that exemplifies irrationality to one that exemplifies rationality.

What has emerged, then, in the relevant examples of the more deliberative[18] revision of belief (which involves the reactive attitudes being exercised) is that one has to be aware of a belief, have self-belief or self-knowledge of a belief, before one can have a reactive attitude toward it. *Now* there *is* some indispensable role for the second-order belief to play. *These* are the actions (certain *distinct* sorts of revisions of first-order intentional states) to which second-order belief is related, actions that cannot be understood except as presupposing that there are such 'embedding' or second-order beliefs. *They* are what reveal the status of and the conditions under which 'embedding' beliefs are present and have point. This last, therefore, finally answers our governing question for authority that we raised above in Section 3 (What sort of animal is an 'embedding' belief?), parallel to the question we had raised and answered for transparency (What sort of animal is an 'embedded' intentional state?).

So once again it becomes clear that the reactive attitudes that are defining of agency, as we have said following Strawson, are essential to the idea of self-knowledge, and that is why it is of no serious point to insist that Oblomov, who lacks such agency, has self-knowledge.

That is why I allowed myself what I called the 'facetious exaggeration' of saying that even if Oblomov had the duet of thoughts (the belief that all men are mortal, the belief that he believes that Socrates is mortal) assail him, he would still not be rightly said to possess self-knowledge. The second of those thoughts, for such a subject, who by definition lacks reactive attitudes and therefore agency, is not something that has any legitimate station or role. And without that, the various changes of intentional states, which Oblomov undergoes, cannot be anything but brute.

To lack this deliberative, evaluative ability is to lack a 'first person point of view', as I am using that term. And as I said, without a first person point of view there is no point of view, not even a third person point of view. It is only creatures who have a first person point of view who can have thoughts, and they can then sometimes (or often) take a *third* person point of view on those thoughts, treating themselves as they treat another. In fact, even when one sometimes takes a third person point of view on oneself and says, "I am thus and so and am disposed to thus and so" (or, for that matter, says something even more *explicitly* third personal, dropping the first person pronoun terms, "AB is thus and so and is disposed to thus and so"), one is *expressing* something in the first person, despite the fact that one is reporting something in the third person about oneself. That is to say, the speaker speaks as an agent even though the angle that he takes on what he speaks about (himself, in this case) is a third personal angle. So even if one takes a third person point of view on oneself, one must possess the point of view of agency. If one lacks agency, one lacks even a third person point of view. One has no point of view. It defeats the imagination to think of a subject like our Oblomov, who is a non-agent and is supposed to have thoughts from a third person point of view only. It defeats the imagination, therefore, to think that he has thoughts of any kind or with any angle. Agency constitutes not just self-knowledge of thought but thought itself. 'Thought', *comprehensively* passive, non-agential, non-deliberative 'thought' that merely *exemplifies* rationality and irrationality, is 'thought' merely so-called.

I have presented the considerations for saying that agency (and the first person point of view of agency) is a necessary condition for thought itself. And that is why the very ask that we imagine our Oblomov is an ask for something that is self-defeating. But let us just pretend a little longer that one can imagine an Oblomov with thoughts that are all possessed in the third person, in order to draw conclusions about self-knowledge. Once the underlying issues of agency and the first person point of view are brought out into the open, it has become clear that self-knowledge and its special character depend not just on considerations of rationality, not just on processes of revision that reveal a rational sensitivity to incoming information, nor on exemplifications of rationality (as found in Oblomov, while we pretend that he has thoughts). It depends on being the subject of reactive evaluative attitudes whether of one's own or (justifiably) of others. This is what Oblomov lacks. It is only this that presupposes or bestows the genuine status of amounting to self-knowledge upon the second of the duet of thoughts, we mentioned earlier. And it is because he lacks it that when it is said that the second in that duet of thoughts assails him, we still want to resist the idea (facetious though it may seem) that it amounts to self-knowledge. It is only this that yields the full prestige of agency. Thus, it is not rationality, but agency, normatively understood, that is *the most general and the deepest underlying element* that makes for the fact that self-knowledge is presupposed constitutively of intentional states. Oblomov (while we pretend that he has 'thoughts') may well be said to 'exemplify' rationality in his 'thoughts'; it is agency that he lacks. That is why he lacks self-knowledge of his 'thoughts' in any constitutive sense. If it were nevertheless insisted that he, even so, has self-knowledge, that self-knowledge would now have to be given a causal-perceptual account, whereby a thought would assail him and it would cause him to be assailed by a second-order belief about it. A constitutive account of self-knowledge proceeds plausibly therefore only in the context of agents. And equally, in the context of agents, as was made clear in the last chapter while discussing transparency, the perceptual account of self-knowledge falls away as beside the point.

Let me take a moment to relate these points to some other very interesting recent writing on self-knowledge. What these points show is that my overall position is in deep sympathy and agreement with many aspects of Shoemaker's, and more recently Burge's,[19] claims that our adjustment to norms of rationality presupposes self-knowledge. But I think the comparative relations between our closely related positions is thrown into visible relief by the example of a radically passive

subject like Oblomov.[20] For, in the example as we have been discussing it, it has emerged explicitly that it is the very thing that Oblomov lacks, the *activity* of, the *agency* involved in, making certain
kinds of rational adjustments that presuppose self-knowledge. And if
this is so, then we can say something *much more general* than Shoemaker and Burge say. We can say (what I have been saying in the last
three chapters) that it is *all* agency—not merely the one in which one
adjusts thoughts to rational norms but *all* thought and action that are
accountable—that presupposes self-knowledge. The relation between
considerations of agency that I have been emphasizing and the sorts
of considerations of rationality that Burge and Shoemaker emphasize
as relevant to self-knowledge can be jointly seen, then, as part of a
single integrated picture of self-knowledge. Something roughly like
the following.

Rationality is, of course, crucial.[21] And rationality is, of course, a
normative phenomenon. But once we understand the fact that a subject like Oblomov who lacks agency may exemplify rationality while
lacking self-knowledge in the constitutive sense, it becomes clearer
that it is not rationality per se, not just adjustment to norms of rationality but the *acts* of adjustment to rational norms via the exercise
of self-reactive attitudes in the process of rational deliberation, that
makes the real and deepest difference. And, as I said, the point—a
point more *generally* illuminating than the one, one finds in Burge
and Shoemaker—that we can extract from this is that it is *all* acts (not
just acts of rational adjustment in our beliefs) and all agency that
provide the site where beliefs and desires are self-known. It is not just
beliefs and desires upon which we make acts of rational adjustment
that are self-known but, as was established in the last chapter, all beliefs and desires that are potentially tied up with any responsible action whatever that are self-known.

That is the first point of comparative advantage of the position I
am presenting over other constitutive positions on self-knowledge,
like Shoemaker's and Burge's—its greater scope and generality. A
second related point of advantage is this. If it is indeed the case that
one can exemplify rationality, as Oblomov does, and show basic rational sensitivity to incoming information, as animals do, without any
role given to second-order beliefs, and if it is indeed true that second-
order belief enters at a point only when rationality takes the form of

being accompanied by agency in the sense of having reactive evaluative attitudes toward oneself, then what we immediately see is that *there is a link between evaluative self-reactive attitudes and self-knowledge.* This link (which I have emphasized in the last sentence), however, is a little shy on the side of information. What the link, baldly stated in the emphasized words, conveys is that self-knowledge is presupposed by self-reactive attitudes. Burge and Shoemaker deliver that conclusion too when they say self-knowledge is grounded not in self-observation but in being critical of our own thoughts in accord with the norms of rationality. But though it is true that we must have *self*-knowledge of our intentional states if we have *self*-reactive attitudes to them, this is surely not the maximally informative and general thing we can say about what makes for this special non-observational character of self-knowledge. In fact, it sounds not very substantial or informative at all to say that *self*-reactive attitudes presuppose *self*-knowledge.

How can more substance be given to this no doubt true but somewhat banal point upon which both I and these other constitutive accounts agree? More substance comes when we introduce a basic lesson of the modified Strawsonian conception of agency that I have been stressing throughout my discussion of self-knowledge. The point of such a conception is that it is not just *self*-reactive attitudes that presuppose self-knowledge but *any justifiable* reactive attitudes—even those that *others* might have toward one's actions and intentional states or that one may have toward *others'* intentional states and actions— that presuppose, respectively, that one has self-knowledge of one's intentional states and that others have self-knowledge of their intentional states. And since (if Strawson is right) being the object of justifiable reactive attitudes *generally* (whether of one's own or of others') is the defining mark of agency, then we have brought together two seemingly different ideas (that of freedom or agency and that of self-knowledge) in a way that makes it clear how the latter may be just a fallout of the former and needs no observational, no causal account, and no superlatively reliable mechanisms to display its special character. To say what I have just said is to say something that *underlies* the claim—and therefore is more general and more informative than the no doubt true but much less interesting claim—that *self*-reactive attitudes involved in adjusting our intentional states to norms of rationality presuppose *self*-knowledge of those intentional states.

Hence, in the more integrated and more informative picture, *both* self-knowledge *and* self-reactive attitudes (the two elements in the link we have just been discussing) are to be understood as something that we ascribe to subjects when their actions seem appropriate objects of justifiable reactive attitudes *generally,* that is, when they are responsible in the general sense that my Strawsonian embedding in freedom for self-knowledge requires. Rationality, stressed by Shoemaker and Burge, if it is to do the work they want it to do in their argument, is a *symptom* of the *underlying* philosophical source of self-knowledge, which is *agency* in the normative sense we have identified in Chapter 2. To point to rationality is undoubtedly to point to something true and relevant in the philosophical study of self-knowledge. (So there is no disagreement between me and Burge and Shoemaker at all.) But it does not say anything as satisfyingly informative and general as we would like until the underlying source is brought into view. I have been using the example of Oblomov to bring it into view, and the point is important enough that I will risk the tax it imposes on endurance, to repeat it. It is brought into view by first observing that even if we credited him with 'thoughts', and with enough rationality and revision of belief in accord with rationality as is present in the sorts of transitions of thought I mentioned above, it would still not follow that he had self-knowledge; and if we added to these transitions a crucial element—that of being transitions that came from critical reactive evaluative attitudes toward one's thoughts—then that *would* require that the subject had self-knowledge, but it would do so precisely because the added element takes us beyond a passive subject like Oblomov to an *agent,* thereby bringing into view that the real work (i.e., the most informative and general work) in the constitutive account was being done by agency.

7. The last section's conclusions about the conceptual relations between intentionality (or thought) and agency are not only important in themselves but also essential to establish this book's view of self-knowledge. For, as I have admitted, if it were *not* the case that agency is a necessary condition for thought, two conclusions counter to the book's view would enter the field with greater plausibility. First, it would introduce scope for a causal-perceptualist rather than constitutive view of the self-knowledge of thought. Second, and alternatively, it might also introduce scope for a constitutive view, only not the

constitutive view being presented in this book, which depends on the centrality of issues of agency and responsibility.

So the stakes are high, and it would be good therefore to secure the conclusion about those conceptual relations. To do so, it is worth giving a fairer run to someone who is skeptical of the conclusion, then responding to their doubts. What argument and resources are available to someone who is not convinced by the remarks of the last many pages to the effect that Oblomov lacks thoughts because he lacks agency, and who wishes to deny that agency is a necessary condition for intentionality?

The considerations offered so far for agency being a necessary condition for intentionality have relied on a conception of intentionality to which normativity and the evaluative reactive attitudes have been central. As we saw, it is these elements that were missing in the 'thoughts' that a purely passive subject, a non-agent such as Oblomov, was supposed to have. And it is the absence of these elements that led one to think that the supposal that he had thoughts was implausible, after all. Therefore, someone who was unpersuaded, and wanted to take up the challenge of showing that agency is not constitutive of thought and intentionality, either (a) would have to show that normativity or the exercise of evaluative attitudes is not central to intentionality or (b) would have to show that even if it is central to intentionality, this normative element is quite possible without agency. The form of the challenge as it is stated in (a) will be addressed in the next chapter, where a thoroughly normative conception of intentionality will be defended against standard naturalistic treatments of the subject. The form of the challenge as expressed by (b) is not easy to pursue, but it is worth trying to do so sympathetically, even if one is not convinced by it in the end, because it will bring to the surface further issues involved in thinking that agency is constitutive of intentionality; and it will provide a natural transition to the theme of the next chapter.

What does make the challenge very hard to pursue is that the role of intentionality, at least in the *practical* domain, the domain of action and of morals, seems very hard to ponder without something like agency well in place. So someone trying to take on the challenge of explaining how it can be denied that agency is constitutive of intentionality might begin by restricting the case to the theoretical domain (or as Kant called it, the domain of 'speculative' thought), at least to begin with, and then extend it, if it is possible, to the harder case of the practical domain.

Here, then, is how the challenge as expressed in (b) might be initially pursued.

"Thinking, in this book, is being presented too much as a kind of 'responsible action'," it might be said.

> Even if thinking is caught up in normativity and even if it is a kind of action, its normativity has nothing to do with *responsibility* as is being presented here; it is purely a matter of what it is correct (justified) and incorrect (unjustified) to think. So the claim that being an agent is necessary for being a thinker reduces to the very thin claim that one cannot be regarded as a thinker unless one is sensitive to the distinction between a correct/incorrect judgment, inference, etc., and that such a sensitivity should manifest itself in a propensity to change one's judgment when it is appropriate to do so. This propensity is not merely the propensity for what was presented above as 'brute change' of judgment by being sensitive merely to new incoming information; it will be a sensitivity to rational norms by which we *assess* our own states of mind as *correct or incorrect*. However, it will *not* require agency and responsibility, only a propensity, a disposition or set of dispositions. Therefore, this changing or revising of one's judgment as a result of assessment by one's rational norms will not be free at all. If one is to be regarded as a thinker, then one has to be responsive to situations in which there is *no choice* but to revise a judgment in accord with one's norms. That is what it is to attribute it all to a disposition. One is '*compelled*' *by reason* to do it. And if one were not so disposed to respond to this pressure, one could not be regarded as a thinker at all. Hence, one could not be blamed for that. Being or not being rational is not something to be praised and blamed. It is something we cannot help be, if we have the right dispositions, and unless they are prevented from being effective by counter-dispositions. Thus very young children and retarded adults do not have the disposition to be rational, and we do not blame them.

That is how the argument would go for those divorcing agency from thought and its normative element in the theoretical domain.

In Chapter 2, it was pointed out that very young children and adults arrested as children may not get counted as *agents* in the normative sense if blame is not appropriate, but the response now will be:

> That is a *further* thing to say about them. The point is that as far as their capacity for thought goes it is not required to bring in their lack of responsible agency. All that is required is to say that they lack certain dispositions. Indeed, even whenever normal adults are irrational, it is because their *dispositions* to be sensitive to rational norms have been jammed and blocked by counter-dispositions (induced by fatigue, say, or a high fever, or inattention, etc.). Intentionality, and the rationality it is subject to, is conceived entirely as being part of a picture of dispositions and counter-dispositions, force and counter-force, which accounts for its rationality and its irrationality. If you are tired or unfit, you may fail to be responsive to norms, you may fail to revise your judgment, but this does not show that you would have failed in normal circumstances. What counts as normal circumstances may be a very hard thing to define in terms that do not go beyond dispositional terms, but those are difficulties of detail.

As I said, the point of presenting the picture of thought that denies that agency is a constitutive feature of thought is not merely to present the eventual prospects of a causal-perceptual account of self-knowledge. It is also to allow space for a picture of self-knowledge that *may even be constitutive* rather than perceptual, that may even assert a special and conceptual link (amounting to transparency and authority) between first-order intentional states and second-order beliefs about them—*it only contests that such links owe to agency, in particular.* They may owe to something like the following instead: As a result of a purely dispositional sensitivity to norms, one's beliefs are always potentially revisable. And in order to revise a first-order belief, one *has* to form a second-order belief about it. That just *is* transparency. As for authority, which is a property of second-order beliefs that they may be presumed to be true, perhaps this picture of thought can say that the second-order belief needed in potential revision of one's judgments in accord with rational norms must have as their object the first-order judgment; and that just *is* authority. Both transparency and authority, thus, have been accounted for by this picture of thought without appeal to agency, only assuming a dispositional and mechanical responsiveness to rational norms. Indeed, this position on

self-knowledge well captures the explicit ambitions of a relatively or-
thodox functionalist about intentionality, like Shoemaker (though not
Burge), to be a constitutive theorist about self-knowledge.

But, as I said, even if the Shoemaker-like constitutive claim fails to
make its case, i.e., even if this purely dispositional account of intentionality and its normative element fails to account for transparency
and authority, there is waiting in the wings the other possibility—
worse, from my point of view—that a purely dispositional and non-
agential picture of intentionality would certainly make plausible an
Armstrong-like causal-perceptual view of self-knowledge.

So, one way or another, this picture of intentionality in the
theoretical domain as presented by this challenge must be squarely
addressed.

As just said, the view to be addressed so far is restricted to denying
that agency constitutes thinking in the *theoretical* domain. Emboldened
by having sketched a view for us to address regarding thought in the
theoretical domain, it may proceed to the more ambitious claim of
denying that agency constitutes intentionality in the practical domain
as well.

Here is roughly how this interlocutor would make out this more
ambitious and radical claim.

If a subject can be imagined to be thinking normatively by compulsion, that amounts to a denial of the claim made earlier that what
Oblomov lacks is the reactive evaluative attitudes. For example, while
discussing his quartet of 'thoughts', I had said that he lacks the crucial
ingredient of having a critical reactive attitude toward the third of his
'thoughts' that would have allowed an agential, deliberative move to
the fourth. This is why, in Oblomov, the fourth thought is merely an
exemplification of rationality. But now we have been told that sensitivity to norms of rationality does not require anything as explicit as
a reactive evaluative attitude reflecting his agency. It could be a far
more dispositional and passively occurrent, non-agential response to
critical norms. On this dispositional picture, all one's critical responses occur passively. Or to put it in the terms I had earlier, they
all assail us. Now, why can't one then extend this idea from the theoretical to the practical domain as well, it might be asked?

So—this interlocutor's challenge continues—imagine that for all
the occasions when an agent, in the sense presented in Chapter 2,

exercises reactive evaluative attitudes in any domain of thought (theoretical or practical) *there is a passive Oblomovian counterpart* to him,
who has all those very attitudes *assail* him. Imagine, that is, a subject
who *perfectly* mimics the evaluative lives of any given agent as portrayed
in Chapter 2, except for one difference: every element of that evaluative life is something that merely *happens* to him. He is 'critical'
(the counterpart of critical) of himself and of others; he 'does' (the
counterpart of does) things on the basis of these evaluations such as
'revise' (the counterpart of revise) his judgments and even 'act' (the
counterpart of act) upon the world. It's just that the 'active' or 'agential' vocabulary to describe all this is erroneous; all this just happens
to him; he is compelled to do these things by his dispositions to be
responsive to the norms of rationality, theoretical *and* practical. In a
word, the more radical challenge just radically expands the Oblomov
figure to be *just like an agent in all respects but the crucial respect of lacking
the first person or agent's point of view.*

My interlocutor continues by admitting that it is true that this passivity might seem more plausible in the realm of the theoretical (ever
since Bernard Williams[22] made so vivid how we do not 'decide to
believe'), but there is no reason to think that a subject who is conceived this way in the practical realm as well is not conceivable or
imaginable (as I was suggesting). He may be *hard* to imagine, and it
is certainly not realistic (as Williams was suggesting, it mostly was in
the theoretical domain), but that still shows that my claim that Oblomov *defeats* the imagination is exaggerated. He is imaginable, and
he does have a point of view, something I denied him. It is just that
he has a third person point of view only. Yet he has thought and
intentionality. Not being an agent in my sense does not prevent him
from having that. He just lacks the point of view of the agent. We do
not attribute to him such a point of view because we do not see any
reason for us to accept anything beyond a purely dispositional understanding of the normative element in thinking, as spelled out
above. What seems like deliberation, revision, etc., in active, agential
terms is all mimicked, only not in those terms but in passive, third
personal terms. It is not thought he lacks, in lacking agency, so it is
not a point of view he lacks, in lacking agency. It is just that he lacks
(ex hypothesi) the point of view that goes beyond the dispositional,
a point of view of agency, as Kant called it, a first person point of

view. He can have all sorts of second-order thoughts and reactive attitudes *assail* him, so he has a full repertory of third personal thoughts about himself and his intentional states, which gives him all the critical standpoint of norms needed to be a thinker in all domains (even the practical) where thought exists.

To say that he has thoughts and a third person point of view should allow one to say that he has self-knowledge of those thoughts—*from that external or third personal perspective on himself.* And we have now a choice as to whether we account for the self-knowledge in Armstrong-like perceptualist terms or in Shoemaker-like constitutive terms, as sketched above.

As for authority in particular, the topic of the present chapter: were we to decide that the causal-perceptualist model of self-knowledge fits the thoroughgoing dispositional picture of intentionality best, we would deny that there is any such thing as authority, and the only task remaining would be to account for the appearance of authority along the lines mentioned earlier in Section 3; i.e., there is an appearance of authority because of our routine expectation that second-order beliefs are true, due to the fact that the causes of our second-order beliefs are routinely the first-order beliefs they are about. Such a causal picture begins to seem much more plausible; in fact, to many (though not Shoemaker) it may be exactly what is called for, given the essentially dispositional picture of intentionality that denies agency as a necessary condition for it.

If all this is right, our efforts to make authority survive the relevant cases of self-deception were quite unnecessary. We had argued in Section 2 of this chapter that we are not required to say that these cases of self-deception undermine authority. And since then, we are embarked on a stronger line of thought—not only is it not required to say that, but we should say the exact opposite. The line of thought, I had said, would depend on the conclusion that agency is necessary for thought, a conclusion based on the argument that our imaginations are defeated by the prospect of a subject that both has thoughts or intentionality and has only a third person point of view. But a picture of intentionality has been presented with all its normative elements apparently in place, where such a subject has now been said to be imaginable, and on that basis, agency has been denied as necessary for intentionality. This puts the stronger line of thought (indeed, even the weaker line of thought), about authority surviving self-deception, in jeopardy. Self-deception on this picture could surely undermine authority, and that is why authority, on this picture, is dismissed as a mere appearance. The relevant cases of self-deception show that though the routine cause of our second-order beliefs may be the first-order beliefs they are about, they need not always be so. When they are not, when we are self-deceived, and yet we avow that we have a certain intentional state sincerely, the second-order belief that the avowal expresses is simply false. It is akin to a perceptual illusion. Since there is only a causal understanding of the link between first-order intentional states and second-order beliefs about them, there is no reason to think that link as conceptual in some way. And if there is no conceptual link, the first-order intentional states, as I said, are not the *unique* causes of the second-order beliefs about them. To say that they are would require going beyond considerations of the contingent and the causal to conceptual considerations linking the first- and second-order states. A thoroughly dispositional picture of intentionality and a causal-perceptual picture of self-knowledge of intentionality are precisely going to withhold such conceptual considerations underlying the link. Authority is therefore undermined.

8. In posing these two challenges, I have presented as sympathetically as I can a conception of intentionality that repudiates a large claim of mine—that agency makes possible intentionality—and repudiates, in turn, a large thesis about one-half of the constitutive nature of self-knowledge that was to be developed on the basis of that claim. I want now to argue against this conception of intentionality that is constructed upon these two versions of the challenge to our view that agency is a necessary condition for intentionality; and then in the next chapter, I want to turn to the more positive task of providing an extended argument for a quite different conception of intentional states, which will be the basis not merely for saying that authority need not be seen as being overturned by the relevant cases of self-deception but for saying that it must be seen as surviving the fact of self-deception.

As I have been saying, should one fail to repudiate these two versions of this challenge and should one have to therefore concede that agency is not a necessary condition for intentionality, a perceptual account of self-knowledge or a constitutive account that does not appeal to agency would begin to loom large with plausibility.

The first and less radical (though radical enough) challenge is that at least as far as *theoretical* reasoning goes one comes to one's conclusions and judgments *compelled* by reason and without any agency, simply due to the *dispositions* that reasoners possess to follow the norms of theoretical rationality. Even the negative reactive attitudes of criticism we have to our mistaken judgments and conclusions are something we are *disposed* to make. They too come helplessly and passively and are not reflective of our agency, as was claimed in the discussion of Oblomov in Section 6.

The second challenge extends the first challenge to *practical* reasoning and to actions as well—indeed, extends it comprehensively to all that counts as 'thought' and 'action', asking, Might it not be that all of our actions are merely the product of intentional states entirely dispositionally conceived, and might it not be therefore that all of our actions and even our reactive attitudes that employ normative concepts merely assail us, just as Oblomov's 'thoughts' are supposed to do?

In general, then, the challenges amount to this. Our denial of intentionality to the non-agent Oblomov had turned on seeing his 'thought' and his 'rationality' as fake because they were unaccompanied by the evaluative reactive attitudes, which are the sign of agency, if Strawson is right. The challenges (posed first in the theoretical domain and then extended to the practical) denied the Strawsonian claim that the evaluative reactive attitudes are the true sign of agency. It is claimed by the challenges that there might be the evaluative and normative element of the reactive attitudes even if there is no agency. You don't need a first person point of view of subjectivity and agency to have reasoning and action and the normative, reactive attitudes. All these might simply *happen to you* in a *comprehensively dispositional* picture of human mentality and behavior.

The first challenge echoes and exploits a point made familiar by Bernard Williams in his well-known article "Deciding to Believe," where he argued that it was quite wrong and unintuitive to think that *believing* something—as opposed to *doing* the things we do—is a matter of decision, thus setting up a distinction in this regard between the theoretical and practical. Note that the regard in which the distinction is set up by him is *not* one of normativity. The idea is not that normativity is absent in the theoretical domain but present in the practical. The idea is, rather, that *agency,* even if present in the practical domain, goes missing in the theoretical.

To respond to this challenge, one need go no further than where one already has been in the long excursus on agency in Chapter 2. The challenge raises no issues that were not settled there and settled quite satisfactorily. Agency or freedom, it was argued there, *is not a matter of being caused by the right kind of cause, independent of the justifiable reactive attitudes we have toward what is caused.* Let it be, then, that we are caused to believe things by our dispositions to be sensitive to norms of rationality and evidence, as the less radical challenge claims. This should not in the end undermine the agency that is essential to thought, including to beliefs. It is not enough, in making the challenge, to simply say that one doesn't agree with Strawson's criterion for what counts as agency. The criterion was grounded in an argument, given in Chapter 2, that showed the shortcomings of other ways of thinking of agency and determinism. It was shown that there was no way to answer the determined incompatibilist who asked, *What about* a cause makes it the right kind of cause that allows for agency? without bringing in the normative element of the justifiable reactive attitudes. The challenge has said nothing to overturn that argument. It has simply turned its back on it and insisted that the causes of one's beliefs are the wrong kind of cause to allow for agency. It has simply asserted without argument that the fact, for instance, that one is caused to have one's beliefs by one's disposition to apply the norms of rationality is sufficient to rule out agency in the theoretical realm. Without being given some argument for why we should doubt the correctness of the Strawsonian conception of agency, which requires more of agency than just a consideration of the right kind of cause, we can remain confident in its correctness.

One must, of course, grant to Williams that we do make an intuitive distinction between belief and action, in the sense that we do think of the former, unlike the latter, as not usually a matter of decision at all. So we are led to say that we may often rightly describe one of the causes of our actions as our decision to act, but we do not typically do so at all in the case of our beliefs. Or (if we don't like to think of the decision itself as a cause) perhaps we are led to say something

slightly different: that once we describe all the causes of one's believing that p, we are not typically tempted to describe the matter as
one of having decided to believe that p, whereas once we have described all the causes of one's actions, one is often correctly given to
describing the matter as one having decided to do the action.

But anyone who has seen the point of the Strawsonian conception
is bound to question an assumption of this challenge and ask, why
insist that *deciding* is the mark of agency? We may arrive at a belief
passively, but what we arrive at is something that is quite within what
is properly described by Kant as the point of view of agency, the first
person point of view. It is just the sort of thing toward which we have
justifiable evaluative reactive attitudes. (Much more will be said in the
next chapter about what sort of thing it is that we arrive at when we
arrive at states like beliefs and desires; and when it is said, it will
become much clearer what underlies the insistence that the point of
view of agency is present wherever such states and whenever theoretical or practical rationality are present.)

Various other things (even other mentalistic things) than coming
to have a belief might happen to us in a state of passivity. And unlike
beliefs, many of these things are not things toward which we have
justifiable reactive attitudes, things such as, say, the coming to have a
stabbing pain in one's appendix. That is why we do *not* say that these
are within the perspective of agency.[23] What makes for the difference
between the case of coming to have a belief and coming to have a
pain or coming to have a belief and coming to lose one's hair is just
as Strawson said. We have justifiable evaluative reactive attitudes to
the beliefs that we come to have happen to us, in a way we do not
have to these other things that happen to us. It is not, then, the
'coming to have' versus 'deciding' that reflects the presence or absence of agency; it is rather the relevance or irrelevance of justifiable
reactive attitudes toward the phenomena that reflect whether or not
they fall within the realm of agency. The question of whether or
not we 'decide' to believe is therefore relevant not to whether or not
believing (and theoretical reasoning generally) is an agential phenomenon but rather to what sort of agential phenomenon it is.

Once this *principled* Strawsonian point against the less radical challenge is firmly understood, the more radical challenge that it is conceivable that *all* our thoughts and actions (*including* all our reactive

evaluative attitudes) assail us should not now look any more threatening *in principle* than the less ambitious one we have just discussed. If being an agent is not a matter of making sure that there is some special form of decision making going on, but rather the justifiable applicability of evaluation, that should apply across the board to all aspects of thought, theoretical or any other. But to say that and just rest there would be incomplete because we need to make clear whether this extension of the Strawsonian response to the more radical challenge is in effect saying that the expanded Oblomov of the challenge is really an agent with an agent's or first person point of view or whether it is in effect denying that the very idea of such an expanded Oblomov is something that we can coherently imagine. The latter, surely, is the effect we want it to have, but we need to spend some time saying how come it can have that effect.

If it were the case, as in the expanded Oblomov presented in Section 7, that *all* of a subject's thoughts (theoretical and practical), *including all of his reactive and self-reactive attitudes,* merely assailed him, then the question might seem to arise: How exactly is he different from one of us, from me, for instance? What is this difference that agency is supposed to make to the possessor of thoughts?

This question can be developed more patiently as follows. In Section 6, we had been withholding the self-reactive attitudes from Oblomov, and we had said that he lacks agency because he lacks them, even if he seems to have 'thoughts' (for example, the trios and quartets of 'thoughts' we discussed there) that exemplify rationality and irrationality. But if one were to expand his mentality and allow him self-reactive attitudes, as my interlocutor did in Section 7, then (as was suggested by my interlocutor) he could be said to have thoughts with all of the normative elements that make for them being rational and irrational. There would no longer be reason to restrict him, as we did in Section 6, to the possession merely of '*thoughts*', which *exemplified* rationality and irrationality. Of course, if we expanded his mentality in this way, we would still have to insist that these 'self-reactive attitudes' are—like all his other thoughts—*simply assailing him.* But that is to be expected since he is not an agent. The point is that once this expansion is made, one can then go all the way with the radical challenge and say that Oblomov is the subject of *all the thoughts* I am the subject of, including the self-reactive attitudes I have, and that he is the subject of *all the actions* I am the subject of. The only difference is that, unlike as with me, *all* of this assails him. But what difference does this last element make? Why should it prevent one from saying that he has thoughts, rationality, normativity, and so on? Why still insist that he merely has 'thoughts'? After all, he has all my speech and behavior. And so, if he is (ex hypothesi) not an agent, is this not proof that agency and thought come apart?

Can one simply deny that thought requires agency in the way that this more radical challenge is doing by asking: why should someone who is passive but just like someone else who is an agent in what he seems to 'do' and 'say' not be said genuinely to have thoughts? Can one claim an intuition that two people alike in all respects of behavior and speech must *both* be genuinely minded with intentionality, even if one of them is comprehensively passive, and then use that intuition to deny that agency is necessary for being minded with intentionality?

This way of putting the radical challenge to the idea that agency constitutes intentionality can be given one of two interpretations.

First, it could be that the challenge is to ask the question, how does anyone of us know that he or she is not a subject like the radically expanded Oblomov, who is wholly passive? For all we know, *we* are not agents; *we* are wholly passive. Yet there is no reason to think that we don't have thoughts or that we don't have a point of view. It's just that we don't have the first person point of view of agency, just as the radical Oblomov does not. What is the proof that *we* are not radical Oblomovs? If the stipulated expanded Oblomov is imaginable, we need to know why we are not such subjects *ourselves.*

The answer to this first interpretation of the radical challenge can only be given by pointing out something that has not surfaced so far but is central to the proper understanding of the very idea of a first person point of view. It has to point out something that, though it is perfectly compatible with the Strawsonian conception of agency that we have invoked against the less radical challenge, is not actually ever made explicit by the Strawsonian conception of agency, not even as it was expounded at length in Chapter 2. (This is why we did not leave things to rest at the point where we extended the Strawsonian response to the more radical challenge.) It has to point out that *it is the nature of a first person point of view that if one has it, one experiences it and knows one has it, and if one thinks one has it or experiences oneself as having it, one has it.* For convenience's sake, I will call this additional feature of the first person point of view the 'self-guaranteeing' feature of agency.

It would be to misunderstand what is meant by the expression 'the first person point of view' to allow that one could have it and not experience oneself as having it, not know that one had it. It would be to equally misunderstand the idea to allow that one thinks one has it and experiences oneself as having it but in fact does not. An agent is not something one could be and not know and experience that one was one; and if one experienced agency and claimed it, one could not be deluded about it. One cannot understand what is meant by the expression 'agent's point of view' or 'first person point of view' and deny these defining claims. It may of course have been the case that there is no such thing as agency or freedom, that there were no first person points of view, but one could not both experience freedom and agency and deny these things. There is no possibility, then, for us to be able to ask meaningfully whether one is not an agent, whether one might be a totally passive subject like the radical Oblomov. The question posed by the first interpretation of the radical challenge is a non-starter.

It may seem as if this response is dogmatic. What is this idea of an agent *experiencing* the point of view of the agent that makes the question a non-starter? Are we not just conveniently inventing a notion of experience to repudiate the challenge posed by the question? We are not. There is absolutely nothing trumped up or even unfamiliar about the notion of experience that is being invoked. Putting aside the extreme cases of comprehensively or *globally* passive agents of the sort we are now considering, the fact is that the experience of agency, and the first person point of view, is a very real thing. It is a very real thing because we know very well what it is like to *locally* fail of it or *lack* it—such as, for instance, when we suffer moments of deep alienation, depression, etc., when we feel as if we lack or are losing control, when we feel that we are passive in our own mentalities. If we can glimpse an imagination, if we can even roughly conceive the radically expanded Oblomov at all, it is only because we can think of the experience of this local loss of agency and local loss of the first person point of view as getting steadily more comprehensive. But even then it will be to imagine that the ladder of agency *as we experience it* is falling away from under us. Even if we slowly lost all our agency and became like the radical Oblomov, it would still be the case that the experience of agency is self-guaranteeing while it is there. By self-guaranteeing, I just mean that if one has the experience of agency, then one is just different from the passive subject; one *is* an agent. If one is different from the passive subject, one knows and experiences oneself to be so. Thus, if the point of the radical challenge is to ask what difference it makes to insist that one has the first person point of view, why can't one have thoughts without it, like the passive subject is imagined to have? The answer provided by this self-guaranteeing feature of the first person point of view is emphatically that it *makes all the difference* to us as thinkers and our relations to the world to be possessed of a first person point of view.

The *second* interpretation of the radical challenge poses a quite different question to the idea that agency constitutes thought and mindedness. This question does not ask, how do we know that *we* are not just like the globally passive expanded Oblomov of the radical challenge? It rather grants the self-guaranteeing feature of the agency and allows that an agent knows that he himself is an agent if he is one. It grants that each person has a first person point of view and often views the world and others from the first person point of view. But then it asks: If, as the radical challenge stipulates, the speech and behavior of the radical Oblomov need be no different from any agent such as, say, myself, how can I tell of someone else that he is not a subject like the radical expanded Oblomov instead of an agent like me? For all I know, he is just like the Oblomov figure and not like me, a subject with thoughts but with only a third personal angle on himself, unlike what I know and experience myself to be. And if that is so, for all I know, he provides the case of someone possessing thoughts without satisfying the allegedly necessary condition for thought, which is agency.

Here the question is not about whether the case of the expanded Oblomov has one asking whether one can know that one is oneself an agent rather than such an Oblomov figure but about whether one knows that *another* is an agent rather than such an Oblomov figure. This question is asked not to make a skeptical point in epistemology, about our knowledge of other agents. It is, rather, asked with a view to just getting clear as to whether agency is supposed to make any difference to thought? Can one simply not leave it out? That is the point of the radical challenge. It is not a question motivated by epistemological skepticism. If that is right, here too the central additional feature of the first person point of view, the self-guaranteeing nature of agency, should help to provide a rather straightforward answer to the challenge. If it really is the case that someone who is an agent knows that he is one and experiences himself as one, and if it really is the case that someone who thinks he is an agent and experiences himself to be an agent is an agent, then all we have to do is to ask *another* question: "Are you an agent?" If the answer is a sincere affirmative, then it expresses the other's belief that he is agent, and given the self-guaranteeing feature, we know that the other is an agent and not an expanded Oblomov. There is nothing unanswerable about the radical challenge under this second interpretation.

I actually do think that things are as simple as this, but not everyone may think so because the fact is that the radical challenge has set up the issue so that the speech and behavior of the expanded Oblomov are exactly the same as the speech of some given agent. (The only difference is that the former's speech and behavior assail him.) The challenge they would raise, then, is, how can we tell which one is the agent and which one is the expanded Oblomov? If their speech and behavior are the same, they will both say, "Yes" to the question, "Are you an agent?" And if so, we cannot tell the difference between the two in the simple and straightforward way I was proposing. No amount of stress on what I have called the self-guaranteeing feature of agency will help in responding to the second interpretation of the radical challenge.

But now this second interpretation of the radical challenge *has* shifted its own question from the initial question to an epistemological one. It is not merely asking, "How do I know that someone else is an agent rather than an expanded Oblomov figure?" with a view to getting clear on whether agency is necessary for thought. It is, rather, asking the question with a view to raising a doubt about whether we can ever know that someone who is an agent is one. For all we know, he is not one. Someone asking this new question need not even want to deny that agency is necessary for thought. For all he is concerned to ask, he could grant that it is. He nevertheless asks how we can ever know whether someone is an agent, given that in all outward appearance and evidence he is just like someone else who is not an agent. To answer this new question, unlike the initial question, we can get no help from the self-guaranteeing nature of agency. We have to respond to it in entirely different terms. This is not surprising even though it seems that the shift in question has come seamlessly from the initial question by way of finding our response that appealed to the self-guaranteeing feature unsatisfactory. This appearance of seamlessness is highly deceptive. The shift it registers is far from seamless; it changes the subject entirely and needs quite other resources to answer.

This new question makes all sorts of assumptions that are highly questionable.

Just because *I know that I am an agent if I am one,* and just because *I am an agent if I think that I am one,* does not mean that others cannot really know that I am an agent or that I cannot know that others are agents. What I have emphasized in the last sentence is what I called a central feature of the first person point of view of agency, the self-guaranteeing feature of agency. But this feature of agency is *not* intended to suggest that there is any problem of privacy whatsoever regarding agency, and it would be quite wrong to interpret it that way.

I know that others are agents when they are because, when I take the first person point of view toward them, I *engage* with them as agents; and I do so because I see in their speech and their behavior, and so on, just the sorts of things that I can and ought to engage with. Their speech and their behavior reveal their mindedness to me and make normative demands on me, and that is why I engage with them. The radical challenger on this second interpretation cannot be questioning this because he has granted me that *I* (and each subject like me) have agency and a first person point of view, and he has granted each subject what I called the self-guaranteeing nature of agency that I invoked in my response to the first interpretation. He cannot therefore deny that when I take the first person point of view I have been granted by him to have, I can experience the world as peopled with others, with whom I *engage.* Anybody with a first person point of view can see the world as containing things to be engaged with, not merely things perceived from a third person, external, objectivist point of view.

The idea that there is an issue of epistemological skepticism about whether or not I am justified in doing so is to assume that if there are agents out there, I can *first* describe them as something that are not the sort of things that I engage with *and then* raise the question, How do I justify going from there to describing them as subjects to engage with, subjects with thoughts, meaningful speech, human actions, and other such things that one engages with? But there *are no such prior descriptions* from which one goes to the subsequent descriptions through some justificatory path. You cannot raise the skeptical question unless you presuppose that there are such prior and neutral descriptions, and that is the wrong presupposition. My experience of the agency of others in my engagement with them is just that—an experience of their agency in my engagement with them. It is not something that comes in two stages, a neutrally described perception of them as non-agential, non-engageable phenomena and then later an engagement with them. The world of others, as I experience it, is not filtered through some first stage like that. It is to misunderstand the epistemology of agency entirely to think that there is such a first stage, and the shift in question from the initial question to the skeptical question precisely presupposes that there is such a first stage.

On such a presupposition, our own example would have to be understood thus: When one says that the agent and the globally passive Oblomov assert "yes" on being asked the question, "Are you an agent?" what we really mean is that there is a first stage, neutral vocabulary to describe what happens, something that Quine once called 'surface assent' (physical sounds, physical noddings of the head, etc.) and that the behaviors of both subjects are described in terms of such 'surface' assent *first,* and the problem (the epistemological problem) is to *then* find out which surface assent expresses *real assent,* i.e., which *surface assent* is a case of *asserting* that one is an agent. It is precisely this framework—a framework that allows a neutral (non-agential and non-intentional) first stage vocabulary to describe the phenomena from which one must then make some claim to a *further* (second stage) right to the agential and intentional descriptions of the phenomena—that is spurious and untenable.

Against this framework, we need to recall the kind of point made by McDowell that we discussed in Chapter 1 regarding other minds and apply it to the question of other *agents.* The framework quite fails to come to grips with, in fact it falsifies, the way subjects with a first person point of view experience and engage with the world of others. I don't experience another agent as a mere body in motion producing sound waves in the air when I am taking a first person point of view on them. There is nothing in my experience of other agents, when I take a first person point of view on them, that can filter out my engagements with them and see them in these other terms. If I were to see them in these other terms, I would not be seeing them from within the first person point of view at all; I would be seeing them from a third person point of view. But seeing them from the first person point of view is not something that is being denied me by the skeptic who has shifted the question of the second interpretation of the radical challenge. He is only questioning with what right I go from a first way of seeing them that is not one of engagement to a second way of seeing them that is one of engagement. But there is no legitimate ground to erect the third person perspective on others as providing a primary and privileged level of description from which one has to go to other levels only if one provides some sort of philosophical justification.

If that is right, this new skeptical question does not get off the ground—no more than a skeptical question could get off the ground about one's own agency. After all, just as one could with others, one can view oneself from the third person point of view. One can see oneself as a body, as putting sounds into the air, as being caused to do things, and so on. But it isn't as if there is any legitimate ground to erect this into some sort of first level of description of oneself as a non-agent that has epistemological privilege and from which one has to justify going to a second level of experiencing one's agency. What is true of oneself as an agent in regard to the skeptical question in epistemology is just as true of the agency of others. There are bound to be all sorts of difference between one's relationship to oneself and one's relations to others, there are bound to be all sorts of differences between one's relations to one's own agency and one's relations to the agency of others, but these differences are not differences that are bound to raise skeptical epistemological questions about others that one cannot and does not raise about oneself.

Once all this is pointed out, the seams in the apparently seamless way in which the skeptical question was drawn from the initial question of the radical challenge in its second interpretation are laid bare. In fact, what is laid bare is that the shift in question is quite illicit.

Therefore, nothing about my claim that the first person point of view is not something that one can be under the impression one has without having it is going to generate any skeptical problem that locks our agency into ourselves as some logically private phenomenon. The response we gave to the more radical challenge by pointing to this central feature of the first person point of view cannot, therefore, simply be fuel for converting the radical challenge to a familiar problem of other minds extended to the notion of agency.

If the relationship between these responses I have been giving in this section to the two (i.e., the more and the less radical) challenges are properly understood, the conclusions we can rest with (in reverse order) are: (1) a *globally* passive subject cannot be a possessor of thoughts nor, once we have a proper understanding of what a first person point of view is, is there any question that we are such globally passive subjects; and (2) a locally *passive* subject *can* be an agent, and all of us are oftentimes locally passive, and as locally passive subjects, we can often possess agency *even on those occasions* when we are *passively* assailed by various thoughts and conclusions, as when we come to have beliefs without deciding to believe and when we are compelled to some conclusion by our rational sensitivity to principles of reasoning.

The responses given in this section to the two challenges now allow us to complete the primary business of delivering on the promised eventual aim of the present as well as the next chapter. What we have been leading up to is an account of the very nature of thought or intentionality, which seems to follow upon the notion of agency and the first person or agent's point of view that has been so basic to the book's argument. The promised eventual aim is to give ourselves the right to the conditional for authority and complete the account of the special nature of self-knowledge, i.e., to justify our intuitions about authority, even in the face of frequent self-deception. I will be arguing that if we understand the nature of intentionality (in particular, of states such as beliefs and desires) as it emerges from the notion of agency that we have established in this chapter as its necessary condition, we will give ourselves this right and justification.

So our next question, bringing with it one more integration of the fundamental themes of this book, is to ask: What is the nature of beliefs and desires that is assumed when we say that they are in the realm of a normative conception of agency, even if they are very often passively acquired? The integration will consist in *quite literally* identifying intentionality with value, in a sense to be elaborated now in the next chapter. This forthcoming integration of intentionality with value, which is itself necessitated by the earlier integration of agency with value in Chapter 2 and the recently concluded constitution of intentionality by agency in this chapter, is what lies behind the second half of the special nature of self-knowledge, i.e., authority.

✦ ✦ ✦

FIVE

The Conceptual Basis for Authority II

Intentionality, Causality, and the Duality of Perspectives

1. SO FAR IT has been argued, among other things, first, that agency is a normative notion (Chapter 2); second, that such a normative notion of agency has, as a fallout, one-half of what makes self-knowledge special, i.e., transparency (Chapter 3); and third, that agency is a necessary condition for intentional states such as beliefs and desires (Chapter 4).

The defining element of the normative conception of agency, which has played such a central role in the argument so far, is that it locates agency in phenomena that are justifiably the target of evaluative reactive and self-reactive attitudes. In the dialectic so far, this is essentially all that makes it a 'normative' conception. We will fill out much more the other aspects of the normative conception of agency in a crucial section of this chapter, Section 4; but in order to do that, we will first have to put in place a very specific understanding of a normative conception of intentionality.

To do this, let's start with and build on what we have: agency as situated in phenomena that can be targeted by our justifiable reactive attitudes. Now, as I have just concluded in the last chapter,[1] even a subject's dispositions and their behavioral outcomes can often be the justifiable targets of evaluative reactive and self-reactive attitudes (i.e., can often be properly described in agential terms) so long as the subject's behavior and 'mentality' are not *wholly* passive and dispositional, as one finds in the figure of the imagined Oblomov. We can, and often do, lament, regret, and criticize our mental dispositions, and we also often criticize the behavior that results from those dispositions. And we can do all this justifiably; we can give justification for these critical reactive attitudes. But if this is so, then the *lights by which we criticize these dispositions cannot themselves be just other dispositions.* Why not? Because if they were, then there is no reason to think that we are not Oblomovs in the comprehensive sense we have shown to be incompatible with the possession of thought. Comprehensive dispositionality with no non-dispositional, normative states would allow for just the comprehensive (as opposed to local) passivity that rules thought out.

If that is right, a question arises: what would a subject's mentality and behavior have to be properly characterized to be *partially* if, as we have resolved, they are *not* to be described *wholly* in dispositional terms and *not* to be viewed *wholly* as the outcome of its dispositions? In other words, where and when the mentality is *not* dispositional and the behavioral outcomes are *not* merely the outcomes of mentality, dispositionally characterized, how is it to be properly described? Oblomov, in our description of him, is globally passive and wholly characterized dispositionally. *We* are not. So how are we to understand that aspect of our mentality, which is not dispositional? That is the main preoccupation of this section and the next two.

The idea, then, is that intentional states such as beliefs and desires will step in to provide what is needed to meet the demand that emerged from the conclusions of the last chapter. What was demanded by the normative conception of agency, as defined thus far and via the dialectic of the last chapter's discussion, is that there be an aspect of our mentality that is not dispositional in any standard sense, that provides us the lights by which we can criticize our dispositional mentality, and that therefore makes possible our agency in its normative aspect. Intentional states will meet that demand, and by showing how they do so (in Sections 1–3), we will have recast intentional states along the lines that I have been periodically threatening in earlier chapters. Then, after seeing the implications of such a recasting for a more fully elaborated normative conception of agency than we have provided so far (in Section 4), it will be argued (in Section 5) that it is only because they are recast in this way that authority holds of intentional states.

Though the time has come to speak more carefully and correctly of intentional states than I have been doing so far, there should be no impression created that I am abandoning any claim made so far about agency, self-knowledge, and their inter-relations. This is important, and it is really worth being clear about it.

So far, the only conclusions I have come to about self-knowledge via the notion of agency have been in Chapter 3, and they have been about the aspect of self-knowledge that we call 'transparency'. No conclusions about authority have been drawn yet. In Chapter 3, I had (with a studied tentativeness, awaiting the present chapter's reconfiguring of intentional states) spoken of intentional states as a species or sub-class of mental states or dispositions; and I had said that mental dispositions were within the realm of agency so long as they could be the objects of justifiable reactive attitudes. I had also said that transparency was a property of mental states, so long as they fell within the *proviso* of the conditional for transparency, which explicitly mentioned agency in its full normative sense. Now, in the present chapter, I will, as I said, be redescribing intentional states, so that they are no longer viewed as dispositions in any standard or substantial sense. But that does not mean that I am abandoning the view that mental dispositions are transparent, under that proviso, and that they are therefore often capable of falling within the domain of agency. The point of the reconfiguration is to say that intentional states are not dispositions, but the reconfiguration *leaves untouched* the claim that mental dispositions can be within the realm of agency and transparency *when they do fall within the proviso*. So one should not conclude that anything said in Chapter 3 about transparency is being retracted. The only right thing to conclude is what I was, in any case, careful to say in Chapter 3—that transparency holds true of a wider class of mental states than just intentional states such as beliefs and desires. Authority is another matter, and that is the subject of the present chapter.

The question of how we are to understand that aspect of our mentality (intentional states such as beliefs and desires, now properly conceived) that is not dispositional can be approached in various ways. One clear and clean way of approaching it can be found in some formulations of a distinction in Kripke's book on Wittgenstein and rule-following.[2] This is the distinction between intentional states (restricted for our purposes to beliefs, desires, and intentions) viewed as dispositional states and viewed as normative states. This distinction invokes the set of considerations in Wittgenstein that, in the last chapter, I had promised would be deeper than the Wittgensteinian considerations discussed there. Wittgenstein's own way of raising these considerations and the distinction between intentional states just mentioned is more masked and contrived than Kripke's clear and vivid formulations of them, so in the discussion to follow, I will rely on the latter.

Kripke points out repeatedly in that work, "[T]he important problem for Wittgenstein is that my present mental state does not determine what I *ought* to do in the future" (p. 56, his emphasis). "The fundamental problem is . . . whether my actual dispositions are 'right' or not, is there anything that mandates what they *ought* to be" (p. 57, his emphasis). "The dispositionalist gives a descriptive account. . . . But this is not the proper account which is *normative*, not *descriptive*" (p. 37, his emphases).

Kripke is talking here (and throughout his book) indifferently about meaning and intentionality. I have argued elsewhere that one has to be very careful about the quite *different* ways in which the question of normativity affects meaning and intentionality, despite the obviously close relation between meaning and intentionality, and Kripke is not always careful to do so.[3] The present discussion will ignore issues of whether and in what way meaning is normative and restrict itself entirely to the normative nature of thought or intentionality. Kripke's general point is that intentionality is a normative notion, and thoughts, therefore, cannot get a dispositional account. He is explicit in his criticisms of functionalism and other such accounts of our intentional states of mind, which stress their dispositional character and their *causal* roles, for completely overlooking and in fact flouting their naturalistically irreducibly normative character.[4]

Well before Kripke, philosophers—such as Davidson, for instance— had pointed out that there is a normative, and even an irreducibly normative, character that is possessed by intentional states. But (and this is a point of real importance that will be stressed throughout this discussion) Kripke's remarks suggest something much more clean and clear than what is often acknowledged by those who think that intentional states are affected by normativity. To illustrate this point, it will be useful to work with a recurring interlocutory contrast between Kripke's way of making the distinction and Davidson's views on the subject. The answer to the question I have posed (How should we think of the mentality of agents when it is not dispositional?) will depend crucially on Kripke's view of the relevance of normativity to intentional states getting things more right than Davidson's view.

Davidson was perhaps the earliest proponent of the explicitly normative element in the characterization of intentional states such as beliefs and desires and intentions. This element was essential to the argument of his celebrated paper "Mental Events,"[5] to the effect that intentional states are not reducible to physical states, that they are not type-identical with physical states. (He actually makes his argument, citing events and not states, but it should be obvious that the argument can be made to apply to states as well.) However, Davidson never took the view that intentional states, if they are normative, cannot be dispositions. That is simply not a conclusion he ever drew from their normative character. In fact, he has always claimed that intentional states *are* dispositions, and he described the relevance of normativity to them in the following further claim: intentional states are mental dispositions that unlike other dispositions are 'constrained' or 'governed' by normative principles of rationality.

Various questions arise. What exactly is this notion of 'constraining' and 'governing' that is done by normative principles of rationality? Dispositions are to be thought of as states defined by their *causal* roles, as second-order properties of the brain, as tendencies in nature? How can—as Kripke puts it—states that are essentially characterized in these descriptive terms, as dispositions are, be thought of as being governed or constrained by normative principles? Of course we may say that a disposition is rational or irrational, but that does not make it constituted by rationality. It does not make it a normative state. It merely says that it either is in accord or fails to be in accord with rationality. So, on this picture, intentional states, being dispositions, are therefore not themselves normative, but they are assessable for whether they are in accord with the normative principles of rationality. I will return to this picture of intentionality in Section 4.

Now, the fact that Davidson says that intentional states are dispositions does not immediately make it *impossible* for them also to be irreducibly normative, since one can characterize dispositions in a way that makes that possible. But even if one did so, one cannot avoid the point, which Kripke has stressed, that dispositions are, at least *prima facie*, just the kinds of states that are thought of in naturalistic terms. So prima facie there is an issue here to be addressed, work to be done, before one can reconcile intentional states—so conceived as dispositions—with their irreducibly normative status. I will return to this question later as well.

Davidson himself does not pause to explicitly address these fundamental questions, despite his insightful insistence on the relevance of normativity to intentional states. His position, therefore, even if not wrong, at the very least is somewhat underdescribed. What makes Kripke's remarks much clearer and more explicit is that he does make a clean distinction between dispositions and intentional states, on grounds of the latter's normativity.

In doing so, he is—implicitly—bringing back to center stage the hallowed wisdom of the 'open question' argument in G. E. Moore. I want to take that as my point of departure.[6]

Despite their similarities, much to be exploited in the next few pages, two basic differences between Moore's and Kripke's interests are obvious and elementary.

First, Moore's theme was not something as general as intentionality, but rather moral values in particular. It was Kripke's innovation (pursuing some remarks in Wittgenstein) to introduce what is rightly described (not that he describes it this way) as the strategy of Moore's open question argument to our understanding of the normative element in intentionality.

Second, Moore's targets of attack were certain naturalistic reductions of normative terms such as 'good' and 'ought' to *external* natural properties. He particularly targeted properties such as social aggregate utility in its Benthamite naturalist versions, though it is a question how external these are in the end. But the argument, as Kripke and Wittgenstein are—implicitly—deploying it, applies equally to reduction of norms or normative properties (such as intentional properties or states) to *internal* natural properties such as (mental) dispositional properties.

With these differences registered, one can present the Moorean structure of argument on behalf of the broadly Kripkean claim, roughly as follows.

It is always a *non*-trivial or open question (always a question that is unlike asking, say, "This is a bachelor, but is he unmarried?) to ask, "I have this disposition to φ, but ought I to φ?" If this is a genuinely non-trivial question, then that is some indication that an affirmative answer to it, "Yes, I ought to φ," expresses a mental state of ours that is *not* a disposition to φ; it is something over and above a disposition to φ. The state that is being expressed by that answer may have various relations to that disposition, but given the fact that it is an answer to a *non*-trivial question, we cannot identify what it expresses with the disposition to φ. And the point is that intentional states are states such as this. They are internal 'oughts' (or, I suppose one must add, 'ought-nots').

Beliefs are oughts of this kind. So are desires.

In order to say this, there is no need to deny that we often use the word 'desire' to describe dispositions such as, say, an urge to smoke a cigarette, which I may have, even if I think I ought not to smoke. But all that shows is that we need to disambiguate the term 'desire' between the term used to describe such urges and the term used to describe the intentional state proper, which is, as Kripke insists, a normative state. Throughout this discussion and for the rest of the book from this point on, I will be using the term 'desire' in this latter sense of an intentional state proper, a fully normative state.

This ambiguity reveals that the point and importance of the Moorean argument are somewhat conditional: if we do already have a sense of the distinction that goes into this ambiguity in the very idea of an intentional state such as a desire (or a belief), the argument helps to bring to the surface what a vast gulf there is between thinking of desires (or beliefs) as dispositions and thinking of desires (or beliefs) as internal oughts. My dialectic in the last chapter and the present one so far has, therefore, been this: to first show in Chapter 4, via a discussion of Oblomov, that we do have a sense of the distinction that goes into this ambiguity. This was done by showing how it is not enough to think of being minded, of being the possessor of thoughts, in terms that are exclusively dispositional, as the radical Oblomov is. That would be to abandon the very notion of being minded and possessing thoughts. We need something over and above dispositions that give us the lights by which we can exercise reactive attitudes toward oneself in a way that Oblomov cannot genuinely do;

and that means thinking of being minded as necessarily also containing states of mind that afford us those lights, states of mind that have the critical power of 'oughts' (and 'ought-nots'). And what the Moorean argument in the present chapter is now allowing us to say is that there is a quite radical distinction and distance between these two aspects that go into being minded. That is the point of my bringing in the Moorean argument only at this late stage, after the conclusions of the last chapter provided the ambiguity between the dispositional sense of intentional states and the 'internal ought' sense. Once this ambiguity has come to the surface, the Moorean argument's point comes fully into view. The term 'desires' exemplifies this ambiguity particularly well in our usage, describing both the dispositions we have as well as those normative states of mind that I am calling 'internal oughts' that provide us the lights by which we take reactive attitudes toward our desires, thought of as dispositions. The open question, when it asks, "I have these dispositions to ϕ, but ought I to ϕ?" is precisely displaying this ambiguity and the distance between these two uses—dispositional and normative.

In this latter normative usage, to desire something, to believe something, is to think that one *ought* to do or think various things, those things that are entailed by those desires and beliefs by the light of certain normative principles of inference (those codifying deductive rationality, decision-theoretic rationality, perhaps inductive rationality, and also perhaps to some broader forms of material inference having to do with the meanings of words as well). It is not to be disposed to do or think those things; it is to think one ought to do and think them.

A good word that is often used to describe such internal oughts that are not defined in terms of the corresponding dispositions is that they are 'commitments',[7] commitments to think various things and to do various things.

If I believe something, say, that there is a table in front of me, then I am committed to believing various other things, such as (to take just one of them) that there is something in front of me. Those commitments characterize the belief. (Two asides regarding the case of belief: (1) Though the example just given only brings in the relevance of logical inference into commitments, obviously more than logical inference will be relevant; various more material sorts of inference will be relevant, depending on what we take tables to be, which will involve other beliefs qua commitments. Thus, for instance, if I believe that there is a table in front of me, then depending on my other beliefs qua commitments, I might be committed to believing that if I run very fast into it, I will be hurt. (2) I am unembarrassed by the fact that the notion of belief is being used in the characterization of beliefs as commitments—to *believe* something is to be committed to *believing* various other things—because I am not trying to provide any sort of explicit definition.)[8]

Desires too are commitments. If I desire something, say, that I should help the poor, then I am committed to doing various things, such as, say, giving money to charity or joining a communist party. As with beliefs, what exactly desires commit us to doing depends (familiarly) both on other intentional states qua commitments we have and on various norms of logic, decision theory, etc.

(Though I will mostly talk of beliefs and desires—except briefly in Section 4, where I will briefly talk about more decisive states—intentions are also commitments, and they too fall under these latter normative codifications, and they too are governed by the holistic constraint coming from the relations they bear to of other commitments. Moreover, as should be familiar from our general understanding of the difference between desires and intentions, intentions are commitments that are undertaken with more specific goals in mind, on more specifically targeted occasions, usually after a weighing of various different, more general sorts of commitments, etc. In a word, they are commitments that stand in greater proximity to decision making than desires.)

Now, of course, those like Davidson and a host of others who think intentional states are dispositions also insist on both the holistic and the logical element, but they do not see those elements as forcing a characterization of beliefs and desires as *themselves being* commitments. On my reading of Kripke's remarks, he, unlike Davidson, is insisting on this latter claim.

This claim that intentional states are commitments does not mean that dispositions do not have a lot to do with intentional states. In fact, as we shall see, it does not even really mean that dispositions are not involved in the characterization of intentional states. But what the Moore and Kripke style of argument establishes is that a certain *simple* (even if holistic) identification of intentional states and dispositions is not possible. What they establish is that one may have a certain first-order intentional state (say, again, a desire that one help the poor), that is a certain sort of commitment, even if one has no corresponding first-order disposition to do anything at all that would count as fulfilling the commitment to help the poor. That is the very least they establish, and it is very important to have done that, for it makes it possible to argue, as I will try and do, that even if there is a more *complex* relevance of dispositions to the characterization of intentional states, its complexity is precisely of the sort that rules out a naturalism and functionalism about intentional states. This will be relevant to the particular argument I have to give to establish the conditional for authority. The importance of the Moore and Kripke style of argument is that it provides the first step toward this anti-naturalism. So, in a sense, what I will be pursuing here is a completion of the argument that Kripke's Moorean remarks, cited earlier, get us started on. If the argument is effective, it should give us the conclusion that Kripke vigorously asserted (see pp. 35–37)—to repeat: it is not possible to entertain the highly prevalent view in philosophy that we may concede that intentional states lack a behavioral or a neurophysiological reduction but nevertheless claim that they have a naturalistic reduction to states characterized in terms of dispositions, in terms of their causal roles. In the end the conceptual basis of authority will depend on establishing a very specific anti-naturalist notion of beliefs and desires.

2. I have said that it is Moore's open question argument that underlies Kripke's remarks against a dispositional view of intentionality.

But it is a striking feature of Moore's argument—and perhaps, from the perspective of the philosophy of mind of the last three or four decades, it will be said that it is a striking *limitation* of Moore's argument—that it is only effective and is only intended to be effective against naturalisms that are *definitional*. It is effective, that is, against reductions of moral properties that proceed via (presumably non-arbitrary) stipulations regarding the meaning or connotation or sense of evaluative terms such as 'good'.

If so, it is a perfectly fair objection that those are not the most interesting forms of naturalism about value, and they are certainly not how the naturalisms of the last few decades present themselves. In keeping with more current thinking, we tend to think of naturalistic treatments of value as proceeding via *discoverable* identities between evaluative properties or states and natural properties or states and as not proceeding via definitional claims about the 'meaning' or the 'sense' of evaluative terms such as 'good'.

Against this, the open question argument will be quite ineffective. That is to say: one might think that there is a naturalistic reduction of good to some natural property via some a posteriori identity claims such as those we have for natural kinds, identities such as, for example, "water = H_2O." This is a reduction that takes good to be a natural kind and 'good' to be a natural kind term that is to be understood in terms of a causal theory of reference of a familiar sort.[9] Such a reduction, which is not dependent on senses or connotation or meaning, is not vulnerable to the open question argument, which only targets definitional reductions. So someone may grant that Moore's argument is fine as far as it goes but object that it does not go far enough to overturn these other more current forms of naturalism about value.[10]

It is important to note that raising this difficulty is not intended to say that there is any fault in Moore's argument itself. It is rather to point out that the argument is only effective against particular kinds of naturalistic reduction, those that depend on definition, meaning, connotation, or senses. It is not effective against reductions based on causal theories of reference yielding only contingent or a posteriori rather than definitional identities.

So far I have raised the question of this limitation only for Moore. But exactly this sort of difficulty can be raised about Kripke's Moorean argument against a dispositional view of intentional properties. In this context, as I said earlier, the open question targets not the identification of good with social aggregate utility but the identification of intentional states qua commitments with certain sorts of dispositions. It is only if this identification was made via meaning or definitional stipulations that the open question argument works. But here too there is no reason to think that those are the best ways to make the identifications. After all, many reductive views of the mind today are based on empirical claims; so here again one might insist that the identification of intentional states (commitments) with dispositions is not definitional but based on a posteriori identities dependent in the familiar way on causal accounts of reference. Against this, the Moorean strategy will be ineffective.

Let us pursue this a little further. For the sake of convenience and abbreviation only, one can restrict oneself to the case of Moore's original argument, which pertains to moral rather than intentional properties. But since intentional properties or states, on the normative picture owing to Kripke, are evaluative properties or states, anything one says about the former will carry over to the latter because the structure of the argument is exactly the same and applies to value in general.

Is this difficulty raised for Moore decisive? I shall be arguing that it is not, and my argument will be based on raising Fregean considerations to supplement the Moorean considerations raised so far. Familiar Fregean considerations[11] raise an issue for these more recent forms of naturalistic reduction of value, even as they seem to have escaped the net of Moore's argument.

Keeping things quite general, instead of taking a very specific property such as social aggregate utility, suppose such a reduction appealed to some a posteriori identity of the form good = x, where x was some natural property.

Now, it is surely possible that someone may without irrationality deny that good = x, just as someone may deny without irrationality that Hesperus is Phosphorus, or deny that London is Londres, or that water is H_2O. To deny these things is not like denying that Hesperus is Hesperus, London is London, water is water. In other words, mere *lack of information* about astronomy or geography or chemistry (or morals) cannot make one *irrational*. But if someone can coherently and meaningfully say, "It is not the case that good is x," then we must ask what the term 'good' in this coherent, meaningful false statement means. Let the term *denote* whatever it is supposed to, given the a posteriori identity. The point is that we need to posit a sense; we need to say what it *connotes,* in order to find the statement coherent and rational, even if it is false. That shows that even in the identity statement "good = x," the term 'good' has a sense over and above a reference.[12] This is an essentially Fregean argument I am invoking, though I have raised it more explicitly in terms of the need to account for the protagonist's *rationality,* something that is only implicit in

Frege's explicit talk of the need to account for the difference in *cognitive significance* of statements such as "Hesperus = Hesperus" and "Hesperus = Phosphorous."

And now the question is, what is this sense or what are these senses (as opposed to the denotation) of 'good' expressing?

Here we have a choice. We can either say that these modes of presentation (which are presumably often specified in descriptions, though one does not *have* to think of them as descriptional) are expressing further *naturalistic* properties, once again. Or we can say that they are expressing moral and evaluative properties.

Either choice leads to serious trouble for the naturalistic reduction.

If we opt for the former, if we say that they express further *naturalistic properties,* then we are back once again to being vulnerable to Moore's open question argument. For recall that Moore's argument was never said to be at fault in itself. That was not the point of the difficulty we raised for Moore. It was only supposed to be *limited* in what it was effective against. It was only effective against definitional reductions that are based on meaning or connotation or senses. But if we grant, under pressure from the Fregean considerations just raised, that our morally badly informed but rational protagonist is rational only because his term 'good' is being given a sense or meaning, then we *cannot* go on to say that that *sense* expresses a naturalistic property. That is just the idea that Moore's argument had undermined.

What if we opt for the other choice? What if we say that the relevant sense (or the descriptions specifying the modes of presentation) does *not* express a naturalistic property? Well, then, there is no fully effective naturalistic reduction in the first place. To choose this second option is to give up on the naturalism.

The point is that if the difficulty was that the Moorean argument was fine as far as it went, but it did not go far enough to overturn this sort of naturalism, the reply is that, with a little help from a familiar Fregean argument, the Moorean argument can be made to go exactly that far.

And as I said, exactly the same structure of argumentation can be made to defend the naturalistic irreducibility of intentional states, under their normative reading, to dispositional states.

It looks, then, as if there is something like a *pincer* effect that disallows any naturalistic reduction of normative notions, whether moral ones or those involved in intentionality. These reductions are either vulnerable to (1) Moore-style arguments or (2) Frege-style arguments. If naturalists think they are not vulnerable to (1), it is only because they are in thrall to a naturalism that is susceptible to (2); and if they think that they can forestall (2) by appealing to the sort of thing (meanings, sense) that (2) demands *while retaining their naturalism,* then they are once again susceptible to (1). In short, naturalism cannot escape the crushing grip of Moore's hand because it is pushed right back there by the other Fregean hand. 'Pincer' is a good word to describe this effect.

Various objections can be raised against the pincer argument, just given, to undermine these naturalisms regarding value in general and intentionality in particular.

(A) Some may resist the pincer dialectic by digging their heels in and saying that there simply are no senses involved at all in our understanding of natural kind terms, and so the Fregean considerations of the pincer need not be taken seriously at all. They were taken seriously at the point where we said that merely being misinformed does not make one irrational; it does not make one's statements denying the relevant a posteriori identities incoherent and meaningless. It is at that point that one appealed to senses or descriptions: to account for their meaningfulness and rationality. But this is all illegitimate, it might be said. At most, descriptions come into originary reference-fixing events, but after that, these descriptions *completely* drop out and in no way amount to modes of presentation or sense. They play no role at all in our understanding of terms like 'water', 'gold', or for that matter, 'good', once the reference-fixing event is over and done with. This is sometimes the view taken by the *strict* forms of the causal theory of reference.[13] If we thought of 'good' along these strict causal-theoretic lines, then there are no senses that hold of 'good', no stereotypes, no descriptions, no modes of presentation, nothing of that sort to which we may tie our term 'good' in a way that has philosophical significance. If so, there is nothing for the other hand of the pincer to come down on. There is no definitional element, no element of Fregean sense to which the Moorean argument can apply.

But if that is really so, it is possible that, once the reference fixing is over and done with, we could be and always have been completely wrong about what good is? If that is really so, there would be nothing in itself incoherent about imagining that every judgment about good we have ever made after the reference fixing might be completely off the mark. We would simply have been fooled into thinking on all occasions of judgment that 'fool's good' is good. Hence, on such a *strict* causal theory of reference, how we conceive of good (or gold or water) can altogether come apart from what good is, what it refers to, what the relevant a posteriori identities reveal it to be identical with.

If the strict causal theories of reference allow for such a consequence, one would have thought that the consequence is quite enough to show that we have here a reductio ad absurdum of the idea that good is a natural kind. It would be bad enough if this were a consequence for gold or water, viz., that it is possible that we are and always have been systematically deceived about them. But about good it seems utterly unacceptable to think that it is possible that we have never gotten it right. *It is unacceptable in the sense that in the face of such a consequence we would be perfectly within our rights to say that the interesting normative notion is 'fool's good' and not good.*

However, precisely because such a consequence threatens to produce a reductio ad absurdum of the very idea of natural kinds, it is not clear that too many people really do hold to such a strict version of a causal theory. Most now think of causal accounts of reference as really only falling back on some idea such as a term referring to *'whatever it is that underlies and explains the stereotypical properties p, q, r . . . to which we tie our term 'water', 'gold', etc.*[14] This is, then, perhaps how they will also think of 'good'. But then that move brings us right back to the idea of senses or definitions. This *non-strict* version of the causal theory of reference is not giving up on reference for sense or for a description theory. It is still a causal theory of reference. But, even so, the stereotypes, descriptions, senses, etc., are *part of the characterization of reference*. If we wanted to avoid the consequence of allowing for the pervasive possibility of 'fool's good' or 'fool's gold' or 'fool's . . . ," then, as these non-strict causal accounts make clear, we will have to build into the characterization of reference these defining and sense-giving stereotypes that the stricter causal accounts of reference left out, once the originary reference-fixing baptisms were over. And if the claim is that a naturalistic reduction of good relies on treating 'good' as a natural kind term with such a *non*-strict causal account of its reference, then the question must arise: are these senses or stereotypes that are built into our characterization of its reference expressing natural properties or not? If they are, then they are vulnerable to Moore's open question argument. If not, there is no naturalistic reduction, in any case. The pincer is effective again.

(B) A second objection to the pincer argument that is bound to be raised is that this entire appeal to Frege and to senses in one hand of the pincer (in order to set things up for the other, Moorean hand of the pincer) is assuming that senses always express properties; and the objection will be to that assumption. If the sense or senses of 'good' were not seen as expressing genuine properties, then the Moorean arm of the pincer (which is intended to undermine a reduction of good to a certain kind of *property*—a natural property—via an appeal to meaning, definition, sense, etc.) would have nothing to work on. No non-natural or any other kind of property is being expressed by the sense of 'good'.[15]

The objection, then, will be that we are never required to say that a sense *always* expresses a property. They often do not, so perhaps they do not in the case of evaluative terms such as 'good' (or 'commitments'). Hence, unless I am taking the quite implausible view that senses always express properties, the pincer is not effective.

Now, of course one needn't deny that some very idiosyncratic senses could be dismissed as not having any corresponding properties or facts that they express. Nor need one deny that there are senses that seem to us to be obviously depicting something false. Those too are similarly dismissable. An example: someone's sense for 'water' might be 'what the Hindu gods drank after their sport'. The claim that this sense and others like it express facts and genuine properties may of course be legitimately dismissed. So in my argument I am talking not only about senses that are communitywide and non-idiosyncratic but also about senses that are not dismissable in this way as not describing facts and properties. If for any relevant natural kind term ('good' included, if that is indeed what 'good' is) there is always a cluster of senses, some of which were and some of which are not dismissable as idiosyncratic and obviously false, then a certain amount of disentangling would have to be done before the force of the Frege-

Moore argument I am presenting can be seen. The Moorean open question applies to the undismissable senses or descriptions remaining, after the disentangling has been done. If *these* express natural properties, then they will be susceptible to Moore's open question; if they do not express natural properties, there is no naturalistic reduction of good in the first place.

(C) It might be said that in saying this I have still not addressed the most principled critical response to this Frege-Moore strategy with which I am confronting the contemporary naturalist. The Fregean part of the strategy has the effect of necessarily throwing up senses, often a cluster of senses, and I have talked of disentangling the dismissable from the undismissable among these senses in order to set things up for the application of the Moorean part of the pincer strategy. The principled objection to all this is to say, "Let the Fregean part of the strategy throw up senses. It still may be the case that the senses involved in the case of 'good' *by their nature are never* undismissable ones, and therefore they *never* express any properties at all, that they are merely concepts and conceptions but there are no corresponding real things, facts, or properties. So one just cannot create the setup for the application of the Moorean part of the pincer strategy."

This echoes what we had said earlier about fool's good, but with a difference. We had said earlier that if senses played no role at all in our understanding of natural kind terms (as claimed by the strict causal theories), then all our judgments regarding what is good could, in principle, be and always have been off the mark, an illusory pursuit of fool's good. Now we are being told that even if we countenance non-strict causal theories where senses *do* play an intrinsic role in natural kind terms, the senses for *'good' in particular* could all be dismissable as never describing real properties. This scenario would really be simply co-extensive with the pervasive fool's good scenario that I was protesting earlier, when senses were not allowed in as relevant at all. The only difference is that it might be thought that being only co-extensive *but not co-intensive* with that scenario that it is not possible to reject this naturalism for being based on a too strict and too implausible causal theory of reference that admits of no senses.

But here a very basic question arises: what could possibly justify this claim that the senses of 'good' are all dismissable out of hand as not really describing properties and facts and real things? We certainly do not say any such thing about senses such as 'the first visible object in the sky in the evening' or 'the city that contains Big Ben' or 'the substance that fills oceans.' If one does not say it of the senses of 'Hesperus' or 'London' or 'water', why does one say it of the sense of 'good'? Nothing else but a scientistic prejudice about the criteria for property existence could lead one to say it. If a sense or description is not purporting to express properties that will play a role (or if it is not expressing properties that are eventually reducible to properties that will play a role)[16] in our basic scientific understanding of the world, if they are not purporting to describe anything that figures in the causal-explanatory scheme of a natural science, then it has nothing but a mere conceptual status. It expresses no real properties. This would be a scientistic prejudice[17] and a question-begging claim on the part of the naturalist. The naturalist was supposed to give an argument for a reduction of value to natural properties and facts by appeal to causal theories of reference and a posteriori identities. Against that argument, a Frege-Moore counter-argument had been presented. If it turns out that in one's response to this counter-argument one is assuming a criterion for property existence that takes for granted the truth of naturalism, the naturalist has begged the question against the counter-argument.

I conclude, then, that the pincer argument, despite these three objections, remains effective, and there is no non-question-begging way out for the naturalist, once one sees its force. I have restricted the presentation of the pincer argument to talk of evaluative notions such as 'good' because that was Moore's target, but the structure of the pincer argument is a perfectly general one and applies to all evaluative notions. So it applies to intentional concepts, if these are indeed normative and not wholly dispositional, i.e., if they are commitments.

3. The last two sections took up Kripke's dialectic of presenting the naturalistically irreducible normativity of intentional states via their contrast with the notion of mental *dispositions*. They have tried to fortify his conclusion with the pincer argument. With that anti-naturalistic argument in place, let me take up the question about how to positively characterize the nature of intentional states if they are not to be characterized naturalistically in terms of dispositions.

In presenting an extension of Moore's argument about values to intentionality in Section 2, I suggested that what it delivers is a notion of beliefs and desires that sees these states as a subject's internal oughts or commitments. This answers the question raised in Section 1: how are we to describe mentality if it is not wholly to be described in dispositional terms, as Oblomov's 'mentality' is? Those aspects of mentality that are not dispositional—and there must be such aspects if we are not all to be thought of as Oblomovs—can now be described as commitments. And I suggested also that once commitments are brought onto center stage in characterizing such states, then, as Kripke rightly pointed out, there is no straightforward naturalistic, functionalist appeal of the relevance of dispositions to intentionality. But I also said there that there is no reason to deny that there are more subtle relations that beliefs and desires, qua commitments, have to the (mental) dispositional states of subjects. Those relations will now be explored.

I have, following some others, called intentional states 'commitments'. What are these?

Take belief. It is sometimes said that when we say that a belief is a commitment, we are saying that we are prepared to defend it against those who deny or challenge it. I should like to disassociate myself from such a conception of commitments. Even if there was something to it, it seems to me to be a superficial feature of commitments. It stresses a social aspect of commitments that does not have to be seen as defining of them, even if it is often true of them. When I think the challenge from another is not worth taking seriously, I would certainly not be prepared to defend my belief. And I may in general not be prepared to listen to others' views. Such indifference to denials of my beliefs cannot possibly threaten the idea of belief as commitment. They do not threaten the claim that I have the beliefs and commitments in question; so it cannot be that being prepared to defend them is a defining feature of commitments. By pointing to the possibility of indifference to denials and challenges to one's beliefs, I don't mean that we could give up on testimony as a source of information and belief acquisition; I mean, rather, that I would not think of my fellows as essential interlocutors, in the sense of questioners and watchdogs of my belief. In general, despite what Rorty and some others say, there is no reason to think that persuading others or justifying oneself to others is an essential aspect of epistemology, even if it is essential to sociability, to intellectual propagation, to self-advancement, etc. And if one sheds the social aspect of this conception of commitment, if one sheds the idea that one justifies and defends one's beliefs against challenges from *others,* then all that is left of the conception is that one would defend a belief against *evidence* to the contrary, and that would in fact be a foolish way to hold a belief qua commitment. Presumably, a commitment should be questioned, not defended, if evidence to the contrary comes in.

This conception of commitments starts off in the wrong direction. Let's try another tack.

A belief or desire, I said in Section 2, was a commitment to believe other things or to do certain things, respectively. And I have denied that we have to be *disposed* to believe or do those things that one is committed to believing and doing by one's beliefs and desires. One *may* be disposed to thinking or doing them, but there is no *requirement* that one be so disposed in order to have the belief or desire, qua commitments. The claim here is quite strong. It says not only that one need not have had to live up to a commitment in order to possess it; one need not even be disposed to do whatever it takes to live up to it.

If that is really so, a question arises as to what really is the difference between someone who has a certain intentional state and someone who lacks it. After all, if one does not have to live up to a commitment in order to have one, and if one does not even have to have the disposition to act so as to live up to it, then it is a real question how one may distinguish the having of the commitment from lacking it.

Simply placing the demand that we can verbalize the commitment with the words "I believe that p" or "I desire that p" will be insufficient, since the words may be phony, and the further demand that the words be sincere does not get us much beyond the initial question. That is to say, to ask, when does someone have a commitment? is not all that far from asking, when is someone's avowal of a commitment sincere? To put it as Polonius might have, "actions speak louder than words," and it is precisely the actions, even potential actions, that go missing if there need be no disposition to act on a commitment in order to have one. So, evidently, some further demand must be placed on the idea of an intentional state than its avowability before one can plausibly be said to think of it as a commitment.

Here is one. We can put it down as a necessary and defining condition of having a commitment. *To have a commitment, one must be prepared to have certain reactive attitudes, minimally to be self-critical or to be accepting of criticism from another, if one fails to live up to the commitment or if one lacks the disposition to do what it takes to live up to it; and one must be prepared to do better by way of trying to live up to it, perhaps by cultivating the disposition to live up to it.*

These defining conditions will play a crucial role in developing the full version of the normative account of agency in Section 4, but in this section, one can see first the sense in which they bring out some part of the normative element of intentional states by stressing the idea of *criticism* of failures. More important, while it brings out the close links between intentional states and dispositions, it does so without abandoning the more crucial normative element, that is, without actually saying that they *are* dispositions, or even saying that they are to be defined *directly* in terms of having the dispositions to do those things that are cases of living up to the commitment.

I say 'directly' because clearly I *have in*directly invoked the idea of dispositions in the characterization of a commitment when I said that in order to be said to have a commitment, one must be prepared to accept criticism for not having the *disposition* to do things that live up to one's commitment or prepared to cultivate the *disposition* to do those things, if one fails to live up to it or if one fails to have the *disposition* to do something that is a living up to it. These are all occurrences of the idea of dispositions in the very characterization of commitments. However, though there is mention of the idea of such dispositions in the characterization of a commitment, there is no requirement that such dispositions actually *be present*. What one is not saying is required in order to have a commitment is that one *has* the disposition to do things that are cases of living up to it. In fact, not only do first-order dispositions not have to be present in order for there to be a first-order commitment, in a sense, they have to be absent for the *in*direct appeal to dispositions above to come into play, since it is the cultivation of absent dispositions that the indirect appeal mentions. To require that those dispositions actually be present would be to invoke dispositions in the 'direct' fashion in the way that I, following Kripke, deny.

But there is an obvious problem here. I have been determined to keep out the *presence* of dispositions in the characterizing of the minimal conditions for having a commitment, but have I not in fact at one level required that dispositions of a certain sort *be* present? How is one to understand the requirement that one be *prepared* to accept criticism for not having lived up to a commitment, when one has failed to live up to it, that one be *prepared* to do better by way of living up to it, etc.? Is this idea of 'preparedness' not just to be thought of as *second-order* dispositions to accept criticism, etc.? And if so, have I not ushered in at the second order precisely what I was keen to keep out at the first, i.e., the presence of dispositions?

I am not particularly invested in keeping out the presence of dispositions at the second order. So I am not invested in resisting this understanding of the idea of 'preparedness' in the minimal conditions characterizing commitments, viz., that the preparedness is just second-order dispositions to accept criticism and to cultivate the necessary first-order dispositions that are absent sometimes[18] when one fails to live up to commitments. Why is that? Doesn't requiring the presence of dispositions at the second order make one vulnerable to the charge that one has in the end conceded everything to the naturalist, who wants to give a dispositionalist analysis of intentional states? It does not. No interesting naturalistic and dispositional analysis of intentional states follows just because one has introduced dispositions into the analysis of intentional states qua commitments in this way. The reason for this is quite straightforward.

If the preparednesses in question were to be understood as the presence of certain sorts of dispositions, dispositions have entered into my characterization of intentional states qua commitments in a way that *is entirely parasitic on first-order commitments.* They have no independent standing, no independent way of being spelled out. They are generated by the simplest and crudest of algorithms that presuppose that something normative like a commitment is inescapably present at the first order.

So, suppose, with me, that intentional states are internal oughts or commitments. And suppose that I have the desires (or beliefs) that p, that q, that r—all of which are to be thought of as commitments. And suppose that I fail to live up to these commitments, and I am not disposed to do anything that lives up to them. I have said that if and when that happens, I must have the 'preparedness' to, among other things, accept criticism for my failure to live up to these commitments. I am worrying now that the preparedness, if it is seen as a second-order disposition, is going to amount to a capitulation to a dispositional analysis of intentional states. And I am soothing my worry with the following thought. The second-order dispositions that each of my preparednesses amounts to can get no characterization but the following: the disposition to accept criticism for not having lived up to the commitment that p, the disposition to accept criticism for not having lived up to the commitment that q, the disposition to accept criticism for not having lived up to the commitment that r.[19] Any effort to characterize the second-order disposition (the preparedness to accept criticism) that leaves out the commitments at the first order from its formulation is going to fall afoul of all the considerations that led one to see intentional states as internal oughts or commitments in the first place, viz., the Kripkean and Moorean open question argument, the Frege style arguments, etc., all of which I mentioned earlier. But if the commitments at the first order always have to be in place in order to characterize the second-order dispositions, then these second-order dispositions (the preparedness to accept criticism for not having lived up to the first-order *commitments,* the preparedness to cultivate the first-order dispositions to do or think things that will live up to the first-order *commitments,* etc.) are simply reeled off algorithmically and parasitically in the manner mentioned above. There is an ineliminable reference to commitments in the analysis of intentional states, even if the analysis requires that dispositions be present at the second order. That is enough to resist the claim that such a dispositional reading of the idea of preparedness in our characterization of commitments capitulates to any interesting naturalistic dispositional analysis of intentional states.[20]

Someone might resist this by insisting that the description of the second-order dispositions that go into the idea of the relevant sorts of preparedness need not ineliminably mention the first-order commitments. The minimal defining conditions for commitments at the first order, on this view, would (in deference to the Moore-Kripke arguments) not require any *first*-order dispositions, but they would require second-order dispositions of various kinds such as the disposition to accept criticism for not having the first-order dispositions to do the actions that the content of the first-order commitments would recognize as livings-up to the commitments. Or they would require second-order dispositions to cultivate first-order dispositions to do those actions. Though I have mentioned the first-order commitments in the description of these second-order dispositions, that mention is eliminable, it will be said. Take my desire (commitment) that I help the poor. The minimal requirement for having this commitment, on this view, would first make clear that actions or sorts of actions satisfy the predicate ("helping the poor') used to specify the content of the commitment. It would then state the requirement that in order to have that commitment I must minimally have a disposition to accept criticism for not having done each of those actions or to accept criticism for not having the disposition to do those actions, and I must have a disposition to cultivate the disposition to do those actions. (And normative talk of accepting 'criticism' would itself have to be redescribed in terms of complex dispositions of various sorts.) In this statement of the minimal defining conditions of a commitment, there will inevitably be a very complicated set of nested and disjunctive dispositions that will have to be mentioned, but if they are complicated enough, no mention at all of the commitment being defined need be made. There might be a problem as to whether what is common to all these dispositions can be made out without mention of the commitment they are trying to define. But that may not seem to the dispositionalist to be an insuperable problem, in principle. We therefore have a naturalistic dispositional analysis of commitments, he will claim.

But we don't have anything of the kind, because *even if* he can overcome the problem just raised, which he has dismissed as not being insuperable in principle (something that is not obvious at all), the Moore-Kripke argument raises its head again.

Suppose that I have these complicated second-order dispositions, purporting to give a naturalistic definitional analysis of commitments. I can still ask non-trivially, "I have all these second-order dispositions, but *ought* I to help the poor?" If that is a genuinely *non*-trivial question, then one cannot define the first-order commitment in terms of (or we cannot identify the first-order commitment with) these complicated second-order dispositions. If I answer "yes" to this non-trivial question, I have announced something *over and above* the complicated second-order dispositions I see myself as having. I have made or announced a commitment. The dispositionalist in order to make his case would have to say that this is a trivial question, akin to asking, "Here is an unmarried man, but is he a bachelor?"; and therefore if the answer is affirmative, *nothing* over and above the possession of the second-order dispositions is announced. But to say that is to misdescribe things. That is the whole point of the Moorean open question argument, and it is force of the remarks from Kripke that I quoted earlier in the chapter. It follows that there is no avoiding mention of the first-order commitments in characterizing the second-order dispositions that constitute the relevant sorts of preparedness that define what commitments are. The only way in which Moore's argument lapses, the only way in which the question Moore raises ceases to be an open or non-trivial question in this context, the only way in which it can be akin to raising the question about bachelors, is if the specification of the second-order dispositions *do* mention the first-order commitments. But in that case there is no problem to begin with, since it in effect thwarts the naturalistic and reductive aspirations of the appeal to dispositions. The lesson in all this is that we can and should, without any anxiety about capitulating to naturalism, allow a *defining* second-order dispositional element in the characterization of intentional states qua commitments.

So the dialectic is really this. In this section I have not tried to give *an argument* for why intentional states, which are normative states, i.e., commitments, cannot be reduced naturalistically to dispositions. That argument was presented over the last two sections, and I have just repeated a fragment of it in the last paragraph. In this section I am only trying to give a characterization of intentional states as commitments, a characterization that if it appeals to dispositions (at the second order) does so without any naturalistic intent. If someone (the interlocutor I have just addressed) says that it *is* quite *possible* to appeal to them at the second order with naturalistic intent, nothing that I have said in this section gives one an argument against that. All I am doing in this section is to say that it is perfectly *possible* to appeal to second-order dispositions in characterizing intentional states *without* that appeal being naturalistic. If my interlocutor insists on the appeal to second-order dispositions being naturalistic, what I need to do (in fact, what I have just done in the last paragraph) is to appeal to (part of) the argument I have already given in the last two sections to show that that appeal must fail.

At the outset, I had said that I would be probing, on behalf of the anti-naturalist convinced of the deep normativity of intentional states, how clean a break intentional states can make from dispositions. It is turning out that the appeal to second order dispositions in characterizing commitments means that it is quite all right to say that the break need not be complete. A less-than-complete break can still leave the naturalistic irreducibility and normative status of intentional states quite intact.

It may seem odd that one is making appeal to a notion of disposition that is *not* naturalistic, since paradigmatically the notion of dispositions is central to naturalistic philosophical treatments of the mind. But that oddity can be amicably resolved by disambiguation.

Dispositions on all accounts of them have a counterfactual component. They are states that in certain circumstances—not necessarily actual, but when actual—will be manifested. But dispositions are *also* widely thought of as states with a causal component, which makes them part of the causal nexus of nature, in a familiar naturalistic understanding of 'nature'. These are two quite different components in our understanding of dispositions, and it is not compulsory that the former component must be understood in terms of the latter, or as requiring or entailing the latter. When philosophers say that the counterfactual component has underlying it a causal mechanism or a scientific-realist causal basis, we are adding a further and substantive component to what we mean by dispositions. So we may, if we wish, speak sometimes of dispositions in very minimal terms, in terms only of the first component, without the second.[21] When we do so, there is no reason to think that dispositions are to be naturalistically understood.

I have made central to one's understanding of intentional states qua normative states or commitments a pair of second-order dispositions. And the challenge to me was, How can I characterize them, and therefore the commitments themselves that are defined in terms of them, in non-naturalistic terms, when the usual understanding of the notion of dispositions in the philosophical study of the mind assumes that mental dispositions are naturalistic states? My answering thought has been that the only sense of dispositions that commitments require in their characterization is one that is minimally characterized in terms of the first, counterfactual component only.

No doubt, and with some right, it will be asked that I say more than

I have about what is meant by a notion of disposition that is not naturalistic and that I do so by saying more about what underlies this counterfactual component, if it is not the standard causal and psychologistic picture familiar from naturalistic conceptions of dispositions. There ought to be no objection even to the use of the term 'cause' in expounding this notion of disposition that is built into the idea of a commitment—so long as the sense of cause it expresses is not spelled out along naturalistic lines. I will say more about this in Section 4. But for now, we may tentatively rest with the conclusion that the normative notion of intentional states such as beliefs and desires, shown by the argument given in Sections 2 and 3 to be naturalistically irreducible, can be characterized as I have in this section in terms that appeal to higher-order dispositions, without spoiling their naturalistically irreducible status.

Let me now fortify the general claims I have been promoting in this chapter so far against objections that might be raised on Davidson's behalf.

To quickly recapitulate those claims: In introducing the distinction between genuinely normative states and dispositions as ordinarily understood, with a view to claiming that intentional states are the former sorts of states, I have been resisting philosophers like Davidson, who have no truck with the idea that intentional states are commitments and would like to retain the idea that intentional states are dispositions and account for the normativity of intentional states in other ways, ways that I have claimed are, in the light of Moore's and Kripke's arguments, misleadingly underdescribed. It would not be a very clear or explicit way of keeping faith with what is established by Moore and Kripke to account for the normativity of intentional states by saying— as Davidson does—that they are dispositions 'governed' by principles of normativity. The clearer and more explicit way of doing so, rather, is to say that intentional states are *themselves* normative states. Having recognized this, calling them internal oughts or 'commitments' is natural and proper.

It is tempting to resist the claim that beliefs and desires are *themselves* commitments by saying that we have no other commitments but commitments to think (believe, desire, etc) in accord with the principles of rationality that govern thought. If we have any commitments, it is to these principles. There are no commitments other than to think logically and rationally, and these minimal commitments do not make the thoughts (which we are committed to being rational) *themselves* commitments. The temptation to say this might be justified as follows:

> It will be said, You began this chapter as follows. We often have critical reactive attitudes to dispositions, even to our own dispositions, and you raised a question, which is, By what lights do we make these critical reactions? And you proceeded to provide an argument (the pincer argument) for the conclusion that these will have to be thought of as normative states or commitments; they cannot themselves be dispositions in some naturalistic sense. Thinkers cannot be like the radical Oblomov; thinkers cannot be creatures of mere and comprehensive dispositionality. They must possess commitments or internal oughts as well as dispositions, and commitments cannot be equated with holistically characterized dispositions, as the naturalist would like. All this is fine. But there is no need to say that *each belief and desire* is itself a commitment. It is enough in answering your question (By what lights do we criticize dispositions?) to concede to you that we do so by normative lights that involve normative states such as commitments but then restrict the normative states of commitments *just to the lights*. That is, restrict commitments to the rational principles by the lights of which we criticize dispositions, when we do. There is no need to also say that each belief and desire is a commitment. We only have commitments to the normative lights by which we criticize dispositions of ours, and those lights are contained in the principles of rationality. Each belief and desire does not have to be a commitment in order to provide the lights by which we criticize our dispositions.

This would capture what Davidson expresses very cryptically and perhaps even misleadingly (at the very least, not very explicitly) by saying that the principles of rationality 'govern' and 'guide' and 'constrain' our beliefs and desires. But even though he may have been cryptic and misleading in the way he expressed it, he would have provided a good reason not to embrace what I am suggesting—that our beliefs and desires are themselves normative states such as commitments. (After reading a draft of this chapter, Davidson did make exactly this point to me.)

But this is not convincing. If thoughts themselves were not commitments, and the only commitments we had were to the principles of logic and of rationality generally, then in the following scenario, we would get quite the wrong instruction. Suppose I believed that p, and in a fit of distraction, I also went on to assent to something inconsistent with 'p' (to put it at its crudest for the sake of convenience, say, 'not-p'). Then the only thing that the commitments to the principles of rationality would oblige me to do would be to get rid of the inconsistency. The only instruction coming from them would be: "Get rid of either the belief that p or withdraw assent from not-p." But it is obvious that in this scenario the fully right instruction is not that; rather, it is much more specific. It is: "Withdraw assent from 'not-p'." Just by the way the scenario has been set up, it is obvious that the instruction, "Clean up your act and get rid of the inconsistency" is not a specific enough instruction. But it is the only instruction that the commitment to the basic principles of rationality gives us. If we want the more specific instruction we should be getting in this scenario, we have to acknowledge that beliefs themselves are commitments. That is to say, we have to acknowledge that all that I *believe* in this scenario is p, which is therefore my only commitment, and that 'not-p' is just a distracted assertion that does not genuinely express a belief, i.e., a commitment.

This gives a compelling reason to think of intentional states as themselves normative states or commitments, and once we do so, the striking relevance of the Moorean and Fregean arguments of Sections 2 and 3 comes into focus. If they are *themselves* values, and Moore's argument (with some help from Frege) is designed to show that values are not natural properties, intentional states are thereby immediately demonstrated to be irreducible to naturalistic dispositional properties.

However, Davidson may still insist that he too has come to the conclusion that beliefs and desires are not naturalistically reducible; and he may deny that he needs to say that they are themselves commitments in order to do so. The argument he provides for this conclusion in fact assumes that intentional states are dispositions, not commitments, and goes on to say that being *mental* dispositions they (unlike physical dispositions and physical states, generally) are constrained by rationality principles that have no echo in the natural sciences, and as a result these mental dispositions will not be integrated in any serious way with the dispositional or categorical states posited by the natural sciences. This is his thesis of the 'anomalousness of the mental'. Quite independently of considering this argument of his, I have tried to give reasons (in the paragraph before the last one) for why he is wrong to deny that mental states are commitments. But now what should we make of this argument from 'the anomalousness of the mental' for the naturalistic irreducibility of intentional states? How does it compare with the argument we have given in Sections 2 and 3 for the same conclusion?

It does not compare favorably precisely because it fails to see a certain integrity or integration, which I have been trying to promote. Let me explain.

We have concluded, via an argument of Moore (with some supplementation by Frege), that value in general is irreducible to natural properties. Davidson no doubt agrees with that general conclusion. (He has to agree with the conclusion since the notion of norm or value plays a role in his own argument for the naturalistic irreducibility of intentionality; so if value was reducible to natural properties, his argument would presumably be rendered ineffective.) He wants to conclude on the basis of his argument from the 'anomalous' nature of the mental that there is *another* irreducibility, that of intentional properties to natural properties. However, if we take intentional states to be commitments *themselves,* we do not need to conclude that there are two irreducibilities here. The first one is enough. If intentional states are commitments, they *are* oughts or values, and the first argument (the Moore-Frege argument) shows that values are naturalistically irreducible. This therefore suggests that Kripke is not merely more clear and explicit; he is simpler and neater about what really is at stake in thinking of intentional states as irreducible. And when we add to this the added advantage of being given the right instruction for what to do when we assent distractedly to things that are inconsistent with our beliefs, the idea that intentional states are themselves commitments begins to look much the more plausible philosophical view of them.

To pursue the contrast between Kripke's and Davidson's picture of the normativity of intentional states a little further, notice that seeing desires and beliefs as commitments requires us to distinguish between two different questions: (1) "Why did someone do what she did?" and

(2) "Did what she did live up to her commitments?" These questions cannot be made to coincide. (This point is not made by Kripke but is surely implied by some of the quotations from Kripke I cited above.) In fact, on a certain interpretation of the issues to be elaborated at length in the next section, the question, "Did her doing live up to her commitments?" is *not really even in view* while we are raising the explanatory question, "Why did someone do what she did?" It is not in view if we interpret the latter question as a demand for an 'explanation' that cites causes, as causes are standardly understood. And equally, on this interpretation, asking the normative question would be out of view while posing the causal-explanatory question. This failure of each question to be in view while asking the other is just a special case of the first person point of view being radically disjoint from the third person point of view. I will say more about such inter-perspectival disjointness in the next section,

In the standard naturalistic picture, the explanatory question about why someone did what she did can be answered by citing such things as dispositions and motives. (They may also in a quite different picture be answered by citing commitments, but it is only after we take up the issue of the perspectival duality I just mentioned that we would be able to say just what sort of illumination this would bring as an answer to the explanatory question.) But the second question is answered by looking to whether actions are in accord with one's intentional states, i.e., with one's commitments. That is a quite different kind of thing than the answer to the first question.

Davidson, however, despite being an anti-naturalist, has nevertheless not been too eager to distinguish between these two questions in the way being insisted on here; and that is of a piece with him not making a clean distinction between dispositions and intentional states. He makes a gesture toward the irreducibly normative status of the mental dispositions that he takes intentional states to be by saying that when one invokes them in answering the first question, one adds a normative element of 'making sense' to the explanations involved that are not present in the explanations in the physical domain. And he says that he prefers, therefore, to use the term 'rationalization' rather than 'explanation' to describe the answers to the first question. But that bit of nomenclature does nothing to distinguish between the two questions in the radical way that is essential to making a clean break between intentional states and dispositional states, as well as essential to understanding what makes intentional states irreducible, i.e., that they are not dispositions at all in the sense that Davidson is willing to say they are. (When, in Chapter 2 during the discussion of transparency, I had not myself made the clean break between viewing intentional state as commitments and as dispositions, I too had used the term 'rationalize' to mark the normative element in the relations between beliefs and desires and the actions they explain. I have nothing against the terminology, but I do insist that terminological moves of that kind don't address the question of the need for the clean break and the need to distinguish sharply between the two questions in a way that Davidson fails to do.) Why, then, does he not distinguish sharply between them?

Because of a firm conviction on his part—a conviction that has pervaded his philosophy of mind and language—*that we are by and large disposed to do what is in accord with our commitments.*

This idea, which he sometimes presents as a necessary form of charity (something that is not an option in interpreting others' words, thoughts, and actions),[22] convinces him that the two questions cannot diverge in any radical sense. And because he thinks the two questions are not really radically divergent, he sees no compulsion to think that beliefs and desires are commitments in the first place.

By contrast, in the picture in which the two questions are radically separated, things are not like that. One does what one does because of one's dispositions, motives, etc. The relations between one's doings and these states we cite in answering the first question are causal. Whether or not these doings are in accord with our commitments is not a question about causality but another question about another relation altogether. However, if one is convinced, as Davidson is, that we do, by and large, do what we are 'committed' to, then one would find it an unnecessary scruple to keep apart the relations between one's doings and their psychological causes from the relations between one's doings and the 'commitments' with which they are (as he sees it) by and large in accord. Given that conviction in the idea of 'charity', we could simply *identify* the 'commitments' with the states that we cite when we answer the question, why did someone do what she did? In other words, one need not feel any particular theoretical pressure to see why 'commitments' and dispositions should be distin-

guished in the first place (thus my placing of 'commitment' in cour-
tesy quotes throughout while expounding his position). This is the
thinking that underlies his identification of intentional states with dispositions, despite recognizing the normative element in intentional
states, despite recognizing that there is a normative question about
actions being *in accord* with one's intentional states.[23]

There is a subtle qualification that is necessary at this point. It is
not that I want to deny Davidson's basic point here, which he erects
into a principle, 'a principle of charity'. (We really should call it the
principle of 'necessary' charity, since he is very clear that it is not an
option, which charity presumably is.) If we formulate the principle of
necessary charity as follows, it does not deserve the notoriety it has
fetched: we cannot be creatures who are massively irrational without
ceasing to be thought of as creatures with a sophisticated level of
intentionality. If this principle were not true, one would be hard put
to say why the maple tree in front of my window does not have all the
sophisticated form of intentionality that I have, hard put to say why
it does not have all of this intentionality but simply sits stationary in
the park outside because it is massively irrational, massively weak-
willed, say. Being weak-willed, it lacks all the dispositions that would
allow it to live up to all these commitments that comprise its intentionality. We could not rule out this absurd hypothesis that the tree
is an intentional creature without admitting to the minimal claim of
his principle. The impossibility of massive irrationality that the principle of necessary charity demands is what allows us to rule out the
hypothesis we find absurd. The principle, therefore, has a point.

If this much is right in what he says, where then does Davidson go
wrong? He goes wrong in drawing quite the wrong conclusion from
this principle; he goes wrong in identifying what exactly it is that this
principle defines. What I have just admitted to being right in the
principle suggests that all it defines is what it is to be a subject with
a sophisticated level of intentionality. To be such a subject one cannot
be massively irrational in just the way that the principle claims. However, Davidson explicitly uses the principle not just to define a *subject*
who can be properly said to possess intentional states of a certain
level of sophistication but to define the very idea of an *intentional
state*. He has repeatedly said that what it shows is that our very idea
of an intentional state is the idea of a state where the dispositional

element and the normative element tend to converge. In other words, the principle of necessary charity has the effect of showing that it is built into the nature of a desire (and a belief) that its possessor will by and large do (and believe) and be disposed to do (and believe), what its normative element requires her to do (and believe).[24] And convinced that it has this effect, he sees no reason to distinguish between the question, 'Why did somebody do what he did?" which is answered by citing his dispositional states, motives, etc., as radically separate from the question, "Did what he do live up to his commitments?" The idea of an intentional state *itself being* an internal ought or commitment, as distinct from a disposition, therefore never so much as occurs to him.

But the principle of charity does not and cannot define *what an intentional state is;* it can only define *what it is to be a creature with intentional states* (of a certain level of complexity). Minimal rationality requirements (even generously understood) can only rule out the absurd hypotheses that certain sorts of subjects such as trees be counted as sophisticated intentional subjects; it cannot rule out the distinction between the very idea of commitments and dispositions. Despite his principle that shows what is required to be a subject of sophisticated intentionality, there is in fact always *enough failure* on the part of such a subject to live up to his commitments to see the distinction between disposition and commitment as having a deep theoretical point and place.[25] If there was *no* failure (or hardly any), then one could perhaps avoid making the distinction and say that intentional states are dispositions, though even that is doubtful.[26] But things are manifestly not like that. Nothing in his principle, therefore, allows it to be used in the way that Davidson does; and it is only his illicit extrapolation from using the principle to define a subject possessing intentional states to using it to define the very nature of intentional states that screens him off from seeing the importance of radically separating the two questions mentioned above and from making the clean distinction between intentional states and dispositions that Kripke is insisting on.

I should add that this view of beliefs and desires as themselves being commitments does not have the problems dealing with the fact of fairly widespread irrationality that Davidson has. For Davidson, because the normativity of intentional states enters as something that (via his principle of charity) constitutes *dispositional* states such as beliefs and desires, he has to deal in some special way with the *fact of irrationality* by a further notorious gerrymandering, whereby human minds are divided in two. With such a division of the mind, *each* divided half of the mind *is* after all rational in line with the constitutive demands of rationality (laid down by his principle of charity), despite the fact of irrationality in the undivided subject.[27] No such gerrymandering is required to deal with the fact of irrationality once we see the normative element in intentionality enter by viewing intentional states such as beliefs and desires as themselves normative states or commitments rather than dispositions. Now irrationality is just the simple and natural and unstrained idea that human subjects have failed to live up to their commitments.

4. There are some highly significant implications—indeed, I should say advances—brought by the broadly Kripkean way of stressing the relevance of normativity to intentional states that I have been pressing over Davidson's way of doing so. The conclusions to follow eventually in the next section regarding the conceptual basis for authority will depend crucially on these advances. They will depend, that is, on the normative relevance yielding the notion of commitments and not a notion of dispositions 'governed' by norms.

There is much to be elaborated in this long section before we derive our conclusions about authority in the next. Thinking of intentional states as commitments has the following implications, which will now be spelled out at length.

First, it will help us to see much more fully and exactly what is meant by the integration of agency with value that was first presented in Chapter 2. And in doing this, it will reveal just how deep and significant the distinction between the first person and the third person point of view is to any anti-naturalist philosophy regarding value and intentionality. This, in turn, will loop back and illuminate the normative conception of agency and freedom by showing what the element of normativity does to transform the notion of causality and causal explanation of behavior so as to allow for agency, a theme that has exercised a number of anti-naturalist philosophers, such as Davidson, McDowell, and others, in a very interesting way.

If all of the criticisms of Davidson in the last section are right, the question arises, what remains of his idea that intentional states cause and are part of the causal explanation of our behavior? Quite apart from Davidson, there is a closely related question that we had left hanging a little while ago. Having admitted that a certain sort of second-order disposition is part of the characterization of commitments, it was also made clear that the relevant notion of disposition was not a naturalistic one in that if it rested on a notion of causality, it was not in any standardly understood sense of causality. At that point, I had said that there was a minimally counterfactual component in the defining of such dispositions, to which one *need or need not* add a further substantive claim that it was underpinned by a *naturalistic* causal element. (However, see note 31 for more on this.) In particular, I went on to say that the sorts of dispositions that were involved in the characterization of commitments do not have such an underpinning. It is a fair demand to ask: what then, is the counterfactual component underpinned by if not *that* sort of causal element?

It has been argued that there are two separable questions: (1) Why did someone do what she did? And (2) did her doing live up to her commitment? If these are so separate, if the former is only a descriptive question as Kripke says and not a normative one like the latter, if commitments are really irrelevant to the former—or if relevant, relevant in a carefully guarded and qualified way to be spelled out soon—then there are at best a very carefully guarded and qualified causal point and efficacy that normative states, which we are insisting beliefs and desires are, have. What point and efficacy do they have?

All the care and the guardedness, obviously, will have to go in making sure that we describe the causal point and efficacy of commitments differently from the causal role of first-order dispositions. What we say about the question of the causal relation between commitments and our doings better keep faith with what we have characterized commitments to be: that they require the presence of no first-order dispositions but, at most, require a preparedness to accept criticism for not having lived up to them and the preparedness to try and do better by way of living up to them. On the basis of this characterization, we can (serially) say *two* things about the causality that attaches to commitments, and I will now elaborate these two things over the rest of this section. (The reader is warned that the passage from the first to the second of these will involve some delay because it will require an extensive intermediate presentation of the idea of a 'duality of perspectives'.)

The first of the two points will be to make clear that commitments have a certain very distinctive and highly insubstantial sort of causal power *built into* them, and its insubstantiality is reflected in the fact that it is only describable in very uninformative terms, such as: *our commitments cause us to try and live up to them.* To make this sort of causal claim is quite different from saying that they cause us to do what we do, where these doings are specified in terms quite independent of the uninformative description of them as 'attempts to live up to the commitments' in question.

And then in the second of the two points, I will try and show later—after some more apparatus is introduced having to do with a certain first and third person perspectival duality—that this first *built-in* aspect of its causal power, this stress on the second-order dispositions to accept criticism and to try and do better when we fail to live up to our commitments, makes an enormous difference to how we are to understand our causal talk regarding commitments that *does* aspire to be *more* informative. That is to say, I will try and show—in a way that others who talk of *singular causal explanation* of human behavior have failed to do—what exactly it is that makes citing a belief and desire as a cause of an action a very different kind of causal talk from the standard causal explanatory talk.

Here is the first point.

Let me expand just a little on what I mean by the 'built-in' causal element. This causal element, registered in the uninformative idea that commitments cause us to live up to them, is something very insubstantial because it points to nothing more than what is already built into the very characterization of a commitment. The kind of second-order dispositions that we built into the characterization of commitments in the form of certain sorts of preparedness yield nothing more than such an uninformative description of the causal role for commitments. Leave alone that the causal role implies no covering laws (something we will discuss when discussing the second of our points), it is much less informative even than that; it is much less informative than most other singular causal statements. *Once we understand what a commitment is,* it adds no extra information, nothing substantial at all, to mention this causal element it has. This should not be surprising. Since, as we saw, commitments are minimally defined in terms of second-order dispositions that we specify in a way that necessarily mentions those very commitments, the causal power that such commitments get from these dispositions is not going to be such that there is any description of those causal powers that can leave out the mention of the commitments themselves. They will have to take the form of saying not that someone's commitment that—or to—x caused him to do y, not even that his commitment to x caused him to do x, but that his commitment to x caused him to try and live up to the commitment to do x. The second-order dispositions (as we have specified them above) that go into characterizing commitments are, after all, specifications of forms of preparedness to accept criticism and to cultivate the dispositions to live up to the commitments. And that just is what is meant by 'trying' to live up to them. The causal power of these second-order dispositions gets us no further than that.

Once we have the notion of commitments in place and, as a result, once we see that intentional states involve dispositions only in a sense that the causal element underlying them is so explanatorily powerless, we get a glimpse of why attempts at explanations citing intentional states were familiarly and routinely found by many to be so unhelpful, compared to other forms of explanation. The relative uninformativeness of *this particular* causal point that is *built into* intentional states viewed as commitments is just a reflection of the fact that it is perhaps more teleological than anything else. All it does is define an area of the mind that is goal directed (though, of course, there is no extrapolation to any generalized teleology in which minds are not in play). Davidson spent a lot of remarkable philosophical effort and ingenuity in seminal and influential papers arguing that a series of 'little red books', as he called them, were completely off the mark in denying that reasons can be causes, which can be invoked in illuminating causal explanations.[28] But I think that Davidson missed the fact that this is the causal aspect of our intentionality that these books were groping for. They had not, of course, formulated the notion of commitments, so this aspect of cause was not very explicit in what they actually said. Yet it is not as if it was altogether undetectable beneath the surface of their somewhat undeveloped talk of 'reasons' standing apart from causes and in one or two cases even talk of a teleological element that 'reasons' bring with them.[29] I will admit that some of the ways in which they did try and develop this core of what they got right was unclear and misleading and laid them open for Davidson's critique of their views. I will try and develop this core somewhat differently in the second point that I make below. Still, I did want to record a note of sympathy with those books, which I think did contain enough hints to allow us the thought that we have been endorsing; viz., "Why did someone do what she did?" and "Is what she did in accord with her commitments" are two questions that cannot be yoked together as Davidson tried to do without doing violence to something basic about the normative element in intentionality.

If that normative element of intentionality involves (second-order) dispositions, thought of in minimal counterfactual terms, it is a fair question, as I admitted, to ask what underpins that minimal counter-factual element. And it has even been admitted that the idea that something causal must underlie it need not be denied. But I have insisted that one clear sense of the causal powers that are *built into* intentional states when they are *themselves thought to be commitments* does not reveal much more than this: in specifying intentional states, we are specifying elements of a sort of goal directedness that is quite peculiar to human beings. That notion of causal power gives no succor to the naturalist.

Let me now move to the second point I mentioned above.

As I said earlier, there is also an intuition that even if we do not think of cause naturalistically, we still have a slightly more informative and more ambitious understanding of the causal relations in which commitments stand to our doings than was just presented in the first point. We have an intuition that we can cite commitments as causes of our actions and say something *more informative* than is allowed by this built-in causal element (which allows us at best to say that a commitment causes us to try and live up to it) *without going over to the idea* that citing such causes implies laws as it does in a Humean and a naturalistic picture of things. And I have said that I have no objection to using the term 'cause' in this more ambitious way, so long as it genuinely squares with the normative nature of the relations at stake. But if they are to square with them, that does, in turn, mean that one's describing them as causal relations should not amount to a complacence about how we are to understand those relations when they are so deeply embedded in the normative. In particular, it is quite misleading to say something like the following, as McDowell, for instance, has.[30] There is a more basic notion of cause that is in-volved in the relations between intentional states and actions, and it is this very notion of cause that is given a different kind of elaboration when we look at relations that hold between states that involve no intentionality. The latter elaboration is a naturalistic one that has the causes implying laws as Hume demands, whereas the former does not.[31]

Before saying why McDowell's position is unsatisfactory, first let's spell out just a little more why, in the first place, there is at least a prima facie problem that *everyone* (naturalist of every kind and anti-naturalist of every kind) faces when they try to give causal explanations citing beliefs and desires. Hume had claimed that cause implies laws, and a familiar Humean tradition down to this day requires that causal explanations have their statements of singular causes subsumed under laws. These laws, in the special sciences particularly, may be quite hedged by ceteris paribus clauses, which hold things steady or equal, but they will nevertheless provide illumination by subsuming the particular case under the true generalization they offer. However, when we cite intentional states such as beliefs and desires as causes of actions, it seems, prima facie at least, that we cannot come up to the demands of this Humean ideal, at least not without spoiling the illumination that the ideal's appeal to covering generalizations is supposed to bring. On the face of it, the citing of a specific intentional cause of an action cannot be subsumed under such generalizations because generalizations about what people will do when they have a certain belief and a certain desire are almost certainly false. To say, for instance, that anyone who desires that he help the poor and believes that giving money to a charity will be the best way to help the poor will give money to a charity is to say something obviously false. And adding a ceteris paribus clause to say that they will give money to charity, all things being equal, is to add something that is too carte blanche to retain the illumination that the generalization is supposed to bring. Ceteris paribus clauses in the cases where intentionality is involved have a "whatever it takes" quality that is quite different from the ceteris paribus clauses in the generalizations in the various special sciences where no intentional states are involved. This is because there is no ex ante specification of the sorts of things that have to be held steady or equal, when we are dealing with explanations invoking intentional states. We have no clear idea in advance of the kinds of things that are to be held steady—there are not only indefinitely many things that could spoil the generalization but also indefinitely many *kinds* of things that do, and so there is no scope for bringing these things under general descriptions in advance and saying that these kinds of things are to be held equal. We can at best, ex post, keep adding to the list of the kind of things to be held steady after a generalization is falsified in specific cases. If we tried to give ex ante general descriptions of what is to be held steady, we would have to say something that is so unspecific and so capacious and accommodating that it would evacuate the generalization of its power to illuminate. Therefore, any ceteris paribus clause that actually made a generalization of the form "If anyone believes x and desires y, he will do z" true will inevitably amount to something like: "If anyone believes x and desires y, then, if he is rational, he will do z." A covering generalization, with such a ceteris paribus clause, is not illuminating at all. It approximates the unilluminating quality of virtus dormativa explanations. This, I think, is the basic ground for thinking that the Humean ideal is highly problematic for explanations that cite intentional states as causes. And it yields the prima facie question for all positions on the explanation of behavior: how can we stick with the idea that it is causal explanation at all if we give up on the Humean ideal? Different positions, Humean and anti-Humean, have given various responses to it.

The response that I am calling complacent simply says and stops at saying that the explanation is provided by citing a cause that is frankly non-Humean and singular, with no claim to generality underlying it. What sort of answer is this? Does it not abandon the notion of cause, as normally understood, for some other? To say 'no' to this (as McDowell does), to say that there is a single notion of cause, which in some cases (the ones that do not involve intentionality) may or in other cases (the ones that do involve intentionality) may not be overlaid with further demands of a Humean kind for covering laws, is what I am finding complacent.

It simply won't do to claim support for this view by suggesting that we have had this notion of cause long before science—understood in terms of laws and generalizations—came into the picture. It won't do because we also had the notion of a star before science in that sense came along, but we are not tempted to say that the ancient notion of a star is the more fundamental one and the modern scientific notion is just a specific elaboration of it for some stars and not others. Rather, we say that science corrected the ancient notion of a star, and the ancient notion of a star must now simply lapse. So if we don't want the singular causal use to lapse in that way, if we want to continue to use the term 'cause' to talk of the relations between commitments and actions, we will have to do some philosophical spadework, which may well involve having to think of it as an essentially different notion and to give a sense of why it seems proper to use it in this quite different way and spell out in what sense it is different.

As will become clearer just below, my own view is that there is no way to do any of this, and indeed, more generally, there is no way to consistently oppose naturalism in the deep way that is required, unless one acknowledges a certain disjointness between the agential, first personal, normative, and engaged perspective, on the one hand, and the third personal and detached perspective, on the other. *And it is in the context of this distinction that we will be able to ground the idea that there are two quite different notions of cause in play* when we talk, on the one hand, of the relations that hold between intentional states and actions and, on the other, of the relations that hold between non-intentional states and events.

McDowell denies that there is any ambiguity in the notion of cause, even though citing some causes makes commitment to laws and citing other causes is done in self-standing singular causal statements. Now, it is not the singularity in itself that is the problem with this view. I myself don't see how the singularity can be avoided. The problem is how it is that it can both be singular and be the same notion of cause as is found when there are covering laws. If the notion of cause is the same as that which applies to cases where subsuming laws are available, we need to know why we have a unitary notion of cause at work here. If it really is a unitary notion of cause, if it really is the same notion of cause as that which is in play in the relations that hold between phenomena studied by natural science, then it is mysterious why the relations that hold in the intentional realm stand apart in this way from the rest.

McDowell will, no doubt, point out that it is the normative aspects of intentional states, the fact that they are, in his phrase, 'answerable to norms' that makes us put aside the Humean demand that causes imply laws. But we need to know, *what about* the normative element forces us to put it aside? After all, Davidson too believed very strongly in the normative aspect of intentional states, but he never thought that it provided any reason to put aside the Humean demand on causality, and it is because he did not do so that he had to claim that mental states were token-identical with physical states. It was this identity that, for him, allowed mental causes to fall under the generalizations that Hume demanded. McDowell opposes Davidson's claims to such identity, and I believe he is right to do so. But then we need to hear more from him—in a way we do not need to hear from Davidson—about why he is adopting the idea that cause does not imply laws and why this is the same notion of cause as when causes do fall under laws. Just pointing to the normative element in intentionality is insufficient.

For Davidson, the problem arises in a slightly different way. If intentional states cause actions in the same sense as other states and events cause other sorts of things, then presumably both intentional states and non-intentional states are one in being causal and dispositional states; they are both tendencies in nature—it's just that the kinds of dispositions intentional states are make them stand apart from the others. They are unintegrated with other dispositions and tendencies in nature studied by the sciences. But, on the face of it, how can one make out the case that intentional psychological dispositions are unintegrated with the others if they are all causal, dispositional states and tendencies in the same sense? Pointing out that mental states are token-identical with physical states does not really help with *this* question because the question of whether or not there are such integrations is at the level of the sciences and their explanations, not at the level of ontology where Davidson himself places the matter of token identity. So Davidson's saying that intentional states, as dispositions, are not integrated with the dispositional (or categorical) states posited by the other sciences, such as biochemistry, say, sounds like a dogmatic assertion of what is needed in order to be an anti-naturalist about intentional states. We don't say solubility is a disposition that is not integrated with the dispositional and categorical states posited by chemistry, so why do we say it of mental dispositions? Here too, pointing out, as he repeatedly did, that intentional states are governed by constitutive principles of rationality does not go far enough because Davidson nowhere makes satisfyingly clear *what about* this fact places them out on a limb, unintegrated with the states posited by other sciences. After all, all of the special sciences have their own constitutive principles that govern the phenomena they study, but one is not forced by that fact to say that the dispositional states that they identify stand out on a limb in this way.

Pointing to the relevance of the normative to intentionality as both McDowell and Davidson do, though it certainly points in the right direction, does not allow us to go as far as is needed to ground the conclusion that singular causal explanations are all that we can have when intentionality is involved. As a result, the conclusion itself sounds like a dogmatic (at the very least, a premature) assertion.

I will in a little while try and say something less dogmatic and peremptory about what underlies the singularity in our understanding of explanations that cite intentional states as causes, by integrating the perfectly correct talk of the relevance of the normative to intentional states with the first person point of view of agency. When I do, it will turn out that, though there is no harm in thinking of them in terms of such singularity, that is only so because the notion of cause involved is quite different from the one embraced by naturalists; this ambiguity in the notion of cause (one involved in such explanations, the other as it is presented in a naturalistic conception) will owe to a duality of first person and third person perspectives.

The perspectival duality on which my claims will be based is a very fundamental element in understanding the normative conception of agency that I have been pursuing since Chapter 2. It is in fact a way of developing that conception more fully. Because it is so fundamental to the kind of anti-naturalist position I am taking, let me first spell out at some length what I have in mind by an anti-naturalism that is based on a difference in perspectives and then return to the matter of causal relations that we have been discussing.

Having integrated a normative notion of intentionality with the notion of agency and the first person point of view of agency as I have in the last two chapters, this avowed anti-naturalism can now be seen as having a more radical form than others. (As we shall see below, it is more extreme even than John McDowell's anti-naturalism, which was more extreme than most philosophers could stand.) To fail to bring this radicalism home would have been to fail to get across the full force of the integrations I have been trying to pursue throughout the book.

Here is how I have allowed myself to think of it.

Naturalist views of mind and value go deep in our philosophical and scientific culture. They are often presented as the most obvious truths, denying which places one in some stubborn, pre-modern cast of mind. After all, in the newest and most sophisticated dress, naturalists are not really any longer explicitly asserting crude reductions of mind and value to matter and measurable utilities. They are asserting far weaker identities or dependencies of value and mind on the states of nature posited by the natural sciences, dependencies that they capture in labels such as 'non-reductive materialism' and 'supervenience', some versions of the latter being the weakest available form of naturalism. The air of plausibility that might seem to emerge with these weaker claims also makes it seem as if the anti-naturalist is some sort of extremist or reactionary for opposing them.

Since I have assimilated (literally identified) the anti-naturalism about intentionality or mind with the anti-naturalism about value, it will not matter that I mostly focus my attention on the latter. The point of these claims to weaker dependencies of values on facts (as they are studied and posited by natural science) is to question the self-standing nature of values. Consider one of the weakest of the claimed dependencies. It is apparently the idea that it is implausible to have all the facts of nature fixed (as the fundamental natural sciences fix them) while one allows for variability among values. One should at least be able to predict from some *global* fixing of facts what the values will be, in the following weak form: If certain values are attributed in a world by the exercise of interpretation, and it is then recorded that they are accompanied by a global range of facts as fixed by natural science in that world, then in another world with the same facts, one should be able to fix the same values. It is said that anti-naturalisms that deny this are incoherent.

But once one understands anti-naturalism in the *integrated* sense I am seeking, such a claim to dependency might just be unassessable. If the integrities I am seeking are there to be found, then talk of the domain of values being (globally) dependent on the domain of facts seems to be not quite so easily assertible or deniable.

Recall that we have integrated the domain of *values* with the perspective of *agency*, which in turn has been integrated with the *first person point of view* that only we have on ourselves (i.e., the perspective that makes our self-knowledge quite unlike the knowledge that others might have of us that *is* in a sense akin to perceptual knowledge where we take a third person stance upon our own minds). Therefore, while in the domain of value, one *is* in the perspective of agency and in the first person perspective. (I will say more about this below. See especially note 36 and the text to which it is attached.)[32] And while in this perspective, we cannot so much as state what the phenomena are that a dependency (such as supervenience) is a dependency on. For that requires being in a third person perspective from which the phenomenon of agency is not available. In other words, while looking at things from the perspective of agency, we cannot take the perspective of a *detached* perceiver (a 'third' person) to describe the non-normative facts that values are dependent on and on the basis of which one is supposed to make the global predictions about values for another world containing the same non-normative facts.

Spinoza famously pointed out that one could not possibly predict while deliberating.[33] That is a very significant insight, much to be exploited here, but it is not an isolated insight; it is, au fond, an insight about why values *are* self-standing. That is to say—and this is the point of crucial importance—once the integrities have been established, the very thesis of the irreducibility of value is not something apart from the thesis of the unavailability of the spectator's or predictor's point of view while one is in the agent's point of view, exercising values, deliberating about one's commitments (what I *ought* to do, not what I am disposed to do), etc. Once the integration of agency with value is in place, there is no way to understand the agent's point of view except in terms of a subject deliberating about what she *ought* to do. Equally with that integration in place, it is no longer possible to think of values except in terms of a person's agential point of view where she deliberates about what she ought to do or is moved to do what she ought to do by the normative demands on her, and where she is prepared to accept criticism and is prepared to try and do better if she fails to do what she ought, and so on.

But this creates a principled obstacle to the sort of weaker dependency of intentionality (qua internal oughts or commitments) on the physical facts that we are discussing. Being able to even state the dependency claim requires one to be able to straddle these perspectives. And it is this straddling that is precisely not possible if Spinoza is right. One perspective cancels the other out.[34]

Here is an analogy. Think of what I am calling the first person point of view in terms analogous to the performative aspect of promising. We may of course talk of promises, even our own, in the third person, but in doing so we will be describing things that are essentially performative. We cannot then in our talk of them claim that they are supervenient on descriptive facts. It is not as if one can deny the supervenience thesis either. By refusing to assert it, one is not forced into denying supervenience and saying what seems absurd: that two worlds may be exactly alike in descriptive facts but not in performative facts. That is what I mean by saying that the thesis might be unassessable. Supervenience is not a thesis that is made for, made to fit, the performative aspect of promising. Whatever it fits, it does not fit the performative aspect. That is exactly analogous to the point about the supervenience of values or of intentionality (thought of as values or commitments) on non-evaluative physical or functional facts.

Now, of course, as I have stressed, this claim about the irrelevance of the supervenience thesis to values and intentionality only holds so long as we think of values in terms of the exercise of our first person point of view in questions such as, "What ought I to do?"—in other words, values and intentionality as they (to use my own term) 'integrate' with agency. Without this integration, the naturalist, presenting himself in this more sober guise, can express puzzlement about why one is bringing in questions of first and third person perspectives at all while the subject is his claim regarding the weak dependence of values on natural facts: "Only a claim about value is being made," he will protest. "Why are we, in the midst of making this claim, suddenly being told to consider the Spinozist claim about the unavailability of third person descriptions while in the first person perspective?" Without the integration of value with the first person perspective, there is no obvious answer to this protest. But with that integration in place, the protest is silenced because the relevant evaluative facts (facts about our deliberative intentional life, which is a life trafficking in commitments, about what ought to be done and thought) *are* first personal facts. While in the realm of these facts, the facts described from a third person perspective are not in view—just as the supervenience base of descriptive elements is irrelevant to the *performative* aspect of promising that is supposed to be supervenient on it.

There is a danger of being misled into a mistake here. All this talk of integrating value with agency, as well as the analogy with performatives, may give (and has given)[35] the impression that what is being said only shows that supervenience about *acts of evaluating* is unassessable. But, it will be said, that would still leave in place a supervenience about values or value properties, still leave in place a supervenience about what is being evaluated. John McDowell, in the paper cited in note 30, makes the following remarks that exemplify well this sort of mistake.

> Bilgrami puts great weight on the agentive character of evaluating. And it is surely right that it makes no sense to affirm, or deny, that *actions* [his emphasis] are supervenient on facts that might be in view from a perspective other than of an agent. Actions, performances, are not the right kind of topic for a supervenience thesis. But the agentive character of evaluating cannot undermine the fact that an evaluator makes a claim, says that things are thus and so—for instance that some action is despicable or heroic. So there is something for a supervenience thesis to be about, notwithstanding Bilgrami's point about the agentive character of evaluating. What supervenes on non-evaluative facts is not the action of evaluating, but the kind of thing that is said to be so, and sometimes is so, when someone evaluates something.

It is to quite fail to get the force of the appeal to the integration of value with agency to think that all it can show is that opposition to supervenience must be restricted to opposition to supervenience about *acts* of evaluation. Nothing about that integration and the appeal to a perspectival duality of first and third person bars one from seeing the point as applying to supervenience about what is judged valuable, that is, values themselves or value-properties. It is the thesis of supervenience of values or value-properties on facts (as studied by natural science) that is unassessable, once one understands the integration I have invoked. Let me explain.

What does the first person or engaged and agential perspective have to do with these values or value-properties? Values or value-properties are, *by their nature* (see note 32), properties that are available to the perception and the apprehension of *agents*. One point of my introducing the Oblomov character in Chapter 4 was to make this clear. Oblomov is a figure who lacks the point of view of agency. Now, this does not simply mean that he lacks the ability to make *acts* of evaluating. It equally means that he is incapable of *perceiving* the world as making any normative demands on him. (Indeed, as we saw in the last chapter, he lacks the capacity even to see the world as making the thinnest sorts of normative demands on him; i.e., he does not even see the world as offering him opportunities for action.) This is exactly what is meant by saying that value and agency are integrated. If you lack the first person point of view on yourself and the world, you will not be able to see the world as a world laden with values and value-properties, since it is those properties that prompt your subjectivity to choice and action. You will not perceive it as offering chances for actions or as making normative demands to act.

Let us bring this out with the restricted understanding of the terms 'first' and 'third' person point of view as it is found in the Spinozist dichotomy of 'agent' and 'spectator'. The spectator views the world in a detached way, including scientifically and predictively, and while he does so he cannot view it as making normative demands on him to act or even to ask what ought I to do and deliberate about how to act.[36] The agent views the world in a deliberative, first person mode and asks how he ought to act, but while doing so he cannot view it in a detached, including scientific and predictive, mode. And now construct an Oblomov figure, who only can do the former. Thus, for instance, imagine a less extreme Oblomov than we imagined earlier, one who has one-half of the Spinozist dichotomy but not the other. He has the third person point of view, the point of view within which he can make detached observations and predictions about the world and himself, but he cannot ask what should or ought I to do. He is 'spectator' but not 'agent'. That is to say, he has enough agency to predict and do science and look at the world in a way that is detached generally, but he perceives nothing that make normative demands for action or more generally as offering opportunities and occasions for actions. Unlike the extreme Oblomov we discussed in the last chapter, he has thoughts, and in particular he has enough thoughts to predict and observe with detachment, but none of the sort that move him to do anything. He is simply blind to those facts in (and aspects of) the world that natural science does not study. The value-properties in the world that others (agents) who do have the other half of the Spinozist dichotomy, the first person point of view, can perceive will be nothing to him; they will not move him to action. This blindness to value-properties is part of what it is to be a subject without a first person point of view in Spinoza's sense, the point of view that *engages* with the world. Therefore, the crucial point of the integration of value with agency is just the point that McDowell misses. The precise point of the integration is that values or value-properties about which supervenience makes its claim are properties of a very special sort: *they are properties that are available only to those who do have the agential half of the Spinozist dichotomy, only to those who do have a first person or subjective point of view of engagement, those upon whom these properties can make normative demands and offer opportunities for actions.*

The world consists of these properties as well as the sorts of properties natural science studies. The supervenience thesis claims that the former are weakly and globally dependent on the latter in ways that are familiar and widely studied. And I am saying that that thesis is not assessable precisely because of the Spinozist duality of the agential, engaged, first personal perspective and the third personal, detached perspective. Once the integration of value with agency (an integration that this Oblomov's lack brings out well) is properly understood, it is just this perspectival duality that reveals the duality of value and facts, as studied by natural science. The duality is a duality of agency and passive detachment. But if values and value-properties are deeply linked to agency (as this Oblomov's case brings out), then that duality itself is equally about value and non-evaluative facts.

It is surprising that McDowell—who was one of the pioneers both in stressing that values are perceptible facts or properties in the world and in stressing that, as such facts and properties, they were not to be modeled on primary qualities—should fail to see this integrating point about their link with the first person, agential perspective. Primary qualities do not depend on the capacities and the sensibilities of the perceiver, and that was McDowell's own point (see note 32 again) in saying that if one thought of values along those lines, one would indeed find them 'queer', to use Mackie's terms. It is a very natural way to think of them, in contrast to primary qualities, as being the kinds of facts or properties for which we must have the appropriate sensibility. It is this sensibility that this Oblomov lacks in lacking the point of view of *agency* and engagement with the world. That is the force of the integration of value and agency I am insisting on. It's a small step to arrive at this idea once one sees how wrong it would be to model values on primary qualities. Thus McDowell's remarks, which I have just quoted at length, suggest that he has not quite understood his own position on the subject. His resistance to my skepticism about supervenience is a sign of such a failure to think through where his own ideas should lead him. The integration of agency with value, far from restricting this skepticism to supervenience about *acts* of evaluating on non-evaluative facts, reveals the skepticism to be precisely one regarding supervenience of values and value-properties on non-evaluative properties and facts.

McDowell adds to the remarks I cited above the following conclusion. "Given an action that is, say, despicable, and another exactly like it in all non-evaluative respects, the second must be despicable too. I cannot see that Bilgrami gives reason not to accept that claim, and others like it, as innocuous." It should be clear by now that on my view one should not *deny* the claim that McDowell finds so sensible and innocuous. If one *assumes,* as he does, that there was no duality of perspectives of the sort that my view has sketched, then it would certainly seem extreme and non-sensible to deny that claim. The point McDowell misses is that one is questioning his assumption within which the denial of the claim gives the impression of being extreme and non-sensible. The point is not to deny the claim—but not to assert it, either. The point is to question the assumption within which these assertions seem to get sensibly made and within which their denials seem wild. As I said at the outset, these claims are neither assertible nor deniable. They are not assessable.

It might be thought that the entire Spinozist duality is not plausible since even when one is deliberating in the first person mode about what one *ought* to do as an *evaluator* and when one decides what *to* do as an *agent,* one is deploying third personal knowledge of others and the world. Thus if I deliberate about whether I ought to help the poor and decide affirmatively and form the intention to do so, I do deploy the third personal observational knowledge of facts of nature such as that this or that person needs aid or food, and so on. There is a subtle confusion here.

I don't have to deny this very last way of describing things at all. But I can point out that it makes all the difference that I am describing the person or persons as being *in need.* To do so is to observe a fact that is *laden with value* in the sense that I perceive it to be making certain *evaluative or normative or imperatival demands on me.* To perceive the world along those lines is *not* to perceive it along lines that are third personal. It is essentially to see the world with a sense of *first* personal *engagement.*[37] What this shows is that just because I am talking about or observing another does not mean that it is always a third person point of view I am taking on the other. It is not as if the first person point of view is a Cartesian or solipsist point of view that leaves the *world and others* out.[38] The first person point of view is not just a point of view in which one asks what one ought to do or think. It is also a point of view in which one takes in or perceives the world, but one does so in a very specifically *engaged* way—one sees the world as making demands on what one or how one *ought* to act or think. That is to say, it sees the world in a way that is laden with value—in a way, therefore, that implicates the perceiving agent, involves the perceiving agent's engagement with it.

By contrast, when one perceives it from the third person point of view, one might (to stick with our example) register such things as the caloric intake of the subjects involved and a prediction of their undernourishment or death and so on. Here there is no engagement with them. Here there is only a perspective of detached observation.

But then, from this, there will have to be a *switch* of perspectives to the agential one of engagement in which one perceives the facts quite differently, as really making normative demands on one, which then in turn leads to forming of decisions and intentions—in this case, to help the poor. That is the switch that comes with describing them as having 'needs' and not just describing them in terms of their caloric intake. The fact that it is a *switch* is absolutely fundamental to the point I am trying to make. It is worth repeating something here, just so as not to be misunderstood on a point that—if misunderstood— will make the scepticism about weaker forms of naturalist dependency seem quite unconvincing: the claim is *not* that the third personal and the scientific knowledge that a person has become inaccessible to her in deliberation. One often needs to and does take those facts into account in deliberation. The point, rather, is that deliberation proceeds in two modes that elbow each other out, so that one switches from one to the other. One doesn't straddle both modes at once; rather, one is in each by turn.

Perhaps the right way to put it is in terms of framing. One may, in one mode or frame, formulate the premises and the conclusions of one's deliberation in scientific vocabulary (where the world is described, as I said, in terms of the caloric intake of populations, predictions about undernourishment, death, etc.) and then one switches modes and frames to describing the world differently in one's premises and conclusions (seeing people as having *needs,* as I said, and, so viewed, the world makes normative demands on one, and that is why in this mode of deliberation we come to conclusions such as that we *ought* to help). So what is being denied is that in practical deliberation one goes directly, without switching perspectives, from premises described in third personal or scientific terms to conclusions about what one ought to do.

The point is not the one famously made by Hume and Richard Hare, viz., that one needs an evaluative major premise to go from the factual premise to the 'ought' conclusion. Instead, the point is that one needs a defection to a different kind of *factual premise* as well, one described (in our example) in terms of needs, in terms of *facts* that make normative demands on one. This is what makes possible the 'ought' conclusion. Words like 'defection' and 'switch' are doing the work here of making clear that the demand is not just the familiar one that you cannot go to evaluative and 'ought' conclusions from merely factual premises. That demand does not have the more radical consequence of questioning the weaker forms of naturalist dependency, such as supervenience. Rather, the demand is that we look at the question in terms of framing. It is only when deliberation switches to this mode of employing the right descriptions in the (factual) *premise itself* and the world is perceived in this way that one's reasoning is evaluative and practical in the full sense. One's perspective on the world is one of engagement rather than detachment, agential and first personal rather than merely third personal.

I admit to using the distinction between 'first personal' and 'third personal' perspectives here in a very specific way, and it ought not to be confused with the quite different use of terms like 'first personal' and 'third personal' in other contexts by others or even by me in other parts of the book. The distinction is intended to mark one's engagement with the world as opposed to one's detached, sometimes even scientific angle on it. And this is intended to be strictly parallel to the Spinozist point I invoked earlier. Just as in the Spinozist point one can have a third person perspective *on oneself* ("This is how I am") and a first person perspective on oneself ("I ought to do . . ."), one can have a third and first person perspective *on the world* (respectively, 'This population's caloric intake is . . . ' and "These people have *needs*"). It is only the latter perspective on the world in which the world is seen as making normative demands on me. Practical deliberation can involve both these perspectives, each on one's self and on the world. In such deliberation I often need to know about myself in a detached way, and I need also to know about the world in a detached, scientific way. But then I also am required (else it would not be practical deliberation at all) to turn to the different, first personal perspective both on the world and on myself. Both perspectives are involved, in these ways, *but only in turn,* as it were.

Hence, even though scientific knowledge is certainly a step in one's thinking, it is the phenomenon of switching modes in deliberation that I am fastening on to raise a question about supervenience. That is to say, if it really is a *switch of perspectives* to go from the scientific facts to the facts that make normative demands on me, then there is something obscure in the idea that the latter kind of facts are supervenient on the former kind of facts precisely because of the Spinozist point (and its parallel) of the unavailability of these perspectives to one another. When the two perspectives are not embraceable at once, and are not, in that sense, available to one another, and when there is no richer perspective to go to (since one is always in one or the other perspective), it is an oddity, a conceptual oddity, to even try and establish that facts that are essentially facts of the one perspective have the requisite naturalist dependency on facts in the other. It would be like trying to establish that facts within the perspective from which the notorious figure is seen as a duck are supervenient (or similarly dependent) on facts within the perspective from which the figure is seen as a rabbit. Duck-facts and rabbit-facts, of course, are both supervenient on a *third* kind of neutral fact that straddles both, and that is just what is missing in the case of the facts within the first person and third person points of view—so the analogy is not meant to be perfect. Since there are no facts that are neutral between first personal and third personal facts, the point of the analogy holds fast: first personal facts cannot meaningfully be said to be dependent by supervenience on third personal facts in just the way that duck-facts cannot meaningfully be said to be dependent by supervenience on rabbit-facts. I repeat: I am claiming only that it's not clear that one can make sense of such talk of dependency. It's not that it is wrong to assert such dependencies. The point is that it seems just as wrong to deny such dependencies. The necessity of perspectival shifts makes claims of this sort of dependency unassessable.[39]

We may at first balk at this idea of switching from one perspective to another in deliberation because it happens so swiftly and so often, but that cannot be a serious objection. As I pointed out in the last chapter, the switch, after all, can even take place in a single utterance sometimes, as when one says, "I predict that I will not meet the deadline." The first occurrence of "I" here is from within a first person point of view of agency, the speaker having and expressing a thought. But the second occurrence of "I" has already switched to a subject that is not viewed as an agent but is viewed in a detached way from a third person point of view. This brings out clearly not only that there is a very rapid switching of perspectives. It also reveals that the term "I" is ambiguous in its reference to an agent and to a more passively viewed subject. Such an ambiguity is basic to the Spinozist thought that I am exploiting. (The example also reveals that it is superficial to equate the first person point of view of agency with something linguistic, i.e., the use of the first person pronoun, since such uses can clearly have a third personal significance as in the second occurrence of the first person pronoun in the example.)

To return now to a subject that we promised to pick up again some pages back, one of the implications of this perspectival duality is that it gives us the ground to distinguish the notion of cause as it occurs in contexts of agency and to say something about the kind of causal relation that holds between commitments and actions. Let me spell out that implication and thereby complete the second of the two points about the causal powers of commitments that I had left incomplete some pages ago. This second point was supposed to say in what sense citing commitments as causes of our actions can tell us something slightly more informative than was allowed in the first point about the causal powers of commitments (which captured only a teleological element that linked commitments to attempts to live up to them) without going over to the very substantial naturalistic and Humean ideal of informativeness that came with nomologicality.

We say such things as, "He gave money to charity *because* he had a commitment to help the poor." Or we say, "The poverty he saw in Calcutta prompted him to give money to charity." These are the singular causal ways of talking that are more ambitious and more informative than the highly uninformative kind of causal talk that I said was *built into* the notion of commitment as a result of defining commitments in terms of certain second-order dispositions: "His commitment to help the poor caused him to try to live up the commitment to help the poor."

I have said that it is odd and complacent to think of the notion of cause (or of a causal state such as a disposition) that one finds in the Humean picture to be the same notion as the one that is operative in these informative examples given above involving agency. That is, it is odd to think of the latter as the same as the one in the Humean picture, only minus the Humean element of implied generality or nomologicality. The idea that it is a singular causal claim as soon as it is intentional states that are involved seems simply an assertion of what one needs to argue for and ground in further considerations, in order to make sense of these causal ways of talking I just cited above. And it is not clear that one has the right to this assertion if it is the same notion of cause that is in play. The explanation that comes with citing causes, if it is indeed the same notion, does seem to bring with it some demand for treating like cases alike and not as distinct singularities. Generalities are built into the idea. So also it is part of the understanding of the standard notion of dispositions or tendencies that they, in principle, integrate with other dispositions (and categorical states); and so it would be odd to think that when dispositions happen to be mental or intentional dispositions, they just simply do not integrate with any other dispositions of any other science. How can we simply just assert that psychology, in its intentional aspect, is set apart in this way?

The causal ways of talking that I gave examples of above ("His commitment to help the poor caused him to give money to charity") reflect the fact that our commitments and our agency make a difference to the world, and we suppose that that is why citing commitments as the causes of our actions should illuminate. It would be absurd, a thoroughly unsatisfactory conception of our capacity for norms and our agency, to think that they make no such difference, that once we form or acquire commitments our agential life is over and done with, the rest is up to causes, dispositions, etc., in the one and only Humean sense of cause that there is. A proper account of agency does not surrender the efficacy of agency, its capacity to transform the world. Our agency is not causally inert nor solipsistically shut off from the world.

In order for our commitments to make a difference to the world, they have to give rise to intentions, which are commitments of a more decisive sort, often a decisiveness that is arrived at by deliberation that consists partly in considering different commitments and weighing them but also often by being moved by the normative demands in the world that we perceive. And when we describe (as in our examples above) the actions that these commitments cause, the one thing that is clear is that they describe our actions as meeting normative demands, as actions done to fulfill commitments (in our example, the commitment to help the poor) and to meet the normative demands made on us by the world around us (in our example, the needs of the poor that one perceives when one is in Calcutta, say). When causes are cited in those examples, they are to be understood necessarily in these normative terms and no other terms. How does that make them distinctive as *causes*?

Certainly, we expect them not to imply nomologicality. McDowell says so and is right to say so. But if we don't dig deeper than that, we have no real ground for claiming its distinctiveness *as causal talk*. And as I said, one has not really dug deeper if one stops with the thought that the ground is given by the fact that these states of mind that cause our actions are 'governed' by or 'constrained by' or 'answerable to' (all phrases from either Davidson or McDowell) normative principles. If these phrases describe a phenomenon that does not affect the kinds of states we are speaking of, and if it does not transform the notion of cause that holds in the relations that these states have with actions, there is no real improvement.

But just as we said about the term "I" and its referent (and I will say more about that further below), the duality of perspectives allows us (indeed, forces us) to see the term 'cause' too as ambiguous. It should be quite possible to say of the term 'cause' too that when we are describing someone as subjects capable of engagement, when we see them as having the perspective of agency in the full-blown sense that involves having commitments and engaging with the world normatively, then we take the relations between them and their actions as being of a different kind than the causal relations that hold when agency, commitments, etc., are not involved. The difference is, of course, that the former has no nomological implications. But we need now to ground the idea of such a peculiar thing as a singular cause (which is so manifestly different from a cause, as Hume has taught us to think of it) in some terms that will help illuminate it as a distinct kind of cause.

We ground things a little when we add to the idea of singularity what is undoubtedly true; viz., there is no echo in the causal talk that involves no agency and normativity, of anything that is analogous to the *weighing of options and deciding between them.* The intentional causes of our actions are the sorts of things that are weighed and decided between by those who possess them, but no such thing holds of the causes that natural science studies. But this fact too describes a symptom, even if an extremely important one.

We don't get to the heart of the matter until we appeal to the duality of perspectives explicitly.

Commitments, when they are decisive, can make a difference to the world, we have said. *What we have to ask to make progress is, what does this sort of idea look like from the first person point of view of the agent?* As Spinoza pointed out, it cannot be viewed by him as something that is in the nature of a prediction. When a subject thinks or says, "I will do this" as an agent exercising his agency to fulfill a decisive commitment, it is clearly not the "will" of prediction. If he were predicting, he would be assuming that there will be causes that bring things about. But when he is not predicting but rather thinking or speaking in the first person mode of agency, what he assumes is quite different; he assumes that his *agency will be effective.* This assumption governs his thought in just the way that the assumption that causes in the standard sense will bring something about, govern his thought, were he to be predicting. The hard question is, what makes one a different kind of cause than the other, and therefore, what makes these different sorts of assumptions? It's not just the singularity, the absence of nomologicality, in one of them. That is part of what needs explaining. It is not the explanation. Here is the explanation. What makes for the underlying difference is not the singularity in the causal talk implicit in thinking, "I will do this" in the first person mode but, rather, that the agent's assumption that she will do the action, the agent's assumption that her agency will be effective, *is not something that she puts aside if she fails to do it.*

The crucial point, the punch line on this matter, then, is this: *The failure is not a refutation of the assumption in the way that a failure of a prediction is a refutation of the assumption that governs the other kind of causal talk (implicit in thinking "I will do it" in the third person mode), with which predictions are made. Rather, the failure is the occasion for self-criticism and for trying to do better to act so as to fulfill her commitment.*

This last sentence, as was spelled out earlier, is the basic defining condition for the very idea of a commitment. I had pledged some pages ago that I would try and show how the much less informative causal talk of how "X's commitment causes him to live up to the commitment" (uninformative because it is *built into* the idea of a commitment as a result of certain specific second-order dispositions that define commitments) would help us understand the nature of the causal talk that aspires to be more informative, such as when we say things like, "His commitment to help the poor caused him to give money to charity." That is the pledge we have just redeemed. The idea behind the second-order dispositions that define commitments is to make clear that failures to live up to commitments lead to the exercise of the second-order dispositions, and these dispositions are rightly seen as ways of conceptually underpinning the idea of the trying to live up to a commitment that is caused by a commitment. If commitments, by their nature, cause us in this uninformative sense (the sense defined by just those second-order dispositions) to try and live up to them, *that trying would be pointless if failures to live up to commitments were counter-instances that refuted the assumptions underlying one's thoughts such as "I will do this" when these thoughts are understood as the decisional thoughts of an agent* rather than a predictor. The agent does not give up the assumption of his *agency's* causal efficaciousness in the face of failures. The obvious appropriateness of giving up the corresponding assumption of causal efficacy in the *predictive* thought "I will do this" in the face of the failure of predictions *is simply not echoed* for the agential thought "I will do this" by someone's failure to live up to a commitment. The former thought *is refuted* by the failure, whereas the latter thought is not, once we understand the nature of commitments as normative states along the lines I have spelled out earlier. The assumption of the effectiveness of the efficacy of agency survives in the agent, despite failures, because that is the nature of commitments; and commitments are, as we have argued, the essential mark of agency in the full-blown sense we are discussing in the book.

The argument that I have italicized at length above makes clear in what sense exactly we think so differently of the notion of cause (and causal efficacy) when commitments and agency are involved. And as should be evident from the way the claim was developed, *there is no way to make it clear without seeing it as an implication of the duality of perspectives* we have been stressing. The perspectival point is essential to the claim and is simply not avoidable.

Someone might persist with the line of thought we are opposing and try and avoid the perspectival point by saying, "Why do you want to insist on this? Why don't you say (as McDowell does) that there is a single notion of cause, and there is only one perspective? It is just that when rational norms govern our causal states, they are not part of a naturalistic causal nexus but allow only singular causal talk." The answer to this objection remains that that sort of position just does not dig deep enough into the source of what makes the naturalistic understanding of cause inadequate to what is needed to talk about how our agency makes a difference to the world. Unless we see the idea of norms governing our beliefs and desires as transforming beliefs and desires into commitments, and then in turn define commitments in a way that affects the causal relations they bear to our actions when viewed from a first person perspective (that stands in contrast with a third person perspective), we will have rested with a premature conclusion. Without bringing in this perspectival point about the assumption that governs the way *agents* (as opposed to detached, unengaged predictors) regard the way in which their commitments and intentions make a causal difference to the world, claims about our beliefs and desires being answerable to norms does nothing (or next to nothing) to tell us about why we should stick with singular causal claims in the explanation of behavior. In other words, what we need to add to this mantra about intentional states being 'answerable to norms' is precisely what this book has been urging from the outset: a more radical *integration* of intentionality with normativity (making it commitmental, as I have) and the integration of both intentionality and norms or values, in turn, with agency and its first person perspective. It is only then that we have the apparatus to say that "she did something *because* she had a certain *commitment*" is very distinctive causal explanatory talk. It is distinctive because the explanation implicitly conveys that what it was like for the agent *from her perspective* is captured by the highly distinctive nature of the governing assumption under which she thinks her decisive intentions, "I will do this." It is this unique form of assumption on the part of the agent about her agency's causal efficacy that makes for a distinctive notion of cause in our normative explanations of a person's behavior. There is no understanding the assumption's unique status, its non-refutability by failures, without (1) seeing it as an assumption held only from the first person point of view of the agent rather than a third person point of view of the predictor and (2) without seeing beliefs and desires themselves as commitments defined along very specific lines that mention certain specific second-order dispositions.

The normative character of freedom and agency, which we first introduced in Chapter 2 with a modification of Strawson's position on freedom, now (and only now) has flowered to its full bloom. There we had said that there is no way to understand agency until we see our actions as the objects of *evaluatively justifiable* reactive attitudes, adding that our values can only justify those actions that are caused by what Hume called *non*-coercive causes such as our states of mind like beliefs, desires, and intentions. But in that chapter, we had not paused to say exactly what beliefs and desires are and what it means to say that they 'cause' our actions. As a result, the normative character of agency was left quite incomplete there, though it was sufficient for the purposes at that point, of establishing transparency in Chapter 3. Since then, by an elaborate dialectic that made appeal to an insuperable challenge posed by a comprehensively passive subject like Oblomov who had only dispositional states, we motivated a very specific conception of intentional states as commitments (to be contrasted with dispositions) that can only be properly understood in the context of their possessors having a point of view that is first personal and agential (to be contrasted with a point of view that is third personal and disengaged). And what we have seen by now in this chapter is that these intentional states, because they are understood as commitments, 'cause' our actions in a highly non-standard sense of that term, a non-standardness that could not be understood except in terms that bring to center stage the irreducibly first person perspective of the agent. It is only after we identified this notion of cause and situated it in a framework characterized by this perspectival duality that we have fully revealed the depth of what underlies the Strawsonian conception of freedom that gives us the right to say that we are free because we are caused by *non*-coercive causes. Strawson himself does not spell any of this out, of course, and the dialectic that threads through Chapters 2, 4, and 5 spells it out in terms that go far beyond Strawson. Even so, all of it is made possible only because of the initial and highly innovative, normative turn he does give to our understanding of agency.

To move away now from the particular considerations of causality and freedom to the more general issues, I have stressed that a perspectival duality is required to pursue any satisfying anti-naturalism that allows space for value (norm), agency, and intentionality when these are all seen as irreducible to causal and dispositional ideas in the standard sense. This trio of irreducible phenomena is highly integrated if the argument so far is right. The irreducibility of intentionality is none other than the irreducibility of value. And as the Moore-Frege-Moore pincer argument presented in this chapter as well as the modified Strawsonian argument presented in Chapter 2 (respectively) make plain, the irreducibility of intentionality and value is deeply linked to the fact that as agents we deliberate about what we *ought* to do and think, and our agency is constituted by the fact that our doings and thoughts are the *justifiable* targets of our reactive evaluative attitudes. But none of these integrated anti-naturalist points could be satisfactorily pursued without the point about perspectival duality, for it is only this that stands in the way of making sense of the weaker dependencies upon which the most contemporary and weaker forms of naturalism depend.

One (that is to say, naturalists) may of course deny the irreducibility of value in the first place. But to do so would require disputing the claims of the last chapter and their consolidation in the Moore-Frege-Moore argument presented earlier in this one, and the theorists who invoke the weaker and more global dependencies (such as supervenience) do not (do not usually, at any rate) feel the need to do that. Indeed, Moore himself was the first to formulate the dependency under the name of the 'supervenience' of values on the facts of nature.[40] So the point of my remarks in this section, expressing skepticism about the weaker dependencies of intentionality on non-intentional facts or values on non-evaluative facts, is not so much to *argue* for the view that values are irreducible (the argument for which has already been given) but to bring out a certain integrity in the conclusions by showing that, properly understood, the argument for the irreducibility contains within it a more radical consequence.

One cannot, strictly cannot, understand the thrust of the Moorean open question argument without fully appreciating that there are these two modes or perspectives involved in deliberation that cannot be occupied at the same time. "I have such and such dispositions, but ought I to do such and such . . . ?" and "X has such and such natural property, but does X have a property that makes such and such normative demands on me?" are open questions that already contain within their passage the perspectival switches that I find significant. Each question moves from one perspective in the first half of its posing to the other in its second half. The significance of this is that it puts into doubt the very assessability of the more sober naturalist strategy, i.e., the strategy that concedes that values are irreducible, then goes on to claim the kinds of weaker naturalism that these weaker claims to dependency offer. It puts it into question by making clear that the irreducibility of value is deeply integrated with the *unique* perspective of agency and of the special character of self-knowledge and the first person point of view. The relevant naturalist dependency, on the other hand, requires a kind of *inter*-perspectival availability, which the irreducibility of value (once understood in its integrated relations to these other things) makes impossible.

However, as we have already seen, it is not just naturalists who will and do resist many of these points about perspectival duality. Anti-naturalists, like McDowell, for instance, are made anxious by it, thinking that it succumbs in some way to a version, even if a distant version, of something that they have developed a distaste for in the last many decades of philosophizing, viz., a Cartesian ego or subject standing in a dualistic contrast with all else that is object or third personal. And they will insist on removing this dualism and finding a common perspective that will allow for an unambiguous use of the term "I."[41] To quote McDowell:

The very capacity of the first person pronoun or other devices to the same effect, to make references, in expressions of first person-thinking, depends on the fact that a first-personal thinker conceives the referent of her self-references as a particular person, an element in the third-personally describable world. Bilgrami's insistence on the uncombin-ability of the perspectives threatens to make it unintelligible how a subject's uses of "I" can refer.

Such a charge is wholly dogmatic. We can simply assert all one likes, that there is an unambiguous use of the term "I" and a monistic per-spective, but it doesn't mean that we will get one. You can't just keep saying that you have something that you would like to have. In any case, nothing is articulated in what I have cited from McDowell that tells one what is so troubling about the ambiguity that the duality of perspectives brings to the first person pronoun; and it leaves us with no option but to see it as a transferred anxiety about a solipsistic Cartesian ego of pure consciousness that makes the reference of "I" highly problematic. But there is nothing even resembling a Cartesian position about the ego in this sort of duality of point of view I am invoking, and there are no insuperable problems about the reference of "I" that are implied by seeing it as ambiguous due to this duality.[42]

As I said, the phobia that dualities of this sort will be problematic go deep in philosophy of the last six or seven decades, which defined itself so much on repudiating two distinct Cartesian polarities, mind and body (the central nervous system and its higher-order causal, or functional, dispositional properties) and the epistemologically more significant distinction between internal (solipsistic) and external, which, though related to the first polarity, was by no means, as Gareth Evans and McDowell himself have rightly pointed out, the same. Put-ting it in broad terms, naturalists have been more keen to deny the first and embrace the second polarity in Descartes, allowing that in-teriority of mind must be conceded if one is to identify mind with body. And it is *anti-naturalist* philosophers like Evans and McDowell who have resisted such an identification partly at least because of a fear of shutting the external world out of our thought and its reach. Now, I think that it is this latter fear of the Cartesian outcome of *losing the world irrecoverably* through a duality of this kind that underlies a good deal of the uncritical dismissal by McDowell of the Spinozist perspectival duality I have been stressing. (After all, we cannot—in our time—pay credence to the theological cheat of recovering the world, as Descartes himself did, via the positing of a non-deceiving deity.) I think a cluster of objections that an anti-naturalist like Mc-Dowell makes to my own anti-naturalism that appeals to this duality can be diagnosed as issuing from this fear.

When McDowell worries about the reference of "I" having to capture at once both the agent and her embodiment in third personally describable ways, he is echoing something that was acutely discussed by Strawson, not only in *Individuals* but also in his insightful and highly influential reading of Kant's First Paralogism in *The Bounds of Sense*.[43] However, Strawson was addressing a Cartesian ego in that reading. He was not addressing issues about agency at all. There is no reason at all to think that when I use the term "I" in what I have called the first person mode of *agency*, there is anything disembodied about its reference in a way that Strawson was quite justifiably made anxious about. Embodiment as opposed to pure Cartesian disembodied consciousness and agency as opposed to third personal detachment are *two* distinctions, *not one*. They don't coincide at all. And there is no reason to think that we cannot scramble them in the way I have all along been doing. There is no more reason to think that "I" uttered in the expression of a thought had in the first person mode of agency cannot refer to something embodied than there is to think that when I am talking in a first person mode of agential engagement about *someone else*, say, about his *needs* (as opposed to his caloric count), I could not be talking about his *bodily* needs. The agential perspective has no such body-excluding or world-excluding implications, and one should not be misled by talk of a 'first person' point of view to think that it must.

There is a conflation of two distinctions on McDowell's part here, and none of the problems of how "I" could refer at all if one embraced Cartesian dualism, which Strawson rightly raised on behalf of Kant, arise as a result of the dualism of *point of view* that renders "I" ambiguous. "I," used in the first person, can refer to something embodied ('to a particular person' as McDowell demands in the cited passage) as much as anyone would want it to. The term 'person' is a term of art in Strawson, to mark something that is the possessor of both states of consciousness and the material states of a body; and nothing I have said rules out that "I" used in the first person, agential perspective would not refer to a person, so understood. The only thing ruled out when "I" is used to refer to a person conceived of in the aspect of agency is that it refers to a person conceived in a detached, impersonal, third personal way as something that is the subject of predictions, etc.

To say, as McDowell does, that "I" couldn't unproblematically refer at all, if it did not in each use refer to both a first personally conceived and third personally conceived referent, needs argument. To assume that if "I" referred to something conceived in the first person mode it would have to refer to something that left the world and body out is to assume something that provides no argument, because it is to assume something false. It is to assume something that is based on a false conflation of two quite different distinctions. Reference of that kind would indeed be problematic, as Strawson and those influenced by him have rightly pointed out. But it is a problem only for Cartesian dualism, which appeals to a special perspective of self-enclosed consciousness, not for a dualism appealing to the special perspective provided by agency.

I suspect that McDowell's mistaken insistence (discussed earlier) that my skepticism about supervenience claims regarding value (a skepticism that also emphasizes the agential perspective) could only undermine supervenience about *acts* of evaluation rather than about value properties *in the world* also owes to a similar confusion or conflation. It comes from a conviction that such a polarized stress on the agent's perspective in the understanding of value will leave *the world* out of value and speak only to *acts* of evaluation on the parts of agents. So also, his insistence (just like his insistence that "I" is univocal) that the notion of cause as it surfaces in agency *is the same notion* as it surfaces in all other contexts—something I denied on grounds that appealed to precisely a perspectival element that stresses the polarity—is driven by a worry that otherwise it would not account for how agency makes a difference to the *world*. I have already had my say against McDowell's objections to my form of anti-naturalism that is skeptical of supervenience as well as against his insistence on a unitary notion of cause. The point here is not to respond to these objections again but only to diagnose these objections as coming from a phobia associating the duality that drives my anti-naturalism with other dualities (rightly feared) with which it has no essential link. To put it as Wittgenstein (and McDowell himself) might, it is this phobia that needs therapy. There is nothing philosophically fearsome about the duality of agential and third personal perspectives, as I have presented it. Such a therapy might arrest a tendency to simply assert without argument univocalities that one would like (but cannot have), even when one's own anti-naturalism is better off without them.

Without them, an anti-naturalism can integrate the four themes I said I would seek to integrate at the beginning of the book: the duality of value and fact; the duality of agency and the detached impersonality of a causally deterministic picture of the world; the duality of intentional states of mind and the body and its causal dispositions; and finally, the asymmetry between self-knowledge and other forms of knowledge. With the first three themes integrated now at length over the last many chapters, it is possible to finally return and complete our claims on the fourth theme of what makes self-knowledge special among all the knowledges we have. The crucial integration that this will rest on is the integration of intentionality and value presented in the first three sections of this chapter. That integration would not have been possible without the others, but it is that one in particular, the viewing of intentional states as themselves evaluative states or commitments, that will provide the conceptual ground for the special character of self-knowledge in the aspect we have so far left ungrounded—the aspect of authority.

5. Authority is that aspect of self-knowledge that holds of second-order beliefs (unlike transparency, which holds of first-order intentional states). It is the property of second-order beliefs being invariably true, and it is a property that is captured in the conditional that we had initially in the first chapter expressed as a presumptive conditional, which read as follows: It is a presumption that: if S believes that she desires (believes) that p, then she desires (believes) that p. We had promised there to find a way to present the property in a rewritten conditional that is not merely a presumption, by giving the conceptual basis for what makes the conditional true. We are now ready to give that conceptual basis.

The last chapter had presented a certain unfinished strategy for upholding the conditional for authority. The first step in this strategy was to deny that authority, something as radical as the invariable truth of second-order beliefs, could be upheld by simply pointing to a contingent fact about the *cause* of our second-order beliefs. It is most unsatisfactory, in other words, to say that we have authority because the cause of our second-order beliefs that go into self-knowledge happen to be the first-order beliefs or desires that they amount to self-knowledge of. That would not get you authority; it would at most get you why it seems to us that we have the intuition that we are authoritative. If it merely 'happens to be' that there is a routine cause of our second-order beliefs, then it might not have been so, and it might not be so in this or that case. We need something more surefire, and giving this sort of account of authority that depends on a property of causes will not do. It will not do for the same reason that giving a causal-reliabilist account of transparency would not do. Transparency and authority need a more principled basis. We have tried to give the principled basis for transparency (in Chapter 3) by appealing to a normative conception of agency. We must now give a principled basis for authority by appealing to a very specific normative notion of intentionality that (over this chapter and the last) we have tried to integrate with and derive from that normative notion of agency.

The very task of seeking and finding a conceptual basis for something as radical as authority rather than a contingent basis for something weaker—our impression of authority—is a task that comes with a certain resolve. The resolve, as expressed in the last chapter, was to pursue a strategy in which the cases of seeming lapses of authority, such as those found in self-deception, were merely and exactly that: *seeming* cases of lapses. They were not really lapses. They are no exceptions to authority, and that is why there is no reason to describe the conditional for authority as a presumption. But that means we have to give an account of self-deception that shows that they do not provide exceptions to authority. In the broad schematic strategy we formulated, it was supposed to come out that they are not exceptions to authority because self-deception need never be taken to show that one's second-order beliefs are false. Rather it need only be taken to show that one had inconsistent first-order intentional states. However, that was only a schema to pursue a strategy for resisting the claim that self-deception thwarted authority. We need to present, as we had pledged to do, what gives us *a right* to that schematically formulated strategy, and we finally have the wherewithal to do so.

Let us work with the example we had given earlier. Someone says he believes that he is healthy. That is his avowal. His behavior, however, suggests that he is very anxious and neurotic about his health. Why does this not make his avowal false? Why is it not just like the case of a perceptual belief that is false, even if perceptual beliefs are much more often than not true?

Now, as I said, one can try and save authority by saying that the behavioral evidence only shows that the avowal is not sincerely made, and therefore there *is no* genuine second-order *belief.* So since authority holds of self-*belief,* the threat to authority is removed. (This borders on a Socratic treatment of the subject.) But it is a treatment that is not always going to work. It is sometimes possible that such behavioral evidence can exist even if the avowal is entirely sincerely made. It is true that it is only the sincerity of an avowal that will establish that a second-order belief really exists. That is a point of some importance. But it is too strong to say, as this treatment does, that there are no cases of sincere avowals, which are accompanied by such behavioral evidence. That is to say, it is too strong to rule out that our protagonist genuinely has a second-order belief about his first-order belief that he is healthy while displaying that behavioral evidence of his anxiety about his health. In these cases, it may seem that the second-order belief is false, just as perceptual beliefs might be.

I now want to argue that it would only seem so if we had not taken in the integrity I have argued for in this chapter, the integration *of intentionality with value* that itself follows from the previous integrations: (1) *of agency with value* (in the discussion of a Strawsonian conception of agency in Chapter 2) and (2) *of intentionality with agency* (in the discussion in Chapter 4 of how Oblomov lacks intentionality and thought because he lacks agency). These three interconnected integrations are all necessary in order to present the conceptual basis for authority. The integration in this chapter (via the Kripke-inspired Moore-Frege-Moore argument and the repudiation of Davidson's way of treating the normative notion of intentionality) has been to show that the irreducibility of intentionality is just a special case of the irreducibility of value itself. And this integration yielded a notion of intentional states like beliefs and desires *as themselves being* evaluative states, i.e., commitments.

Once this is established, we have a way of dealing with the behavioral evidence that is involved in the cases of self-deception. We have a way of refusing to see the evidence as evidence for the falsity of second-order beliefs. Recall that in presenting this last integration of intentionality with value, we had—following Kripke—distinguished between dispositions and commitments via the Moore-Frege-Moore argument. Exploiting that, we can now say that the behavioral evidence does not provide any evidence that the person lacks the *commitment* that he has sincerely affirmed in his avowal. It only shows that he has not lived up to the commitment in his behavior. What his behavior reflects is some of his *dispositions,* which of course he may not be aware of. And these will conflict with his commitments. If he becomes aware of them, all we need to find in order to attribute the *commitment* to him is that he accepts criticism for not living up to his commitments and tries to do better by way of living up to them, by perhaps cultivating the dispositions to do what it takes to live up to them, etc., these being the required conditions for possessing the commitment. And so even when he is not aware of his dispositions and his failures, so long as he is *prepared* to accept criticism, etc., were he to become aware of this, that is sufficient to attribute the commitment to him. If he meets these conditions for having the commitment (i.e., if he has this preparedness), his behavior can no longer be seen as evidence for his second-order belief being false, only of him not having lived up to his commitment. That is to say, if beliefs and desires are commitments, then he possesses the first-order belief that he is healthy, which makes his (sincere) avowal and the second-order belief that he expresses in the avowal (viz., that he believes that he believes he is healthy) true.

Here is another way of putting the point. We have established that when our protagonist avows a belief in his health, he is avowing a commitment. Two things must be established to conclude that there is authority—his avowal must be sincere (otherwise, there is nothing—there is no second-order belief—to be authoritative), and the conditions for his having the commitment must be met. Let us assume that the avowal is sincere despite the behavioral evidence, because if it were not, there would be no question, as I said, of something being either authoritatively true or being false; i.e., there would be no dispute. Now, what are the conditions for the sincerity of his avowal, given the behavioral evidence that suggests anxiety on his part about his health? The answer here is revealing: there can be no conditions that would establish the sincerity of his avowal *that would not also be the conditions that establish that he has the commitment he is avowing*. The conditions for having the commitment, I said, would be his preparedness (were he to become aware that he is not living up to his commitment) to accept criticism for not having lived up to it and his preparedness to try and do better by way of living up to it. These preparednesses, I am now saying, are the *very conditions* that would establish that his avowal of the commitment is sincere. What else could establish its sincerity?

When we ask whether a person's avowal of her beliefs or desires is sincere, we often look to her previous or subsequent actions as criteria. Actions speak louder than words, we say. But which actions? If beliefs and desires are commitments, then always demanding actions that *fulfill* the commitments will be quite wrong unless we think that a subject always has to be rational in order to be sincere about what she says she believes and desires—an absurd assumption. Were we to view beliefs and desires as dispositions, the matter would be quite different. Why should we assess a person's avowal of her dispositions to be sincere if she is not acting as she says she is disposed to do? Well, perhaps she is sincere about having the disposition in question but has counter-dispositions as well that prevent her acting on the disposition in question. So at least we need some explanation of that kind to establish her sincerity in her avowal. No such explanation is required to assess the avowal of beliefs and desires, qua commitments. A person can quite sincerely avow her commitment without acting on her commitment and needs no explanation to account for her failure to so act. Well, what then is the sign of sincerity of an avowal of the commitment if explanation-less failures to act do not put into doubt that sincerity? The answer can only be that the actions that are relevant for sincerity of avowal when there are no commitment-fulfilling actions are those actions where a person criticizes herself for not fulfilling her commitments and makes various efforts to try and do better, perhaps by doing what it might take to cultivate the right dispositions that would lead to actions that *would* fulfill the commitments. These would surely reflect the sincerity of her avowal of the commitment.

Now, let's turn to ask not when an avowal of a commitment is sincere but when someone is properly attributed a commitment. It cannot be that a person is not properly attributed a commitment if he fails to act so as to live up to it. All that would show is that he is irrational by his own lights. The notion of commitment, as I pointed out, is precisely meant to allow for irrationality without going into the odd and unnecessary complications that Davidson does to allow for it on his *dispositional* view of beliefs and desires, where these dispositions are supposed to be constituted by rational principles. Being so constituted, Davidson has to divide the mind into two, each of which meets the requirements of being rationally constituted. A commitmental view of beliefs and desires needs to make no such fanciful philosophical maneuvers. A person is irrational when she does not live up to her commitments. Since her beliefs and desires are commitments, if her actions do not live up to them, she is irrational, but there is no implication that she does not really have the commitments. It is only if one thought that beliefs and desires are *dispositions* constituted by rational norms of logic and decision theory that we need to explain away why one is not producing the actions that the dispositions are dispositions to. Without explaining it away, we put into doubt that the beliefs and desires (dispositionally conceived) were properly attributed in the first place, when the actions are not present. But no such implication exists for beliefs and desires (commitmentally conceived) when one's actions don't live up to them. The commitments are perfectly well attributed even if there are no such actions. So here too the question arises: well, what are the signs that a person has a commitment (i.e., is properly attributed a commitment) if it is not the case that he needs actually to act so as to be living up to the commitment? And here too the answer is exactly the same. As I said, when defining the nature of commitments, the conditions for having a commitment are that one is prepared to criticize oneself when one fails to live up to it and that one tries to do better by, say, cultivating the dispositions that would lead to one's doing what it takes to live up to the commitment. *These are the very same conditions as those for the sincerity of avowal.*[44]

Sincere avowals, therefore, cannot come apart from what they are avowals of, once one sees that what they are avowals of (beliefs and desires) are commitments. That means sincere avowals of beliefs and desires are always true. And since sincere avowals express second-

order beliefs, second-order beliefs that take first-order beliefs and desires as their objects are always true. That is what is expressed in the
authority conditional. The conditional was formulated initially in
Chapter 1 in the form of a presumption in order to deal with cases
like self-deception that seem to provide exceptions to the conditional.
But now we have given an argument by which we can conclude that
there is no need for the presumption.

In the last chapter, we had presented a strategy that showed why
we *need* not view self-deception as providing exceptions to the conditional. But in this chapter, in the argument just given, we have
shown why we *should* not view it as providing exceptions. The strategy
of the last chapter was incomplete not merely in being weaker in the
sense just emphasized in the last two sentences. It was also incomplete
in another sense. In pursuing the strategy, it was argued that authority
survives self-deception because self-deception need not be seen as
showing that the first-order states that our second-order beliefs are
about don't exist. All that cases of self-deception need be taken as
showing is that a self-deceived subject has inconsistent first-order intentional states, including the one that she has a second-order belief
about. But with all the conceptual apparatus we were able to lay bare
in the argument given in this chapter, we can now say something
more correct and more precise about that point. It is no longer correct to describe the situation as the strategy did in the last chapter. It
is no longer correct to say that there are two inconsistent first-order
intentional states (such as she believes that she is healthy and she
believes that she is not healthy, to continue with our example discussed over these two chapters) in cases of self-deception. The correct
and precise thing to say is that she has a first-order commitment that
she sincerely avows and has a true second-order belief about, and she
has a disposition that is at odds with her commitment, that does not
allow her to live up to it, and that is manifested in her behavior. That
behavior, in the last chapter, was seen as a reason to think that she
believed that she is not healthy. But that is now at best an ambiguous
and, at worst and more correctly, an incorrect thing to say. It is more
correct to say unambiguously that she has a disposition that leads to
behavior that fails to live up to the commitment. Only seeing beliefs
and desires as commitments, something we have only argued for in
this chapter, makes this correction and precisification possible.

The strategy of the last chapter has therefore been developed to a point that it allows for the strong conclusion that self-deception does not (over and above, need not) provide any exceptions to the authority conditional. The conditional need not therefore be expressed as a presumption since that was only done to allow for exceptions. In Chapter 1, there was a pledge that the presumptively formulated conditional for authority would get a *rewrite* once authority's grounds had been laid out. The conditional there read as follows. It is a presumption that: if S believes that she desires (believes) that p, then she desires (believes) that p. Here, then, is the rewritten conditional for authority.

(A). If S believes that she desires (believes) that p, then she desires (believes) that p.

This stark conditional has now been established by the slowly developed argument of these last two chapters, culminating in the claims of the last few pages. It has taken nothing less than a reorientation of the notion of intentionality as commitments in the light of a normative conception of agency to do so. (I say that this rewritten conditional for authority is stark because the reader would have noticed that it is distinctly more straightforward than the rewritten conditional for transparency in Chapter 2, the conditional (T). I will return to this difference between the two conditionals in Section 6 below.)

It is simply impossible, then, to embrace the integration I have proposed, i.e., to view intentional states themselves as commitments while denying that we have authority regarding our own intentional states.

In a sense, but only in a very restricted sense, this implies that the Cartesian position, which says that one's self-knowledge of intentionality is infallible, is quite correct. We cannot be wrong about our intentional states. But in crucial other respects it is not Cartesian at all.

For one thing, the claim that one's second-order beliefs cannot be wrong depends here on giving up a conception of intentional states as dispositions. There is no echo of this in the Cartesian position, no derivation of that claim from a normative notion of intentional states as commitments. On the present picture, dispositions need not be the sort of thing one is authoritative over at all. Only commitments are authoritatively known by their possessors. Thus self-deception is allowed on the present view because it is restricted to dispositions, and that means that self-deception does not get counted as providing exceptions to authority over intentional states. But the Cartesian position can make no such allowance since it has no such distinction in place between dispositions and commitments. Thus the position is refuted by the familiar Freudian cases, while the position presented here is not. That is why we said in Chapter 1 that Cartesian claims to infallibility were too obviously wrong and must be made over. We have made them over into the present position, and it is not really recognizable as a Cartesian position at all. There is no backsliding on our acknowledgment that Cartesian infallibility is obviously wrong if we ground the idea of the invariable truth of second-order beliefs on a distinction to which the Cartesian position is simply blind.

For another, in Descartes 'infallibility' came from a substantial epistemology of inner *perception* of one's inner states; it was the perception that was infallible. But on the position presented here, that is not the case at all. The invariable truth of our second-order beliefs is not owed to an infallible faculty of inner perception; it is owed to the very nature of intentional states, thought of as normative states or commitments. So the right thing to say, perhaps, is that it is coextensive but not cointensive with the Cartesian position. Both positions end up with the invariable truth of our second-order beliefs, but the grounds for this outcome are so different that it is wrong to even use the same word 'infallibility' to describe both. The term 'infallibilist' is best restricted to describe an outcome that is supposed to be the result of an infallible faculty of inner perception. When instead it is due to the very nature of what is self-known, neutral terms like 'authority' are better for describing the outcome. The term 'authority' is neutral because it does not carry the suggestion that there is any infallible faculty of perception or infallibly reliable mechanism that is responsible for the outcome. Authority could then be viewed as a consequence of the fact that there is no right understanding of the nature of second-order beliefs (and the sincere avowals that express them) that does not also produce the outcome that the first-order beliefs and desires that they are about are also present. That echoes the notion of a 'constitutive' notion of self-knowledge, which was spelled out in Chapter 1. In that chapter, I had said that the Cartesian position had both the perceptual understanding of self-knowledge and the constitutive understanding of it, and these were impossible to reconcile. I had promised to extract the constitutive claim from the rest of its Cartesian setting of notions of the *infallibility* of our inner *perception of* our mental states. We have now done that. What we have done is to show that one can redeem the constitutive claim, first, by contrasting it with the perceptual claim and, then, grounding it in considerations that are not Cartesian at all. That grounding has been hard earned; it has consisted in an *integration* of the notion of intentionality with the notion of value. And once so grounded, the claim to authority that emerges need not be described in the misleading vocabulary of 'infallibility'.

Resistance to authority, as a property of our second-order beliefs, must therefore be viewed as a failure to grasp the significance and the implications of this integration.

Resistance, though, is bound to come easily to those who are unprepared for this integration, and it may be worth spelling out patiently just how we should respond to it. Someone resisting the idea that authority is a property of our second-order beliefs might devise scenarios of various kinds to put it into doubt. Here is one.[45]

Suppose someone to have long had a commitment to, i.e., a belief in, Christianity. (I am encapsulating and summarizing for the sake of convenience here by talking of 'belief-*in*' something as omnibus as Christianity—obviously, this would have to get a breakdown into a series of beliefs-*that,* all of which are commitments in the sense characterized earlier in this chapter.) Suppose also that he has for some years now lost or shed this commitment and that, though he is not hostile to Christianity, he has been indifferent or somewhat skeptical of it for some years. Thus, at present he lacks the first-order belief in or commitment to Christianity. Suppose, however, that he nevertheless sincerely avows that he is a Christian, and therefore we can truly say that he believes that he believes in Christianity. And finally suppose that this second-order belief leads him by the following reasoning to go to church, to pray, and to do other 'Christian' actions: he believes that he believes that he is a Christian; he believes that anyone who believes he is a Christian should go to church; etc.; so he does all these Christian actions. But since he is somewhat skeptical of Christianity now, these actions are merely going through the motions; they are not really revealing of any first-order Christian beliefs or commitments. So his second-order belief *is in place, but it is false.* Thus my conditional for authority is not exceptionlessly true. Leave alone dispositions, even commitments, therefore, may not be something we are authoritative about in our second-order beliefs.

My claim has been that the presence of the second-order belief ensures that there is a first-order commitment (though not necessarily a first-order disposition). If this person believes that he believes he is committed to Christianity, nothing else is needed in order for him to be so committed except that he is prepared to accept criticism if he were not to live up to his commitment, and he is prepared to try and do better. Living up to one's Christian beliefs is done by things such as going to church, etc. However, in the scenario just sketched, this person *is* going to church, etc.; it's just that these actions are phony—he is merely going through the motions of living up to a commitment, not really living up to them. Now, I would argue that if he really does have a second-order belief that he believes that he is a Christian, then the following counterfactual is true of him: should it become clear to him that he is merely going through the motions, he would criticize himself and try and do better, thereby revealing that he met the minimal conditions of having the first-order belief in or commitment to Christianity. He thus has the commitment, and the second-order belief is true.

But in response, suppose one further thing on behalf of the resistance. Suppose our protagonist, when he comes to understand that he is merely going through the motions, does *not* criticize himself for having failed to live up to his first-order commitment, but instead simply sheds his second-order belief that he has the first-order commitment. Does not that show that he did not have the first-order belief or commitment?

It does not. If he met the minimal conditions for sincerity of avowal when he avowed the commitment, then he has the commitment and he has a second-order belief expressed by the avowal that is true—and if, on realizing that he is going through the motions in his actions, he simply sheds his second-order belief, that does not show that his second-order belief when he held it was false; it just shows that he has now changed his own mind. That is, he has moved from a first-order commitment to Christianity to a skepticism or to an indifference about Christianity. He therefore has moved from a second-order belief that was true to shedding that second-order belief. It won't do to say, "Well, but he was going through the motions even before he realized that he was and shed his second-order belief, so why is it a change of mind? Why doesn't the fact of his simply going through the motions at that stage not show that lacked the commitment at that stage?" It won't do to say this because the fact that he was going through the motions showed only that he lacked the *dispositions* to act in a way that would live up to the Christian commitments that he had. It would *not* show that he lacked the *commitments*.

The resistance to authority might respond by saying: What if even before he realized that he was going through the motions, he assented to the following counterfactual: If I come to know that I am going through the motions in my actions such as going to church, then I will shed my second-order belief that I believe in Christianity (i.e., I will shed my second-order belief that I have a commitment to Christianity). Assenting to this counterfactual at that stage is of course inconsistent with the commitment to Christianity and the expression of it in a sincere avowal. It is inconsistent with it because the condition for having the commitment and the sincerity of the avowal is that a quite different counterfactual holds of him, viz., that were he to discover that he was merely going through the motions, then he would criticize himself for not having lived up to the commitment and would try and do better by way of living up to it. So if he did sincerely avow the commitment and therefore possessed the commitment, then the situation is just like the situation that I had raised for Davidson. That was the situation of someone believing that p (in the sense of commitment) but assenting in a fit of distraction to not-p. So our response has to be that the commitment expressed in the sincere avowal of his Christian beliefs is such that it implies that he should be discarding his assent to the counterfactual that has it that he would shed his second-order belief, were he to discover that he was merely going through the motions. That assent must have been made in a fit of distraction or some other such condition, and it is inconsistent with one's commitments. Unlike with Davidson, who does not view beliefs (and desires) as commitments, we have no choice but to say that the assent was not serious. If this is right, then the second-order belief that we attribute to him on the basis of his having made a sincere avowal remains true at that stage, and it is authoritative of his commitment. My conditional for authority thus remains unharmed.

Patiently responding to this resistance to authority brings out the fact again that the conditional for authority has its conceptual basis in the idea that beliefs and desires are commitments. In fact, it is really only because we implicitly *do* view them as normative states such as commitments (and if the pincer argument is correct, we view them so with some right) that we have such strong intuitions about authority in our knowledge of our own intentional states. I myself doubt that anything short of this view of beliefs and desires will satisfyingly capture the intuition, but it would be dogmatic to put this in any other terms than a doubt, without saying much more than I can here.

6. Before closing this chapter, something needs to be said now about the relations between transparency and authority, which we identified at the outset as the two properties that make self-knowledge special among all knowledges.

These two properties I had promised would be redeemed in two conditionals, and I have done so now over four chapters. In Chapter 3, I redeemed transparency in the conditional (T), after having provided its conceptual basis in Chapter 2 via an integration of agency with value. In the present chapter, I have redeemed authority in the conditional (A) above, after having provided its conceptual basis in an integration of intentionality with value earlier in this chapter, an integration that itself first needed an integration of intentionality and thought in the very condition of agency and a first-person point of view, which was presented in Chapter 4. Both conditionals now are in place, with their conceptual basis revealed, and they each have shown how self-knowledge has the properties of transparency and authority, respectively, possessed by no other kind of knowledge.

Each conditional began its formulated life in this book with a qualifying, presumptive status. Each began with the words "It is a presumption that. . . ." This qualified status was necessary in order to accommodate the fact of exceptions to transparency and authority. Because there were exceptions, one could not assert the conditionals outright but merely as presumptions.

But, on the other hand, the fact of the exceptions did not inhibit one from thinking that there was not something special to self-knowledge, did not inhibit one from thinking that transparency and authority really held of it. That is why one has thought it perfectly appropriate to formulate conditionals to express these two properties—it's just that one was forced to formulate the conditionals, at least initially, as mere presumptions. By contrast, in the case of perceptual knowledge, there is no temptation to formulate conditionals expressing transparency and authority. In other words, exceptions to transparency and authority in self-knowledge were not like exceptions to the truth of our perceptual beliefs, and that is why we are not even tempted to say of our perceptual beliefs that they are *presumed* to be transparent or authoritative. That is why self-knowledge, unlike perceptual knowledge of the world, is special. We don't have any temptation to say that there is a presumption that if there is an object or fact in the external vicinity of a subject, then she will believe that it is there. Nor are we tempted to say that there is a presumption that if a subject believes that there is a fact of object in the external vicinity, then it is there. Our intuition that there is something special about self-knowledge therefore lies in the fact that the many exceptions to transparency and authority in the perceptual case are not something we are even tempted to accommodate in conditionals with a presumptive status, as we are in the case of transparency and authority in self-knowledge.

But all that is merely to assert the intuitive specialness of self-knowledge. That was just the starting point laid out in the first chapter. The goal we set ourselves for the rest of the book was to consolidate this intuition in an underlying conceptual basis that would give us the right to remove the merely presumptive status of these conditionals, to formulate the conditionals without the words "It is a presumption that . . ." by giving an account of the exceptions to transparency and authority on a more principled basis, thereby accommodating the exceptions. *However, it is a very interesting fact that, having now provided that basis, we find that the conditionals (T) and (A) for transparency and authority, respectively, read somewhat differently and that therefore the exceptions, at least at first sight, have been accommodated somewhat differently in each case.* That difference is revealing.

In Chapter 3, we arrived at the conditional for transparency in the following formulation:

(T). Given agency, if S desires (believes) that p, then S believes that she desires (believes) that p.

(Fully written out, the conditional should read: To the extent that an intentional state is part of a rationalization [or potential rationalization][46] of an action or conclusion, which is or can be the object of justifiable reactive attitudes, or to the extent that an intentional state itself is or can be the object of justifiable reactive attitudes, then that intentional state is known to its possessor. We will work with the more abbreviated version above, for the sake of convenience.)

But in the previous section of the present chapter, we arrived at the conditional for authority in a formulation that is without any proviso regarding agency. The conditional for authority we arrived at is:

(A). If S believes that she desires (believes) that p, then she desires (believes) that p.

There is no proviso "Given agency . . ." in (A) as there is in (T). Why not?

In the case of (T), the proviso, as I said, is there to deal with exceptions to transparency. But with authority, I *did not allow for any exceptions*. I claimed instead that *once we understand that intentional states such as beliefs and desires are commitments* in the sense we have characterized them, there are no exceptions to authority. Self-deception and other such phenomena, though quite widespread, do not provide exceptions to authority.

This difference in our treatment of the transparency and the authority conditional is explained first of all by the fact that when we were dealing with transparency, we were not restricting the conditional to talk of beliefs and desires *qua commitments*. At that earlier stage (Chapter 3), there was no mention of commitments. The notion of commitments and our rationale for introducing them in the first place was given over a long discussion in the present chapter, and it owed to a line of argument going back to Chapter 4.

Were we to have restricted the transparency conditional to cover beliefs and desires qua commitments, we would not have needed the proviso "Given agency . . ." for the transparency conditional, either. Why? The reason should be obvious. It is the nature of commitments that they are transparent. We have characterized commitments as states that, were we not to live up to them, we should be prepared to criticize ourselves and be prepared also to try and do better, by way of living up to them by, say, cultivating the dispositions to live up to them. We cannot therefore have commitments without believing that we have them. I cannot be prepared to be critical of myself for not having lived up to a commitment if I did not believe that I had that commitment. Thus the very condition for having a commitment pre-supposes that one has a second-order belief that one has that commitment. However, in Chapter 2, we did not have the conceptual wherewithal laid out to introduce the notion of commitments nor the rationale to introduce it. To introduce commitments, it was necessary to have the entire discussion of Oblomov and why, lacking agency, he lacks thought and intentionality and how that implies that agents are subjects whose mentality cannot be wholly dispositional and therefore in particular that agents are subjects who necessarily possess states such as commitments. None of this ground had been laid as early as Chapter 3.

Someone might, then, wonder: Why was this ground for intro-ducing commitments not laid out earlier before presenting the trans-parency conditional? Why was it delayed till the authority conditional became the issue of focus? There is a point and purpose in having delayed that ground and not presented it for the discussion of trans-parency. This is because there *is* a real difference—it is perhaps even an asymmetry—between transparency and authority. When it comes to transparency, we can produce an interesting conditional such as (T) that holds for beliefs and desires *even if they are considered as dis-positions*. This is important. As was pointed out in Chapter 3, we do have self-knowledge of intentional states (even conceived disposition-ally) so long as (and this is the proviso of agency understood in mod-ified Strawsonian terms) they are the justifiable targets of the reactive attitudes. We have no justification for blaming or resenting actions that flow from mental dispositions that are not self-known to the agent. We can only justify these reactive attitudes to actions that flow from dispositions that are self-known, and *there are* dispositions of this kind that are often the justifiable target of the reactive attitudes. So we do have transparent self-knowledge of mental dispositions. We can, as a result, make the more ambitious claim that (T) holds of beliefs and desires, even if they are conceived as dispositions.

By contrast, authority does not hold over dispositions. If we thought beliefs and desires were dispositions, we would not have a right to say that my belief that I have a belief or a desire is authoritative. Cases of self-deception, cases such as the case of a person's Christian beliefs discussed above, and so on, would provide exceptions to authority. And no proviso about agency would accommodate these exceptions. That proviso is meant to summarize the presence of justifiable reactive attitudes to actions and states of mind. If I believe that I have a set of Christian beliefs and desires (dispositionally, not commitmentally, conceived) and my behavior shows that I am merely going through the motions and in fact don't have them, no such proviso will help to accommodate this and make the conditional true nevertheless. How could it help? Suppose someone justifiably blamed my behavior of merely going through the motions. That would not show that I had authority over my Christian beliefs (dispositionally conceived). It would show the opposite. It would show that I did not have Christian beliefs and that I was in fact blameworthy for thinking that I do and pretending that I do.

So there is a real difference, even an asymmetry. Considerations of agency, i.e., of being the justifiable object of reactive attitudes, can show certain dispositions to be transparent; they can show that we must have some second-order beliefs about these dispositions; but they cannot show that we have any authority over them when we have second-order beliefs about our dispositions. This is because we may not have the dispositions that we think we have, even when agency is all in place and reactive attitudes are quite appropriate and justified. Authority of our second-order beliefs only comes when it is *commitments* that we have second-order beliefs about.

What this shows is that the role of agency in the matter of authority is a role that is not immediately visible in the conditional itself. We do not need to mention agency explicitly in any proviso in (A) because *there are no* exceptions to authority once it is formulated with beliefs and desires viewed as commitments. The relevance of agency to authority is a much more *background* relevance, in the sense that the very idea of beliefs and desires as commitments is introduced *only because* we understand that there can be no beliefs and desires without there being agency (as the whole discussion of Oblomov in Chapter 4 makes clear), and the notion of beliefs and desires that must be introduced if agency is to be in place at all is a commitmental one. That was the conclusion earlier in this chapter. So in a sense, what one may conclude here is that though there is no need, unlike as in (T) to have an agency proviso in (A) because there are no exceptions to authority that have to be accommodated, we need to understand that *the reason why there are no exceptions to authority* owes in the end to matters of agency. In other words, the asymmetry is this: considerations of agency show that the exceptions to transparency are not threats to the conditional for transparency because we build in considerations of agency into the conditional itself. Considerations of agency are not required to be *built into* the conditional for authority because there are *no exceptions* to authority at all, but the *explanation* for why there are no exceptions to authority owes in the end to considerations of agency. Put another way: (T), being more ambitious than (A) in covering beliefs and desires qua commitment *and* disposition, needs a proviso with explicit mention of considerations of agency. (A) is less ambitious than (T) in restricting its formulation to beliefs and desires qua commitments only, but there is no rationale for the very notion of commitments that is so crucial to its formulation, unless there is an implicit understanding of the deep relevance and importance of considerations of agency in the *background* that force that notion on us.

Thus agency, value, and the very nature of beliefs and desires as commitments all go in an integrated relation into our understanding of and accounting for the properties of transparency and authority that make self-knowledge special. In a very short concluding chapter of the book that follows immediately now, I will pull these large strands of the argument together in a brief summary.

SIX

❖ ❖ ❖

Conclusion: Philosophical Integrations

THIS BOOK HAS been as much about the relation of agency and intentionality to the notion of norm or value as it has been about the nature of self-knowledge. That is not surprising since it was stated at the outset that self-knowledge, despite being knowledge, cannot be viewed as a standard subject merely within epistemology. There is not much that is standard about self-knowledge. It stands out as special among all the other kinds of knowledge that we have.

That it is special is not something that can in any *obvious or quick* way be put into doubt. All the intuitions are that it is special in some way. If it is not special, that would have to be shown by real philosophical effort that would have the task of *battling these intuitions* and showing in some way that it is akin to perceptual knowledge (as Armstrong tried to show) or akin to knowledge by inference (as Ryle tried to show) or some combination of both (as Gopnik tried to show). Were their efforts successful, they would have shown that the intuitions don't stand up to the philosophy that these efforts produce. The intuitions were first formulated in Chapter 1 of this book in the form of two properties (transparency and authority) expressed in two presumptions, each of which took a conditional form. I have had my say against those efforts to undermine the intuitions and done my bit to show that these presumptions are not overturned by these philosophers, nor in principle could they be by the impressive edifice of cognitive scientific notions and theories that have been built on the more philosophical claims by Armstrong, Ryle, and Gopnik.

The efforts in philosophy on the part of those who share the intuitions and do not want to battle them have to be of a quite different kind. They have to be efforts to *ground these intuitions* about what is special about knowledge in philosophical argument. This book has tried to produce such an argument by a series of philosophical moves that I have claimed are best understood as amounting to a project of philosophical *integration* of different philosophical notions. Once the notion of self-knowledge is integrated with the notions of agency, value, and intentionality (viewed in the light of agency and value), the intuitions about self-knowledge will be grounded.

This grounding of the intuitions allows us to cease seeing them merely as presumptions; it allows us to see them as philosophical theses expressed in two conditionals, now no longer characterized presumptively. The (non-presumptively expressed) conditionals without the grounding are obviously false. With the grounding, they are invulnerable.

The grounding consisted first in situating one of these conditionals, the one for transparency, in a very specific normative conception of agency (i.e., a Strawsonian conception modified along very specific radically normativist lines). This happened over Chapters 2 and 3, and it allowed one to see transparency as simply a fallout of such a conception of agency. Just as Strawson had shown agency to be a fallout of a set of normative or evaluative attitudes (what he called the 'reactive' attitudes), the strategy was to take this one step further: by making the agency-constituting evaluative attitudes themselves rest on further values, it allowed one to see self-knowledge (in the aspect of transparency) as a fallout of such a radically evaluative notion of agency. Thus, in this first stage of the grounding, agency was *integrated* with value, and self-knowledge (in the aspect of transparency) was in turn integrated with such an evaluative notion of agency.

The grounding consisted next in drawing out the implications of this specific normative notion of agency for the notion of intentionality. This happened in Chapters 4 and 5. Via a discussion of an imaginary subject wholly lacking agency, it was shown how deeply the very notion of thought or intentionality turns on possessing the point of view of agency, of subjectivity, the point of view of the first, rather than the third, person. And it was then shown via an argument owing to a Fregean extension of G. E. Moore's anti-naturalism that such a picture of intentionality required ceasing to see intentional subjects in wholly dispositional terms and, indeed, required seeing intentional states such as beliefs and desires as *themselves* normative states or commitments. When so viewed, intentional states are very different from how they appear even to a range of philosophers who think of them along normative lines, such as Davidson. When so viewed they are not only irreducible to and non-identical with the physical and causal states of subjects; they cannot even be clearly assessed to be dependent on such states in the specific ways that philosophers like to capture with such terms as 'supervenience'. (There are of course all sorts of other dependencies that intentional states have on the states of the central nervous system, which do not amount to anything like the relation or relations that go by the name of 'supervenience'.) This is because when they are so viewed, they are essentially first personal phenomena, phenomena whose claims to supervenient dependence on third person states such as physical or causal properties of subjects are neither stateable nor deniable. (Therefore, not assessable.) This duality of perspectives, which puts into doubt notions of supervenience, is also essential to understanding the nature of value and to understanding more fully the normative conception of agency first expounded in Chapter 2. The perspective of agency is vital to how we understand values because it is from this perspective (and this perspective alone) that we can ask and answer the question, "What *ought* I to do or think?" And it is from this perspective (and this perspective alone) that the value properties in the world are so much as perceptible, which is why Oblomov, who lacks this perspective, cannot see the world as offering opportunities to act or making normative demands for actions on his part. The perspectival element fills out and completes the normative conception of agency that was first presented in Chapter 2 by making clear that it is from the first person perspective alone that we can understand how it is that the non-coercive causes of our behavior (our intentional states), we saw in Chapter 2 to be compatible with freedom, have the causal efficacy to make a difference to the world via our behavior. The non-naturalistic sense in which our intentional states or commitments cause our behavior cannot be elaborated just in terms of the idea of singular causal statements. That idea, though correct, is superficial if it is not consolidated with an analysis of the nature of such a cause as it surfaces in the point of view of the agent, and only when that analysis is given do we get a full grip on the normative notion of agency and intentionality.

With all of this presented in Chapter 5, the wherewithal for the conceptual basis or grounding of our intuitions about self-knowledge is now complete. When intentional states are viewed in this light, when they are themselves normative states or commitments, as I characterized them, the conditions for possessing intentional states are no different from the conditions for the sincerity of the avowals by which we express our second-order beliefs about these intentional states. These second-order beliefs therefore are invariably true. Their invariable truth is precisely what is claimed by the conditional that states the other half of what makes self-knowledge special, the aspect of authority. By showing that intentionality has agency as a necessary condition and by showing that agency (when already understood to be the thoroughly normative phenomenon it is) requires that the intentional states it is a necessary condition for must themselves be evaluative states rather than dispositions, a quite literal integration of intentionality with value has been achieved. It is this integration that allows the grounding of the other half of the special nature of self-knowledge, the aspect of 'authority'.

Is what emerges in these conditionals for transparency and authority, then, rightly described as an '*explanation*' of self-knowledge? This terminological issue can now be put to rest.

In a real sense, these are not explanations if explanations require causal-explanatory satisfaction. In Chapters 3, 4, and 5, it has been shown how causal mechanisms connecting intentional states to second-order beliefs about them are not to the point in coming to grips with the nature of transparency, nor is the standardness or uniqueness of the cause of our second-order beliefs to the point in accounting for the nature of authority. Since authority and transparency are the properties that mark self-knowledge as special, and since they are grounded in these quite radically normative notions, causality, even where it exists, is not what is doing the work of illumination.

But there need be no disappointment in this because genuine illumination can come from the fact that a phenomenon (self-knowledge) is located in its relations with other phenomena (agency, intentionality, value) as they relate to one another in turn. Self-

knowledge is precisely illuminated by this network of integral relations. To find no illumination in the philosophical work that goes
into such a detailed locating is to be driven by the ideological conviction that illumination in a subject where knowledge is in play can
only in the end come from a broadly causal-explanatory account. This
is to assume *from the outset* that self-knowledge cannot be as special as
our intuitions initially suggest, that if it is special, it is only because
of such things as the greater reliability of the causal mechanisms connecting intentional states with second-order beliefs about them and
the standardness and uniqueness of the cause of our second-order
beliefs. If the passage of argument from Chapters 2 to 5 carries any
conviction, that ideological conviction (if it is held from the outset,
turning a deaf ear to these integrating efforts at locating self-
knowledge in a network of related concepts) amounts to a tiresome
prejudice, a surrender, really, of one's philosophical intelligence.[1]
That being said, the question of whether the term 'explanation' best
captures the sort of illumination that location among these other concepts provides may be resolved amicably in the word.

A more substantial question is not about 'explanation' but about
whether the treatment of self-knowledge offered in the grounding of
our two conditionals amounts to a 'response-dependent' treatment of
intentional states. The idea of 'response-dependence' owes to Crispin
Wright[2] and his ambitious efforts to identify a class of phenomena
regarding which our judgments about them are not to be seen as
tracking an independent realm of facts, but rather as determining
what the facts are. Thus, on many current treatments of secondary
qualities, intentionality, value, even perhaps agency, if Strawson is
right—these would all belong to such a class of phenomena.

Is my treatment of intentional states such as beliefs and desires as
being in some sense 'constituted' by our self-knowledge of them such
a treatment of intentionality?

This is very hard to answer without being very clear about what
exactly motivates the idea of response-dependence. Is it intended to
formulate a refined, contemporary version of anti-realism about the
phenomena concerned? Is the idea that judgment determines rather
than tracks an independent realm of facts supposed to be announcing
this anti-realism?

What is clear from these last five chapters is the relatively restricted and neutral claim that beliefs and desires are the kinds of things that, unlike stools and chairs, are transparent. And what is clear too is that when we judge or believe that we have a belief or desire, we do have it; i.e., our second-order beliefs about these intentional states are authoritative in a way that our beliefs about whether there is a stool or table in the carpentry shed is not. Does this clarity on these points carry over to any clarity about claims to an anti-realism about intentionality (or color or value or agency) that does not hold of stools and tables?

It is not at all obvious that it does.

There is, to begin with, a real question as to whether there is a *kind*, which we may properly call 'response-dependent' phenomena. The examples of color, agency, value, and intentionality do not seem to be characterizable in terms that are usefully uniform.

There is, to begin with, an obvious thing (there are others) that spoils the aspiration to uniformity and complicates any aspiration to classing these phenomena into a kind. The judgments that are supposed to determine rather than track an independent domain of color facts are perceptual judgments, but it is my whole point (and Wright's too) that my second-order judgments about my beliefs and desires are precisely not perceptual judgments; they are constitutive of intentional states precisely because they are not like perceptual judgments.

This might seem to make matters better, not worse, for the claim to anti-realism, since something that is not perceived is more likely to be susceptible to anti-realist treatment. So, it might be said, though it is true that response-dependence phenomena are not uniformly treatable in all ways, what you have just noticed about intentionality is particularly apt for a response-dependence treatment that has as its motivation to establish an anti-realism about the relevant phenomenon. But that thought too is spoiled by a complication. *Others can know my intentional states by perception even if I don't know them by perception.* And that presumably then restores a realism about intentional states.

What then, if someone protested that others cannot really *perceive* my intentional states—they can only infer them from my behavior which they perceive? (This protest is something I have considered and expressed my doubts about when considering the relation between Gopnik's and McDowell's views on the matter in Chapter 3; but right now I am not concerned with whether or not it is correct, rather simply with the fact that no clarity on the question of realism and anti-realism is forthcoming from the idea that my account of the self-knowledge of intentional states is a constitutive one.) The protest seems to be granting that were others to be able to perceive my intentional states, a realism about them could be restored; but since they are not really perceiving them, only inferring them from what they perceive—a person's behavior—realism is not restored at all, and on the contrary, an anti-realism is asserted. But now it seems that realism about some phenomena lies in the non-inferential availability of the phenomena to one's judgment.[3] If so, then one may after all restore the realism about intentional states once again by pointing out that the availability of my intentional states to *my* judgment is indeed non-inferential because of the constitutive thesis for which I have been arguing.

The dilemma for the anti-realist, then, is this: If one takes response-dependence to be a mark of anti-realism, then the fact that one's intentional states (unlike colors, say) are not dependent on the response of others (but only our own) and yet are perceivable by others is proof that they are real things independent of responses. On the other hand, if this claim to realism is answered by insisting that intentional states are not in fact perceivable by others, they are merely inferred from what is perceivable by others (i.e., one's behavior), then the mark of anti-realism is not response-dependence but *in*direct availability to one's judgment and perception. And if so, then once again intentional states cannot get an anti-realist treatment since they are available to one's judgment without any indirection or inference—at least if my argument in this book has been right.

There are other reasons too for worrying about assimilating disparate phenomena under the rubric of response-dependence, worries about assimilating intentional states with secondary qualities in particular. Much of the point of the idea of secondary qualities is that though they contrast with primary qualities in being response-dependent, they are supervenient on them. But, as I argued in Chapter 5, it is precisely supervenience that cannot be assessed for phenomena like intentionality (or for agency and value with which it stands in integral relations in the ways that I presented).

All this I say by way of saying that 'response-dependence' should not be thought of as picking out a kind, nor if it is intended to an-nounce an anti-realism should it be seen as applying to intentional phenomena on the grounds that such phenomena stand in constitu-tive relations to our self-knowledge of them. If the description 'response-dependence' *only* describes these constitutive relations, if it only describes the fact that the two conditionals I have established hold of the relations between intentional states and second-order judgments about them, I would be happy to accept that 'response-dependence' is a good description of my treatment. But there is not much beyond that which I would embrace in accepting the descrip-tion. My acceptance of it may therefore disappoint someone who has in mind to register more ambitious things with the description, and worse, it may mislead others into thinking that I have those more ambitious things in mind. If so, it would be best, then, not to accept the description. That is why, just as I avoided words like 'entitlement', which, as I pointed out in Chapter 3, has implications that would mislead others about my treatment of transparency there, I have also avoided words like 'response-dependence' in elaborating my treat-ment of self-knowledge of intentionality in general.

The two conditionals and the large conceptual integrations from which they emerge are interesting and ambitious enough, I hope, without having to line them up with yet more ambitious thematic considerations of realism and anti-realism.

What, in sum, then, is the ambition behind establishing the two conditionals via the elaborate path that these chapters have taken?

Four perennially vexing issues have emerged as deeply linked. There is, of course, the issue of the place, the special place, of self-knowledge among other forms of knowledge, which is the subject of the book. There is the issue of the place of freedom and agency in a deterministic universe. There is the issue of the place of value in a world of nature. And there is the issue of the place of intentional states among the states of the central nervous system. If the argument provided over this book's many pages has been effective, these are *not* a *miscellany* of issues.

The point can be put more provocatively and only slightly mislead-ingly because of the obvious encapsulations involved.

Philosophy over the centuries has drawn four prima facie distinc-tions of interest and importance, which have then been dissected to see whether they are tenable as distinctions and in what exact form they are tenable, if they are: the distinction between value and nature, the distinction between freedom and determinism, the distinction between mind (intentionality) and body (the causal and physical properties of the brain), and the deep and intuitive difference between self-knowledge and other kinds of knowledge. It would be too misleading to say that the integration I have tried to achieve shows that these are at bottom the same distinction. But what it shows is something roughly like this. There has been a tendency among philosophers to find one side of each of these distinctions to be intrinsically problematic and mysterious. How is value so much as possible in a natural world? we ask. And in the same vexed spirit, How is freedom possible in a deterministic universe? How can the mental, the intentional, not be reducible to events and states and properties in the material world? And finally, how can an epistemological notion such as self-knowledge not be just like all other knowledge, perceptually, inferentially, and generally cognitively achieved? Thus to think there is a distinction at all in each case is to think that there is a problem or mystery to be confronted. If the integrations of this book have a point to make, it is that these are at bottom the same mystery. Once one grants the irreducibility of value to the facts of nature as the natural sciences conceive of those facts, and once one integrates the notions of agency and intentionality and self-knowledge to the notion of value in the nested way that I have done, we can with right see these seemingly differentiated mysteries as being, at the last, the same. And reducing the numbers of mysteries there are can surely only be a good thing.

In one sense the book's efforts to show that self-knowledge is special by these *integrative* means have yielded a rather modest result. They have merely shown that were we to make these integrations between the notions of agency, value, intentionality, and self-knowledge, then self-knowledge is special in being constitutive of intentional states rather than something gained by a form of perception of them or by any other form of cognition or causal connection. They have shown that were we to make these integrations, standard descriptions by which knowledge is described—as the outcome of a 'justification' and an 'entitlement' (in the case of perceptual knowledge, an entitlement drawn from the objects or facts given in experience; in the case of self-knowledge, from the presence of intentional states)—are not quite apt to describe it. And they have presented reasons to embrace these integrations.

What they have not done is to *demonstrate* that there are *no other ways* of establishing that self-knowledge is special in these senses. It is not obvious what general form such a demonstration would take. Perhaps there is no general demonstration of that kind, and to look to more specific demonstrations would have required that one consider each such way present in the philosophical literature and repudiate it. The book did not set out to do anything like that, and in any case, to do that would require a temperament that its author frankly does not possess. Yet, though nothing like that exclusiveness has been demonstrated, I do have a very strong hunch that other ways of establishing the special character of self-knowledge, even if they do not eventually rest on the truth of these integrations, will be strengthened and deepened by them.

At the very least, what has been shown is that no other way of establishing what is genuinely special about self-knowledge can *fall afoul* of these ways of thinking about intentionality, agency, and value and their inter-relations. In other words, there may be other ways of establishing what is special about self-knowledge, but I would deny that they are *incompatible* with the larger claims that have been proposed here.[4] So I am immodest enough to think that the book has shown that were we to deny its large claims about agency, intentionality, and value and their inter-relations, then the honest thing to do would be to say that self-knowledge is after all akin to the perceptual and inferential forms of knowledge we possess, that it is after all not all that special, and that claims to it being special are a mere Cartesian residue that modern developments in philosophy and cognitive science would be quite right to discard.

And the interesting point is that the integrations show that even for those who wish to discard its special character as an illusion and who are unconvinced by the argument given in this book, they would have to at least acknowledge that in discarding it they are discarding much more than a certain view of self-knowledge; they are resisting the stance taken here on a range of other issues as well. That, though not my maximal ambition for the book, would at least remain as a small but satisfying compensation. For it would mark its own kind of progress and illumination.

It has always worried those of us who do philosophy that its issues are so perennial, that it has no results, that most readers of any but the most trivial book will go away unconvinced by its argument, that there is no cumulative and progressive knowledge in the sense of building on consensual results and leaving behind once and for all the issues that have been resolved. But perhaps we would feel less worried in the face of this lack of accumulation and resolution if we were reassured that a different kind of progress might come from such integration as I have tried to provide. The integration would at least allow us to say to someone who is unconvinced by one's argument: Look *how much* you are giving up by being unconvinced. That is progress of a sort, something in which philosophy can take satisfaction.

◆ ◆ ◆

When Self-Knowledge Is Not Special
(with a Short Essay on Psychoanalysis)

1. THE TWO CONDITIONALS, now stated, elaborated, and defended over five chapters, were intended to establish that self-knowledge is not (paradigmatically) a cognitive achievement, that it is (paradigmatically) a fallout of the fact that our intentional states are caught up in normative notions of agency and the implications of that notion. These parenthetical qualifiers such as 'paradigmatically' that were assumed to be in place throughout this work were intended from the outset to allow that there are exceptions to the paradigm, to allow that there are cases of self-knowledge that are not a fallout of our agency, but that were achieved in ways that were at least in some minimal part similar to other forms of knowledge such as our perceptual cum inferential knowledge of the external world and of the minds of others. The work would not be complete therefore without some word about these cases of self-knowledge and how they fit in, in detail, with the paradigmatic cases.

I used the qualifier 'paradigmatic' cases of self-knowledge of intentional states only *before* I introduced and argued for the thesis that intentional states are themselves normative states, i.e., commitments. The qualifier is not needed once that thesis has been established. This is because intentional states, qua commitments, are *all* self-known without cognitive effort in the way that those states I was calling the 'paradigmatic' intentional states are self-known. Because until I introduced the thesis intentional states were being viewed as they are usually but wrongly viewed—as 'dispositional' states, in the standard and substantial sense of that term—the qualifier 'paradigmatic' was needed. While viewed dispositionally rather than commitmentally, only some intentional states are known without cognitive achievement, the ones caught up with agency, and so they alone provided the paradigmatic cases of self-knowledge. But once intentional states are viewed as commitments, they are, as I pointed out at the end of Chapter 5, all known without cognitive effort because it is part of the very understanding of what commitments are that they are self-known to their possessors. One needs to know what one's commitments are if one is to meet the conditions for having a commitment, viz., that one would be prepared, for instance, to criticize oneself for not having lived up to it. One could not be prepared to do this if one did not know what the commitment was.

The fact is, however, that though there is no reason to retain the qualifier '*paradigmatic* cases of self-knowledge of intentional states', once one understands that intentional states are commitments, our interest in self-knowledge is not circumscribed just to self-knowledge of intentional states. This is because intentionality, even when viewed as commitments, is thoroughly caught up with one's dispositions. This is a point of some real importance. What do I mean by 'caught up'? Commitments are the sorts of things that one lives up to or fails to live up to. When one does either of these it is because (respectively) one does or does not possess the dispositions to act so as to live up to them. So a question also arises about our self-knowledge of those dispositional states. And as I said in Chapter 2, those dispositional states are transparent so long as they are in the domain of agency. The proviso in (T), discussed in that chapter, makes this clear. Thus, since even mental dispositions are transparent, under certain conditions, one needs to mark out the cases of those mental dispositions that are transparent and those that are not. 'Paradigmatic' is a term that can be retained to mark out the ones that are transparent. Given that stipulation, self-knowledge of our mental states, when viewed as dispositions, is paradigmatically transparent, is paradigmatically not a product of cognitive effort. And the condition of agency as spelled out in the full version of that proviso is what spells out, in turn, the conditions for the presence of these 'paradigmatic' cases of self-knowledge.

So our question for this chapter now has to be: What happens when we are dealing neither with the cases of self-knowledge of commitments nor with the paradigmatic cases of self-knowledge of mental dispositions? What happens when we are dealing with cases of self-knowledge of mental dispositions that are *not* caught up with agency at all and therefore are not transparent at all? These are mental states that fall afoul of the proviso in (T). They exist, but they need not be self-known. And so if and when one does get to know them, that is due to cognitive effort. And, as I said, it is very important to point out that one cannot dismiss them as being irrelevant to our subject (which is the self-knowledge of intentional states—now understood as commitments) because these mental dispositions that need not be self-known may well be highly relevant to whether we are or are not living up to the commitments that our intentional states are.

In the next section, I will start with and spend some time on one of the most interesting and theorized of these cases in which self-knowledge is a cognitive achievement—psychoanalysis. And then, in the third and last section, something more general will be said about all cases, including the less interesting and more mundane ones.

Part of what makes self-knowledge in psychoanalysis interesting for non-philosophers is that it is tied intrinsically to a distinct kind of therapy. I will be making a generalization of this point of its interest and will try and show why 'therapy' is a fair general description of what *all* non-paradigmatic, cognitively acquired cases of self knowledge amount to.

Psychoanalysis is a very special case of cognitive acquisition self-knowledge, a highly regimented and institutional way. And, of course, the point of the regimen is not to stop at the self-knowledge but to proceed from there to providing a therapeutic cure for various forms of neurosis. This entire regimen can be illuminated and put in its theoretical place by bringing to bear upon it the framework from Chapter 5, consisting of the distinctions we have been making and the relations we have been drawing between commitments and dispositions and our self-knowledge of them. Theorists and philosophers writing about psychoanalysis have paid very little attention to these issues. That is unfortunate. How we understand the place of intentionality among the totality of our mental states and in our psychology in general is essential to coming to philosophical grips with the form of self-knowledge that is intrinsically caught up with the forms of therapy that comprise psychoanalysis. I will try and provide that understanding, and the generalization of the therapeutic point from psychoanalysis to all other cases of cognitively acquired self-knowledge will then follow upon such an understanding.

2. Some years ago the well-known psychoanalytic theorist Roy Schafer (in an influential book called *A New Language for Psychoanalysis*)[1] wrote to lament the tendency in psychoanalysis and its theorists to a discourse that leaves out too much the perspective of agency for a too passive understanding of human mentality and behavior; and he urged instead a turn or return to a more active voice. I want to applaud that sentiment, but I am not at all sure that what I have to say by way of developing it is what Schafer had in mind. In fact, I am certain that he did not have it in mind.[2] All the same, I think it is strictly implied by the theoretical sentiment he expressed.

Oblomov must return to the stage, at this point. We had described him as a figure of total passivity, precisely lacking in the agency that Schafer is commending. Of course, as a conceit of imagination, Oblomov is hyperbole, and in fact, as became clear in Chapter 4, he is not even so much as coherently imaginable. But it is the effort (in the name of science) to approximate in our theoretical descriptions what the conceit represents as an ideal (or a scientific ideal-type), from which Schafer is asking us to recoil. What lesson are we to learn, then, from his methodological advice? Nothing less than this: the more we approximate this ideal, the closer we are to negating the very idea of mind, at least to the extent that we think of intentionality as an essential feature of the mind. This much is clear from the points we made earlier about how a subject such as Oblomov who is purely passive or, to put it differently, who has *only* a third person perspective and no first person perspective on himself lacks thought and intentionality.

What relevance does this have for psychoanalysis? Its relevance can be sighted first in a paradox in the way we understand the effects of the disciplinary regimes of psychoanalytic and psychiatric disciplines. I have said earlier in the book and will repeat it here because it is directly relevant: Ever since Spinoza and most explicitly since Freud, we have been familiar with the idea that our *agency*, that is to say, our *autonomy and self-governance, is enhanced* by coming to know the ways

in which we are *caused* by various mental states, conscious and unconscious, to do the things we do. In other words, the very way in which
Oblomov thinks of himself—*in the third person, as a product of such
causes*—when exercised in these disciplinary formats to unearth and
bring to our own grasp the relevance of our own mental histories, is
liberating. Freud stressed this as being very much the motive for engaging in psychoanalysis, and Spinoza, without making a regime out
of the process, nevertheless anticipated Freud's general idea that we
increase our freedom and agency by the acquisition of such knowledge. And the paradox is this. This third person exercise that we
perform upon ourselves is the genuinely liberating thing that Spinoza
and Freud claimed for it, *only so long* as it is not elevated into some
sort of ideology about the nature of mind itself, only so long as it is
not, as Schafer puts it, erected into a discourse or language of mentality. The conceit shows that decisively. Oblomov, in the exaggerated
version I have presented, is, after all, the very antithesis of agency and
autonomy; he is just the logical end, and the *ideological* by-product, of
precisely such a third person point of view.

So, once again, we are presented with a deep but undiagnosed
curiosity (if not quite a paradox) as to why the *very thing* that, when
writ small, *induces* agency should, when writ large, *reduce* it. This is a
rather fascinating problem that I had mentioned in Chapter 3, and I
want to say something about it now by way of providing a diagnosis.

The main thesis I want to claim is that *psychoanalysis is really a form
of technology—it is not concerned in its methods with reasoning, and its
targets are not a person's commitments, even though it indispensably presupposes commitments and reason or reasoning in the background.* This thesis
will help to give the diagnosis of what I have called a 'curiosity'.

The statement of the thesis just coupled 'reasoning' with normative
states such as 'commitments', and the coupling is obvious and familiar
to philosophers, as are the codifications of reasoning that hold between these commitments such as beliefs, desires, and intentions or
choices. The codifications of deductive (and inductive) rationality, for
instance, hold between beliefs; the codifications of decision theory
hold between beliefs and desires and choices; and there ought to be
some codification, however rudimentary, that adds to these familiar
ones and that systematically links the rational relations between desires themselves. (These relations among desires or values that make

for their rationality would have to be relations of coherence analogous in some way—though which exact way needs to be thought through with some care—to coherence relations that hold between beliefs. That is an area not much worked on but desperately in need of work.)[3]

The coupling of reasoning with normative states is so obvious because when one *reasons* with someone, with a view, say, to changing their mind, one tells them that they have some commitment (which one thinks they *ought* to shed) because it does not follow deductively or inductively from or does not cohere with other commitments of theirs. Or one tells them that they do not have a commitment (which they *ought* to acquire) because it follows deductively, inductively, or coherentistically, from other commitments of theirs. Or one tells them that they *ought* to choose to act in a certain way that they have not, or ought not to choose something that they have, because that is what is sanctioned by the codified norms of coherence and decision theory to be in accord with their commitments.

None of these reasonings could apply to Oblomov. Oblomov does not reason. He has no intentional states, no commitments, which could be the vehicles of reasoning. As was said in Chapter 4, if he is rational, it is only in the sense that his states of mind, such as dispositions, *exemplify* rationality. Intentional states such as beliefs, desires, choices, toward which the norms of rationality are directed in reasoning, are states upon which we cannot have an exclusively third person angle, and so we cannot merely be passively assailed by them, at best observing them when that happens but taking no more active stance toward them. In other words, they cannot be dispositions, which Oblomov has in abundance; they have to be commitments, of which he has none. It's not that we *cannot* have a third person angle on our own commitments. I can say or think to myself, "That is a commitment I have" as a bit of unengaged observation. But of course unengaged observation is not active, in the sense that Schafer demands. It is passive, since to observe oneself in that way is to treat oneself as another. But that is not the only angle that we have on our intentional states. What makes them intentional states proper is that they are the sorts of things on which we can also have a first person angle, precisely what Oblomov lacks, an angle not of observation as a bystander but rather of an endorser, the angle of one who takes it up as a commitment and *in doing so* makes it (and the dispositions that are or are not in accord with it) the sort of thing that can be the justifiable object of someone's (including one's own) reactive attitudes, thereby making one an agent.

This, then, is how a deep trinity is formed. This is how (1) *value* (or commitment), (2) *freedom,* and (3) *the first person perspective* (a perspective that makes self-knowledge different from all other knowledge, such as, say, observational knowledge of the world) all reduce to a single and highly integrated package of elements, all of which Oblomov lacks. Lacking one, he lacks all three, since these are not separable elements. What I am taking pains to say, then, is that Schafer's methodological proposal, though he does not present it that way, is a highly omnibus one: it integrates with other elements that he does not explicitly draw out himself. On the face of it, his proposal is about agency. But we have found underneath that agency is equally about value or commitments and about the nature of the unique angle that an agent can have only on herself. Let's put the point another way. We might have thought that there are three distinctions of interest: first, the distinction between agency or freedom as opposed to passivity or determinism; second, the distinction between norm or value and natural fact; and third, the distinction between our own angles on ourselves (the first person angle, which makes self-knowledge special) as opposed to our angle on others and the world (the third person or observer's angle). But if I am right, these are all at bottom the same distinction. There is no freedom and agency if all we have are dispositions and no evaluative states, and there is no role or point for a first person perspective if we are passive creatures with only dispositions and no normative states. The implications of Schafer's remark that we need to acknowledge agency, therefore, brings with it an acknowledgment of *much else* besides.

The idea of rationality issues directly from saying that our intentional states are commitments because it is rational to be in accord with your commitments and irrational to fail to be in accord with them. In this picture of rationality, what is rational does not come from any standard *outside* of our own commitments. We may be committed to certain things quite rationally so long as they cohere with other commitments of ours, even if they do not square with the trends and tenets of culture and morality. Of course, what we are committed

to could be much influenced by those external things; that is not
ruled out as an empirical fact about us, and is no doubt often true of
us, but there is nothing about rationality so conceived that necessarily
issues from influences outside. Rationality itself is internal to the commitments of the individual, even if many commitments she embraces
are influenced by external standards. Actually, there is no need here
to overstate the case: I don't want to particularly deny that there is a
notion of rationality that is constituted by external sources and not
merely historically influenced by external sources. But at least as far
as psychoanalysis and these cognitive forms of self knowledge are concerned, we do not have to make any appeal to rationality in that
strongly external sense.

The relevance of this internalist picture of rationality to psychoanalysis is that a person's mental well-being can now be seen as *coin-
ciding* with her rationality, *so defined*. Since the demands of rationality
relevant to psychoanalysis are not demands that are external, they
merely tell her what she herself believes and values or desires and
what their implications are for her actions and her other beliefs,
values, or desires. So also *failures* of mental health coincide with failures of accord with one's commitments. These failures of accord with
one's commitments can be found in one's actions, in one's dispositions, and of course in one's commitments themselves when they lack
coherence with each other. I should be a little more clear by what I
mean by 'coincide'. I am not suggesting at all that every such failure
is of interest to psychoanalysis. Many such failures lead to no neurosis
or anxiety at all of the sort that prompts the relevance of psychoanalysis. What I am suggesting is that things hold the other way round.
There can be no understanding neuroses or anxieties of the sort that
prompt the relevance of psychoanalysis for an agent unless there exist
failures of internal rationality, i.e., unless there is some failure of his
actions and dispositions (or even his commitments) to square with
his (other) commitments. Why would he seek therapy if there was not
some internal tension, some disequilibrium of the sort that we have
just described in the most general possible terms as failures of his
'internal rationality'? There would no doubt have to be all sorts of
further things than a failure of internal rationality before something
like neurosis or anxiety sets in. But the idea that there can be neurosis
or anxiety, that there can be a search for therapy, when there is per-

fect internal equilibrium, makes no sense. And the notion of mental health or internal equilibrium, I am saying, can only be seen as defined in terms of the relations that exist or do not exist between one's commitments, on the one hand, and one's doings, dispositions, and other commitments, on the other. That is the very general and rudimentary relevance of what was said in the last chapter to psychoanalysis, and I now want to build upon this a somewhat more detailed framework to understand the regime's method and point.

Two broad kinds of failures have just been mentioned—when our actions and dispositions do not accord with our commitments, and when our commitments do not cohere with our other commitments. The latter form of irrationality is fundamentally different from the former. Why? Because only *reasoning* will alter the situation since *both* sides of the conflict involve normative states. The former is a different matter altogether, since it is a form of irrationality in which things that are not essentially normative, things such as the dispositions and the motives that cause our actions, are in conflict with our commitments. Here reason has only a limited function. It can only point out to us that conflict exists, and it can point out to us that we ought to get rid of it, by changing our dispositions and motives.[4] But that is not sufficient to bring about such a change. And reasoning will not help with the rest; it will not help to bring about the change. The rest comes from control, and control sometimes is hard to achieve without some form of what I am provocatively calling 'technology'.

Why this nomenclature? When one is dealing with changes of normative states, only deliberation about them is to the point. The kind of irrationality in which control is necessary has to deal not with normative states but with purely causal states, dispositions and motives, to which deliberation cannot possibly make any difference, after a point. What is needed here is to bring dispositions into line with what our commitments sanction, and bringing them into line means either curbing or getting rid of the dispositions that conflict with our commitments or acquiring dispositions that we lack but that our commitments require (acquiring them, say, by cultivation of certain *habits* of behavior). All this involves not reasoning but drill of one kind or another. That the drill is psychological and not physical should not mislead us into thinking that it is not a technology. The idea that if it is not physical (if it is not manipulation, say, by hypnosis or by medication) it must be *deliberative* is an impoverished conception of the options. If this is right, the refinements that Freud visited upon his own methods from the early phase of post-hypnotic suggestion to the fully psychoanalytic methodology is a sophistication and development *within* a technology, not a shift in direction from technology or manipulation (hypnosis) to deliberation (psychoanalysis).

Nothing in the idea of a technique requires that it must be physical. Perhaps in the (barely conceivable at present) fullness of time and knowledge, eventually only medication will be necessary to bring our dispositions into line with our commitments. But until we have that full knowledge, we have to exercise forms of technique that are psychological rather than physical. The important point is that we should not get confused into thinking therefore that just because we lack the full physical knowledge, that until we acquire it, what we are doing is something other than technology. The distinction between the physical and psychological does not coincide with the distinction between that to which technology is relevant and that to which deliberation and reason are relevant. This is because, as I have said, the psychological is a domain that is deeply divided by the dual aspect of the intentional and the dispositional. Because the latter aspect by itself requires neither norm nor the first person deliberative angle, both of which constitute agency, it is an aspect that is quite as susceptible to technology as the realm of the physical. It's just that the disciplinary regimes and the techniques used are bound to be very different and perhaps far more interesting and subtle than anything that is used in the physical realm.

Some of the interest and subtlety comes from the fact that the realm of dispositions and motives is a realm that, while we are in a position of epistemic weakness, that is to say, while we lack the full reductive knowledge of its categorical, biochemical basis,[5] leaves us no other option but to use propositions to specify what they are. Thus it is that we describe mental dispositions in contentful terms, just as we do normative states such as commitments. That is the source, or one source, of the widespread conflation of intentional states with dispositions, which Kripke was decrying. Given the inevitable specification of dispositions in contentful linguistic terms while we are epistemically weak, any efforts we may bring to the task of aligning our dispositions with our commitments will involve techniques that are radically different from material technologies. The technologies, after all, are addressing not the balance of chemicals, nor the configurations of cells and neurons, but propositionally specified phenomena, by which I don't mean just linguistically described phenomena but phenomena that take linguistic objects such as propositions as their contents.

Dispositions that get such a description are thus rightly described as objects of interpretation. (Psychoanalytical theorists are often keen to describe them as having 'meaning'.)[6] But, if I am right, the interpretation of dispositions by assigning propositional contents (or 'meaning') to them is, in one crucial sense of the term, 'unprincipled'—since it is something that we do only out of a position of epistemic weakness. There would be no reason for such interpretation if we had the full knowledge of their underlying basis, which we lack. During this period of ignorance, the assignment of content to them is an *instrument* by which we can come to an understanding of them in our efforts (among other things) to bring them in line with our commitments. So the interpretation of dispositions, the assigning of propositional content to them, being an *instrumental* matter, is not a matter of principled description of a phenomenon that is stably and ultimately *irreducibly* propositional. It lacks that full prestige that is reserved for what is (if Kripke and Moore are right) genuinely irreducible, i.e., normative states.

This point, though it may seem controversial at first sight, follows naturally from the claims and distinctions argued for in Chapter 5. Philosophers like Davidson and many others would be highly suspicious of the idea that these mental dispositions are only instrumentally and provisionally described in propositional terms. They argue that mental dispositions do not have a biochemical basis and are irreducible. That is a very mysterious position. It would be very mysterious if there were a level of mental dispositions that has no categorical basis underlying it; or at any rate, as I say in note 5, it would be very mysterious if mental dispositions did not have *another level of dispositions* studied and described by a more basic science such as biochemistry underlying it. For that would leave us hanging with *no theoretically integrated* scientific picture within which to assimilate a naturalistic phenomenon like a mental disposition. If this were really so, it's hard not to be sympathetic with the eliminativists who say that if mental dispositions are irreducible, we should eventually eliminate them from our scientific aspirations. How can science tolerate an essentially naturalistic phenomenon as *in principle* standing out on a limb in the way that intentionality qua dispositions is supposed to be, according to Davidson?

Davidson himself, unlike others who hold this position, of course, does *not* want to think of mental disposition as an essentially naturalistic phenomenon. This is why, as I said in Chapter 5, he sees two irreducibilities (the irreducibility of mental dispositions to biochemical states, the irreducibility of value to facts of nature), whereas if Kripke's Moorean position is right, there is one. And once we see the point of that position, we see intentional states as commitments and not dispositions, so there is no question of eliminating them on the ground that it is intolerable that there be a *naturalistic* phenomenon that we do not seek to integrate at all with the rest of one's scientific aspirations. Once we see them as commitments, they are frankly outside of scientific aspirations and of naturalistic concerns, and so they are *not* naturalistic phenomena in that sense. To want to eliminate them in the name of science would now be for science to arrogate rather than for it to merely insist on its own integrity by the lights of which irreducibly mental *dispositions* are mysterious. (For a fine and unjustly neglected early work, not particularly on mental dispositions but generally on dispositions, tying them to this sort of scientific integrity, the reader is directed to Levi and Morgenbesser's paper "Belief and Disposition.")[7]

A note of caution should be registered about this talk of integrity and integration, for someone might respond to what I have been saying by allowing that there might be *non*-reductive integrations of mental dispositions with physical states and protest that the impression I have given is that much stronger integrations must be assumed for them. The word 'integration' that I have been using is a very general term and can cover more and less interesting sorts of links between phenomena at different levels. It is true that the integration of mental dispositions with the dispositional or the categorical states described by a more basic science need not amount to the strictest of reductions, but I would insist that if they were interesting theoretical integrations at all, they would make dispositions essentially different from what Kripke and Moore think of as evaluative states, which could not possibly be integrated in *those* ways with physical states. Hence, there is no need for me to deny that there are all sorts of 'integrations' that may exist between mental phenomena (even normative mental phenomena such as intentional states seen as commitments) and the phenomena studied by the physical sciences. The term 'integration' is general enough to allow for that. But if Kripke and Moore are right, whatever integrations we can provide for evaluative states with physical states would not be, and could not be, the sorts of interesting theoretical integrations that we aspire to provide for mental *dispositions* with those states, even if these latter fall short of reductions.

If all this is right, then that means that the domain to which psychoanalysis gives its most assiduous and creative attention—the unconscious—involves 'interpretation' only in a sense that is instrumental and opportunistic, something forced on us only while we are in a position of epistemic weakness. The point of saying this is not to suggest that the weakness will turn to strength any time soon; the point is more to make the conceptual point that we should not think of this as interpretation in the full and ineliminable and irreducible sense that goes on when we are dealing with the attributing of intentional states, proper. This is because unconscious mental states cannot possibly have the normative property of commitments as I have defined them, and it is only states with such a property that are in a principled way the objects of interpretation and reasoning. Why do I say that unconscious states cannot be normative states such as commitments?

To repeat from Chapter 5, the defining property of commitments is not that we are disposed to act on our commitments. If it were, many of our unconscious mental states could well be commitments, since there is no gainsaying the fact that many of our dispositions are unconscious. The defining property of commitments is that they and the acts that are in (or not in) accord with them are the sorts of things to which we have justifiable reactive attitudes of praise and blame and indignation and resentment and that we ourselves are prepared to accept criticism for failing to live up to them when we do fail and to try and do better by cultivating the dispositions that will cause us to live up to them. But none of these things are appropriate to unconscious mental states, since it makes no sense to say that I am prepared to accept criticism for failing to live up to a state of which I am unconscious and might even deny as possessing. These states are thus fully dispositional but altogether lack the defining normative element that makes for genuine intentionality. Even where relative coherence exists among our unconscious states, their intentionality is only a form of *mimicry* of the real thing. As with Oblomov, the unconscious may exemplify rationality but not possess it.[8]

Almost from the moment that Freud formulated his systematic thoughts on the unconscious to this very day, philosophers and others have wrestled with the question of whether intentional states can be unconscious, and many have doubted that they can be so. But none of those who have doubted it have given a completely convincing reason for doing so, because every one of them (whom I have read, anyway) has also assumed that intentional states are dispositions, in some sophisticated sense. On that assumption, nothing whatever could prevent the unconscious from containing intentionality. Nothing we could add to the idea of a disposition by way of sophisticating it could make a principled requirement that one *must* have self-awareness of it, nothing at any rate that does not sophisticate it so much that it is no longer recognizable as a disposition. Those who are intuitively skeptical of the idea of unconscious intentional states, I think, will find *no principle* to ground their skepticism unless they come around to the criterion for intentionality that we have adopted, viz., that states possessing intentionality are themselves commitments defined as the sort of thing that we are prepared to accept criticism for not having lived up to them and to try and do better by way of living up to them. One could of course complain about my view that it rules out too much that is intentional by insisting on this version of the normative criterion for it. But the onus is on those who make this complaint to show how any notion of the intentional that is more accommodating than mine does not fall afoul of Kripke's Moorean (and in the end, as I argued, Fregean) demand that we distinguish the intentional from the dispositional.

It is a highly revealing fact, however, that such a high level of mimicry can exist at all at the unconscious level. And one thing it reveals is that a technology that we bring to bear on unconscious mental states (states that I have been saying are necessarily dispositional and only intentional manqué) must work on these dispositions holistically and speak to the patterns of inferential links that are *exemplified* by these dispositions. A great deal of the techniques of psychoanalysis are geared to do just that, both in the bringing to the surface of awareness unconscious dispositions as well as in the aligning of these dispositions (once they are brought to the surface) with the commitments, when they conflict with them.

A very crude framework is now emerging within which we may see the relations between the subject of psychoanalysis and the larger setting of mentality in its intentional aspects—something roughly with the following elements.

- Our conscious mentality consists partly of intentional states, properly so-called and not merely instrumentally attributed. These states are inherently normative and not merely dispositions that seem to exemplify the patterns of inference. They are commitments to actions of either one or another sort or to other intentional states, which are implied by the norms of one or other codified forms of reasoning.

- There are other mental states that are not intentional but dispositional. They are psychological tendencies that have an underlying basis; just like the physical tendencies of physical nature, such as, say, solubility, they too have an underlying basis. But while we are in a position of epistemic weakness regarding their (biochemical) basis, they are necessarily of a far greater subtlety and complexity than straightforwardly physical dispositions, and they need contentful description mimicking the contentful specification of intentional states properly so-called, such as beliefs and desires.

- There can be deep conflict between our commitments and our dispositions, which can sometimes (though by no means always) give rise to anxieties and neuroses of a wide variety. All neuroses fit this general framework. That is to say, ex hypothesi, the idea of a neurosis is a special case of the sort of disequilibrium that comes from a clash of dispositions with 'commitments', in the broadly defined sense I have given that term.

- Some of these conflicts are between our commitments and *un-*

conscious dispositions, and the neuroses *they* give rise to are typically of the sort that decades of sophisticated theory, building
upon the pioneering work of Freud, have studied.

All this suggests, roughly speaking, that the analytical method has
three central *conceptual* moments (though, of course, the actual *tem-
poral* chronology is bound to be much untidier, involving much back
and forth among these moments).

First is the discovery by the patient of some hitherto unconscious
mental state (or set of inferentially linked states) that is a necessarily
dispositional and motivational state but not a normative state such as
a commitment. The path to this discovery is via a technology, a set
of techniques, which have been much studied. *It is this first stage in
which self-knowledge is cognitively acquired.* It is acquired by combinations
of inference from one's behavior, including one's childhood behavior, and by inner introspection that is akin in some ways to perception.

At this point, a *second* conceptual moment sets in, which is normative and not technological, and it is where takes place deliberation
that requires the analysand to consider first whether the discovered
dispositional or motivational mental state is in conflict with her commitments, then, if it is, to see whether she wishes to bring the conflicted disposition in alignment with her commitments by changing
the commitment or by changing the disposition. All this falls in the
intentional realm, in the full and genuine (that is to say, non-
instrumental) sense of that term. Wittgenstein once said in his critical
remarks on Freud that, ultimately, *assent* on the part of the analysand
is the only criterion for the existence of unconscious states. Presumably he meant potential assent, and if so, the point is not all that
controversial. The deeper point is that he leaves it completely unclear
whether by assent he meant what I have in mind by the first conceptual moment or by the second. For those are two quite different
things: to assent to whether one has a disposition that has hitherto
been unconscious (the first stage) and to assent in the sense of endorse that disposition, thereby making it a commitment (the second
stage). In this second stage, one could endorse the disposition that
one has discovered oneself to have, or one could reject it. If one
endorses it, one has made it a commitment. That *is* what it is to

endorse. In that case, the only thing left to reach an equilibrium is to make sure that this newly acquired commitment does not conflict with other commitments, and that task falls within the normative realm of reasoning. However, if one does not endorse the disposition but rather rejects it, there may well be more to be done, and what more there is to be done has nothing to do with reasoning, and further technology is required.

This last is the *third* central moment or stage in psychoanalysis: the path from self-knowledge of one's hitherto unconscious states to the actual reaching of a situation of equilibrium, the removing of conflict by getting rid of the conflicting disposition that one's commitments have rejected. The technologies involved in doing this during the third stage are also much studied by the theory of psychoanalysis.

So technology is relevant to two key moments, the first and the third.

In the first stage certain unconscious states are uncovered, and they are uncovered by a cognitive way of acquiring self-knowledge. These uncovered states are necessarily dispositional states, since being initially un-self-known they cannot meet the basic requirements of commitments, which has it that commitments must be known to their possessors. And while unknown, these states are *not* caught up with agency in the way that the proviso to my conditionals demands—since only commitments and dispositions that are self-known fall within the coverage of the proviso. Not being caught up with agency, these states fall outside of the constitutive paradigm for self-knowledge. Thus they are *necessarily* uncovered by a *cognitively gained* self-knowledge. Unlike commitments, these uncovered states might be uncovered slowly and in degrees; they might go in and out of the focus of our self-knowledge, a point well understood in therapeutic and analytic regimes. No such thing is possible with commitments, which are, ex hypothesi, that is, by their very nature, as sketched in the last chapter, self-known. Such grades of self-knowledge can only be something that holds therefore of states that are acquired through a cognitive process. I will explain in a moment how psychoanalysis introduces a technology for the gaining of self-knowledge of these states.

Technology is also relevant to the third stage, or conceptual moment. This is the stage during which, if certain discovered dispositions (knowledge of which is acquired cognitively by the aid of technology in the first stage) have been rejected by the assessments carried out in the second normative stage, then they need to actually be *discarded* from the psychological economy, and this is done again by the technologies of this third stage.

Let us glance briefly at just one salient example of what I have in mind by technologies: transference. I don't mean the everyday phenomenon of transference but the clinical one.

Transference provides a technique relevant to both the first and third stages or conceptual moments. It is a specific form of a *reliving* of certain relations (sometimes past relationships) within the context of the relationship that a patient has come to develop with the analyst. This reliving can, in the first stage, help bring to the surface and the awareness of a patient's mind a number of mental states (necessarily dispositional) that have hitherto been unconscious. Such cognitive acquisition of self-knowledge of hitherto unconscious states is actually *facilitated by the technique* of inducing a reliving in the analytical relationship of relationships elsewhere in which many of those states unconsciously occur and thrive. Moreover, once so available to the agent, Freud then describes, in what I am calling 'the third stage', the '*working through*' of these dispositions (again via transference, via the reliving) as something necessary for the patient to undergo in order to be *relieved of* them. Thus during transference there is a specific sort of 'reliving' that (in the first stage) brings to the surface long repressed states of mind, and the continuing of the transference past this gaining of self-knowledge of these hitherto repressed mental states helps the patient (in the third stage) to 'work through', in Freud's phrase, those mental states and thereby to ease them out of one's psychological economy (if that is what the non-technological and deliberative second stage has decided should happen to them).

Here are Freud's own words for the manifestly technological elements in the third conceptual moment. They are from his essay "Recollecting, Repetition and Working-Through":[9]

The first step toward overcoming the resistance is made by the analyst's discovering the resistance, which is never recognized by the patient, and acquainting him with it. Now it seems that beginners in analytical practice are inclined to look upon this as the end of the work. I have often been asked to advise upon cases in which the physician complained that the resistance had been made aware to the patient and all the same no change had set in. . . . The gloomy foreboding has always proved mistaken. The treatment as a rule was progressing quite satisfactorily. Only the analyst had forgotten that naming the resistance could not result in its immediate suspension. One must allow the patient time to get to know its resistance of which he is ignorant, to "*work through it*," in order to overcome it . . . only when *it has come to its height* can one, with the patient's cooperation, discover the repressed instinctual trends which are feeding the resistance, and only by living through them again will the patient be convinced by their existence and power. This "working through" of the resistance may in practice amount to an arduous task for the patient and a trial of patience for the analyst. Nevertheless it is the part of the work that effects the greatest changes in the patient and which distinguishes analytic treatment from every kind of suggestive treatment.

In early writings, Freud often talked of 'catharsis'. That this earlier terminology denoted a kind of technology (by contrast with deliberation) is perhaps obvious. But the later idea of 'working through', as this passage shows, is not in essence different from it. In both, one is describing techniques for controlling dispositions. The entire vocabulary here and in several other passages is one of force (of unwelcome dispositions) and counterforce (of 'working through' them via transference). Technology against natural forces.

In his autobiographical study of 1925,[10] Freud explicitly uses both terms ('catharsis' and 'working through') in the context of discussing transference, and then in a more general context he explicitly links the two ideas when discussing the passage in his own intellectual development from stress on hypnosis to analysis proper, under the influence of Bernheim. And my point is that neither in the idea of catharsis nor in that of 'working through' is there *any* central (or even peripheral) place given to *reasoning* with a patient to curb or remove one or another mental state or attitude. I don't mean that an analyst never actually reasons with a patient, never actually says that he ought to do this or that, given what his commitments are. Of course, analysts may well do so. But when they do so, they are not particularly doing what their theory is about. They are engaging with a patient in a way that anyone else might, and that is hardly surprising, given how much time they spend together, I suppose. The point is only that the general and detailed claims of psychoanalytic theory do not conceive of the analyst in these terms at all. His or her function, rather, is a facilitator, via certain *techniques,* of the cognitive gaining of self-knowledge of certain unconscious mental states, then of 'working through' them again via certain *techniques,* to get rid of them in a form of 'catharsis', if that is what the patient—in the second intermediate phase—decides should happen to them.

So the reason why it is technology in this third stage is that it is not a matter of reasoning that is involved; it is a matter of letting the disposition *'come to its height'* (as he says in the passage I have cited) and thereby having it *eased* out of you; and Freud is explicit in saying that transference is one absolutely central technique in carrying out this task.

Many more examples could and should be given to bring this point about technology decisively home, but I cannot now. In fact, I have no doubt that I have been crude here in the hope of making the basic elements in the framework I want to impose on psychoanalysis come to light. A great deal needs to be said by way of qualification, further examples, and other detail. I have even less doubt, however, that those details would not impeach the general claims of the framework.

If the third stage is pure technology, that means that the normative element is over once the second stage is over, once one has deliberated as to whether an uncovered mental state—some feeling of hostility, say—is to be endorsed as consistent and coherent with one's commitments or rejected as conflicting with them. Perhaps this is obvious, perhaps no one needs convincing that the last stage (and the first stage) is a technology. It may simply be obvious just from reading the various descriptions of (or from undergoing) the dynamics of the analytical process. My point, however, is this. We do not have a *theoretical right* to this seemingly obvious conviction until we grasp the full contrast with the notion of agency that Schafer urges upon us and all that it implies about the normativity of mind.

Psychoanalysis is pervasively silent on the matter of the normative element relevant to the second stage, focusing all its theoretical and strategic energies on the first and third stages, where the tools of uncovering states of mind (what amounts to a cognitive acquisition of self-knowledge) and then 'working through' them are most relevant. *But the second stage is indispensable.* If there were no second stage, the whole process could be performed by an Oblomov, since the first and third stages require no more than an observational or third person perspective on oneself. Agency surfaces in the second stage, and that is vitally necessary for what allows the first and third stages to be the sort of liberating stages that Spinoza and Freud had claimed that they would be. It is the presence of the second stage that prevents the psychoanalytical method from deteriorating into the ideological picture of the mind, which Schafer was lamenting and which creates the 'curiosity' or paradox I mentioned at the beginning of this discussion.

In short, the normative element is an unerasable backdrop, both to the very idea of what counts as a neurosis in the first place and to the task of achieving or approximating the goal of equilibrium, which is supposed to ease the neurosis. Why is it crucial to defining neurosis? Because *accord of one's dispositions with one's commitments* is the standard of health, departure from which is a necessary (though, of course, by no means sufficient) condition for neurosis to even so much as arise. Without a standard of health, there could be no lack of mental health, no notion of neurosis. That specific kind of accord alone provides our idea of health, which is relevant to psychoanalysis. Nothing else can provide the relevant standard. Mere accord between dispositions could not be the standard of health, since consistent and coherent dispositions may still conflict with one's commitments. For that matter, mere accord among commitments could not be either the *complete* standard of health or the *relevant* one. It is irrelevant because even if our commitments are conflicted, that normatively unsatisfactory state is something against which psychoanalysis is helpless. It being entirely in the normative realm, only reasoning could resolve it. But coherence among commitments is in any case not a complete standard of health, simply because one could have perfectly coherent commitments and yet have dispositions that conflicted with them. It's the alignment of *disposition with commitment* that provides that further standard of health, departure from which may give rise to the kind of neuroses to which the techniques of psychoanalysis are relevant. And the point is that psychoanalysis would have no subject matter if there was not this background of a standard of health provided by the normative ideal of the equilibrium or alignment itself.

Freud himself, perhaps because of his avowed distaste for philosophy, did not say much about this element of norm or value that lay
behind the entire point of his repertory of structural claims, empirical
hypotheses, and techniques for discovery and curative therapy. They
were unspoken assumptions. The reason for the silence may well have
come from certain prejudices he had about the nature of value, which
distracted him from seeing the role for value that I am stressing.

First, the notion of a norm he often wrote about was an external
one, norm as morality, as issuing from conventional, social, and public
demands. But that is not the notion of norm that surfaces in the
framework I am placing on his ideas at all. That is not the notion of
norm that is built into the idea of an intentional state, the notion of
norm that comes from the idea of a commitment. Here it is entirely
internal to the psychological economy of an agent, even if external
influences may shape what one's commitments are, as they are bound
to. Once the influence is in place, the point is that the notion of
norm comes in with the idea of *accord with* one's *own* commitments.
The normative idea of that accord or failure of accord is not at all
the normative idea of an external moral value.

Second, Freud goes on to give a reductive view of norms. Once he
sees norms generally only in moral and external terms, he finds himself bound to give an explanation of them in terms of his own basic
concepts, and so he sees them as having their source in an external-
ization of the id-restricting tasks of the superego. For him, this was
no mere genetic point. He thought of norm (or conscience, as he
often called it in *Future of an Illusion*)[11] as *being* a second-order disposition or drive that is defined in terms of a function to curb one's
first-order drives, which are highly destabilizing. This is a thoroughly
disappointing, naturalistic view of normativity that reveals the very
point where Freud's scientific ambitions became outsize. It is not the
point on which those who think he should be a hermeneuticist or a
narrativist, rather than a scientist, focus[12] but the point where he
simply thought that norms were themselves natural facts, second-
order dispositions of a naturalistic sort.

Those who hanker for narrative and hermeneutics in psychoanalysis
are saying something banal and perfectly compatible with Freud the
scientist. Of course we *interpret* our unconscious states of mind and *tell
a story* about what underlies our behavior. How could this possibly
conflict with anything scientific? Mental dispositions, so long as we

are epistemically positioned so as to know nothing or nothing much about their detailed biochemical basis, leave us no choice but to see them as objects of interpretation, to which we assign meaningful propositions with inferential links to one another. That does not mean that dispositions are irreducible to natural facts. What is the argument that they are not? Mere dispositions do not even yield agency, as the extreme and radical version of Oblomov discussed in Chapter 4 makes clear, so why should it provide any principled obstacle to scientific reduction? Just because we have to exercise our hermeneutical abilities to grasp what these dispositions are until we gain more scientific knowledge cannot be an argument for their irreducibility, in principle. It is only commitments, the genuinely normative elements that come with agency and the first person perspective, that are unyielding to reduction, and it is this point that escaped Freud.

Keen to put in their place the demands of *external,* moral norms, Freud confusedly then also aspired to reduce the *very idea of norm or value* to second-order naturalistic drives to curb first-order drives. That is misplaced science. Even if he were right that our *interest* in morals is entirely a product of our need to curb our drives (and even if it were the case that such an interest was hardwired into us genetically), the Moorean/Fregean argument of Chapter 5 would remain untouched. Therefore, even if he were right about these other things, he would still be wrong about the reduction—what I am calling commitments would still remain irreducible to second-order, naturalistically conceived drives and dispositions. If they were not, he himself would not be able to give sense to the idea of his own key interests; he would not be able to make sense either of the idea of neurosis or the idea of its elimination in the providing of mental *health.*

So to begin to sum things up in this discussion of psychoanalysis, Schafer had proposed that the concept and the conceptual vocabulary of agency, rather than passivity, should govern our understanding of psychoanalysis. I have tried to redeem that proposal in a specific way, showing how if we understand agency properly in all its implications, then that introduces a normative, first personal element as standing behind a way of understanding the basic elements of neurosis and the various third personal and technological and non-normative forms of dealing with it.

For many, this contrast of third personal dispositional and first person normative will seem too crude and too sharp. I have talked of recognizing unwelcome dispositions in one's self as though it were entirely a third personal matter. I have not allowed any place for the idea of acknowledging and articulating 'from the inside' hitherto unacknowledged features of one's consciousness of the world. From the way I have talked, it might have seemed that an 'unconscious' fear was something like an unfortunate behavioral tic that impinges on one's awareness of the world only insofar as one perceives its behavioral manifestations in oneself. Otherwise, it is like having a small mole in the middle of one's back. And this is surely not being fair to the way an unconscious fear is part of *one's experience,* for it may in fact infuse one's whole experience of the world. But, in fact, I don't wish to or need to deny that there is this quality to one's experience of the unconscious in order to make the point I am making about psychoanalysis. There is no doubt that self-knowledge is a capacious enough notion that it accommodates both states that are captured with such words as "I have the fear that . . ." as well as states where someone has nothing like this level of acknowledgment and articulation. I have said so at various points in the text when I said that self-knowledge may come in degrees.

The fact is that in any case the point may not even be one that is always best captured in talk of degrees. The experience of the world that is shot through with an 'unconscious fear', because it is an *experience,* may be said to bring with it some more primitive and less articulated awareness of the fear too. To say the notion of self-knowledge is capacious, however, is not to deny that what its capaciousness accommodates may be things that are quite different from each other, with different theoretical and philosophical implications, and that, therefore, for many theoretical purposes can be analyzed differently. In this book, I have openly and frankly focused on the more articulated form of self-knowledge with distinct theoretical purposes in mind, which I have throughout declared as being my purposes. And in particular, in this appendix I have tried to analyze what happens and what is required when unconscious states such as fears, even when they pervade our experience of the world (but that, after all with good reason, we still describe with the term 'unconscious'), become conscious in the sense that involves a fuller acknowledgment and articulability. The point is that we are able to take a normative stand on them, endorsing them or wishing to rid oneself of them, only if one has this fuller sense of self-knowledge. And however much one experiences the 'unconscious' fear 'from the inside', the coming to full awareness of them cannot just be a greater flowering of the very same thing that is already felt from the inside but, rather; requires having (however fleetingly) an angle on them that is not 'from the inside', an angle captured only with third personal formulations such as, "This is how it is with me"—which then allows the assertive normative responses in the first person such as, "And that is fine," or its opposite. These distinctions between the first and the third personal that I have tied to the distinction between the normative and the dispositional are the further distinctions that are crying to get out from within Schafer's one-dimensionally described distinction between agency and passivity when he laments the domination of the latter over the former in our language and understanding of psychoanalysis.

I suppose no one can write philosophically as I have about psychoanalysis and its methodology without running up against the neverending controversy about the scientific status of psychoanalytic theory. But if it is true that a much richer framework of the sort being proposed here follows from Schafer's proposal, then it reconciles what it is that some theorists find both attractively scientific about psychoanalysis with what other theorists insist should be irreducibly humanistic in it. Once we see the relations between the normative and the technological in this unified framework, many of these old disputes in psychoanalytical theory between the 'scientific', on the one hand, and the 'humanistic', on the other, should be seen as unnecessarily adversarial. The first and third stages I identified speak to the scientific side of the dispute because they deal with naturalistic phenomena; the second stage speaks to the humanistic because it deals with naturalistically irreducible phenomena. The theories and practices Freud generated contain both sides without any conflict between them, and each is indispensable to the other.

What, then, of the continuing debate, the controversy going back to criticisms made by Popper[13] and others that the specific claims of psychoanalysis are unfalsifiable and unverifiable, criticisms followed up in the writings of Grunbaum[14] and then, with an almost mystifying zeal in the pages of literary magazines, by such commentators as Fred-

eric Crews? I don't doubt that the irreducibly normative, agential, first
personal element I think of as an indispensable part of the framework
will raise the Crews and the Grunbaums to new heights of denunciation. They will no doubt find it to be a distastefully unscientific element. But that denunciation could no longer have its source in anxieties that were initially raised by Popper or by Grunbaum himself. It
could no longer be targeting purportedly empirical hypotheses that
turn out, on inspection, to be unempirical because unfalsifiable. That
criticism is now wholly beside the point since the normative element
relevant to psychoanalysis, unlike the dispositional element relevant
to it, is not pretending to be scientifically or causally tractable. Unlike
various other hypotheses put out by the doctrine of psychoanalysis, it
is not making claims for which we seek *confirmation* by clinical or other
forms of evidence. So Grunbaum's anxieties about it not getting that
confirmation by the standards of scientific confirmation are, as far as
this normative element is concerned, beside the point. It is precisely
my point that it is just as wrong (and wrong in mirror image of one
another) to say that the normative element in the background falls
within the naturalistic domain as it is to say that the dispositional
element falls in anything but the technological domain. The normative domain therefore frankly announces itself as standing in a principled way *outside* the purview of scientific ambitions. Grunbaum and
others—for all I say in the last many pages—may be right in some of
the things they target for their criticism. But there is nothing in what
I do say in these pages that provides them with those targets for their
criticism. After all, as I have already said in an earlier chapter and as
anti-naturalists keep pointing out quite correctly: it cannot be unscientific to insist that not all themes are scientific themes. It is only
unscientific to give unscientific responses to *science's* themes.

3. The short essay on the theme of psychoanalysis that made up the
last section applied some of the distinctions and claims I made about
intentionality, agency, and value in Chapter 5 to that theme. Apart
from the intrinsic interest of the subject of psychoanalysis, and of this
application of those claims to it, my eventual hope has been to work
up to saying something about how it relates to the book's more general subject of self-knowledge of our states of mind. If I am right about
how to view psychoanalysis as a general framework, then self-

knowledge enters into that framework, I said, at a certain stage—what I called the *first* stage or conceptual moment that the framework provides. I described this stage as being one in which there is a gaining of self-knowledge of states that were hitherto unknown, and I said that therefore it was necessarily self-knowledge of dispositions, not commitments (commitments being necessarily transparent and self-known without any need of the *gaining* of such knowledge). I tried to show that the gaining of such self-knowledge was a cognitive achievement that fell under the (inner) perceptual and inferential paradigm and not the constitutive paradigm where agency was necessarily in play; and I argued, moreover, that the inferential, causal, and (inner) perceptual processes could be aided and effected by technologies of the very sort that psychoanalysis famously provided. And, finally, once again using the tools and distinctions of the last chapter, I tried to show how the framework also situated this cognitively acquired self-knowledge in the broader *point* of psychoanalysis (the third stage), where the therapeutic goals of the regime enter. The point of the therapeutic goals is always to deal with and to remove phenomena properly describable as neurotic and pathological, i.e., to restore mental health, and I had argued that the idea of a lapse from mental health could only be made sense of as indispensably involving a failure of an internal sort of rationality, i.e., a failure to keep faith with the demands of one's own commitments. If one were not in some way failing in some commitment or other, it is hard to understand what could prompt the search for therapy and cure. The anxiety or neuroses that prompt the relevance of the regimes of psychoanalysis are only to be understood as issuing (in part, but the indispensable part) from a failure to do or be disposed to do what some commitment or set of commitments we have demand of one. Without such internal tension or disequilibrium, we cannot make sense of the idea that one seeks cure for something one feels as a pathology. Others may of course by their lights think one to be pathological even if they find one to be internally perfectly rational (in the broad sense of 'rational', which we have defined in terms of a range of different codifications), but one cannot find oneself *pathological* under conditions where one has lived up to one's commitments, find oneself to be in any need for therapy. If rationality, defined upon living up to one's commitments, is what provides for the standard of mental health that leads one to get therapy, then the therapeutic aspect of the cognitive seeking of this self-knowledge is that such *cognitive seeking of self-knowledge is part of one's effort to live up to one's commitments* and thereby come to achieve that mental health.

This last point I have italicized is the *basic core* of how self-knowledge enters into the general framework of psychoanalysis, and it is absolutely crucial to the rest of what I am going to say.

Psychoanalysis (and psychiatry and psychotherapy) is only one form of cognitively acquired self-knowledge, a form that is highly specific in its methods, highly selective in the states of mind whose self-knowledge it is interested in gaining (the repressed, i.e., the motivatedly unconscious ones), and highly specific in the eventual goals it has (the cure of specific forms of mental illness involving neuroses, anxieties, etc.) for seeking such self-knowledge in the first place. Cognitively acquired self-knowledge is a much broader notion than this specific instance of it, and it is exemplified in many more cases than those that surface in the narrower interests of these disciplinary regimes. What are we to say of the *general* class of cognitively acquired self-knowledge? How does it fit in with what we have said so far?

The general class, including the psychoanalytic cases, consists of cases of self-knowledge that I have described as exceptions, as extra- or non-ordinary cases of self-knowledge because they do not fit the paradigm as it is found in the two conditionals that I have tried to establish over the five chapters of this book. The paradigm shows self-knowledge of intentionality to come 'for free', to come with intentionality itself, without cognitive gaining or achievement. As I and other philosophers have put it, it shows self-knowledge to be "constitutive" of the very idea of intentionality. By contrast, what we are considering now are all cases of its cognitive acquisition, and so they all raise a potential embarrassment to the paradigm unless their relation to the paradigm is described in a way that leaves the paradigm unhurt.

To do this I will have to return to some of the points I was making in Chapter 2 about the nature of agency and say more than I had there about its relations to self-knowledge.

In that chapter, I had tried to argue for an essentially Strawsonian line on freedom and agency. I had tried to show how Strawson had changed the direction of the subject of agency as it had hitherto been discussed by philosophers, that he had done so by rightly pointing out that such things as the practices of praise, blame, and punishment, as well as the reactive attitudes that underlie them, were a necessary element in agency, and that in doing so he had made agency a normative notion. And I had claimed that self-knowledge, in the paradigm, was simply a *fallout* of such a notion of agency. I formulated two conditionals that in one way or another depended on and were derived from a notion of agency in order to consolidate that claim. But the sort of fallout it is depends a great deal on how we are to understand exactly what it is falling out of, the notion of agency.

In showing how it ought to be understood, I had made the criticism of Strawson that after having changed the direction of the subject of agency by stressing the evaluative reactive attitudes rather than metaphysical properties of our actions and their causes, he had not taken that direction as far as it goes. He does not ask the question (or at any rate, he does not give the proper response to the question): With what right do we have our practices of praise and blame, and with what right do we have these reactive attitudes that lie behind these practices—what justifies *them*? This question, I argued, was something that was bound to be posed by an incompatibilist about freedom and determinism, the philosopher who opposed Strawson's radically unorthodox way of reconciling agency with determinism by essentially changing the subject of agency from a contra-causal one to a normative one. Such a philosopher, I said, may invoke the psychiatric zealot whose slogan is "Cure, don't criticize, blame and resent!" or he may invoke the highly alienated attitude "Who cares enough about anything to criticize, blame, and resent!" in order to say that there is nothing unshakeable about the evaluative reactive attitudes that Strawson thinks are defining of agency. He may, that is, invoke the (no doubt remote) possibility of what I called 'rational or evaluative suicide' to say that there is no ground floor fact about our being creatures with reactive attitudes such that these reactive attitudes neither need nor get any further (internal) justification. And I said, in turn, that it would be wrong to respond to this by saying that what such a philosopher was proposing was impossible since, despite being remote, it was not impossible. Such zealotry or such alienation is not conceptually incoherent, and it needed a philosophical response.

The obvious response is that if we do not adopt these zealous or alienated ideological stances, it is only because we do not *want* to, because *our values* tell us that we ought not to. Thus I argued that agency is not merely a normative notion in that it is necessarily identified with our normative practices of criticism, of praise and blame and the reactive attitudes, but it is more radically normative than that because these practices and attitudes are *themselves* justified by further (necessarily more specific) values or norms that we have, in a way that I tried to spell out. This modification and extension of Strawson, therefore, adds to his view one very important thing: it adds to the idea that the notion of agency is an evaluative notion, the claim that *we are committed to this evaluative notion of agency itself* because of further values we have. The evaluative notion of agency is not a stopping point. It is internally justified by further values. *It is itself a value commitment.*

If self-knowledge is a fallout of *such* a notion of agency, then what theoretical consequence would this have for the notion of self-knowledge? Self-knowledge is, as I said in the discussion of transparency in the subsequent chapter, a necessary condition of agency, so understood. So to the extent that our states of mind were caught up in our agency, we had self-knowledge of them. Putting this point and the point of the previous paragraph together, we can conclude that to the extent that we are committed to agency (the point of the previous paragraph), *we are also committed to self-knowledge of our intentional states.* Self-knowledge, if it is necessary to have the agency we are committed to having, is something that we are also *committed* to having. It is something that we *ought* to try and gain. This is a point that has not been made before in any of the chapters of this book so far.

So it is beginning to emerge now that the book has argued for *two separate theses.* Most of the book focused on (1): There is the constitutive thesis encapsulated in the two conditionals. That thesis asserts, among other things, that so long as *agency* is in the offing, if I have an intentional state, then I believe that I have it. But I am now also saying that over and above the constitutive thesis there is another thesis, (2), which asserts a quite different thing about our mentality and its self-knowledge, viz., that so long as a *commitment to agency* is in the offing, if I have a mental state, then I am committed to believing that I have it.

Notice a couple of things here, one small and one large.

To begin with, I have formulated the first thesis in terms of 'intentional' states specifically, and I have formulated the second thesis in terms of 'mental' states more generally. Why this is so should be obvious from what I have already said in the last section of Chapter 5. Intentional states (such as beliefs and desires, anyway) have been characterized in such a way in the last chapter that, *by their very nature, they cannot fail to be known to their possessors.* They are commitments, and commitments are characterized as involving a preparedness on our part, among other things, to accept criticism for not having lived up to them. One cannot be prepared to accept criticism for something that one has no knowledge of. If that is right, if it is right that we cannot fail to know our intentional states, then it makes no sense to say (as the second thesis aspires to do) that we are *committed* to knowing them. We could, I suppose, say that we have a commitment to believing that we have an intentional state whenever we have it, then add that we cannot fail to live up to that commitment. But if we can't fail to live up to a commitment, then there is not much point in calling it a commitment. For that reason, I have not formulated the second thesis as a thesis holding of intentional states but, more generally, of mental states so as to include mental dispositions as well. As the last chapter made clear, mental dispositions, unlike commitments, are *not* the sort of things that are by their very nature self-known. And as the reference to Spinoza and Freud in this appendix has made clear, self-knowledge of them in fact *enhances* our agency. So putting these two things together, the point of the second thesis is that if there are mental states, having self-knowledge of which enhances our agency, and those states are *not* the sorts of states that are *by their very characterization* self-known by their possessors, then to the extent that we are committed to agency, we are committed to self-knowledge of those states. Hence, there is a real point to the second thesis, so long as we formulate it as holding of mental dispositions. (And that point is something that other philosophers who do not believe that there are any such things as commitments, who think that even intentional states are dispositions, will want to formulate as being one about intentional states as well.)

Another thing (of greater consequence) to notice is that I have been careful all along to say such things as, "*To the extent that one is committed to agency,* one is committed to self-knowledge of our intentional states." This qualifier is necessary because it was part of my point against Strawson that agency is not a transcendentally justified fact standing outside our commitments, but rather it is one among our commitments, and like all other values and commitments, it has internal support and justification from within our other values and commitments. But even if it is a commitment, I don't want to deny at all that as commitments and values of ours go, it is a far more general and fundamental commitment of ours than other commitments of ours. The fact that we have to appeal to something as drastic as the prospect of what I called 'rational or evaluative suicide' to bring out that it was itself a commitment makes clear that it is not (except in a theoretical sense, forced by the theoretical possibility of 'rational or evaluative suicide') just another commitment, just any old commitment. I think we can take for granted in the ordinary course of things that we are all committed to agency in a way that we are not committed, say, to studying history or philosophy, to reading novels, to going to the opera, to playing cricket, to taking an interest in public life, etc., cherished though these commitments may be for particular persons. And since self-knowledge is a necessary condition for agency, it too is a commitment in just the sense (which Strawson failed to recognize for agency) as agency itself is; and, moreover, it too, like agency, is not just another commitment but is, in a sense to be made clear, a more general and deep and fundamental commitment than the other sorts of commitments I just mentioned above.

Here is a way, a not-unfamiliar way, of describing clearly the sense in which it is more fundamental than they are.

I don't want to deny, however deep and general and fundamental the commitment to self-knowledge may be, that it has *excusing* conditions. Sometimes the costs are too high to fulfill the commitment, where by 'cost' I mean, of course, something rather broad (though thinking of the expense it takes to go to a New York psychoanalyst, its narrower meaning is by no means always irrelevant). One may be too busy and one may have other things to do. These costs provide the excusing conditions. Even so, the commitment to self-knowledge, unlike, say, someone's commitment to know a lot about Indian history, is a more fundamental commitment because it is in primary place, with these conditions coming in secondarily as exactly what they are properly called, *"excusing"* conditions for something *already in primary place*. The desire to know Indian history, to take just one example, even if it is intense and even if some people believe they *ought* to pursue it, is simply not a commitment in this more fundamental sense. People pursue such a commitment and others like it as and when their specific interests dictate, without there being any philosophical ground upon which we must say that when they do not pursue it, their reasons for not doing so count as excusing conditions for a commitment to know something (Indian history) that is already in primary place. *"Do x, unless the costs are high"* and *"If you are interested, do x"* are forms of imperative that have a very different place and role in our psychological economies. A commitment taking the former imperatival form is quite rightly seen as being more fundamental or basic in our evaluative economies than one taking the latter. It is not more fundamental in the sense that it is always in the forefront of one's mind, as the commitment to pursue Indian history or a host of other such commitments might sometimes be. Nor is it the case that what makes it more fundamental is that it, unlike other values, yields some sort of strict liability. Not at all. As I said, one can often be excused from not having pursued self-knowledge of our dispositions if the costs are too high. But the right formulation of the imperative, which puts the value in place as a default, nevertheless shows that it has a special philosophical status that comes from the generality and importance of agency (and therefore of self-knowledge, which is a necessary condition for agency) in our lives. Understood this way, the idea of its being more fundamental cannot be spoiled at all by the fact that it *has* excusing conditions, nor is it spoiled by my insistence (against Strawson) that even the more fundamental commitments to agency (and therefore to self-knowledge) are, in the end, supported and justified by further values. Rather, what it means is this: for the reasons I have given, the commitment to self-knowledge (and to agency, for which self-knowledge is a necessary condition) is more fundamental than the values that *support and justify it*.[15] As discussed in Chapter 2, that is often the case when you have non-foundationalist and coherentist forms of justification, where there is no requirement that something more general and fundamental support and justify what is less so.

And so, once we understand that due to its deep connections with

agency self-knowledge is itself a commitment and a rather fundamental commitment, we are finally in a better position to say something more general about the question we posed at the beginning of
this section: how does one deal with the *general* class of exceptional
and cognitive cases of self-knowledge?

What is meant by this talk of the 'general' class of exceptional cases
of self-knowledge, where self-knowledge is cognitively acquired and
does not come for free, as it were? Psychoanalysis, I said, is only a
specific and the most institutional and interesting of cognitive forms
of self-inquiry; there are the much more numerous and more everyday forms such as when we find ourselves often asking in more ordinary ways, "What was I thinking?" "Do I really feel angry with him?"
Even such things as, "Where did I put my keys? (asked in circumstances where attention and memory would dredge up an image, say,
of walking into a room and placing keys on a table). These are also
all forms of cognitive self-inquiry that are often exercised and exercised fruitfully. They may be less interesting because they are less
theorized, less institutional, less tied to neurosis and anxiety than
those that get the focus of psychoanalysis, but we must have an account of them too, an account that cannot be discontinuous with what
we have said about psychoanalysis—or else we will have no unified
understanding of the general class of exceptions to the paradigm.

What my modified Strawsonian framework that I have just been
reminding us of allows me to say of all these other exceptions to the
constitutive thesis (all these other cases where *cognitive* gainings of self-
knowledge are involved, just as they are involved in psychoanalysis) is
that they *too* are forms of *cognitive therapy*,[16] which we undertake in
order *to live up to the commitment to self-knowledge* when we have failed
to live up to it. The modification to Strawson allowed us to think of
self-knowledge as itself a commitment, and that, in turn, allows us to
make just such a therapeutic claim regarding all these cognitive cases.
That is its continuity with psychoanalysis.

This will seem to be a very odd claim, at first sight. What do I mean
by it exactly? Freud saw the acquisition of certain kinds of cognitively
achieved self-knowledge (via the technologies of psychoanalysis) as
therapy, and it is obvious why he did so. But I think that the less
obvious idea of therapy that is relevant to self-knowledge is much
more general than the more obvious notion of therapy *he* had in

mind, which was to remove neuroses and anxiety that often accompany specific cases of lack of self-knowledge. The normative framework I have briefly sketched in my modification and extension of Strawson's picture gives us the right to say that because the commitment to self-knowledge is much more general and in a sense much more fundamental than the desire to alleviate the neuroses sometimes engendered by certain kinds of lack of self-knowledge. And as a result, the notion of cognitive therapy I am invoking is much more general than Freud's framework allowed, general enough to see these other more routine and quotidian exercises I mentioned as *also* falling under the notion of cognitive therapy.

To fulfill our commitment to rid ourselves of certain neuroses, we are no doubt required to go through the elaborate and interesting cognitive acquisitions of self-knowledge of motives and beliefs that the process of psychoanalysis provides. To live up to the *very much more general* commitment to self-knowledge (established by my modification of Strawson) requires not merely the psychoanalytic cognitive acquisitions but also the much less interesting sorts of everyday cognitive inquiries I have listed. That these cognitive inquiries are less interesting and that they are not related to curing neuroses should not distract us from seeing that they too are forms of therapy. *They too,* just like the Freudian cases, *are cognitive efforts to live up to a certain commitment (to self-knowledge) when we have failed to do so.* In the opening paragraph of the present section of this chapter, I had emphasized (and italicized) that just such a commitment is the *core* to understanding Freud's claims for the method and point of psychoanalysis. The fact that, in psychoanalysis, the core has a lot of *surround* such as involving certain technologies to cognitively achieve the self-knowledge, and such as going on to alleviate neuroses and anxiety by gaining the self-knowledge, may distract us from the core because the surround is so interesting in itself. But we should resist the distraction. The core is there, and it is shared by the uninteresting and non-psychoanalytical cases of cognitive self-knowledge. Just because in these cases the core does not mention the interesting fact (mentioned in the surround), viz., that cognitive seekings of self-knowledge *can be aided by certain technologies,* that does not mean that there are not the cognitive efforts that are shared by both the specifically psychoanalytic and the more general cases. And just because the core does not mention the interesting fact (that the surround mentions), viz., that the cognitive seekings of self-knowledge are there to fulfill a commitment to self-knowledge and *thereby provide a very specific kind of therapy to alleviate neuroses and anxieties,* that does not mean that the cognitive seekings of self-knowledge are not there precisely for the much *more general therapeutic effect* of overcoming a lapse, of trying to do better to fulfill a commitment to self-knowledge that one has failed to live up to.

To object that this talk of 'therapy' is eccentric when it is deployed outside of the context of such regimes and forms of inquiry as is found in psychoanalysis, psychotherapy, etc., would now be a superficial objection because it would not have taken in the sense in which the exercise of the more general class of cognitive acquisitions of self-knowledge is a way of fulfilling our own commitment to self-knowledge. We seek therapy in general to fulfill our commitments. That the therapy does not always come in regimes, that it does not always get rid of states such as neuroses and anxieties, and so on, does not mean that it does not have a right to be called a 'therapy'. It is self-improvement necessary to live up to a commitment to self-knowledge. One would be failing to take in the fact that self-knowledge is itself a commitment, and failing to take in the full implications of the modifications that were made to the Strawsonian picture of agency in Chapter 2, if one made this superficial objection.

Let me sum up by repeating that the claim (which issues from the modification of Strawson) that self-knowledge is itself to be thought of as a commitment is a claim that stands *over and above* the constitutive thesis about self-knowledge.

Thus in the picture of self-knowledge I have been sketching through the book there are three elements.

They are: (1) There is a commitment of the sort I have just mentioned to self-knowledge. Then (2) there is a separate claim, which I have called the "constitutive thesis" (formulated in the two conditionals, one of which has a proviso explicitly mentioning considerations of agency). Element (2), in the context of (1), i.e., in the context of the idea of self-knowledge being a commitment, says that we ordinarily (paradigmatically) *live up* to this commitment, and we do so *not* by the exercise of some cognitive capacity, nor by the operation of a causal mechanism, *but simply to the extent that we think and act as free and responsible agents.* Thus, the constitutive claim mentioned in (2) is a claim about the nature of *livings-up-to* the commitment to self-knowledge mentioned in (1). And finally, (3), when we do *not* live up to the commitment in the way that the constitutive thesis claims, when we fall outside of the proviso of agency mentioned in one of the conditionals (the conditional for transparency) that present the constitutive claim, we have to undertake forms *either* of everyday cognitive therapy *or* of a more institutionalized cognitive therapy in order to do better and to live up to it. These cases mentioned in (3) are the exceptional cases of cognitive self-knowledge. They are exceptional and non-paradigmatic.

The idea that cognitive acquisitions of self-knowledge are exceptional and peripheral *despite their frequency* can now be characterized without embarrassment for any theorist who takes self-knowledge to be constitutive of self-knowledge. The notion of 'exceptional' here is not meant to suggest necessarily that these are *rare* exceptions to the constitutive thesis, for they may *not* be rare. So (2), which is the main claim of the book, represents a position that is very far from being Cartesian. It acknowledges a phenomenon that Cartesian notions of infallibility denied and moreover admits that their occurrence is not merely rare but quite widespread. So the sense in which the phenomenon is exceptional is not a frequentist one. It is exceptional in the sense that these cognitive exercises do not provide the paradigm for self-knowledge; the paradigm for self-knowledge is, rather, that it is a form of *commitment* that we *necessarily live up to* simply by having intentional states that are essentially linked with our agency. In other words, it is exceptional in the sense that the cognitive exercises, however frequent, are nevertheless to be understood as *merely* picking up a very specific sort of *slack:* they are forms of cognitive therapy that help us to live up to this commitment when we have failed to do so, i.e., when our mental states have fallen outside the conditions of responsible agency that define the paradigm of self-knowledge.

Element (1), therefore, gives a context and a gloss to the book's main constitutive thesis (2), and in doing so it helps to explain why (2) need not be embarrassed by what is acknowledged as being widespread by (3). And (1), which does this vital work, is itself fully justified by the modification made to Strawson's normative conception of agency in Chapter 2, which has been so central to the book's argument. Thus it is that self-knowledge is indeed special, and when it is not, its specialness is not compromised. Descartes had no resources to say anything like this, and that is why his view of the mind could make nothing sensible out of his own perfectly correct intuition that our knowledge of our own mind is special.

♦ ♦ ♦

Does the Debate about Internal versus External Reasons Rest on a Mistake?

THIS BOOK HAS had much to say about intentionality and about agency, but it has not had much to say explicitly about 'reasons'. Yet reasons are centrally linked to a person's intentional states and to his or her agency. The weakest link is that one could not have reasons to do or think things if one were not an agent with intentional states. Are there much stronger links than that? That is a question that has been central to recent debates between Humean and Kantian ways of thinking, especially about what is sometimes called 'practical' reason.

My insistence that intentional states are not dispositions but commitments, and that the intentional aspect of the mind is not exhausted by causal, dispositional, and motivational states, as standardly conceived, but is also populated by states that are themselves irreducibly normative, has a striking implication for these debates. This implication flows specifically from the idea that commitments force us to a notion of explanation or rationalizing that stands apart from the standard explanatory or rationalizing ideals in Humean (and more recently Davidsonian) conceptions of intentional psychology. Let me explore that very briefly in this short appendix. The subject is part of a much larger project of mine that spans both philosophy and politics. Here I only want to put down a preliminary ground clearing for that larger project because it has an intrinsic interest for anyone engaged in the study of practical rationality.

In his brilliant and widely discussed sophistication of Hume's thinking on reasons in "Internal and External Reasons,"[1] Bernard Williams distinguishes between two kinds of reasons, expressed in two different interpretations of the statement "A has a reason to φ." One interpretation is that it is true under the condition that A has some motive that will be furthered by φing. This expresses the idea of internal reasons. The other interpretation, which expresses the idea of external reasons, denies that it is any part of the statement's truth-conditions that there be any such motive that is furthered by φing. As Williams puts it, the idea of internal reasons is just the insistence that there be something in the 'motivational set' of the agent, which sanctions φing, and the idea of external reasons is a denial of that. His paper's claim is that there are only internal reasons, that the very idea of external reasons is of precarious coherence. Williams is happy to be broadminded about what is included in the motivational set, allowing in a variety of dispositions, emotions, and even, as he puts it, 'commitments'. (I will return to the last in a moment.) What he is against is the idea that facts that speak not at all to what is *within* an agent's *motivational* psychology, facts external to her, which need not even be known by her, can provide reasons for her to act. I have emphasized both 'within' and 'motivational' quite deliberately, since that is central to the point I make in this brief appendix.

The paper has generated much distinguished opposition, most notably by Nagel, Scanlon, Korsgaard, Parfit, and McDowell. All of them say that it is in some sense to misunderstand the very idea of reasons, which is an essentially *normative* idea, to think that reasons flow in the way Williams suggests, from causal-psychological internal states such as our motivations, dispositions, etc.

I want to argue that there is something ill-configured in this dispute and that there might just be scope for a set of theoretically liberating possibilities in moral psychology (and eventually in politics, though I will not pursue that here) if we notice this. Notice, that is, that there is something uncompulsory in the way that the dispute has been set up.

Both parties to the dispute are guilty of conflating two separate distinctions. The words 'internal' and 'external' are actually each marking two different theoretical places in the very dispute whose official proceedings, as conducted by the disputants, mention only one. The two distinctions are as follows: (1) the idea that reasons are irreducibly normative (one notion of external) versus the idea that they get their point and 'rationale' from descriptive psychological facts about us such as our motives, dispositions, etc. (one notion of internal); (2) the idea that reasons are external to and independent of our substantive evaluative mental lives, such that they are reasons for all of us to the extent that we are creatures capable of rationality and therefore of grasping their normative force (the other notion of external) versus the idea that they are not thus external but are instead internal to our substantive evaluative mental lives and may thus be held variably by some of us and not others, depending on whether the substantive elements are present in our specific evaluative economies (the other notion of internal).[2]

I claim that these distinctions *do not coincide*. To say that they are not coincident is to allow that we may scramble them. And the particular scrambling that I think is both interesting and true is that there might be reasons that are external in the first sense but internal in the second. There might be reasons, which are fully and irreducibly normative, that do not essentially owe to our dispositions and motives but, nevertheless, are *not* independent of our mental lives as facts in the external world, which might be unknown to us, are. In other words, it is perfectly possible to think of our internal and mental or psychological lives as being populated not just by states such as dispositions and motives[3] but also by irreducibly normative states.

This, of course, complicates how we must think of the very nature of psychology. Williams himself actually pays lip service to this complication by saying that his conception of a 'motivational set' is intended by him as being broad enough to include what he—with no philosophical studiedness—calls 'commitments'. At the same time, he says that for reasons to be 'internal', which is all that they can be for him, they must figure in the explanations of the actions (or thoughts) of the subject for whom they are reasons. But precisely because his use of the term 'commitments' is casual and carries no philosophical weight of the sort that we gave it in our discussion in Chapter 5, he pays no serious attention whatsoever to what is implied by it for his own framework for thinking about psychological states and the explanations they figure in. In that framework, there is no clarity about the status of what he has in mind by the word 'commitments' and how they might be explanatory. In fact, as his critics point out, his framework is in essence Humean or, to use McDowell's term for it, 'psychologistic', and in being so, these 'commitments' could only be dispositions that we characterize in an unprincipled way with evaluative terminology—unprincipled because it is not clear what that vocabulary really marks out if the states being characterized are essentially dispositions or tendencies and motives. If, on the other hand, one's psychology was populated not just by dispositions and motives (with an unprincipled veneer of evaluative vocabulary characterizing some of them) but also by genuinely normative states, a question is raised about how this enriches or changes the very idea of psychological explanation along the lines spelled out by me in Chapter 5.

Williams's critics, as I said, are much better on this point and see the difficulty that Williams does not—of how claims to normativity are spoiled by equating them or deriving them from the descriptive and explanatory psychological apparatus of motives, dispositions, etc.

On the other hand, and this is a crucial part of what I want to say about this debate, Williams's critics, though they are indeed sensitive to the incompatibility of norms and dispositional/motivational states, because they think of norms as not being internal but given in *external* facts, they leave no scope for allowing for a properly moral *psychology*, at least until these facts move into a second stage, where they come to be apprehended by subjects with a psychology. The point being made here against them is that there is (often) *no need* for a second stage because there are plenty of cases of genuine and irreducible normativity, where there is no first (external) stage at all. So there is no question of having (always) to postpone the relevance of norms to psychology till this second stage. A subject (often) has irreducibly normative states *internal* to him or her, and these can differ from subject to subject, providing internal reasons quite differentially, and therefore are *not* a matter of subject-independent external facts providing the same reasons for everyone and providing internal reasons *only* when they are apprehended by subjects and made internal.

A very important caveat must be registered in order to avoid misunderstanding. I am by no means saying that there is *no* such externally located source of reasons. Far from it. In Chapter 5, I argued how—if we are agents—we will see facts in the world, evaluative facts, making normative demands on us. But that does not mean that agents do not also have internal normative states, which are *not* formed by his or her perception of external evaluative facts. It may be that we could not *in general* have internal normative states without having the capacity to see external facts as making normative demands on one. But that is a general dependency of internal reasons on external evaluative facts. It is not a specific and distributed dependency whereby *each* internal normative state or commitment issues from the perception of an external evaluative fact making a normative demand on one.

Therefore, without in any way contradicting or denying the notion of external reasons as described in Chapter 5, I want to mark out a space for a quite different notion of properly and genuinely internal reasons. But these internal reasons, on the other hand, are not quite what Williams offers up when he talks of 'internal reasons', nor are they what his externalist critics allow for when they say that reasons are irreducibly normative states owing to facts external to and independent of a subject's psychology and that become internal to their psychology only when they are apprehended by subjects.

It is a space that is not available in their official dispute.

Armed, then, with the *two* notions of 'internal' and two notions of 'external' (which in the official dispute is hidden as only *one* conflated distinction), my main claim in this appendix is that we may now agree with Williams's critics that it is intolerable that reasons should be thought of as, in the end, having their normative source in something quite non-normative such as one's dispositions and motives but agree with Williams that, in order to say so, *we do not have to think of them as external to our mentalities, as owing to facts that are external and quite possibly unbeknownst to the agent for whom it is a reason.* A sympathetic (and no doubt revisionary) reading of Williams therefore can see him as struggling to express only this last thought (the one I have just italicized) by his talk of internal reasons, which talk is marred by his own conflation of this good thought with a quite different Humean thought: that reasons owe to motives and dispositions. And I am saying that this sympathetic reading of Williams does not so much as occur to his opponents since they too are guilty of a parallel conflation. They too spoil their own good externalist thought that the normative standing of reasons would be demeaned by seeing them as beholden to our motives and dispositions, when they identify that thought (literally equate it) with the quite distinct thought that therefore reasons must owe to facts external and quite possibly even unbeknownst to those for whom they are reasons.

So, to repeat, the debate between Williams and his critics leaves no space for the notion of internal reasons that (1) have all the irreducible normativity that one would expect reasons to have because it is not based on any Humean motivational psychology and that (2) at the same time can be entirely internal to a subject, in the sense that they may be reasons for some subjects and not others because they are not based in external facts that make normative demands on all subjects independent of their other commitments. In other words, there is a notion of reasons that is neither Humean nor Kantian, which the contemporary dispute's renewed and sophisticated elaboration of Humean and Kantian arguments deprive us of. The notion of commitments or internal oughts first argued for in Chapter 5 is what makes this scrambled position on reasons possible. Both 'internal' and 'ought' were crucial to the idea of a commitment, and both these aspects are crucial to the argument of this appendix. Being a genuine ought and not just a psychologistic state, to use McDowell's term, it is not a Humean notion of internal reason of the kind Williams promotes. Being genuinely 'internal', it is not a Kantian notion of reason that Williams's critics promote.

That is the main point of this appendix, but let me raise one more issue. A question arises: From *whence* comes the normativity of commitments or reasons if it is not always and necessarily from external sources that make for a normativity *for all others* as well, as in Kant's way of thinking of norm? This 'whence' question, which is about the sources of normativity, is not something that I can pursue in a short discussion appended to a book. It is to be pursued in another work. But it should be recorded here that it would, on the face of it, be dogmatic to think there can be no understanding of the normativity of a commitment of mine (an irreducible internal 'ought' of mine) that does not have external sources that make it a commitment of all others as well, so long as they were sighted enough to see it. I think the idea of being sighted to see external evaluative facts is a good one, but it does not settle the issue against internalism, for it still may be the case that what makes someone sighted to see something external may have to do with internal factors that have to do with other internal oughts they have. Externalism and perceptualism about reasons, therefore, cannot remove the *aspectual* element in seeing, which may come from internal differences among rational subjects.

Thus so-called 'externalism' about reasons has more than one motive fueling it. One is simply to make it possible to say that one might derive one's sources of reasons or internal oughts from the world, which may often be given to us in different aspects depending on other internal normative factors (which I cannot say more about here). The other is to say that the world gives *everyone* the same reasons and commitments, and what makes them internal is merely our perception of something that is the same for all. The latter motive stands in deep opposition to any form of internalism. The former motive does not.

Notes

Preface

1. Noam Chomsky has often described freedom as a mystery. He himself is not made particularly anxious or dogmatic, as some naturalists are, by viewing it to be a mystery. But what he means by it is that, from the point of view of the kind of theoretical understanding that one tries to gain in the natural sciences, freedom seems quite intractable. This book's entire argument may be viewed as systematizing and, therefore, to some extent, domesticating and demystifying this idea by showing that in some deep sense the conviction that freedom is a mystery is inseparable from our conviction that values are irreducible to the properties that natural science studies; and, in turn, by showing that such convictions that we might have that intentionality is irreducible and not a proper subject for scientific study is no other than the conviction that value is irreducible and unfit for such study; and finally, by showing that our intuitions about the specially authoritative and transparent character of our knowledge of our own intentional states derives strictly from the foregoing integration of agency, value, and intentionality.
2. Akeel Bilgrami, *Belief and Meaning* (Oxford: Blackwell, 1992).

1. What Makes Self-Knowledge Special?

1. René Descartes, *Meditations on First Philosophy: The Philosophical Writings of Descartes,* vol. II, ed. John Cottingham, Robert Stoothoff, and Dugald Murdoch (Cambridge: Cambridge University Press, 1984).
2. I say guardedly 'it is said' in order to avoid scholarly controversy. In

general, the remarks in this chapter about Descartes do not aspire to great scholarly scruple, though it is hoped that they are not irresponsible in the attributions that they make to him. At the very least, they do not depart from the standard attributions to be found in the position that goes under the label "Cartesian" in so much contemporary Philosophy of Mind. Perhaps this position is not an accurate picture of the historical Descartes. It is a much derided position in this century's philosophy, so it would not come as a surprise if scholars of Descartes found it to be a caricature in one or another respect. But this chapter, whose purpose is not scholarly, will leave that question alone since its author is not really knowledgeable enough to address it.

3. There is a question, of course, that can be raised about whether the method of hyperbolical doubt that gets started in the First Meditation can have the sort of dialectic it gets there without something like the problematic subjectivist conception of mental states (as being conceived from the strictly first person perspective) defined in the Second Meditation seeming inevitable. Here is how someone might pursue this. Does one have to think that one cannot doubt that one *has* the beliefs one has about the external world in order to doubt the *truth* of these latter beliefs in the way that Descartes asks us to? And if so, does this imply (with the *external* world now in doubt) that the idea of our own beliefs and their contents, which are not in doubt, cannot therefore depend on anything but one's *internal* perspective on oneself? And isn't this last implication just the problematic subjectivist assumption that is made explicit in the Second Meditation? I think we have to tread carefully here before coming to any conclusion, but I will not take this matter up any further. I present the opposite view in note 6 below.

4. Such a reading was first made, of course, most elaborately by Wittgenstein in his *Philosophical Investigations* (Oxford: Basil Blackwell, 1953), where it was also given its most famous and extensive critique. It might have, and has, been said that John Locke in Book IV of his *An Essay Concerning Human Understanding*, ed. P. H. Nidditch (Oxford: Oxford University Press, 1975), did actually make something like that same elaboration with much greater sympathy into a positive Philosophy of Language and that, therefore, he too is a target of the critique found in Wittgenstein.

5. For the earlier view, see A. J. Ayer, *Language, Truth and Logic* (London: Gollancz, 1946). For the later view, see A. J. Ayer, "One's Knowledge of Other Minds," *Theoria* 19 (1953): 1–20.

6. The 'First Meditation' on the face of it (though see note 3 for a question about this) merely presents an 'internalist' conception of the mind,

which is neutral between the first person, subjectivist conception and a more objectivist one. Here the mind is such that it could be what it is whether or not the external world can be said to exist. Hyperbolic doubt puts the world's existence into question, and so it is implied that the mind is not dependent on the world for its existence and its characterization. This is 'internalism', and as such, this doctrine of a world-independent mind says nothing about the mind's subjectivity. Fastening on such an internalist doctrine, modern theories of the mind, such as reductive materialism and functionalism, could characterize the mind in thoroughly anti-subjectivist terms. Indeed, philosophers such as Evans and McDowell have claimed that Cartesian internalism is of a piece with these modern forms of materialism, and just because the latter are modern developments, that should not hide the fact that they owe to a quite traditional internalism to be found in Descartes. See Gareth Evans, "Comment on Jerry Fodor's *Methodological Solipsism as a Research Strategy in Cognitive Psychology*," *Behavioral and Brain Sciences* 3 (1980): 79–80; John McDowell, "Singular Thought and the Extent of Inner Space," in *Meaning, Knowledge, and Reality* (Cambridge, Mass.: Harvard University Press, 1998). But what I am insisting on is that it is the Descartes of the 'First Meditation', not the 'Second', to which it is owed, where subjectivity is not written into the idea of mental states, but only interiority is. And it is the 'Second' where our concerns in this chapter really begin.

7. We want to say: the very same thing that I describe when I say "Carol is in pain" is what Carol describes when she says, "I am in pain." But it's not clear what gives us the right to say this if pain is conceived in the way mental states generally are conceived in the 'Second Meditation'. The argument from analogy, which was first formulated by John Stuart Mill in *An Examination of Sir William Hamilton's Philosophy* (London: Longmans, 1867), is intended to give us that right. It proceeds from the observation of a causal connection between one's own mental states and one's bodily behavior, and the observation of similar forms of behavior in other bodies, to a conclusion about mental states of others similarly causing their behavior. For Wittgenstein, this argument does not even acknowledge that, in the projection onto others by analogy that it proposes, the term 'pain' or the term 'mind' generally could not mean the same as it does when it is applied by us to ourselves. Given the Cartesian assumption of subjectivity, this is necessarily so, for if the terms get their meaning conferred on them by states that are logically private, then nothing (no sort of projection, and indeed nothing else at all) *could* bridge the gap that gives rise to the problem.

There are other less fundamental criticisms of the argument from analogy (such as that it is an induction based on a single case), but, by Wittgenstein's lights, they seem to proceed without recognizing the fact that what I called the 'distinctive' problem of other minds is not even taken up by the argument.

8. Although it is not the place here to discuss how successful the argument against the first personal assumption is, it should at least be stated in the briefest of terms. Earlier I had said that, under the first personal assumption, attributions of pain, say, to others were made without access to that which made those attributions true or false. Wittgenstein thought that this made it impossible to have a distinction between when a judgment attributing such pain was correct or incorrect, and that made for an intolerable conception of the meaning of the terms used in the judgment since the concept of meaning and of language generally required that we have the right to the distinction between a correct and a mistaken judgment. Those who have found this argument unconvincing have, among other things, questioned whether the passage from not having *access* to that which makes these attributions correct or incorrect to not having the *distinction itself* between the attributions' truth and falsity harbors a controversially verificationist premise.

9. This connection, often known as 'criterial,' is much discussed in the secondary literature on Wittgenstein.

10. The subtle as well as stark differences among these philosophers should not go unrecorded, despite their all joining in with the reversal of direction. The difference between Ryle and the strict behaviorist (among other things) is that Ryle (like Wittgenstein, as mentioned above) never demanded, as they did, that the behavior in terms of which inner mental states must be reductively understood is to be described in nonintentional vocabulary. What the functionalists crucially and explicitly added to Ryle was, first, a frank acceptance of inner states as irreducibly inner and, second, a holism by which an intentional state was related to behavior. But most of them *subtracted* two things from Ryle as well. First they subtracted the allowance of intentional vocabulary in describing the behavior (and the inner states) when they claimed that in the end the intentional vocabulary could be jettisoned for a purely functional or causal one (for example, by an application of a method akin to the one by which Ramsey replaced the theoretical vocabulary in scientific theories for a purely observational one). Behavior was defined by them relationally and abstractly as the output of holistically related causes, which were themselves defined relationally to these out-

puts and non-intentionally described inputs. Second, unlike anything in Ryle, who was, as I said, skeptical of the inner altogether, it was part of their eventual programmatic ideal that the inner mental states of a person could be broken down into the causal states of sub-personal systems within a person. Like the functionalists, Quine and Davidson both embraced the holistic feature, but they embraced—like Brentano much before them—that the intentional vocabulary is irreducible not only to the physical but even to the causal and functional. However, Davidson (unlike Quine, who often proposed its elimination) thought that the intentional vocabulary is also ineliminable. Despite all these genuine and intricate differences, all these philosophical positions fall within the shift in direction to a broadly third personal conception of mental states. Here are some references: J. B. Watson, *Behaviorism*, rev. ed. (Chicago: University of Chicago Press, 1958); B. F. Skinner, *Verbal Behavior* (New York: Appleton Century Crofts, 1957); Gilbert Ryle, *The Concept of Mind* (London: Penguin, 1949); D. M. Armstrong, *A Materialist Theory of Mind* (London: Routledge and Kegan Paul, 1983); David Lewis, "An Argument for the Identity Theory," in *Philosophical Papers*, vol. 1 (New York: Oxford University Press, 1983); M. V. O. Quine, *Word and Object* (Cambridge, Mass.: MIT Press, 1960); Donald Davidson, "Mental Events," in *Essays on Actions and Events* (Oxford: Oxford University Press, 1980).

11. In this expository chapter, I am restricting the use of the expression 'first person' approach to the specific Cartesian subjectivist conception of how to understand the meaning of mental concepts. This is the idea of 'first person' that underlies the conception of mentality that gives rise to the problem of other minds. In subsequent chapters, most explicitly in Chapter 5 but also earlier in Chapters 3 and 4, I will be using the expression 'first person' to talk of a first person perspective that is an entirely different idea. It has not to do with subjectivity in the Cartesian sense made much of by recent philosophers such as Tom Nagel and David Chalmers but, rather, has to do with the deliberative perspective of the agent, the perspective of freedom, as Kant put it. Thus, by that stage of the book, the expression would be tracking a quite different phenomenon, not the inner life of consciousness understood in narrow Cartesian terms but the unique perspective each of us has in the exercise of deliberation, norm, and agency, most explicitly formulated by Kant in the third section of his *Groundwork*, and before him by Spinoza. The issues of a 'logically' private mentality raised by Wittgenstein against the Cartesian notion of a first person understanding of mentality are irrelevant to this quite other understanding of what is

meant by the 'first person', though of course other issues will arise for it, such as its naturalistic irreducibility to anything third personal. All this will be discussed in Chapters 4 and 5.

12. I am being careful to say 'states of mind' here rather than the more specific 'intentional states' because I want to leave it open till very much later in the book as to whether it is indeed intentional states or something else that we fail to know and then come to know as a result of cognitive acts of inquiry of various sorts, including psychoanalysis (but including many more quotidian forms of cognitive self-inquiry as well).

13. See chapter 6 in Ryle, *The Concept of Mind.*

14. Alison Gopnik, "How We Know Our Minds: The Illusion of First-Person Knowledge of Intentionality," *Behavioral and Brain Sciences* 16, no. 6 (1993): 1–15, 90–101.

15. See the articles in Peter Carruthers and Peter K. Smith (eds.), *Theories of Theories of Mind* (New York: Cambridge University Press, 1996), in particular the article by Martin Davies and the two articles by Peter Carruthers himself.

16. Perception is at least phenomenologically different from inference, and this phenomenological difference is often thought to make a difference to epistemology. Knowledge by perception and knowledge by inference are often said to be direct and indirect forms of gaining knowledge, respectively. This distinction is sometimes rejected by those who think that all perception involves some inference, from some background theoretical commitments. They claim that because the inference is from commitments that are in the *background,* there is no phenomenological sense of an inference (which there would be if they were in the *foreground,* explicitly in the form of something like premises). But they insist that the fact that there is inference present, even if not felt to be so, means that the phenomenology is not reflected in any epistemology. Gopnik, on self-knowledge, clearly falls within the latter group. If Gopnik is right, the most plausible position denying any special character to self-knowledge embraces not just the inferential but *also* the perceptual forms of knowledge in a single, integrated position. If she is right, the usual contrast "either perceptual or inferential" is not warranted since her position is both. However, I am speaking in a very interim neutral voice here, and I don't actually mean to suggest that Gopnik is right and that any perceptual view of self-knowledge must look like hers. In fact, below in the text, I look at another form of the perceptual view of self-knowledge (owing to David Armstrong) that seems to me a more plausible view because it has no inferential ele-

ment, though it is not plausible enough in the end to be convincing. The point, however, is that her view seems prima facie more plausible than *Ryle's* because it brings something to his idea of inferential self-knowledge, something more plausible than his simple description of it. In other words, the point is not so much that I want to record sympathy with the idea that the most plausible perceptual view of self-knowledge is in some sense to be an inferential view, but rather that if one is going to take an inferential view of self-knowledge, the most plausible such view better also be a perceptual view.

John McDowell traverses some of the difficulties involved in insisting that perception is inferential in his many writings on epistemology, not just of perception of the external world but in the perception of mind, meaning, and value as well. I discuss his views below in the text, and once we see their relevance, it turns out that what seems prima facie the case, viz., that Gopnik improves on Ryle, is actually not necessarily the case. (McDowell's articles are collected in his volume of papers cited in note 6.) For the present purpose of discussing self-knowledge, my interest is only to say that there *may* be a problem about the usual distinction between perceptual and inferential knowledge that is found in the literature on self-knowledge, when it is said so often that there are two *distinct* ways of knowing, perceptual and inferential, and self-knowledge is *either* one of these or neither of them and therefore some third thing. See particularly Crispin Wright on this way of setting up the issue of self-knowledge in his "Wittgenstein's Rule-Following Considerations and the Project of Theoretical Linguistics," in Alexander George (ed.), *Reflections on Chomsky* (Oxford: Blackwell, 1989).

Here, then, is how things divide up on the issue. If Gopnik's arguments are effective and so if self-knowledge is inferential, it had *also* better be perceptual. And so the standard way of setting up the issue (either perceptual or inferential) may not leave the inferentialist scope to move beyond Ryle to something more like Gopnik's (*both* inferential and conceptual) perceptual refinement upon his inferentialist view. On the other hand, if McDowell is right in denying that perception of other minds and the external world ordinarily involves inference, then the entire terminology that describes self-knowledge as being special and different from these knowledges, because it is not based on evidence and is somehow more direct than they are, is misleading. That is, if ordinary perception of other minds and objects in the external world is itself direct and not derived by inference from evidence, then whatever is special about self-knowledge had better not be described (as it is by many) in such terminology. More on this later in the chapter.

17. When I say that we must decide which of Descartes' two enduring features today—the perceptual or the constitutive—are right and show how they look *in a non-Cartesian setting*, I most immediately mean how either would look without infallibility. But this implies something a little less immediately non-Cartesian; it implies that, without infallibility, neither feature will afford any foundationalist hopes. For the infallibilist feature in Descartes is much motivated by his epistemological project that has come to be called 'foundationalism'. He is looking for certainties ('indubitabilities') that can be the foundation of other kinds of knowledge. It is too obvious why the perceptual feature without infallibility could not provide for any foundationalism. But the constitutive feature without Cartesian ideas about infallibility would not provide much hope or scope for foundationalism, either. Why this is so will not emerge until a full account of what makes any constitutive view possible and plausible is spelled out. For now, it would be enough to say that the constitutive view of self-knowledge presented in this book, and by others today who subscribe to it, is a view that has no underlying foundationalist motivation and is merely motivated to get right what the nature of self-knowledge is. It should also go without saying that there is a more distant element in the Cartesian setting that all these issues about self-knowledge need to be separated from, and that is his dualism about mind and body. No one wanting to retain the constitutive feature of self-knowledge need have anything to do with his ontological dualism.

18. See McDowell, "Criteria, Defeasibility, and Knowledge," in *Meaning, Knowledge, and Reality.*

19. See Saul Kripke, *Wittgenstein on Rules and Private Language* (Oxford: Blackwell, 1982).

20. Though she did not see it as deriving from McDowell's argument, Annalisa Coliva made such an argument against inferential accounts of self-knowledge in a recent talk at a workshop on the subject of self-knowledge in Lugano, Switzerland: "Self-Knowledge and the Self," August 3, 2004.

21. It is true that analogues such as, say, "I remembered" might apply sometimes. I might say on occasion, "I remember that I once believed. . . . ' But there are any number of cases of self-knowledge of intentionality where no such analogues are apt or forthcoming. So, here again, one should guard against taking exceptional cases and erecting them into a—perceptual—paradigm for self-knowledge.

22. I have not said anything so far about other forms of knowledge about the external world than the perceptual, such as those based on testi-

mony. Those too are cognitive achievements and make such knowledge stand apart from self-knowledge. It is to keep things simple that I have restricted the contrast in our governing disjunction as between constitutive views and *perceptual* views only.

23. Pointing out that these analogues are missing in self-knowledge is helpful because it adds a factor to the notion of non-independence that went into our initial characterization of the constitutive view. By itself, the idea that our intentional states lack an independence from our self-knowledge of them that external objects have from our knowledge of them does not distinguish self-knowledge from certain views of secondary qualities in the external world, according to which these qualities lack an independence from our perceptual responses to them. And if it does not distinguish this, we cannot have the general contrast between the constitutive view and the perceptual view, on which I have pinned so much. But once we point out that self-knowledge lacks the analogues to seeing, looking, etc., we can distinguish the dependence that intentional states have on our knowledge, and responses to them form the dependence that secondary qualities have on our responses to them. So the contrast that we want for the constitutive view from the perceptual view remains. I will take this question up again at the very end of the book (in the "Conclusion") when I briefly consider the difference between my way of grounding a constitutive account of self-knowledge and Crispin Wright's.

24. See the chapter "Introspection," in Armstrong, *A Materialist Theory of Mind.*

25. So, for instance, someone might say that for all the distinctiveness that human beings are endowed with in terms of second-order mental states and the full and rich notion of first-order intentionality that they bring in their wake, human beings, after all, do share some first-order mental states with animals. Of these states it might be said that the causal-perceptual view of self-knowledge should hold. Even if it were the case that there are mental states properly describable as being 'shared' by both human and non-human animals, this does not affect the point I am making, since I am making claims only about the authority and transparency that hold regarding intentional states in the full and rich sense that human beings uniquely possess (at least so far as we know). A great number of philosophers hold a causal-perceptual account of these intentional states, and that is what I am opposing by giving a constitutive account of them along my distinctive lines. In any case, it should be pointed out that the idea that we 'share' a certain kind of intentional state with animals has not gone unquestioned. John Mc-

Dowell in many papers (see all the papers in section III of his *Mind, Value and Reality* [Cambridge, Mass.: Harvard University Press, 1998], without questioning that non-human animals have intentional states in some sense, has questioned the idea that our own mental states that do not have the full and rich intentional status could be thought of as being 'shared' by non-human animals. This is because our possession of these states, when placed in the surround of a full and rich intentionality also possessed by us, would spoil them for that shared status. I have sympathy with McDowell's writings on this theme, but my claims in this book don't turn on that sympathy being borne out as a philosophically correct position. As I have said repeatedly, my claims about transparency and authority are restricted to intentional states in the full sense.

26. To complete the asymmetry, one should make the contrast not just with knowledge of others but also with knowledge of the external world. The full asymmetry, then, is that we know what others think by inferring it from their behavior or perceiving it in their behavior, and we know what there is in the external world by perceiving things in the external world and inferring other things from the perception, but we know self-knowledge without any such perception or inference.

27. P. F. Strawson, *Individuals* (London: Methuen, 1959).

2. The Conceptual Basis for Transparency I

1. P. F. Strawson, "Freedom and Resentment," *Proceedings of the British Academy,* reprinted in his *Freedom and Resentment and Other Essays* (London: Methuen, 1974).

2. P. F. Strawson, *Individuals* (London: Methuen, 1959).

3. It should be obvious that I am being highly selective about what I am calling 'traditional'. Talk of causality has not been uniformly present in the traditional contrast of freedom and determinism. 'Predestination', 'fate', and other such notions defined the contrast, without any explicit mention of causality. It is a real question, however, how much something like causality was always implicit in these other traditional ways of setting up the contrast.

4. David Hume, *A Treatise of Human Nature,* Part III, Sections I and II (Oxford: Oxford University Press, 1978).

5. A. J. Ayer, "Freedom and Necessity," in *Philosophical Essays* (London: Macmillan, 1954).

6. I say 'excusing' and mean it to contrast with something like 'forgiving' because the latter, unlike the former, seems to suggest that the action

is considered blameworthy, but special circumstances and considerations, possibly having to do with contingent relations between the re-actor and the actor whose action is being judged—a good friend, perhaps, or someone whom she is otherwise beholden to, etc.—have entered in forming the reactive attitude.

7. John McDowell, "Reply to Bilgrami," in Cynthia Macdonald and Graham Macdonald (eds.), *McDowell and His Critics* (Oxford: Blackwell, 2006).

8. See note 11 below for a direct remark about the case of reactive attitudes toward children.

9. In Chapter 5, I will repeat a thought-experiment I had made in earlier papers of mine of a subject, 'Oblomov', who has not so much committed normative or rational suicide but who, contrary to appearances, lacks a normative and rational life, whether practical or theoretical, because he is wholly passive. My claim there will be that such a subject lacks intentionality. That is, the claim will be that it is not possible to imagine a subject who is both intentional and completely passive. However, there is no reason to think that such a passive and non-intentional subject cannot be imagined to exist or to survive physically. It can be imagined to have various dispositions, and it can have its sensations gratified, without it making normative judgments about what is correct or incorrect thought and action. And so there is no reason to think that one cannot imagine oneself becoming a subject who sheds one's intentional life for a purely passive subjectivity.

10. See Jay Wallace, *Responsibility and the Moral Sentiments* (Cambridge, Mass.: Harvard University Press, 1994), for such an appeal to these more general sorts of value. I have some doubts about how Wallace addresses this question, but quite apart from my doubts, I would commend Wallace's book to the reader for a contrastingly more guarded and more conventional reading of Strawson than mine, one that I know would resist the extension and modification that I am giving to Strawson.

11. The rejection of this utilitarian justification of our evaluative reactions raises an instructive, if obvious, point. When I gave a paper recently on this subject, Ned Block pressed me with the point that not only do we have reactive attitudes to very young children (say, two-year-olds), but we are able to justify having them in just the way I was demanding that Strawson spell out. The justification consists of the fact that it will *help them* to *develop* a sense of norm—of the distinction between right and wrong—at a stage when they lack the distinction and also, perhaps, encourage them to find the one less attractive than the other. This problem surfaced famously in what seemed to be a glaring paradox in

the world's most famous book, when a woman was punished by expulsion from a garden for eating an apple from one of its trees, which eating was supposed to have given her a certain knowledge, the knowledge of the distinction between right and wrong. The paradox consists in her being punished for an act that was ex hypothesi committed before she had this sense of right and wrong, since the act was supposed to have imparted that sense. The only excuse for the punishment (if punishment coming from the source it did needed an excuse) would have to be (just as in Block's point) a utilitarian one. We have negative reactive attitudes toward children and express them openly sometimes because they are useful in having just the effect that Block suggests. But to say all this is itself to acknowledge the difference between reactive attitudes conceived of in utilitarian terms and reactive attitudes conceived of as expressive of our sense of norm, of right and wrong. What we are interested in is the latter, since they alone are justified when their targets are creatures who do possess the distinction between right and wrong; what we have when we deal with children, perhaps even animals, is the former. And it is the latter, not the former, that will help us define a compatibilism that keeps the ideological incompatibilist at bay. The former will only feed into this ideologue's 'objectified' picture of things, which Strawson quite rightly finds shocking and repugnant, because it spells destruction for the very possibility of the latter (the reactive attitudes as expressions of our normative selves) and indeed, therefore, for the very notion of agency.

12. In raising this line of inquiry that led to the modification I have made of Strawson's notion of agency, I began with the question of our often helplessly arising reactive attitudes toward cats and pianos, for example. It might be said that lumping cats and pianos is not quite right. Such attitudes toward cats, even if unjustified, quite rightly see in cats some real agency, which pianos do not have, and that agency is different from full and free responsible agency. Or perhaps the objection might be put slightly differently. Unlike as with pianos, toward cats we may have attitudes of a more primitive emotional sort involving affection and dislike, if not the more evaluatively loaded forms of blaming that go with the attitudes on which I have focused. This reflects a more primitive notion of agency that cats might possess. And inasmuch as in many areas of our lives we are like cats, this holds of us too, viz., a more diverse conception of agency than I am allowing.

I am not disallowing such further notions of agency, no more than I am disallowing to animals other notions of intentionality than the one that is the focus of this book. The point, rather, is this: These further notions of agency cannot carry the burden of Strawson's argument since the reactive attitudes that reflect them lack the fully critical, normative dimensions that do carry the burden of his argument to which I am appealing. My argument (the one that modifies Strawson) has been that our *further* values tell us that the fully evaluatively loaded reactive attitudes are *justifiably* had only toward subjects that are themselves capable of apprehending that they are the targets or recipients of such attitudes and of accepting these attitudes toward them as justified or of rejecting them as unjustified. Cats and dogs may even in some sense grasp the more primitive emotional reactions we have toward them, but it is only subjects who can grasp the more evaluatively loaded and critical attitudes that may be justifiably directed toward them that have the requisite kind of agency that Strawson's argument rests on. And it is that notion of agency that yields the account of self-knowledge that I will be pursuing in the rest of the book. (This distinctiveness of the fully normative and critical reactive attitudes surfaces in the last footnote as well and will recur at various other points in the book, including the next chapter at the point where I discuss the objection from the asymmetry of praise and blame.)

It will not do to say that I have conveniently and circularly focused on the richer notion of responsible agency to make my claims about the radically normative nature of agency. There is nothing circular about the appeal to this notion of agency because most philosophers believe that this very notion of agency depends on non-normative metaphysical considerations that have nothing to do with the reactive attitudes. Whether or not one agrees with it, the illumination and innovation and the substantial surprise that was created by the entire Strawsonian line of thinking on agency can hardly be denied. In fact, the widespread disagreement to be found regarding his line of thinking is proof that there is nothing trivial or circular about my appeal to Strawsonian considerations.

13. Though it does not matter for the point I am making here about his identifying freedom with certain practices surrounding responsibility, I should admit that I am imposing a bit on Strawson when I say that he brings in the reactive attitudes to 'justify' these practices. I think perhaps it would be better to say that he wants to 'ground' them in our reactive attitudes. I say this because the main rationale of my modification of his view in Section 4 is the criticism that he does *not* ask the question about what justifies the practices; he merely seems to be filling in what it is to have these practices by pointing to the reactive attitudes. 'Grounding' seems a better term to describe that. In fact, it is because

I think that they actually *justify* the practices that I can and must go on to ask, "Well, then, what justifies the justifiers?"—something Strawson does not think of asking because he never put the initial question in terms of justifying. And to ask that is precisely to get on to the path of my more thoroughgoing evaluative and coherentist modification of his view. In general, I conjecture that the very special naturalism of philosophers like Strawson and others such as McDowell and perhaps Wittgenstein—to be sharply distinguished, of course, from naturalism as it is normally and pervasively understood, in terms of the scientist attitudes toward mind and value—will want to shun the demand for 'justification' at these basic levels and will want instead to 'ground' these basic levels in human nature, in 'how we are'. I suppose, then, that my modification of Strawson is just a way of expressing my dissatisfaction even with this more rarefied naturalism.

14. Some of these issues are, of course, related to the general issue of punishment and what justifies it, as it has been discussed over the years. Familiar theories of punishment appealed to such justifications as retributive or utilitarian ones. There might be a tendency therefore to think that Strawson's rejection of utilitarian justifications and his appeal to reactive attitudes such as resentment to say what underlies the practices surrounding responsibility such as punishment, is an echo of the *retributive* variety of justification for punishment. But that would be a quite gross confusion. I will not distract myself to say why.

15. See McDowell's "Reply to Bilgrami."

16. Even if one took the view that there was no parity on these points between science and values, even if one took the view that in science there is a fact of the matter as to whether two conflicting theories are true that is simply missing in the case of conflicting values, relativism does not follow for values. Even assuming that particular lack of parity, relativism would still only be interesting and vexing if there could be a value conflict (to take the present case, say, a conflict about whether blame and punishment are justified in some case) in which the two conflicting views were *in principle unreachable*, one by the other. And there is no reason in general to think that they would be unreachable, in principle. Viewed dynamically, conflict may be resolved if one of the conflicting parties—as a result of future incoming states of information—develops inner conflicts *within* its values, reflection on which then allows it to see its way to the point of the other party's position. This is always a permanent possibility if we view value conflict in dynamic terms. So viewed, unless there is some sort of impossibility theorem regarding the prospects of such resolution of present conflict in

the future, there is never any reason to admit to an in principle un-reachable impasse in the conflict—no reason, that is, to admit to rel-ativism regarding value. See my "Secularism and Relativism," in *Politics and the Moral Psychology of Identity* (Cambridge, Mass.: Harvard University Press, forthcoming).

17. The reader has perhaps noticed by the end of this chapter that I have been using the terms 'freedom', 'responsibility', and 'agency' inter-changeably. The recent discussion should have helped to make clear why. I will continue to do so throughout the book. Of course, any one wanting to preserve some notion of agency that is non-normative, or some notion of freedom that is non-normative, may do so without any disagreement with what is said here, so long as terms are kept distinct.

18. Thus, for instance, philosophers like Wittgenstein and McDowell and more recently Barry Stroud use the term 'naturalism' not only narrowly in the sense I have just mentioned (McDowell calls that narrow sense 'bald naturalism') but in a wider sense to include their own position as a kind of non-reductive naturalism. This wider kind of naturalism is not the target of criticism at all in *this chapter's* opposition to naturalism. (In Chapter 5, some versions of such a broader naturalism are criti-cized.) That still leaves plenty of other philosophers—by far the ma-jority among philosophers, I would say—who are being targeted in this chapter.

19. There are many other contemporary philosophers who have claimed that values are irreducible and have written eloquently about it. See particularly any of the many articles on the subject by philosophers such as John McDowell, Donald Davidson, Isaac Levi, and Robert Brandom. Davidson, on this subject, is discussed critically in Chapter 5.

3. The Conceptual Basis for Transparency II

1. Strictly speaking, the phrase 'beliefs about the first-order intentional states' is misleadingly general. It should be replaced by 'beliefs that the first-order intentional states are there' or 'beliefs that we have the first-order intentional states'. The rule-like quality does not hold between intentional states and *any* or *all* of our beliefs about them. It only holds between our intentional states and our beliefs that *we have those inten-tional states*. There is no need to make a corresponding caveat about the misleadingness of the phrase 'beliefs about them' as it occurs when I say in the text that the rule-like quality fails to hold between facts and objects in the external world and our beliefs about them. If it fails to hold of even the belief that the facts and objects 'are there', it is bound

to fail to hold of *all* beliefs about them. However, the point of contrast still remains that it fails to hold between the facts and objects in the world and the beliefs that they are there, while it holds of our own intentional states and the beliefs that *they* are there. I say all this to warn against being misled by the locution ('beliefs about them') because I will continue to use it since the more correct alternative ('beliefs that they are there') is a stylistic blight.

2. Actually, as will emerge in Chapter 5, the proviso is necessary to accommodate exceptions only to the transparency conditional. The proviso is not needed for the authority conditional in order to accommodate the exceptions. It is needed for a quite different reason.

3. See note 13 for what is being marked by the use of the word 'potential' here.

4. See, for example, David Rosenthal, "Thinking that One Thinks," in M. Davies and G. Humphrey (eds.), *Consciousness* (Oxford: Blackwell, 1992).

5. I am not offering this as an analysis of the notion of an 'unembedded' state. Just as I said of efforts to invoke the notion of the conscious to analyze the notion of 'embedded' states, to invoke the notion of the unconscious here would presumably give no more than a synonym. I am happy to use the term 'unconscious' as a synonym rather than as a bit of analysis, since I don't want to be giving an analysis when I say it. I just want to pick out the class of unembedded states in more familiar terms since the term 'unembedded' is a term of art devised just for the purposes of this discussion. And the fact is that the word 'unconscious' has a popular usage to describe, for example, the sorts of states that Freud was interested in, and that at least marks a sub-class of states that are unembedded, even if it offers no analysis of the term 'unembedded'.

6. I put this in parenthesis very deliberately because, as will emerge in Chapter 5, it is better perhaps to restrict the term 'rationalize' to describe what happens between states that I will there call 'commitments' and that are fully self-known and our actions. The better term here might just be the term 'explains' rather than 'rationalizes'. As I said, there is a lot more on this in Chapter 5. Until then, I will rest with the parenthetical caveat.

7. Tyler Burge and Christopher Peacocke, for instance, tend to start with something that they call the "basic case." See Burge, "Individualism and Self-Knowledge," *Journal of Philosophy* 85 (1988): 649–663: also Christopher Peacocke, *Being Known* (Oxford: Oxford University Press, 1999).

8. The general demand for a state of mind in criminal liability (mens rea) may be elaborated in terms of intention as well as in terms of self-knowledge. It should go without saying that these are not equivalent. The self-knowledge demand can be met without the demand for intention being met. Someone may know that his actions have certain obvious consequences, but he may not actually intend those consequences. Yet he may be liable for those actions. Equally, lots of philosophers think that one may have intentions that one has no knowledge of. That is not my own view, but it is by no means the case that my view of the matter is widely held, so, prima facie at least, that provides another reason to think that the two demands are not equivalent. However, it is perhaps safe to say that the actions that meet each demand very often coincide.

9. It is interesting that these very reasons that surface in criminal law where blame and punishment are the issue crop up also when praise and reward are the issue. For example, a world in which individual authorship has no central place, and where works of literature and art, say, are viewed more as the productions of a culture of zeitgeist, would be a world that our values find unattractive because we do not as individuals want to be so alienated from our own creations and want to be admired and rewarded for them as individuals. And so for this reason too we will demand the notions of individual responsibility grounded in intention and self-knowledge as being necessary to our notions of praise and reward.

10. Nor, by the way, will it be a world in which the 'law and economics' ideology will have any governing or central theoretical place, since (presumably) the demand for self-knowledge and intention is quite simply 'inefficient'.

11. In Chapter 5, I will briefly take up this question again and will want to say that degrees of self-knowledge apply to self-knowledge of dispositions but not to self-knowledge of intentional states viewed in normative terms, as commitments.

12. See Susan Wolf, "Asymmetrical Freedom," *The Journal of Philosophy* 77 (1980): 151–166.

13. In this context, I use the term 'potential' here and elsewhere in the text to talk about intentional states rationalizing actions, and it is a very general term that can cover a lot of things. But it should be obvious that by 'potential' in this context I mean something very specific and tightly controlled. By an intentional state 'potentially' rationalizing an action I mean an 'intentional state if *in its present status* in the moral

psychology of an agent it were to rationalize an action that it has not actually so far done.' What I do not mean by it is 'if it were to rationalize an action that it has not actually done so far, *after having altered its status.*' I mention this for the following reason. Mental states that are not self-known have a status *different* from the states whose potential to rationalize I am claiming is caught up with agency. Yet these unself-known mental states may *come to be* self-known by cognitive (e.g., psychoanalytical) inquiry, and then they too might rationalize, which they have not actually so far done. When they do become self-known and when they then actually rationalize an action, those actions would be the object of justifiable reactive attitudes. So while they are still unself-known, in one sense of the term they still have the 'potential' to rationalize actions that are the objects of justifiable reactive attitudes. However, they would have this potential only in the sense that in order for the potential to be actualized, they would have to first change their status from unself-known to self-known; otherwise, the actions they rationalize would not be the objects of justifiable reactive attitudes. That is a sense of 'potential' quite different from the one I intend. What I intend is a distinction between actual and potential within the same status of intentional states. Perhaps one should drop the word 'potential' and find another if this distinction is easily lost sight of.

14. Only in Chapter 5, after fully justifying the conditional for authority, will I be able to show how we may go from viewing the second-order beliefs in these conditionals as true self-*beliefs* to viewing them as cases of self-*knowledge.* Till then, however, I will not maintain the scruple of only using the expression 'true self-belief' instead of 'self-knowledge' when describing these second-order beliefs. This, entirely for reasons of convenience and felicity of expression.

15. See Crispin Wright, "Wittgenstein's Rule-Following Considerations and the Central Project of Theoretical Linguistics," in Alexander George (ed.), *Reflections on Chomsky* (Oxford: Oxford University Press, 1989), who explicitly formulates conditionals too but has no such proviso and explanation as the one I am offering.

16. H. P. Grice, "Meaning," *Philosophical Review* 66 (1957): 337–388.

17. See, in particular, the project in Brian Loar's *Mind and Meaning* (Cambridge: Cambridge University Press, 1981).

18. See Wright, "Wittgenstein's Rule-Following Considerations."

19. See Peacocke, *Being Known.*

20. Ibid. See also John McDowell, *Mind and World* (Cambridge, Mass.: Harvard University Press, 1994).

4. The Conceptual Basis for Authority I

1. Sounding off is not the same as lying, of course. Lying implies one cares for the truth and is concealing or inventing it. Sounding off implies one has no regard for the truth; one is simply speaking for the sake of speaking.

2. Gareth Evans, *The Varieties of Reference*, ed. John McDowell (New York: Oxford University Press, 1982), p. 225.

3. Ivan Goncharov, *Oblomov*, trans. Natalie Duddington (New York: Dutton, 1959).

4. Carol Rovane, *The Bounds of Agency: An Essay in Revisionary Metaphysics* (Princeton, N.J.: Princeton University Press, 1998).

5. This is to be found in a familiar and much discussed line of argument both in Wittgenstein's *The Blue and Brown Books* (Oxford: Basil Blackwell, 1958) and in his *Philosophical Investigations* (Oxford: Basil Blackwell, 1953). I should warn: there is no doubt that some devotees of Wittgenstein will think that I am doing some violence to his thinking in saying that this strand of argument is separable from what I called the deeper strand and that I will take up in the next chapter. But the fact is that Wittgenstein is so inexplicit about how the two strands are to be integrated that it is perfectly possible to separate them, however we interpret *him*. And many philosophers have indeed separated them. In fact, many philosophers think that the present strand is right, while they reject the second strand, which I am describing as deeper. That is why I have thought it best to present things as if they were separable. For a very interesting integrated account of these issues in Wittgenstein, which I am perhaps artificially separating out, see the essays on Wittgenstein in John McDowell's volume *Meaning, Knowledge, and Reality* (Cambridge, Mass.: Harvard University Press, 1998). See also Saul Kripke's by now classic *Wittgenstein on Rules and Private Language* (Oxford: Blackwell, 1982), where the second strand surfaces very forcefully for the first time, but no very great effort is made toward an explicit integration of the two strands. I must conclude this note by apologizing for referring to strands of arguments that I have not even spelled out yet, and one of which I won't spell out till the next chapter. Such are the handicaps of proceeding dialectically. I will say something again in the next chapter to redeem myself. I nevertheless mention all this now as well just to guard myself against those who find the first strand of argument as I present it too narrow and incomplete—to say to them that I am perfectly aware that there are further elements in Wittgenstein that some philosophers have thought to be integral to this strand

but that are not obviously so and that are not very explicitly so by any means in his own texts.

6. Of course, the difference intended in the two thought-experiments is that the imagined Oblomov is proposed with a view to raising a question as to whether comprehensive passivity can be compatible with claims about the possession of a mind, and the brain in a vat is proposed with a view to raising the question as to whether exclusive interiority is compatible with claims about the possession of a mind. And the idea is that if possession of mind consisted in having dispositions regarded as being dependent in certain ways on the brain, then there is no problem about these claims to the possession of minds by either sort of subject. This strand in Wittgenstein has it come out that such a conception of dispositions is illicit, that mental dispositions are not dependent on the brain in one or another of these ways, and they are not to be thought of as genuinely mental states unless the public manifestations and the behavioral productions of the subject are in place. The idea that a completely passive subject that has the same brain states as an active one is as minded as the active one, or that a brain in a vat that has the same brain states as a brain in a body in a normal environment is as minded as the latter, is a misguided idea precisely because the dispositions that amount to possession of mind are not to be understood in terms of these sorts of defining dependency relations to states of the brain.

On this Wittgensteinian view that some, I suppose, would like to describe as an 'anti-realist' view of dispositions, there is no question of saying that Oblomov (or the brain in a vat) is fully minded but simply awaiting behavior (or a body and an environment) to fully realize the mind in behavior (and in behavioral actions upon the external world). It's worth adding as an aside that the two thought-experiments could be made to come closer together in their points, if one also required that behavior was not behavior unless it was behavior upon an environment. On this there is another bit of inexplicitness in Wittgenstein— when he says inner states need to meet an outer criterion, does he by 'outer' mean to include behavior that is described in terms that necessarily include the external environment? There is nothing explicit in any of his texts, as far as I know, as to whether he is an 'externalist' in this sense. The term 'outer' by itself does not imply externalism, even if it is natural to assume that he would not have opposed such externalism.

7. I say behavior in the 'ordinary sense' to rule out counting as behavior the case of movement of the sort I mentioned when setting up Oblomov, movement produced by being blown about by gusts of wind, say.

8. Immanuel Kant, *Grounding of the Metaphysics of Morals*, trans. and ed. Mary Gregor (New York: Cambridge University Press, 1998).

9. Immanuel Kant, *Critique of Pure Reason*, trans. Norman Kemp Smith (London: Macmillan, 1978).

10. Bernard Williams, *Descartes: The Project of Pure Inquiry* (Harmondsworth: Penguin, 1978).

11. Immanuel Kant, *Critique of Practical Reason*, trans. Lewis White Beck (Indianapolis: Bobbs-Merrill, 1956), p. 7.

12. This point is important because it allows me to accommodate Kant's sometimes explicit statements that the idea of freedom (like the ideas of God and of the immortality of the soul) is not a necessary condition for knowledge (see, for instance, *Critique of Pure Reason*, A799/B827) with my own reading of him precisely because one may read 'necessary condition' there narrowly as the sort of thing provided by concepts of the understanding only and not by ideas of reason.

13. Allen Wood, *Kant's Ethical Thought* (Cambridge: Cambridge University Press, 1999).

14. Cited in ibid., p. 203, from Kant's *Lectures on Anthropology*, Ak 25 in *Kant's Gesammelte Schriften* (Berlin: Akademie Press, 1902).

15. Sydney Shoemaker, "Self-Knowledge and 'Inner Sense'," *Philosophy and Phenomenological Research* 54 (1994): 289.

16. They play this role vis-à-vis the actions to which they are directed not just by themselves but via relations they bear with other first-order intentional states. This familiar point will obviously apply to second-order beliefs and the role they play vis-à-vis the actions to which they are directed.

17. To be scrupulous, I should add that, for animals, the idea that the new incoming information might come not only from the senses but from 'testimony' may require a correspondingly special use of the term 'testimony' as is given to the idea that it is 'beliefs' the testimony succeeds in revising. That is, I take it that if the squawk of fear in a bird alerts other birds of a predator, that is to say, causes complacent birds to go into a change of mind by acquiring the new belief that there is a predator in the vicinity, the use of the term 'testimony' to plausibly describe what the squawk provides matches the special use of the word 'belief' that is plausibly used to describe what is acquired on its basis.

18. By 'deliberative' I don't mean that it has to be very conscious and attentive and explicit deliberation. What it has to be to be deliberative, as opposed to 'brute' revision, is that it is not just mediated by sensitivity to new incoming forms of information but by the exercise of reactive evaluative attitudes toward one's own thoughts. Many revisions that are mediated by reactive attitudes of criticism do not involve explicit and

highly conscious deliberations. They are nevertheless revisions that are deliberative.

19. See Tyler Burge's excellent article "Our Entitlement to Self-Knowledge," *Proceedings of the Aristotelian Society* 96 (1996): 91–116. For the reference to Shoemaker, see note 16.

20. Some fifteen years ago at a conference in Frankfurt, I raised questions about Oblomov and about agency, generally, for Burge's views on self-knowledge, in much the way I am about to raise them in the text just below. Burge on that occasion said that he would ponder its consequences for his own position on self-knowledge. I have not kept up with all of Burge's recent writings on the subject to see if he has a view or a response, but it does seem to me that there is no deep problem created for his position by what I have to say below. Shoemaker's position is a quite different matter, since Shoemaker cannot possibly take within his overall functionalist stride the points about agency being made in this book.

21. In chapter 2 of my book *Belief and Meaning* (Oxford: Blackwell, 1992), I had tied self-knowledge conceptually to questions of rationality and then situated that tie in an overly elaborate discussion of the *lack* of self-knowledge that must account for the irrationality of the protagonist Pierre in Kripke's puzzle about belief. When I wrote that, I had not read Shoemaker's elaborate discussion of the relation between rationality and self-knowledge, which was already in print in some papers of his; had I read it, my discussion would have been much more brief and elegant. However, even then, in the appendix to *Belief and Meaning*, which was also on the subject of self-knowledge, I had explicitly seen the more critical points I am making here about Shoemaker's views and my own claims in chapter 2 of that book about the relation between self-knowledge and rationality, viz., that it is necessary to produce the more integrated picture and to situate the point about the relationship of self-knowledge to rationality in the more general relation of self-knowledge to agency. Most of the present book is an elaboration of that appendix.

22. See Bernard Williams, "Deciding to Believe," in *Problems of the Self* (Cambridge: Cambridge University Press, 1971).

23. This, of course, immediately marks a distinction within the subjective or first person point of view between the point of view of agency and the phenomenological point of view. I have already spoken to this distinction, when I first introduced the idea of a point of view in the last chapter. As I said there, I will be restricting my use of the term 'point of view' to exclude the non-intentional, non-agential, phenomenolog-

ical phenomena of pains, etc. This is not because of any conviction that the latter are not subjective phenomena. The restriction is entirely a matter of focusing on what is relevant to this book, relevant to self-knowledge of intentional states, and its links with agency and normativity or value.

5. The Conceptual Basis for Authority II

1. It should have also been plain from the conclusions of Chapter 3.
2. Saul Kripke, *Wittgenstein on Rules and Private Language* (Oxford: Blackwell, 1982).
3. Akeel Bilgrami, *Belief and Meaning* (Oxford: Blackwell, 1992). For a more specific and pointed discussion of just this point, see my "Precis of 'Belief and Meaning' " in the symposium on the book in *Philosophy and Phenomenological Research* 58, no. 3 (1998): 595–605, and in "Norms and Meaning," in Ralph Stoecker (ed.), *Reflecting Davidson* (Berlin: de Gruyter, 1993). For a very plausible and congenial discussion of this point, see the discussion of rules and norms of meaning by Noam Chomsky in his *Knowledge of Language* (New York: Praeger, 1986) and the discussion of conventions in Donald Davidson's "A Nice Derangement of Epitaphs," in Ernest Lepore (ed.), *Perspectives on Truth and Interpretation* (Oxford: Blackwell, 1986).
4. See Kripke, *Wittgenstein on Rules and Private Language,* pp. 35–37.
5. Donald Davidson, "Mental Events," in his *Essays on Actions and Events* (Oxford: Oxford University Press, 1981).
6. The Moorean nature of Kripke's points are never made explicit by him, but they are clearly assumed in his arguments, and I will draw them out in this chapter. For Moore, see the first two chapters of his *Principia Ethica* (Cambridge: Cambridge University Press, 1903).
7. The first philosopher to have systematically treated intentional states as 'commitments' is Isaac Levi. See his *Enterprise of Knowledge* (Cambridge, Mass.: MIT Press, 1983). I differ from Levi on issues having to do with the extent of what count as commitments, and these differences issue from the fact that our interest in the notion seems to come from different contexts. Levi's primary use of the notion is situated in his interest in belief revision. He is skeptical of my interest in situating the idea in a notion of intentionality as commitment derived in part from a modified Strawsonian notion of agency in terms of the reactive attitudes. One consequence of this difference is that though on my view a belief or a desire is a commitment in the sense that its possessor is committed to various things in possessing it, the things she is committed

to in having the belief are not, on my conception, themselves properly thought of as 'commitments' in the same sense. This is because they (unlike the belief that generates my being committed to them) may well not be the justifiable objects of reactive attitudes—if one had no self-knowledge of them, for instance, as one often may not. Levi, who does not situate the notion of intentional states as commitments in the notion of agency and responsibility along these Strawsonian lines, has no such qualm about thinking of these things as themselves commitments in the same sense. See note 20 for another difference between our views. Despite these differences, I have been much influenced by his general stress on commitments in the study of intentionality. Robert Brandom in his *Making Explicit* (Cambridge, Mass.: Harvard University Press, 1994) also makes elaborate and interesting use of the notion of commitment, though not in the service of an account of self-knowledge. There are some disagreements I have with the notion of commitment to be found in Brandom, only one of which emerges fleetingly in some critical remarks I make in this chapter against the tendency to situate commitments in social frameworks ever since Rorty.

8. Two questions about commitments may be raised. First, if one's beliefs are commitments generated by principles of rationality, including inference, a question looms about whether one is committed to the logical consequences of one's beliefs. Some may doubt this on the grounds that there are too many of these that are unknown, and we may be too busy with other worthwhile things to work them out. So there is a question as to whether we can be said to have obligations to believe such unknown consequences. This familiar question has an answer. If the Moore-Frege-Moore argument I have given is right, then we have an argument for putting commitments in place when the subject is intentionality. To say they are put in place is not necessarily to say that one cannot always put them aside under excusing conditions. One may, if the costs are high, as is suggested by the question being raised ('we may be too busy with other worthwhile things . . . '), be excused from living up to one's commitments without them ceasing to be commitments. What makes something a commitment as opposed to a mere hypothetical imperative is that it is in place, and there are excusing conditions for something already in place. It is not merely that one should do what is suggested by the commitment if one feels like or has an interest in doing so. That is too conditional to make talk of 'commitments' genuine. "If you have an interest and desire to do x, do it" is a quite different kind of animal than "Do x, unless the costs are high." Only formulations of the latter kind of imperative mark what are prop-

erly called 'commitments'. But, nevertheless, things marked that way do allow for excusing conditions, and so the question being raised here has an answer, if the Moore-Frege-Moore strategy provides a good argument for putting commitments in place, in the first instant. Moreover, one should distinguish between the kinds of things that one is committed to (the logical consequences of one's beliefs) and the kinds of states that yield those things that we are committed to. Only the latter are properly called commitments. The former are essential to understanding what makes the latter commitments but are not themselves properly called 'commitments'. This last point is important to various issues that have to do with responsibility and blame that were discussed in Chapter 2, but I will not pursue them.

Second, it may be asked of commitments: surely there is no more obvious consequence of p than p. That means that I ought to have any belief that I in fact do have, including false ones, formed stupidly, and this cannot be right. But from the point of view of the subject in question, it is indeed right. I cannot apologize for having the commitments I have if it is indeed *commitments* I have. Someone else might find them stupid and objectionable in various ways. But the whole idea of a commitment is that it is something that is possessed within a point of view. It is a value that is held by someone, a state of mind that issues from her endorsement. Within that deliberative point of view, one cannot fail to think that one ought to have the belief, at least unless it is, from *within that point of view*, brought into question by some conflict injected into the point of view. But as soon as it is, it ceases to be a commitment. One might suspend it as a commitment as a result of such conflict and, after subsequent deliberation from the perspective of other commitments, even shed it as a commitment (or of course once could re-recruit it as a commitment after deliberation while it is suspended). But while it is a commitment, and qua commitment, from my point of view, I certainly ought to have the belief. To not think so is to not quite have comprehended the concept being discussed.

9. The locus classicus is of course "Naming and Necessity" by Kripke himself, in Donald Davidson and Gilbert Harman (eds.), *Semantics for Natural Language* (Boston: Reidl, 1972). Also Hilary Putnam's "The Meaning of Meaning," in Keith Gunderson (ed.), *Language, Mind and Knowledge* (Minneapolis: University of Minnesota Press, 1975). It is mildly ironic that causal theories of reference formulated by Kripke might be relevant in this way to recent versions of naturalism about value, a naturalism that Kripke opposes. The irony is going to get a little less mild just below in the text, when I actually exploit a Fregean

argument of the sort Kripke has deeply opposed in his writings on reference, in order to support Kripke's Moorean anti-naturalism about intentionality and value.

10. Recent work by Richard Boyd is a good example of this second and more recent strain of naturalism about value. See his "How to Be a Moral Realist," in G. Sayre-McCord (ed.), *Essays on Moral Realism* (Ithaca, N.Y.: Cornell University Press, 1980). Sturgeon, Railton, and Brink are other philosophers writing within this broadly characterized form of ethical naturalism, despite the detailed differences among their positions.

11. See Gottlob Frege, "On Sense and Reference," in his *Philosophical Writings*, ed. Peter Geach and Max Black (Oxford: Blackwell, 1952).

12. This Fregean argument is of course a perfectly general one, and I have been deploying it for various ends against naturalist and certain forms of externalist accounts of mind in a number of my writings on the subject of intentionality. With somewhat other purposes in mind, Brian Loar used Fregean arguments of this kind very instructively and in detail in a paper titled "Social Content and Psychological Content," which I commented on at the Oberlin Colloquium, subsequently published as an exchange in Patrick Grimm et al. (eds.), *Contents of Thought* (Tucson: University of Arizona Press, 1985). But, following Loar, I have restricted my use of it to the study of intentional states. J. J. C. Smart, "Sensation and Brain Processes," *Philosophical Review* 68 (1959): 141–156, and Stephen White, "Curse of the Qualia," *Synthese* 68 (1986): 333–368, apply it to phenomenal states.

13. Michael Devitt, for example, in his *Designation* (New York: Columbia University Press, 1981), explicitly says that this view is what is entailed by any workable causal-theoretic notion of the reference of terms. Kripke himself, to whom we owe the causal view of reference, treaded much more carefully on this and various other matters about which philosophers like Devitt have rushed in on his behalf.

14. For a detailed presentation of this view, see P. Kyle Stanford and Philip Kitcher, "Refining the Causal Theory of Reference for Natural Kind Terms," *Philosophical Studies* 97 (2000): 99–129.

15. John McDowell expresses this sort of objection, and he invokes Davidson's distinction between conceptual commitments and ontological commitments to do so. "But what is the point of claiming that the naturalizing identification holds only a posteriori? Surely the point is to enable the theorist to concede that the conceptual apparatus is not naturalistic in the relevant sense, while maintaining that the terms that satisfy those concepts also satisfy concepts that place the items in a

naturalistically conceived causal nexus. In this way of thinking there is no intention to propose a naturalistic reduction and, for all Bilgrami says, the second horn of the dilemma is a comfortable resting place. It is where Davidson places himself." See McDowell, "Reply to Bilgrami," in Cynthia Macdonald and Graham Macdonald (eds.), *McDowell and His Critics* (Oxford: Blackwell, 2006). McDowell wrote this in response to a paper I wrote that gave a very highly encapsulated argument version of the pincer argument. The fuller version is given in my paper "Intentionality and Norm," in Mario De Caro and David Macarthur (eds.), *Naturalism and Its Discontents* (Cambridge, Mass.: Harvard University Press, 2004), in which I myself raise objections of the sort McDowell gives, and I respond to it in detail, as I will do now in the text in my responses to objection (B) and objection (C). It is understandable that McDowell should raise this objection, since he was not aware of the kinds of responses I had formulated elsewhere to such an objection. Even so, simply to say, as he does, that the very point of the a posteriori identifications is to have a strategy that makes a distinction along the Davidsonian lines that he describes is to assume that there is nothing uncontroversial about such a strategy. That cannot possibly be right. The strategy assumes a nominalism in what it takes to be our ontological commitments, whereby what 'satisfies' the concepts will be natural objects; but no properties, natural or non-natural, are implied by the concepts. The whole point of the Fregean arm of the pincer is to raise at least a prima facie question about this by forcing the notion of sense and to suggest that the relevant senses might express value *properties* (and if they did not and expressed natural *properties*, they would be susceptible to Moore's arm of the pincer). Davidson was not aware of nor responding to the pincer argument and the Fregean difficulties being raised by it, which make his nominalism in this context controversial. So it is understandable that Davidson should not have worried about this issue. But McDowell is responding to the pincer argument, and his simply citing the Davidsonian position, as he does in that quotation, seems just a little insouciant.

16. In this parenthesis, I say this guarded thing because terms like 'sky', 'city', 'ocean', etc., themselves will not figure in the ultimate scientific description of the world either, but for many, there is an assumption regarding their broadly reductive relation to the terms that *will* figure in that description, an assumption that, it is being claimed by me, does not hold of evaluative terms on grounds of principle. For a forceful expression of a quite plausible view that denies that the very notion of reference has any role to play in any scientific study of language pre-

cisely because even terms like 'sky', 'city', etc., are not assimilable (re-ductively) into a genuinely scientific vocabulary, see various essays by Chomsky in his *New Horizons in the Study of Language and Mind* (Cam-bridge: Cambridge University Press, 2000).

17. What I am saying here is intended to be sympathetic to something that John McDowell has said in response to John Mackie's claim that eval-uative facts would be 'queer' sorts of facts. McDowell, as is well known, compares evaluative terms to terms describing secondary qualities. Of course we would find evaluative facts 'queer' if we modeled them on primary qualities, he argues, but we need not find them queer if we modeled them on secondary qualities. It is his further claim that terms like 'red' and 'good' describe something just as real as 'square' even if terms like 'red' and 'good' do not figure in the conceptual vocabulary of fundamental science. To deny this last claim is to express the same prejudice as the one I am inveighing against when I say that my natu-ralist opponent is working with a criterion for property existence that is scientistic when he says that the senses I have shown to be necessary by my argument do not describe anything real; they do not describe any evaluative properties.

18. I say 'sometimes' because they clearly don't always have to be absent whenever there is a failure. They can be present, but the failure is due to some other factor.

19. In making this point, I have restricted the discussion to the second-order disposition underlying the preparedness to accept criticism, but the same point apples equally to the second-order disposition under-lying the preparedness to cultivate the relevant first-order dispositions. Here too there is no way to characterize the second-order dispositions, except as the disposition to cultivate the first-order disposition to live up to the commitment that p, the disposition to cultivate the first-order disposition to live up to the commitment that q, the disposition to cultivate the first-order disposition to live up the commitment that r, and so on.

20. The preparedness, I am saying, is a second-order disposition, and saying so makes no concession to a naturalistic program. Isaac Levi and I disagree on this point. He thinks that the preparedness should only be viewed as another commitment, a second-order commitment, and not a second-order disposition. That is a far less ambitious claim regarding self-knowledge than I want to make. I want to say that we fulfill this second-order commitment by having a disposition at the second-order, and saying so makes no concession to naturalism. Levi's view amounts only to saying that we have a commitment to self-knowledge, a com-

mitment to believing that we have the first-order state we do, whereas I want to say that the second-order state is a true belief. It's not that I don't deny that we have the second-order commitment to know our first-order intentional states. I certainly do, and I elaborate on that important point in Appendix I of this book. It is just that I also want to say, as I have been saying in the present chapter, that *we do live up to that commitment*. That is the more ambitious and the right thing to say, though Levi finds it implausible.

21. Ryle did so when he talked of dispositions merely as inference tickets. When it came to mental dispositions, he was in fact quite skeptical of the psychologistic, naturalistic underpinning of dispositions in causal terms. That development of giving it that underpinning came only with philosophers much later who developed the doctrine of functionalism along non-Rylean lines, even though Dennett, among them, is in some ways a functionalist who has kept faith with some aspects of Ryle in an interesting attempt at a hybrid position, whether or not in the end successful.

22. References to this principle can be found in many papers of his both in the philosophy of language and in the theory of action. They are pervasive and too numerous to mention. See the essays in Davidson's two volumes, *Essays on Actions and Events* and *Inquiries into Truth and Interpretation* (Oxford: Oxford University Press, 1981).

23. In fact, because Davidson is convinced that we cannot but be living up to the principles of rationality (necessary charity, as he thinks of it), he does not even feel much pressure to think that we have a minimal commitment to the principles of rationality, let alone beliefs and desires being commitments. The idea of a commitment simply does not figure in his work.

24. When charity takes in not just rationality but truth, Davidson also says things such as: 'a belief, by its nature, tends to be true'. But our concern here is just his use of charity in the rationality involved in living up to our commitments.

25. Davidson's complacence here, the refusal to draw the right lesson from the fairly widespread fact of irrationality, is of course a kind of complacence that characterizes a lot of assumptions, such as the basic assumptions of rational choice theory in the social sciences. In fact, I should add that in another, quite different area, Davidson shows the same structures of complacency. This is when he refuses to take seriously the lessons of the Frege and Kripke puzzles for the truth-conditional theory of meaning and intentional content. There are not enough such puzzle cases, and so there is no need to worry that a truth-conditional view of

meaning has to address them. It is remarkable that despite a lifelong—at any rate, a career-long—commitment to such a view of meaning, he never once addressed the Frege puzzle, thinking that they did not arise often enough to worry about. It may be possible to accommodate the puzzle within a modified truth-theoretic view of meaning, but it is complacence to think that the issue is not to be addressed. It is a similar complacence (via the notion of charity) that leads to his insouciance about the radical distinction between the two questions I have been discussing. A proper appreciation of the distinctness of the questions might have led him to a commitmental rather than a dispositional view of beliefs and desires.

26. It is doubtful since it is always *possible* that we fail to live up to our commitments.

27. Davidson struggles with the widespread fact of irrationality and proposes the divided mind thesis in his essay "The Paradoxes of Irrationality," in Richard Wollheim and James Hopkins (eds.), *Philosophical Essays on Freud* (Cambridge: Cambridge University Press, 1982).

28. A. I. Melden, R. S. Peters, and Peter Winch are three among other authors in that series who expressed some suspicion of the idea that reasons are causes.

29. These criticisms are partially of a piece with the criticisms that John McDowell has made of Davidson's view of intentional explanation when he faults him for a wholly unnecessary metaphysical commitment to a Humean notion of cause, in which causality implies laws, and faults him also for a monism about the mind that is forced on Davidson once this faulty Humean assumption about cause is in place. See the concluding paragraphs of John McDowell's "Functionalism and Anomalous Monism," in his *Mind, Value, and Reality* (Cambridge, Mass.: Harvard University Press, 1998). But as I will argue below in the text, there are many implications of such a criticism of Davidson that McDowell does not see his way through to at all, and in fact he resists these implications, some of which are quite radical and which I will discuss in much of the rest of this chapter.

30. See John McDowell in various places but in particular in his "Reply to Bilgrami." I have no quarrel with McDowell insisting that intentional states cause actions and that we are illuminated when we are told of specific instances of their doing so. I in fact give reasons below for why the illumination is nothing as powerful as the normal illumination we hold out for when causes are cited. What I oppose in McDowell is his view that the notion of cause is the same notion of cause whether or not intentional causes are involved.

31. There is an asymmetry here in the way I talked of counterfactuals a little while ago and the way I am talking now of cause in the disagreement with McDowell that I have just registered. Though it is right to say, as I have, that there is a unitary notion of a counterfactual that can respectively get a more and less minimal description, depending on whether it is not or is underpinned by a naturalistic notion of causality, it is quite wrong to think that the notion of *cause* can be described that way. It is quite wrong to think that there is a basic notion of cause that may or may not be thought of naturalistically. A proper understanding of the difference between the naturalistic and the anti-naturalistic notion of cause puts into doubt that there is a single notion of cause here, and this is because that proper understanding of the difference depends on an appreciation of a radical perspectival duality between the first and third person point of view. I will, as I said, be elaborating that difference along those lines below. The point being stressed here is that this disunity in the notion of cause does not have the effect of producing the same disunity in the notion of a counterfactual, which can quite properly be described as we have, viz., as a single notion with a minimal description, which then gets to be more than merely minimal when it is underpinned by the naturalistic notion of cause. Why this asymmetry? Because the notion of a counterfactual can be characterized in purely formal terms, which can capture our more and less minimal understanding of it. But 'cause' is a metaphysical idea, not a formal idea, and whether it is to be treated as a single notion or an ambiguous notion depends, respectively, on whether we do not or do accept the fact that our understanding of it is affected by the duality of perspectives. But nothing much hangs on this asymmetry. If someone were to feel strongly that the duality of perspectives, if it is to have any effect, should have an effect not just on the notion of cause but all the way up to the notion of counterfactuals, thus introducing disunity in that notion too, I have no strong investment in denying this. It just seems to me that less is given away in the domain of metaphysics, and indeed eventually epistemology, if one allows that the notion of counterfactuals is unaffected by the duality of perspectives.

32. Of course, to think of values in this way as being of a piece with the first person point of view is to give up on certain hyper-objectivist conceptions of value that certain positions describing themselves as 'Kantian' have adopted. In a paper on Bernard Williams ("Might There Be External Reasons?" in the volume *Mind, Value, and Reality*), McDowell, despite some of his criticisms of Williams's Humean psychologism about values, is also critical of many of Williams's objectivist critics and op-

ponents, who would divorce values from our perspective on them. In this, McDowell is insightfully right. There is much to be discussed here, but for the purposes of this book, I will simply admit that when I make these integrating claims regarding value and the first person point of view, I am restricting myself to value commitments of agents and am excluding certain highly objectivist conceptions of value from the claim. Perhaps the clearest example of a position being excluded is the objectivist position taken by Derek Parfit in recent papers. See his "Reasons and Motivation," *Proceedings of the Aristotelian Society* 71 (Supplement, 1997): 99–130. I will say more about this soon in this chapter to show that McDowell himself has not fully understood the significance of his own criticisms here.

33. I am focusing only on this duality of perspectives in Spinoza's discussion of freedom and agency and not his eventual monism in the ontological aspects of his doctrine, which may or may not be consistent with the duality.

34. I say more on this Spinozist point and its implications for anti-naturalism and intentionality in my "Psychoanalysis as Technology," in Erik J. Olsson (ed.), *Knowledge and Inquiry: Essays on the Pragmatism of Isaac Levi* (Cambridge: Cambridge University Press, 2006).

35. See McDowell, "Reply to Bilgrami."

36. I do certainly grant that if one is viewing the world in a detached way as, say, a natural scientist or as Spinoza's 'spectator' or 'predictor' does, then one will at least see the world as making normative demands on one's capacity for detached observation. This will take the form of the world (or one's perceptions of the world) demanding one to form the 'commitments' that we have said beliefs, even natural scientific beliefs and predictions about the world, are. So in that restricted sense, even the 'spectator' or detached observer is an agent and is in the normative realm. If he were not an agent at all and if he were not at all in the normative realm, he would not be a thinker at all. We already granted this in the last chapter when we granted that the really extreme case of the passive Oblomov is an incoherent figure who has no thoughts at all.

What I am focusing on now is the more specific distinction between the first/third person point of view, or the agent/spectator distinction, one that is tied only to Spinoza's dichotomy, which says you can't intend and predict at the same time. Predicting involves agency, of course. When I say "I predict that I will do . . . ," the first use of the first person pronoun refers to an agent, only the second does not. The second does not because the agent referred to by the first use of "I" has a spectator's angle on himself. So also, if I say 'I believe that this population will die of starvation' (a prediction about them), I *as an agent* am taking a *spectator's* angle on the world. But now contrast both these claims with the claim that I *ought or intend* to do something or the claim that I make when I say, "Those people *need* food." Here, as before, one speaks as an agent, of course, but one *adds* an *agent's angle of engagement* on oneself and on the world, as one did not before. That brings a further and more specific element of normativity and agency than in the previous statements. One thinks one *ought* to do something rather than predicts that one will do it, and one sees the world as making normative demands on one by describing the people as having *needs*. So, unlike the case of the extreme and incoherent Oblomov discussed in the last chapter, who is only useful in making the agent/non-agent distinction, the Spinoza point brings out the more specific idea of *an agent* who can be detached as opposed to an *agent* who can be engaged. And my point is that of the *detached* agent one has to be careful to say two things. (1) Because he is an *agent*, he does, of course, see the world as making normative demands on him. (2) But because he is a *detached* agent, he sees the world as making no normative demands on him over and above those that demand that he get the world right as a detached observer of the world. His perceptions of the world do not view the world as making any other sorts of normative demands on him, such as those of acting. He does not even view the world as offering him opportunities to act, at least not while he is detached. That is what is meant by 'detached' or by Spinoza's 'spectator'.

It would be foolish to insist that if he is observing the world at all, he cannot be detached because he is forming beliefs that are normative states or commitments and that rules out detachment. It would be foolish because we do talk of 'detachment' in Spinoza's sense, and to think that it is impossible to have that detachment (contrasted with engagement) is to trample over a commonsense as well as a philosophical distinction that Spinoza very sensibly makes. Once we grant that the extreme Oblomov is incoherent and has no thoughts and that even prediction and detached observation involve thought and agency, we do not need to destroy the obvious distinction between detachment and engagement altogether, nor between a spectator's and an 'agent's' point of view in a narrower and more specific sense of 'agent'—as someone with a sense of engagement with the world. This distinction may crudely coincide with our usual distinction between the realm of theoretical reason and the realm of the practical reason, as Kant and others have drawn it. But I won't pursue that point here, since it needs many careful and detailed qualifications.

37. I say more about this theme of viewing the world with a sense of en-

gagement in my contribution to a forthcoming volume of essays on "transitional justice," edited by Jon Elster, with title and other details to be announced.

38. Anticipating a point made below in the text: It does not leave out the body of the first person, either. By 'world' here I mean to include the body of the agent himself as well as the environment he perceives with a sense of his own engagement with it. That is how Descartes understood 'the world', and so therefore, anti-Cartesians, among whom I count myself, have to mean the same thing by the 'world'. There is no reason to think—in fact, there are good reasons not to think—that the first person point of view leaves the subject or agent as disembodied. There is nothing Cartesian about the first person point of view.

39. Stephen White, who has independently taken this view of things, has suggested to me that the view is best expressed as a form of Kuhnian incommensurability. I have qualms about that way of putting the point. I have preferred to put the point in Spinozist terms, which are I think best understood in terms of an issue about frames rather than incommensurability. The fact is that incommensurability was intended to attach to scientific theories, and scientific theories are *fragments* of a *third* person discourse and third person point of view on the world, whereas the point here is about the unavailability of the entire first and third personal discourses and points of view to one another. Because they are fragments within a third personal discourse, it is hard to actually be convinced that there *are* cases of the complete and principled unavailability of one scientific theory to another. Surely, we want to say, there is always scope to retreat to some minimal belief or set of beliefs that both theories share, then deliberate from there on. Surely, we want to say, there is always an open possibility that one theory will be able to offer the other theory at least some internal argument to bring it around. But none of these deflationary and skeptical responses are possible in the case of inter-perspectival unavailability that holds for the first and third person points of view. Here there really is no question of finding a common ground, and there is no other perspective to go to. So my own inclination is to resist too much talk of incommensurability—at any rate, to insist that if we fall into that talk, then the notion of incommensurability should be restricted to whole discourses, to the discourse of facts as the natural sciences study them and the discourse of value or (what is the same thing, once my integrations have been made) to first personal, agential descriptions and third personal descriptions. In other words, talk of incommensurability is fine, but only so long as we make clear that it applies not to what it was initially

thought to apply to when it was introduced by Kuhn and Feyerabend but to something much broader and more general and basic than they had in mind.

40. Whatever Moore had in mind by that formulation better not be, if I am right, in the service of these weaker forms of naturalism. His remarks are too brief on the subject of supervenience for us to figure out what his motivations were. But, in any case, the fact remains that even if his motivations were simply to say that we should not differ in our judgments of evaluation in two cases, if all the non-evaluative facts are the same in the two cases, it is precisely that sort of claim whose assessment is put into doubt by my remarks about supervenience.

41. See McDowell, "Reply to Bilgrami."

42. There are complications about the relations between some of the different uses of "I"—as when one talks in the present of one's past actions or thoughts, for instance, which may not be quite the same as one's talking of other persons, since one bears a certain relationship to one's past that one doesn't to others—but these are complications that need patient spelling out; they are not difficulties that overturn the idea of the ambiguity in the term that is forced by the perspectival duality.

43. See P. F. Strawson, *The Bounds of Sense* (London: Methuen, 1966). Also see his *Individuals* (London: Methuen, 1959).

44. In the last chapter, I had raised an objection to my own strategy for showing that one need not ever allow that self-deception threatens authority. The strategy had claimed that whenever there was a second-order belief about a first-order intentional state of mind such as a belief or desire, we need never deny that this second-order belief was true, even if we were self-deceived. That is, we need never deny that the first-order state of mind did not exist; we could always say that the self-deception was accounted for by the fact that there was another first-order state of mind inconsistent with the one that one's second-order belief was about. The objection to this strategy was that this strategy worked only for those cases of second-order beliefs that were about beliefs or desires, not about the absence of beliefs or desires, i.e., second-order beliefs, with negative formulations such as "X believes that she does not believe that p." In that discussion, I had tried to show that even in these negatively formulated cases, one *need not* ever abandon the strategy, even in cases where there was self-deception. But now that the question is not about what we need or need not do, now that we have given an argument to show how we *should and should not* think about authority, we can say something slightly different about these cases, even if we need not think of them as threatening authority.

The argument we just gave for authority relies on the fact that the specifically normative sense of intentionality we have now provided has it that the conditions under which second-order beliefs hold are the very same conditions under which the intentional states of mind (commitments) they are about *exist*. It does not show anything about second-order beliefs about states of mind in which *no* first-order state of mind exists. If we understand the nature of the argument, just given, for authority, it may be unmotivated to insist that all second- order beliefs are true. It is only plausibly motivated to claim that those second-order beliefs that are about existing intentional states of mind are true. Only these latter are grounded in the normative nature of intentionality, and so only these latter can lay claim to authority. For those who want the stronger claim that all second-order beliefs must be true, even when no intentional first-order state exists, some other sort of motivation for their claim will have to be provided, and I don't myself find any compelling reason to claim such a thing. There may even be good grounds not to claim it, but I will not pursue that here.

45. The example was suggested to me by Philip Kitcher.

46. In this context, I use the term 'potential' here and elsewhere in the text to talk about intentional states rationalizing actions, and it is a very general term that can cover a lot of things. But it should be obvious that by 'potential' in this context I mean something very specific and tightly controlled. I mean: an intentional state, *in its present status* in the moral psychology of an agent, that could rationalize an action, which it has not actually so far done, . . . What I do not mean by 'potential' is that it could rationalize an action that it has not actually done so far, *after having altered its status*. I mention this for the following reason: Mental states that are not self-known have a status different from the states whose potential to rationalize I am claiming is caught up with agency. Yet these unself-known mental states may *come to be* self-known by cognitive (e.g., psychoanalytical inquiry), and then they too might rationalize behavior, which they have not actually so far done. When they do become self-known and when they then actually rationalize an action, those actions would be the object of justifiable reactive attitudes. So while they are still unself-known, in one sense of the term they still have the 'potential' to rationalize actions that are the objects of justifiable reactive attitudes. However, they would have this potential only in the sense that in order for the potential to be actualized, they would have to first change their status from unself-known to self-known; otherwise, the actions they rationalize would not be the objects of justifiable reactive attitudes. That is a sense of potential quite different from the one I intend. What I intend is a distinction between actual and

potential within the same status of intentional states. Perhaps one should drop the word 'potential' and find another if this distinction is easily lost sight of.

6. Conclusion

1. See Michael McKinsey, "On Knowing Our Own Minds," *Philosophical Quarterly* 52 (January 2002): 107–116, for repeated signs of such a prejudice.
2. Crispin Wright expresses this in many papers, but see specifically his "Wittgenstein's Rule-Following Considerations and the Central Project of Theoretical Linguistics," in Alexander George (ed.), *Reflections on Chomsky* (Oxford: Basil Blackwell, 1989). For reasons that I am about to give in the main body of the text of this concluding chapter, I do not follow Wright in the idiom of 'response-dependence' to describe my own constitutive account of self-knowledge, which I share with him. But that essay (rather than anything by other constitutive theorists of self-knowledge such as Burge and Shoemaker, whom I did not read till very much later), when it first came out, was an inspiration to me, and in the appendix to my last book, I had promised to write the present book and take up the issues that it had inspired. My efforts here to say what is special about self-knowledge by lodging it in the two conditionals owes to that inspiration. But as I said in that appendix written seventeen years ago, I don't think that Wright offers a "substantial enough" account of the intuitions we have that the conditionals, characterized as presumptions, capture. In fact, it is because I do try and offer a more substantial account in this book that I can actually rewrite the conditionals as I have, something Wright does not do. After my rewrite, there are no exceptions to the conditionals. But Wright wants to allow for exceptions, and so (in my way of putting things) he must conceive of them in presumptive terms till the end. My rewrite removes their presumptive status, and by providing a substantial account in the philosophical integrations that I am now summing up in this concluding chapter, it shows what allows us to think of them as exceptionless. No doubt, Wright will find this whole approach far too ambitious and bound for failure. Even so, I did want to put it on record that the ambition was generated by his remarks pursuing the special character of self-knowledge in the framework of such conditionals.
3. This is a familiar criterion for anti-realism that Michael Dummett has presented in many writings of his, and Crispin Wright himself has pursued it in many of his writings inspired by Dummett.
4. For this reason, despite my deep sympathy and admiration for Shoe-

maker's writing on the subject of self-knowledge, I am very skeptical that his own conclusions on the subject—in particular, his excellent denial of the possibility of what he calls 'self-blindness'—can be reconciled with the pervasive causal, functional picture of the mind within which he presents these conclusions. This skepticism of mine can be inferred at some points where I have discussed Shoemaker specifically in the book but also more generally at those points where I have claimed that the normative and agential accounts are incompatible with causal accounts of self-knowledge. See especially Chapters 3 and 4.

Appendix I

1. Roy Schafer, *A New Language for Psychoanalysis* (New Haven, Conn.: Yale University Press, 1976).
2. This became clear recently when these ideas were presented at a conference of philosophers and psychoanalysts where he was a panelist. In writing up this section of this chapter, I have been much helped by many helpful and interesting conversations over some years with Garrett Deckel, who wrote a dissertation on the subject of the moral psychology surrounding psychoanalysis. On that occasion, we made a presentation jointly expressing these ideas.
3. It is a subject I discuss in a longer work on the nature of internal rationality and its relation to various issues in moral psychology and politics to be published under the title *Politics and the Moral Psychology of Identity* (forthcoming, Harvard University Press).
4. We could also resolve things by changing our commitments, of course.
5. It need not necessarily be a categorical basis. It could simply be that the basis consists of *further* dispositions that are described in biochemical terms. So though the basis need not be categorical, without at least some basis in the dispositional states studied by a more basic science, mental dispositions would be danglers in a way that is most implausible. See further below in the text for more on this.
6. See Jonathan Lear, *Open Minded* (Cambridge, Mass.: Harvard University Press, 2000).
7. Isaac Levi and Sidney Morgenbesser, "Belief and Disposition," *American Philosophical Quarterly* 1 (1964): 221–232.
8. A possible objection to this might come from the phenomenon of unconscious guilt. It might seem that if we have a first-order unconscious state (say, a hostile and poor opinion of a parent) and feel some *unconscious* guilt about having it, then we have the sort of self-criticism and self-reactive attitude at the level of the unconscious, that should allow that first-order unconscious state (the belief about the parent) to

meet my defining condition of a commitment. But the fact is that the guilt itself is not something we could see as being rightly or wrongly held if we were not aware of having it. No praise or blame for having it or for actions that flow from it would be justifiable. But, as the discussion of Strawson made clear, it is only *justifiable* praise and blame that define agency and commitment. The normative element at the unconscious level is at best superficial, at worst, and more correctly, fake.

9. Sigmund Freud, "Recollecting, Repetition and Working-Through," in his *Collected Papers*, vol. 2 (New York: Basic Books, 1959), p. 375.

10. Ibid.

11. Sigmund Freud, *Future of an Illusion* (New York: W. W. Norton, 1961).

12. See especially Donald Spence, *Narrative Truth and Historical Truth* (New York: W. W. Norton, 1982).

13. See Karl Popper, *Conjectures and Refutations* (London: Routledge and Kegan Paul, 1963).

14. A. Grunbaum, *The Foundations of Psychoanalysis* (Berkeley: University of California Press, 1984); also Grunbaum, "Meaning Connections and Causal Connections in the Social Science: The Poverty of Hermeneutic Philosophy," *Journal of the American Psychoanalytic Association* 38 (1990): 559–577. Grunbaum's criticisms are different from Popper's in that he does not deny that psychoanalysis is in the realm of science at all, but rather that its main claims are not confirmed by the standards of scientific confirmation.

15. This was why I said when making this criticism of Strawson that a genuinely coherentist understanding of the rational relations between values shows that values and commitments much less general and fundamental (of which I gave various examples) can be brought in to support and justify something much more general and fundamental (such as the commitment to agency and self-knowledge).

16. I realize that the term 'cognitive therapy' has a meaning of its own in the diverse spread of available psychotherapeutic and psychoanalytic theories and practices prevalent today, but here I use the term strictly to mean a therapy that involves cognition—and nothing else more specific.

Appendix II

1. Bernard Williams, "Internal and External Reasons," in his *Moral Luck: Philosophical Papers, 1973–1980* (Cambridge: Cambridge University Press, 1981), pp. 101–113.

2. I am assuming here that if reasons are dependent on and issue from

elements internal to our evaluative mental lives, then they may differ
from person to person, depending on whether or not those elements
are present in a person. Thus it is that we find ourselves saying such
things as, "It's a reason for him to do it but not for her." But of course
it may be that reasons owe to some internal element that happens to
be present in all of us, in which case these would coincide in their
universality with the outcome of the second notion of *external* reasons
without actually being external. This point echoes the point that we
often make when we say that consensus in a value among all has the
same universalist outcome as an objective value, without being objective.

3. I use the word 'motives' here in just the way that Williams uses it—to
refer to a state understood in Humean terms. Since I will be arguing
in this appendix that commitments can be viewed as internal states that
provide reasons, it may seem that if commitments have motivational
power, then they will satisfy Williams's demand that they are beholden
to one's motivational psychology. But because I view commitments as
irreducibly normative states, and because I do not understand them in
a Humean sense at all, what I mean by their motivational power is not
at all what Hume and Williams understand by them. It is not even what
Davidson understands by them, as was made clear by the elaborate discussion in Chapter 5 of the sense in which commitments caused our
actions. The kind of motivational power that commitments, as I characterized the term in Chapter 5, have has nothing like the motivational
element that Williams demands of internal reasons in his sophisticated
Humean picture of internal reasons. What sophistication he brings to
Hume by introducing his own casual and breezy talk of 'commitments'
as being in our motivational set does nothing to make commitments
the kind of irreducibly normative states or internal oughts I have said
they are.

Index

389

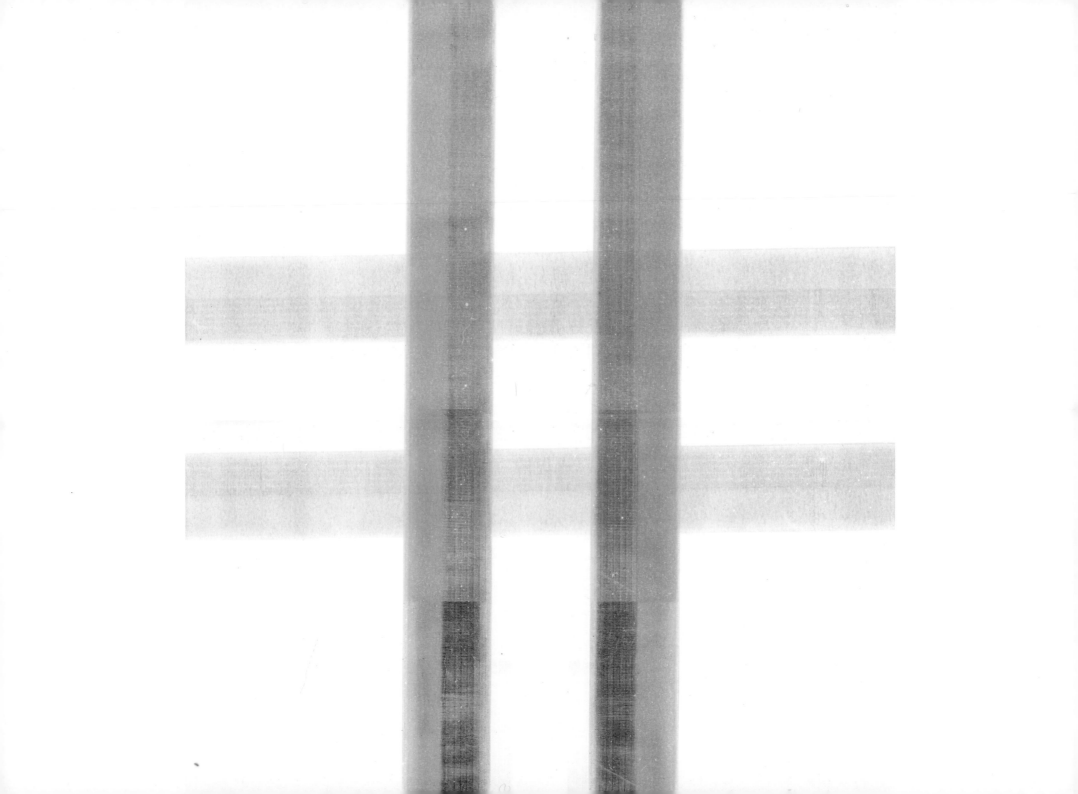

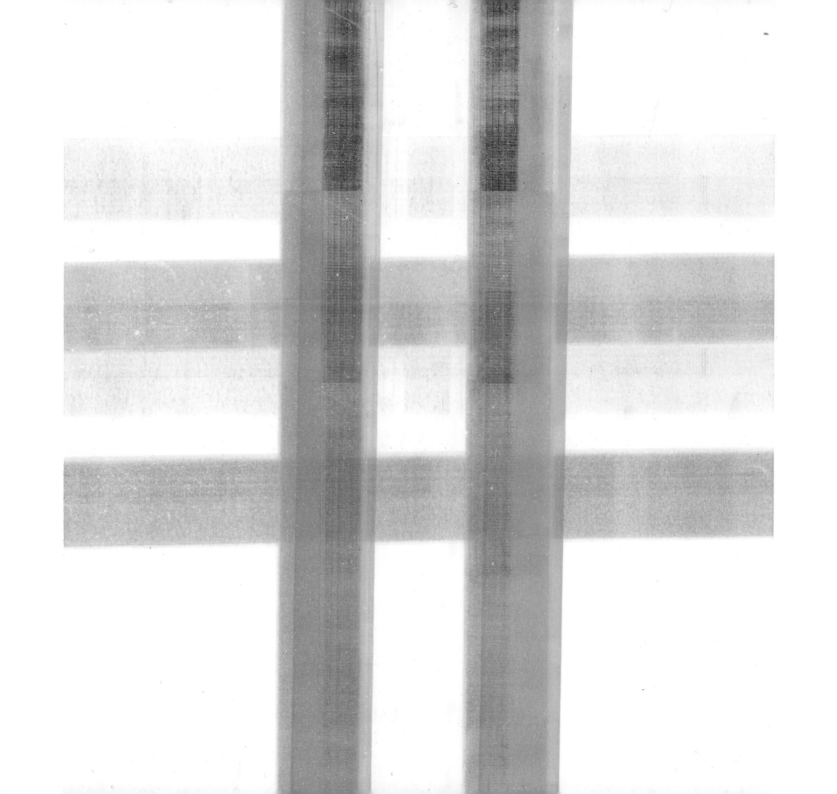